# GERIATRICS *At Your* FINGERTIPS®

## 2005, 7th EDITION

D1506491

# GERIATRICS *At Your* FINGERTIPS®

## 2005, 7th EDITION

**AUTHORS:**

David B. Reuben, MD

Keela A. Herr, PhD, RN

James T. Pacala, MD, MS

Bruce G. Pollock, MD, PhD

Jane F. Potter, MD

Todd P. Semla, MS, PharmD

Citation: Reuben DB, Herr KA, Pacala JT, *et al. Geriatrics At Your Fingertips: 2005, 7th Edition. The American Geriatrics Society; 2005.*

ISBN 1-886775-12-5
Library of Congress Control Number 2004114463
Printed in the U.S.A.

# TABLE OF CONTENTS

**Abbreviations** . . . . . . . . . . . . . . . . . . . . . . . . . . . . . . . . . . . . . . . . . . . . . . . . . . . iii
    Drug Prescribing and Elimination . . . . . . . . . . . . . . . . . . . . . . . . . . . . . . . . . vi
Introduction . . . . . . . . . . . . . . . . . . . . . . . . . . . . . . . . . . . . . . . . . . . . . . . . . . . . . viii
**Formulas and Reference Information** . . . . . . . . . . . . . . . . . . . . . . . . . . . . . . . . . 1
Assessment and Approach . . . . . . . . . . . . . . . . . . . . . . . . . . . . . . . . . . . . . . . . . . . 4
Appropriate Prescribing, Drug Interactions, and Adverse Events . . . . . . . . . . . . . . 9
Alcohol and Tobacco Abuse . . . . . . . . . . . . . . . . . . . . . . . . . . . . . . . . . . . . . . . . . 15
Anticoagulation . . . . . . . . . . . . . . . . . . . . . . . . . . . . . . . . . . . . . . . . . . . . . . . . . . 18
Anxiety . . . . . . . . . . . . . . . . . . . . . . . . . . . . . . . . . . . . . . . . . . . . . . . . . . . . . . . . 21
Cardiovascular Diseases . . . . . . . . . . . . . . . . . . . . . . . . . . . . . . . . . . . . . . . . . . . 24
Delirium . . . . . . . . . . . . . . . . . . . . . . . . . . . . . . . . . . . . . . . . . . . . . . . . . . . . . . . . 42
Dementia . . . . . . . . . . . . . . . . . . . . . . . . . . . . . . . . . . . . . . . . . . . . . . . . . . . . . . . 44
Depression . . . . . . . . . . . . . . . . . . . . . . . . . . . . . . . . . . . . . . . . . . . . . . . . . . . . . . 49
Dermatologic Conditions . . . . . . . . . . . . . . . . . . . . . . . . . . . . . . . . . . . . . . . . . . . 54
Endocrine Disorders . . . . . . . . . . . . . . . . . . . . . . . . . . . . . . . . . . . . . . . . . . . . . . 59
Falls . . . . . . . . . . . . . . . . . . . . . . . . . . . . . . . . . . . . . . . . . . . . . . . . . . . . . . . . . . 65
Gastrointestinal Diseases . . . . . . . . . . . . . . . . . . . . . . . . . . . . . . . . . . . . . . . . . . 70
Hearing Impairment . . . . . . . . . . . . . . . . . . . . . . . . . . . . . . . . . . . . . . . . . . . . . . 78
Hematologic Disorders . . . . . . . . . . . . . . . . . . . . . . . . . . . . . . . . . . . . . . . . . . . . 81
Incontinence—Urinary and Fecal . . . . . . . . . . . . . . . . . . . . . . . . . . . . . . . . . . . . 85
Infectious Diseases . . . . . . . . . . . . . . . . . . . . . . . . . . . . . . . . . . . . . . . . . . . . . . . 91
Kidney Disorders . . . . . . . . . . . . . . . . . . . . . . . . . . . . . . . . . . . . . . . . . . . . . . . . 107
Malnutrition . . . . . . . . . . . . . . . . . . . . . . . . . . . . . . . . . . . . . . . . . . . . . . . . . . . . 114
Musculoskeletal Disorders . . . . . . . . . . . . . . . . . . . . . . . . . . . . . . . . . . . . . . . . 118
Neurologic Disorders . . . . . . . . . . . . . . . . . . . . . . . . . . . . . . . . . . . . . . . . . . . . 129
Osteoporosis . . . . . . . . . . . . . . . . . . . . . . . . . . . . . . . . . . . . . . . . . . . . . . . . . . 138
Pain . . . . . . . . . . . . . . . . . . . . . . . . . . . . . . . . . . . . . . . . . . . . . . . . . . . . . . . . . . 141
Palliative and End-of-Life Care . . . . . . . . . . . . . . . . . . . . . . . . . . . . . . . . . . . . . 150
Preoperative and Perioperative Care . . . . . . . . . . . . . . . . . . . . . . . . . . . . . . . . . 156
Prevention . . . . . . . . . . . . . . . . . . . . . . . . . . . . . . . . . . . . . . . . . . . . . . . . . . . . . 159
Prostate Disorders . . . . . . . . . . . . . . . . . . . . . . . . . . . . . . . . . . . . . . . . . . . . . . 163
Psychotic Disorders . . . . . . . . . . . . . . . . . . . . . . . . . . . . . . . . . . . . . . . . . . . . . 165
Respiratory Diseases . . . . . . . . . . . . . . . . . . . . . . . . . . . . . . . . . . . . . . . . . . . . 167
Sexual Dysfunction . . . . . . . . . . . . . . . . . . . . . . . . . . . . . . . . . . . . . . . . . . . . . . 177
Skin Ulcers . . . . . . . . . . . . . . . . . . . . . . . . . . . . . . . . . . . . . . . . . . . . . . . . . . . . 180
Sleep Disorders . . . . . . . . . . . . . . . . . . . . . . . . . . . . . . . . . . . . . . . . . . . . . . . . 190
Visual Impairment . . . . . . . . . . . . . . . . . . . . . . . . . . . . . . . . . . . . . . . . . . . . . . . 194
Women's Health . . . . . . . . . . . . . . . . . . . . . . . . . . . . . . . . . . . . . . . . . . . . . . . . 199
**Appendixes**
    Assessment Instruments . . . . . . . . . . . . . . . . . . . . . . . . . . . . . . . . . . . . . . . . 204
        Mini-Cog Assessment Instrument for Dementia . . . . . . . . . . . . . . . . . . . 204
        Physical Self-Maintenance Scale (Activities of Daily Living, or ADLs) . . . . 204
        Instrumental Activities of Daily Living Scale (IADLs) . . . . . . . . . . . . . . . . 205
        Geriatric Depression Scale (GDS, Short Form) . . . . . . . . . . . . . . . . . . . . 206
        Brief Hearing Loss Screener . . . . . . . . . . . . . . . . . . . . . . . . . . . . . . . . . 207
        Performance-Oriented Mobility Assessment (POMA) . . . . . . . . . . . . . . . 208
        Abnormal Involuntary Movement Scale (AIMS) . . . . . . . . . . . . . . . . . . . 210
        Pain Scales for Assessing Pain Intensity . . . . . . . . . . . . . . . . . . . . . . . . 212
        Brief Pain Inventory (Short Form) . . . . . . . . . . . . . . . . . . . . . . . . . . . . . 214
        Karnofsky Scale . . . . . . . . . . . . . . . . . . . . . . . . . . . . . . . . . . . . . . . . . . 216
        Palliative Performance Scale (PPS) . . . . . . . . . . . . . . . . . . . . . . . . . . . . 216
        Reisberg Functional Assessment Staging (FAST) Scale . . . . . . . . . . . . . 217
        AUA Symptom Index for BPH . . . . . . . . . . . . . . . . . . . . . . . . . . . . . . . 217
        Medication Appropriateness Assessment . . . . . . . . . . . . . . . . . . . . . . . 218
    OBRA Regulations . . . . . . . . . . . . . . . . . . . . . . . . . . . . . . . . . . . . . . . . . . . . 219
    CMS Criteria: Inappropriate Drug Use in Nursing Homes . . . . . . . . . . . . . . . 223
**Important Telephone Numbers and Web Sites** . . . . . . . . . . . . . . . . . . . . . . . . . 226
**Index** . . . . . . . . . . . . . . . . . . . . . . . . . . . . . . . . . . . . . . . . . . . . . . . . . . . . . . . . 228

# AUTHORS

**David B. Reuben, MD**
Director, Multicampus Program in Geriatric Medicine and Gerontology
Chief, Division of Geriatrics
Archstone Foundation Chair
Professor of Medicine
David Geffen School of Medicine at UCLA
Los Angeles, CA

**Keela A. Herr, PhD, RN**
Professor
Chair, Adult and Gerontological Nursing
College of Nursing
The University of Iowa
Iowa City, IA

**James T. Pacala, MD, MS**
Associate Professor
Distinguished Teaching Professor
Department of Family Medicine and Community Health
University of Minnesota School of Medicine
Minneapolis, MN

**Bruce G. Pollock, MD, PhD**
Professor of Psychiatry, Pharmacology, and Pharmaceutical Sciences
Chief, Academic Division of Geriatrics and Neuropsychiatry
Department of Psychiatry, University of Pittsburgh
Pittsburgh, PA

**Jane F. Potter, MD**
Chief, Section of Geriatrics and Gerontology
Harris Professor of Geriatric Medicine
University of Nebraska Medical Center
Omaha, NE

**Todd P. Semla, MS, PharmD**
Associate Professor
The Feinberg School of Medicine
Northwestern University
Chicago, IL

| | |
|---|---|
| ABG | arterial blood gas |
| ABI | ankle-brachial index |
| ACC | American College of Cardiology |
| ACE | angiotensin-converting enzyme |
| ACIP | Advisory Committee on Immunization Practices |
| ACOG | American College of Obstetrics and Gynecology |
| ACTH | adrenocorticotropic hormone |
| ACR | American College of Rheumatology |
| AD | Alzheimer's disease |
| ADA | American Diabetes Association |
| ADLs | activities of daily living |
| AFB | acid-fast bacillus |
| AGS | American Geriatrics Society |
| AHA | American Heart Association |
| AHRQ | Agency for Healthcare Research and Quality (formerly, Agency for Health Care Policy and Research) |
| AIDS | acquired immune deficiency syndrome |
| AIMS | Abnormal Involuntary Movement Scale |
| ALT | alanine aminotransferase |
| APAP | acetaminophen |
| ARB | angiotensin receptor blocker |
| AS | aortic stenosis |
| ASA | acetylsalicylic acid or aspirin |
| ASA class | American Society of Anesthesiologists grading scale for surgical patients |
| ATA | American Thyroid Association |
| ATS | American Thoracic Society |
| AUA | American Urological Association |
| BMD | bone mineral density |
| BMI | body mass index |
| BP | blood pressure |
| BPH | benign prostatic hyperplasia |
| BUN | blood urea nitrogen |
| C&S | culture and sensitivity |
| CABG | coronary artery bypass graft |
| CAD | coronary artery disease |
| CBC | complete blood cell count |
| cfu | colony-forming unit |
| CHD | coronary heart disease |
| CI | confidence interval |
| CMS | Centers for Medicare and Medicaid Services (formerly, US Health Care Financing Administration, or HCFA) |
| CNS | central nervous system |
| COPD | chronic obstructive pulmonary disease |
| CPAP | continuous positive airway pressure |

| CPK | creatine phosphokinase |
|---|---|
| CPR | cardiopulmonary resuscitation |
| Cr | creatinine |
| CrCl | creatinine clearance |
| CT | computed tomography |
| CXR | chest x-ray |
| CYP | cytochrome P-450 |
| D&C | dilation and curettage |
| D5W | dextrose 5% in water |
| DBP | diastolic blood pressure |
| D/C | discontinue |
| DHIC | detrusor hyperactivity with impaired contractility |
| *DSM-IV* | *Diagnostic and Statistical Manual of Mental Disorders*, 4th ed. |
| | (Washington, DC: American Psychiatric Association; 1994) |
| DVT | deep-vein thrombosis |
| ECF | extracellular fluid |
| ECG | electrocardiogram, electrocardiography |
| EEG | electroencephalogram |
| EF | ejection fraction |
| EPS | extrapyramidal symptoms |
| ESR | erythrocyte sedimentation rate |
| FDA | Food and Drug Administration |
| $FEV_1$ | forced expiratory volume in 1 sec |
| FI | fecal incontinence |
| FOBT | fecal occult blood test |
| FVC | forced vital capacity |
| GAD | generalized anxiety disorder |
| GDS | Geriatric Depression Scale |
| GERD | gastroesophageal reflux disease |
| GFR | glomerular filtration rate |
| GI | gastrointestinal |
| GnRH | gonadotropin-releasing hormone |
| GU | genitourinary |
| Hb | hemoglobin |
| $HbA_{1c}$ | glycosylated hemoglobin |
| HCFA | *See* CMS |
| HCTZ | hydrochlorothiazide |
| HDL | high-density lipoprotein |
| HF | heart failure |
| HR | heart rate |
| HT | hormone therapy |
| HTN | hypertension |
| hx | history |
| IADLs | instrumental activities of daily living |
| IBW | ideal body weight |
| ICD | implantable cardiac defibrillator |
| INH | isoniazid |
| INR | international normalized ratio |

| IOP | intraocular pressure |
|---|---|
| iPTH | intact parathyroid hormone |
| JNC 7 | Seventh Joint National Committee on Prevention, Detection, Evaluation, and Treatment of High Blood Pressure |
| $K^+$ | potassium ion |
| LBW | lean body weight |
| LDL | low-density lipoprotein |
| LFT | liver function test |
| LMWH | low-molecular-weight heparin |
| LVEF | left ventricular ejection fraction |
| LVH | left ventricular hypertrophy |
| MAOI | monoamine oxidase inhibitor |
| MDI | metered-dose inhaler |
| MI | myocardial infarction |
| MMA | methylmalonic acid |
| MMSE | Mini-Mental State Examination (Folstein's) |
| MRA | magnetic resonance angiography |
| MRI | magnetic resonance imaging |
| MSE | mental status examination |
| NG | nasogastric |
| NSAIDs | nonsteroidal anti-inflammatory drugs |
| NPH | neutral protamine Hagedorn (insulin) |
| OCD | obsessive-compulsive disorder |
| OGTT | oral glucose tolerance test |
| OT | occupational therapy |
| PAD | peripheral arterial disease |
| PCA | patient-controlled analgesia |
| PE | pulmonary embolism |
| PEF | peak expiratory flow |
| PNS | peripheral nervous system |
| POMA | Performance-Oriented Mobility Assessment |
| PPD | purified protein derivative (of tuberculin) |
| PSA | prostate-specific antigen |
| PT | prothrombin time *or* physical therapy |
| PTCA | percutaneous transluminal coronary angioplasty |
| PTH | parathyroid hormone |
| PTT | partial thromboplastin time |
| PUVA | psoralen plus ultraviolet light of A wavelength |
| $QT_c$ | QT (cardiac output) corrected for heart rate |
| RBC | red blood cells *or* ranitidine bismuth citrate |
| sats | saturations |
| SBP | systolic blood pressure |
| SD | standard deviation |
| SIADH | syndrome of inappropriate secretion of antidiuretic hormone |
| SPEP | serum protein electrophoresis |
| SSRIs | selective serotonin-reuptake inhibitors |
| TCA | tricyclic antidepressant |
| TD | tardive dyskinesia |

| | | | |
|---|---|---|---|
| TDD | telephone device for the deaf | | |
| TG | triglycerides | | |
| TIA | transient ischemic attack | | |
| TSG | thyroid-stimulating globulin | | |
| TSH | thyroid-stimulating hormone | | |
| TTP | thrombotic thrombocytopenic purpura | | |
| TUIP | transurethral incision of the prostate | | |
| TURP | transurethral resection of the prostate | | |
| U | unit(s) | | |
| UA | urinalysis | | |
| UI | urinary incontinence | | |
| UV | ultraviolet | | |
| VF | ventricular fibrillation | | |
| VIN | vulvar intraepithelial neoplasia | | |
| VT | ventricular tachycardia | | |
| WHO | World Health Organization | | |
| wt | weight | | |

**Drug Prescribing and Elimination**
Drugs are listed by generic names; trade names are in *italics*. Check marks (✔)
indicate drugs preferred for treating older persons. Formulations in text are
bracketed and expressed in milligrams (mg) unless otherwise specified.
Abbreviations for dosing, formulations, and route of elimination are defined below.

| | | | |
|---|---|---|---|
| ac | before meals | min | minute(s) |
| bid | twice a day | mo | month(s) |
| C | capsule, caplet | npo | nothing by mouth |
| conc | concentrate | NS | normal saline |
| CR | controlled release | oint | ointment |
| crm | cream | OTC | over-the-counter |
| ChT | chewable tablet | OU | both eyes |
| d | day(s) | pc | after a meal |
| ER | extended release | Pch | patch |
| F | fecal elimination | pk | pack, packet |
| g | gram(s) | po | by mouth |
| gran | granules | pr | per rectum |
| gtt | drop(s) | prn | as needed |
| h | hour(s) | pwd | powder |
| hs | at bedtime | qam | every morning |
| IM | intramuscular(ly) | qd | every day |
| Inj | injectable(s) | qhs | each bedtime |
| IT | intrathecal(ly) | qid | four times a day |
| IV | intravenous(ly) | qod | every other day |
| K | renal elimination | S | liquid (includes |
| L | hepatic elimination | | concentrate, elixir, |
| lot | lotion | | solution, suspension, |
| max | maximum | | syrup, tincture) |
| MDI | metered-dose inhaler | SC | subcutaneousl(ly) |

| | |
|---|---|
| sec | second(s) |
| shp | shampoo |
| sl | sublingual |
| sol | solution |
| Sp | suppository |
| spr | spray(s) |
| SR | sustained release |
| sus | suspension |
| syr | syrup |
| T | tablet |
| tbsp | tablespoon(s) |
| tinc | tincture |
| tid | three times a day |
| TR | timed release |
| tsp | teaspoon(s) |
| wk | week(s) |
| yr | year(s) |

# INTRODUCTION

Providing high-quality medical care for older persons requires a special set of knowledge, clinical skills, and attitudes. Many resources contain current, accurate information on evaluation and management of the older patient. However, few are portable enough to be used in the examining room, on nursing home or hospital rounds, or when the clinician is on call outside the office.

In 1998, the American Geriatrics Society (AGS) first published *Geriatrics At Your Fingertips® (GAYF)*, a pocket guide that provides immediate access to specific information needed to care for older persons in various health care settings. The response was extraordinary, and *GAYF* soon became the society's best-selling publication. During the past two years, the AGS has created new platforms for *GAYF* to take advantage of the expanding integration of electronic mediums into clinical practice. Specifically, beginning in 2002, *GAYF* became available on the Internet (http://www.geriatricsatyourfingertips.org) and in 2004, Palm and Windows CE operating systems versions of GAYF were released (available for download at the Web site listed above). Clinicians can now have *GAYF* instantly available on their PDAs.

In this edition, we have reorganized some material, creating new chapters on incontinence (including fecal) and prostate disorders (including prostate cancer). Breast cancer has been moved to Women's Health, and Renal Disorders has been renamed Kidney Disorders. New sections on tinnitus, bipolar disorder, skin and soft-tissue infections, chronic kidney failure, and hyperkalemia have also been added. We have updated information throughout the text and tables, including recommended diagnostic tests, management strategies, and assessment instruments. Tables and lists of drugs are designed to facilitate appropriate prescribing. Generic and trade names are provided, as well as information on dosages, how the drugs are metabolized or excreted, and which formulations are available. Specific caveats and cautions to be observed when using the medication in older persons are also included.

The goal of *GAYF* is to reduce to a minimum the amount of time that a practicing clinician must spend searching for specific information that is needed immediately to make patient care decisions. Accordingly, *GAYF* does not attempt to explain in detail the rationale underlying the strategies presented. In many instances, these strategies have been derived from guidelines published by organizations such as the Agency for Healthcare Research and Quality, the American Geriatrics Society, the American Heart Association, and the American Diabetes Association. Many of the guidelines can be obtained from the National Guidelines Clearinghouse (http://www.guideline.gov). When no such guidelines exist, the strategies recommended herein represent the best opinions of the authors and the experts they have asked to review the chapters. In an effort to be comprehensive yet concise, references have been provided sparingly, but many others that are relevant are available from the organizations mentioned or in the most recent edition of the AGS *Geriatrics Review Syllabus*.

The authors welcome comments about the format and content of this edition of *GAYF* that may guide the preparation of future editions. All comments should be addressed to the American Geriatrics Society, Empire State Building, 350 Fifth Avenue, Suite 801, New York, NY 10118.

The authors are particularly grateful to Nancy Lundebjerg at the AGS, who has served a vital role in the development of this book and its readership. We are also grateful to the John A. Hartford Foundation for support in distributing *GAYF* to residents and medical and nurse practitioner students across the nation and for generously supporting the development of PDA versions.

We would also like to thank the following persons who have reviewed parts of this edition:

Perry Fine, MD
Rita A. Frantz, PhD, RN
Gail Greendale, MD
Catherine MacLean, MD, PhD
Elizabeth C. Reed, MD

Larissa Rodriguez, MD
Jules Rosen, MD
Ruth Wintz, MD
Thomas T. Yoshikawa, MD

Guidelines of the following organizations are the basis of parts of specific chapters:

Advisory Committee on Immunization Practices
Agency for Healthcare Research and Quality
   (formerly, Agency for Health Care Policy and Research)
Alzheimer's Association
Amercian Academy of Neurology
American Association for Geriatric Psychiatry
American College of Cardiology
American College of Chest Physicians
American College of Gastroenterology
American College of Obstetrics and Gynecology
American College of Rheumatology
American Diabetes Association
American Geriatrics Society
American Heart Association
American Lung Association
American Pain Society
American Psychiatric Association
American Society of Anesthesiologists
American Thyroid Association
American Urological Association
Ethnogeriatrics Committee, American Geriatrics Society
National Cholesterol Education Program
National Heart, Lung, and Blood Institute
U.S. Preventive Services Task Force
World Health Organization

**Staff**
Managing Editor (all versions): Carol S. Goodwin
Medical Editor (print version): Susan E. Aiello, DVM, ELS
Medical Editor (PDA and Web versions): Barbara B. Reitt, PhD, ELS(D)
Medical Indexer (all versions): L. Pilar Wyman

**Fry Communications, Inc.**
Technical development and production of print and electronic versions:
Robyn Diven, Composition
Melissa Durborow, Group Manager
Gwen Eckenrode, Composition
Jason Hughes, Technical Services Manager
Scott McCaughey, Account Adminstrator
Terry Plyler, Systems Architect/Engineer

# FORMULAS AND REFERENCE INFORMATION

## Table 1. Conversions

| Temperature | Liquid | Weight |
|---|---|---|
| F = (1.8)C + 32 | 1 fl dram = 4 mL | 1 lb = 0.453 kg |
| C = (F − 32) / (1.8) | 1 fl oz = 30 mL | 1 kg = 2.2 lb |
| | 1 tsp = 5 mL | 1 oz = 30 g |
| | 1 tbsp = 15 mL | 1 grain = 60 mg |

**Alveolar-Arterial Oxygen Gradient**
A − a = 148 − 1.2($Paco_2$) − $Pao_2$
[normal = 10 − 20 mm Hg, breathing room air at sea level]

**Calculated Osmolality**
2Na + glucose / 18 + BUN / 2.8 + ethanol / 4.6 + isopropanol / 6 + methanol / 3.2 + ethylene glycol / 6.2  [normal = 280–295]

**Golden Rules of Arterial Blood Gases**
• $Pco_2$ change of 10 corresponds to a pH change of 0.08.
• pH change of 0.15 corresponds to base excess change of 10 mEq/L.

**Creatinine Clearance**
For renally eliminated drugs, dosage adjustments may be necessary if CrCl <60.

$$\frac{IBW(140 - age)\ (0.85\ if\ female)}{(72)\ (stable\ serum\ creatinine)}$$

**Erythrocyte Sedimentation Rate**
Westergren: women = (age + 10) / 2
men = age / 2

**Ideal Body Weight**
• Male = 50 kg + (2.3 kg) (each inch of height >5 feet)
• Female = 45.5 kg + (2.3 kg) (each inch of height >5 feet)

**Lean Body Weight**
IBW + 0.4 (actual body weight − IBW)

**Body Mass Index**

$$\frac{weight\ in\ kg}{(height\ in\ meters)^2} \quad or \quad \frac{weight\ in\ lb}{(height\ in\ inches)^2} \times 704.5$$

**Partial Pressure of Oxygen, Arterial ($Pao_2$) While Breathing Room Air**
100 − (age/3) estimates decline

### Table 2. Motor Function by Nerve Roots

| Level | Motor Function | Level | Motor Function |
|---|---|---|---|
| C4 | Spontaneous breathing | L1–L2 | Hip flexion |
| C5 | Shoulder shrug | L3 | Hip adduction |
| C6 | Elbow flexion | L4 | Hip abduction |
| C7 | Elbow extension | L5 | Great toe dorsiflexion |
| C8/T1 | Finger flexion | S1–S2 | Foot plantar flexion |
| T1–T12 | Intercostal abdominal muscles | S2–S4 | Rectal tone |

### Table 3. Lumbosacral Nerve Root Compression

| Root | Motor | Sensory | Reflex |
|---|---|---|---|
| L4 | Quadriceps | Medial foot | Knee-jerk |
| L5 | Dorsiflexors | Dorsum of foot | Medial hamstring |
| S1 | Plantar flexors | Lateral foot | Ankle-jerk |

# Figure 1. Dermatomes

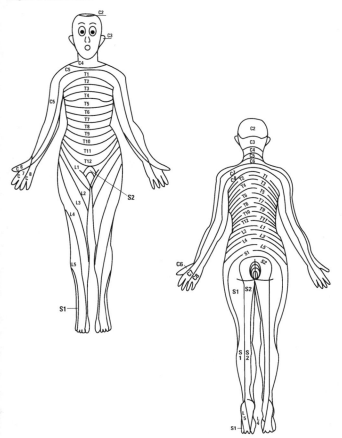

Source: *The Tarascon Pocket Pharmacopoeia*, 2004 classic shirt-pocket edition. Lompoc, CA: Tarascon Publishing, 2004:88. Reprinted with permission.

## ASSESSMENT

### Table 4. Assessing Older Adults*

| Assessment Domain | Screening Methods | Further Assessment (if screen is positive) | See Page(s) |
|---|---|---|---|
| **Medical** | | | |
| Medical illnesses | Hx, screening physical examination | Additional targeted physical examination, laboratory and imaging tests | |
| Medications | Medications review | Pharmacy referral | 9, 218 |
| Nutrition | Inquire about weight loss (>10 lbs in past 6 mo), weigh patient | Dietary hx, malnutrition evaluation | 114 |
| Dentition | Oral examination | Dentistry referral | |
| Hearing | Handheld audioscope, Brief Hearing Loss Screener, whisper test | Ear examination, audiology referral | 78, 207 |
| Vision | Inquire about vision changes, Snellen chart testing | Eye examination, ophthalmology referral | 194 |
| Pain | Inquire about pain | Pain inventory | 141 |
| Urinary incontinence | Inquire if patient has lost urine >5 times in past year | UI evaluation | 85 |
| **Mental** | | | |
| Cognitive status | 3-item recall, Mini-Cog, MMSE | Mental status examination, dementia evaluation | 204 |
| Emotional status | GDS or other depression screen, inquire "Do you ever feel sad or blue?" | In-depth interview | 206 |
| Spiritual status | Spiritual hx | In-depth interview, chaplain or spiritual advisor referral | |
| **Physical** | | | |
| Functional status | ADLs, IADLs | PT/OT referral | 204–206 |
| Balance and gait | Observe patient getting up and walking, orthostatic BP and HR | POMA scale | 208 |
| Falls | Inquire about falls in past year | Falls evaluation | 65 |
| **Environmental** | | | |
| Social, financial status | Social hx | In-depth interview, social work referral | |
| Environmental hazards | Inquire about living situation, home safety checklist | Home evaluation | **Table 36** |

*See also Assessment Instruments, pp 204–218.

## HOUSING ALTERNATIVES FOR OLDER PERSONS

Depending on need for assistance and financial resources, various options are available. Specific names may differ by region, and some may be combinations of various types (see also **Table 69**).

- **Home** with support, if necessary, including caregiver (PP or limited hours if on Medicaid), home-delivered meals (usually PP with sliding scale), homemaker (usually PP with sliding scale)
- **Senior citizen housing** typically does not provide individual services although some may have a social worker available and may provide access to hiring help (PP, may be subsidized for elders spending over one third of income for rent)
- **Continuing care retirement communities** provide living arrangements ranging from independent to skilled (PP)
- **Assisted living facilities, residential care facilities, board-and-cares** provide meals, housekeeping services, and medication management (PP and Medicaid for some facilities)
- **Nursing homes** provide skilled and custodial care, some have separate units for dementia and behavioral problems (PP, Medicaid, Medicare only if following a 3-day or longer hospital stay and only for a limited duration)

    PP = private pay

## SCHEDULED NURSING HOME VISIT CHECKLIST

1. Evaluate patient for interval functional change
2. Check vital signs, weight, laboratory tests, consultant reports since last visit
3. Review medications (correlate to active diagnoses)
4. Sign orders
5. Address nursing staff concerns
6. Write a SOAP note (subjective data, objective data, assessment, plan)
7. Revise problem list as needed
8. Update advance directives at least yearly
9. Update resident; update family member(s) as needed

## INFORMED DECISION MAKING

Physicians have no ethical obligation to offer care that is judged to be futile.
Three elements are needed for a patient's choices to be legally, ethically valid:

- A capable decision maker: Capacity is to the decision being made; patient may be capable of making some but not all decisions. For a sufficiently impaired person, a surrogate decision maker must be involved. (See also **Figure 2**)
- Patient's voluntary participation in the decision-making process.
- Sufficient information: Patient must be sufficiently informed; items to disclose in informed consent include:
  - Diagnosis
  - Nature, risks, costs, and benefits of possible interventions
  - Alternative treatments; relative benefits, risks, and costs
  - Likely results of no treatment
  - Likelihood of success
  - Advice or recommendation of the clinician

## Figure 2. Informed Decision Making

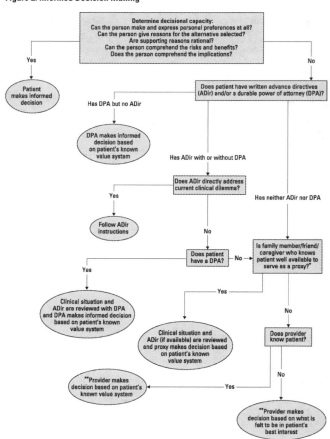

Determine decisional capacity:
Can the person make and express personal preferences at all?
Can the person give reasons for the alternative selected?
Are supporting reasons rational?
Can the person comprehend the risks and benefits?
Does the person comprehend the implications?

Yes → Patient makes informed decision

No → Does patient have written advance directives (ADir) and/or a durable power of attorney (DPA)?

Has DPA but no ADir → DPA makes informed decision based on patient's known value system

Has ADir with or without DPA → Does ADir directly address current clinical dilemma?

Yes → Follow ADir instructions

No → Does patient have a DPA?

Has neither ADir nor DPA → Is family member/friend/caregiver who knows patient well available to serve as a proxy?*

Does patient have a DPA?
Yes → Clinical situation and ADir are reviewed with DPA and DPA makes informed decision based on patient's known value system
No → Is family member/friend/caregiver who knows patient well available to serve as a proxy?*

Is family member/friend/caregiver who knows patient well available to serve as a proxy?*
Yes → Clinical situation and ADir (if available) are reviewed and proxy makes decision based on patient's known value system
No → Does provider know patient?

Does provider know patient?
Yes → **Provider makes decision based on patient's known value system
No → **Provider makes decision based on what is felt to be in patient's best interest

* State laws may dictate who is legal proxy
** Or court-appointed decision maker; laws vary by state

## ELDER MISTREATMENT
### Risk Factors for Inadequate or Abusive Caregiving
- Cognitive impairment in patient, caregiver, or both
- Dependency (financial, psychological, etc) of caregiver on elderly patient, or vice versa
- Family conflict
- Family history of abusive behavior, alcohol or drug problems, mental illness, or mental retardation
- Financial stress
- Isolation of patient or caregiver, or both
- Depression or malnutrition in the patient
- Living arrangements inadequate for needs of the ill person
- Stressful events in the family, such as death of a loved one or loss of employment

Source: Fulmer T. Elder mistreatment. In: Cobbs EL, Duthie ED, Murphy JB, eds. *Geriatrics Review Syllabus: A Core Curriculum in Geriatric Medicine, 5th ed.* Malden, MA: Blackwell Publishing for the American Geriatrics Society; 2002:55. Reprinted with permission.

Table 5. Signs that Raise Suspicion of Elder Mistreatment

| Type of Mistreatment | Some Clinical Signs of Possible Mistreatment | Questions to Ask Patient to Gather more Hx |
|---|---|---|
| Abandonment | Evidence that patient is left alone unsafely<br>Evidence of sudden withdrawal of care by caregiver<br>Statements about abandonment by patient | Is there anyone you can call to come and take care of you? |
| Abuse | Anxiety, nervousness, especially toward caregiver<br>Bruising, in various healing stages, especially bilateral or on inner arms or thighs<br>Fractures, especially in various healing stages<br>Lacerations<br>Repeated emergency department visits<br>Repeated falls<br>Signs of sexual abuse<br>Statements about abuse by patient | Has anyone at home ever hit you or hurt you? |
| Exploitation | Evidence of misuse of patient's assets<br>Inability of patient to account for money and property or to pay for essential care<br>Reports of demands for money or goods in exchange for caregiving or services<br>Unexplained loss of Social Security, pension checks<br>Statements about exploitation by patient | Has anyone taken your things? |
| Neglect | Contractures<br>Dehydration<br>Depression<br>Diarrhea<br>Failure to respond to warning of obvious disease<br>Fecal impaction<br>Inappropriate use of medications<br>Malnutrition<br>Poor hygiene<br>Pressure ulcers<br>Repeated falls<br>Repeated hospital admissions<br>Statements about neglect by patient<br>Urine burns | Are you receiving enough care at home? |

(cont.)

| Type of Mistreatment | Some Clinical Signs of Possible Mistreatment | Questions to Ask Patient to Gather more Hx |
|---|---|---|
| Psychological abuse | Observed impatience, irritability, or demeaning behavior toward patient by caregiver<br>Anxiety, fearfulness, ambivalence, or anger shown by patient about caregiver | Has anyone ever scolded or threatened you? Has anyone made fun of you? |

Table 5. Signs that Raise Suspicion of Elder Mistreatment (cont.)

Source: Adapted from Fulmer T. Elder mistreatment. In: Cobbs EL, Duthie ED, Murphy JB, eds. *Geriatrics Review Syllabus: A Core Curriculum in Geriatric Medicine, 5th ed.* Malden, MA: Blackwell Publishing for the American Geriatrics Society; 2002:55–56. Reprinted with permission.

## Assessment and Management
- Interview patient and caregiver separately.
- Ask patient some general screening questions, such as, "Are there any problems with family or household members that you would like to tell me about?" Follow up a positive response with more direct questions such as those suggested in **Table 5**.
- On physical examination, look for any unusual marks, signs of injury, or conditions listed in **Table 5**.
- If mistreatment is suspected, report case to Adult Protective Services (most states have mandatory reporting laws).
- If patient is in immediate danger of harm, create and implement plan to remove patient from danger (hospital admission, court protective order, placement in safe environment, etc).

## CROSS-CULTURAL GERIATRICS
Clinicians should remember that:
- Wide differences appear among the individuals in every ethnic group.
- Familiarity with a patient's background is useful only if his or her preferences are linked to the cultural heritage.
- Ethnic groups differ widely in
  - approach to decision making (eg, involvement of family and friends),
  - disclosure of medical information (eg, cancer diagnosis),
  - end-of-life care (eg, advance directives and resuscitation preferences).

In caring for patients of any ethnicity:
- Use the patient's preferred terminology for his or her cultural identity in conversation and in health records.
- Determine whether interpretation services are needed; if possible use professional interpreter rather than family member.
- Recognize that the patient may not conceive of illness in Western terms.
- Determine whether the patient is a refugee or survivor of violence or genocide.
- Explore early on the patient's preferences for disclosure of serious clinical findings and reconfirm at intervals.
- Ask if the patient prefers to involve or defer to others in the decision-making process.
- Follow the patient's preferences regarding gender roles.

# APPROPRIATE PRESCRIBING, DRUG INTERACTIONS, AND ADVERSE EVENTS

## HOW TO PRESCRIBE APPROPRIATELY
- **Obtain a complete drug history.** Ask about previous treatments and responses as well as about other prescribers. Ask about allergies, OTC drugs, nutritional supplements, alternative medications, alcohol, tobacco, caffeine, and recreational drugs.
- **Avoid prescribing before a diagnosis is made.** Consider nondrug therapy. Eliminate drugs for which no diagnosis can be identified.
- **Review medications regularly and before prescribing a new medication.** D/C medications that have not had the intended response or are no longer needed. Monitor the use of prn and OTC drugs.
- **Know the actions, adverse effects, and toxicity profiles of the medications you prescribe.** Consider how these might interact or complement existing drug therapy.
- **Start chronic drug therapy at a low dose and titrate dose on the basis of tolerability and response.** Use drug levels when available.
- **Attempt to reach a therapeutic dose before switching or adding another drug.**
- **Educate patient and/or caregiver about each medication.** Include the regimen, the therapeutic goal, the cost, and potential adverse effects or drug interactions. Provide written instructions.
- **Avoid using one drug to treat the adverse events caused by another.**
- **Attempt to use one drug to treat two or more conditions.**
- **Use combination products cautiously.** Establish need for more than one drug. Titrate individual drugs to therapeutic doses and switch to combinations if appropriate.
- **Communicate with other prescribers.** Don't assume patients will—they assume you do!
- **Avoid using drugs from the same class or with similar actions** (eg, alprazolam and zolpidem).

See also Medication Appropriateness Assessment, p 218. For more on drugs that should be avoided in all elderly patients, see p 223.

## WAYS TO REDUCE MEDICATION ERRORS
- Be knowledgeable about the medication's dose, adverse events, interactions, and monitoring.
- Write legibly to avoid misreading of the drug name (*Celexa* versus *Celebrex*).
- Write out the directions, strength, route, quantity, and number of refills.
- Always precede a decimal expression of <1 with a zero (0); never use a zero after a decimal.
- Avoid abbreviations, especially easily confused ones (qd and qid).
- Do not use ambiguous directions, eg, as directed (ud) or as needed.
- Include the medication's purpose in the directions (eg, for high blood pressure).
- Write dosages for thyroid replacement therapy in μg not mg.
- Always re-read what you've written.

## CRITERIA FOR DRUGS OF CHOICE FOR OLDER ADULTS
- Established efficacy
- Compatible safety and adverse-event profile

- Low risk of drug or nutrient interactions
- Half-life <24 h with no active metabolites
- Elimination does not change with age or known dose adjustments for renal or hepatic function
- Convenient dosing—single or twice daily
- Strength and dosage forms match recommended doses for older adults
- Affordable to the patient

## PHARMACOLOGIC THERAPY AND AGE-ASSOCIATED CHANGES

**Table 6. Age-Associated Changes in Pharmacokinetics and Pharmacodynamics**

| Parameter | Age Effect | Disease, Factor Effect | Prescribing Implications |
|---|---|---|---|
| Absorption | Rate and extent are usually unaffected | Achlorhydria, concurrent medications, tube feedings | Drug-drug and drug-food interactions are more likely to alter absorption |
| Distribution | Increase in fat:water ratio; decreased plasma protein, particularly albumin | HF, ascites, and other conditions will increase body water | Fat-soluble drugs have a larger volume of distribution; highly protein-bound drugs have a greater (active) free concentration |
| Metabolism | Decreases in liver mass and liver blood flow may decrease drug metabolism | Smoking, genotype, concurrent drug therapy, alcohol and caffeine intake may have more effect than aging | Lower doses may be therapeutic |
| Elimination | Primarily renal; age-related decrease in GFR | Kidney impairment with acute and chronic diseases; decreased muscle mass results in less Cr production | Serum creatinine not a reliable measure of kidney function; best to estimate CrCl using formula (see p 1) |
| Pharmaco-dynamics | Less predictable and often altered drug response at usual or lower concentrations | Drug-drug and drug-disease interactions may alter responses | Prolonged pain relief with opioids at lower doses; increased sedation and postural instability to benzodiazepines; altered sensitivity to $\beta$-blockers |

## COMPLICATING FACTORS

### Drug-Food or -Nutrient Interactions

***Physical Interactions:*** $Mg^{++}$, $Ca^{++}$, $Fe^{++}$, $Al^{++}$, or zinc can lower oral absorption of levothyroxine and some quinolone antibiotics. Tube feedings decrease absorption of oral phenytoin and levothyroxine.

***Decreased Drug Effect:*** Warfarin and vitamin K-containing foods (eg, green leafy vegetables, broccoli, brussels sprouts, greens, cabbage).

***Decreased Oral Intake or Appetite:*** Drugs can alter the taste of food (dysgeusia) or decrease saliva production (xerostomia), making mastication and swallowing difficult. Drugs associated with dysgeusia include captopril and clarithromycin. Drugs that can cause xerostomia include antihistamines, antidepressants, antipsychotics, clonidine, and diuretics.

## Drug-Drug Interactions

A drug's effect can be increased or decreased by another drug because of impaired absorption (eg, sucralfate and ciprofloxacin), displacement from protein-binding sites (eg, warfarin and sulfonamides), inhibition or induction of metabolic enzymes (see **Table 7**), or because two or more drugs have a similar pharmacologic effect (eg, potassium-sparing diuretics, potassium supplements, and ACE inhibitors).

***Digoxin:*** Digoxin levels must be monitored with concomitant administration of many other drugs.

The following **increase** digoxin concentration or effect, or both:

| | | |
|---|---|---|
| amiodarone | hydroxychloroquine | quinine |
| diltiazem | ibuprofen | spironolactone |
| erythromycin | indomethacin | tetracycline |
| esmolol | nifedipine | tolbutamide |
| flecainide | quinidine | verapamil |

The following **decrease** digoxin concentration or effect, or both:

| | | |
|---|---|---|
| aminosalicylic acid | colestipol | psyllium |
| antacids | kaolin pectin | sulfasalazine |
| antineoplastics | metoclopramide | St. John's wort |
| cholestyramine | | |

***Enzyme Inhibitors and Inducers:*** **Table 7** is a list of common drug-drug interactions via this mechanism.

| Table 7. Selected CYP Isozyme Substrates, Inducers, and Inhibitors | | | | |
|---|---|---|---|---|
| Substrates* | | Isozyme | Inducers** | Inhibitors† |
| Amitriptyline<br>APAP<br>Clozapine<br>Estradiol<br>Imipramine | Nortriptyline<br>Olanzapine<br>Warfarin-R‡ | CYP1A2 | Carbamazepine<br>Cigarette smoke<br>Omeprazole<br>Phenobarbital<br>Phenytoin<br>Rifampin | Amiodarone<br>Cimetidine<br>Diltiazem<br>Estradiol<br>Fluoroquinolones<br>Fluvoxamine<br>Isoniazid<br>Ketoconazole<br>Ticlopidine |
| Celecoxib<br>Fluvastatin<br>Glipizide<br>Ibuprofen<br>Irbesartan<br>Losartan<br>Phenytoin<br>Piroxicam<br>Tamoxifen | | CYP2C9 | Carbamazepine<br>Phenobarbital<br>Phenytoin<br>Rifampin | Amiodarone<br>Cimetidine<br>Fluconazole<br>Fluvoxamine<br>Isoniazid<br>Omeprazole<br>Propoxyphene<br>Ticlopidine<br>Valproic acid |

*(cont.)*

**Table 7. Selected CYP Isozyme Substrates, Inducers, and Inhibitors (cont.)**

| Substrates* | | Isozyme | Inducers** | Inhibitors† |
|---|---|---|---|---|
| Amitriptyline | Paroxetine | CYP2D6 | | Amiodarone |
| Codeine‡ | Risperidone | | | Bupropion |
| Clomipramine | Tamoxifen | | | Celecoxib |
| Desipramine | Timolol | | | Chlorpheniramine |
| Dextromethorphan | Tramadol§ | | | Cimetidine |
| Donepezil | Venlafaxine | | | Clomipramine |
| Haloperidol | | | | Diltiazem |
| Imipramine | | | | Fluoxetine |
| Metoprolol | | | | Haloperidol |
| | | | | Paroxetine |
| | | | | Propoxyphene |
| | | | | Quinidine |
| | | | | Valproic acid |
| Alprazolam | Lovastatin | CYP3A4,5,7 | Carbamazepine | Amiodarone |
| Amiodarone | Nefazodone | | Glucocorticoids | Cimetidine |
| Atorvastatin | Omeprazole | | Griseofulvin | Clarithromycin |
| Buspirone | Pioglitazone | | Oxcarbazepine | Cyclosporine |
| Carbamazepine | Quetiapine | | Phenobarbital | Diltiazem |
| Chlorpheniramine | Quinidine | | Phenytoin | Erythromycin |
| Clarithromycin | Risperidone | | Pioglitazone | Fluconazole |
| Clozapine | Sildenafil | | Rifabutin | Fluoxetine |
| Codeine | Simvastatin | | Rifampin | Fluvoxamine |
| Cyclosporine | Tacrolimus | | St. John's wort | Grapefruit juice |
| Diazepam | Trazodone | | | Haloperidol |
| Dihydropyridine | Triazolam | | | Isoniazid |
| calcium channel | Venlafaxine | | | Itraconazole |
| blockers | Verapamil | | | Ketoconazole |
| Diltiazem | Warfarin | | | Nefazodone |
| Donepezil | Ziprasidone | | | Propoxyphene |
| Erythromycin | Zolpidem | | | Quinidine |
| Estradiol | | | | Telithromycin |
| Fluoxetine | | | | Verapamil |
| Haloperidol | | | | |
| Itraconazole | | | | |
| Ketoconazole | | | | |

* Substrate: a drug metabolized by the isozyme.
** Inducer: a drug that increases the capacity of the isozyme to metabolize the substrate and potentially decreases the therapeutic effect of the substrate.
† Inhibitor: a drug that prevents the isozyme from metabolizing the substrate and increases the risk for toxicity or therapeutic failure of the substrate.
‡ R-isomer
§ Analgesic effect decreased because of inhibition of substrate metabolism to its active metabolite by an inhibitor.
Note: The list of medications is not comprehensive, but represents medications often prescribed for older patients or medications involved in very serious drug interactions (eg, cyclosporine). Some interactions have in vivo or in vitro documentation, whereas others are theoretical. For more information, consult a drug-drug interaction text or Internet resource, eg, http://medicine.iupui.edu/flockhart/.

Table 8. Common Herbal and Alternative Medications Used by Older Adults

| Product | Common Uses | Adverse Events | Drug Interactions | Cautions |
|---------|-------------|----------------|-------------------|----------|
| Chondroitin | Osteoarthritis | Nausea, dyspepsia, changes in intraocular pressure | | |
| Echinacea | Immune stimulant | Hepatotoxicity | Immuno-suppressants | D/C ≥2 wk before surgery; cross-sensitivity with chrysanthemum, ragweed, daisy, and aster allergies; kidney disease; immuno-suppression |
| Feverfew | Anti-inflammatory, migraine prophylaxis | Platelet inhibition, bleeding, GI upset | NSAIDs, antiplatelet agents, anticoagulants | D/C 7 d before surgery, active bleeding |
| Garlic | Hypertension, hypercholesterolemia, platelet inhibitor | Bleeding, GI upset, hypoglycemia | NSAIDs, antiplatelet agents, anticoagulants | D/C 7 d before surgery |
| Ginger | Antiemetic, anti-inflammatory, dyspepsia | Bleeding | NSAIDs, antiplatelet agents, anticoagulants | D/C 7 d before surgery |
| Ginkgo | Alzheimer's disease, memory, intermittent claudication, macular degeneration | Bleeding, nausea, headache, GI upset, diarrhea, anxiety | MAOIs | D/C 36 h before surgery |
| Ginseng | Physical and mental performance enhancer | Hypertension, tachycardia | Antiplatelet agents, anticoagulants, NSAIDs, MAOIs | D/C 7 d before surgery, kidney failure |
| Glucosamine | Osteoarthritis, rheumatoid arthritis | GI distress, anorexia, insomnia, painful and itchy skin, peripheral edema, tachycardia | | Allergy to shellfish |
| Kava kava | Anxiety, sedative | Sedation, hepatotoxicity | Anticonvulsants (increased effect) | D/C 24 h before surgery |
| SAMe (S-adenosyl-methionine) | Depression, fibromyalgia, insomnia, osteoarthritis, rheumatoid arthritis | GI distress, insomnia, dizziness, dry mouth, headache, restlessness | Antidepressants, St. John's wort, NSAIDS, antiplatelet agents, anticoagulants | Not effective for bipolar depression, hyperhomo-cysteinemia (theoretical), D/C at least 14 d before surgery |

(cont.)

**Table 8. Common Herbal and Alternative Medications Used by Older Adults (cont.)**

| Product | Common Uses | Adverse Events | Drug Interactions | Cautions |
|---------|-------------|----------------|-------------------|----------|
| Saw palmetto | BPH | Headache, nausea, GI distress, erectile dysfunction | Finasteride, $\alpha_1$-adrenergic agonist properties in vitro may decrease efficacy | |
| St. John's wort | Depression, anxiety | Photosensitivity, hypomania | Potent CYP inducer (see **Table 7**) | Wear sunscreen, avoid in fair-skinned patients, D/C 5 d before surgery |
| Valerian | Anxiety, insomnia | Sedation, benzodiazepine-like withdrawal | | Taper dose several weeks before surgery |

# ALCOHOL AND TOBACCO ABUSE

## ALCOHOL ABUSE
### Definition
***Possible Alcohol Dependence—DSM-IV:*** Three or more of the following:
- Tolerance, requiring more alcohol to get "high"
- Withdrawal, or drinking to relieve, prevent withdrawal
- Drinking in larger amounts, or for a longer time than intended
- Persistent desire to drink, or unsuccessful efforts to control drinking
- Spending a lot of time obtaining, using alcohol, or recovering from effects
- Giving up important occupational, social, or recreational activities because of drinking
- Drinking despite persistent or recurrent physical or psychologic problems caused or worsened by alcohol

***Possible Alcohol Abuse—DSM-IV:*** Recurring problems with one or more of the following:
- Drinking resulting in the failure to fulfill major obligations at work or in the home
- Drinking in situations where it is physically hazardous
- Alcohol-related legal problems
- Continued drinking despite social problems caused or worsened by alcohol

***Hazardous Drinking:*** WHO definition—use of alcohol that places a person at risk of physical or psychologic complications. Increases risk of HTN, some cancers (eg, head and neck, esophagus, breast in women), and cirrhosis (higher in women). Possible increased risk for hip fracture and other injury.

### Evaluation
Alcohol dependence or abuse is often missed in older persons because of reduced social and occupational functioning; signs more often are poor self-care, malnutrition, and medical illness.

***Alcohol Misuse Screening:*** CAGE questionnaire has been validated in the older population.

**C** Have you ever felt you should **C**ut down?
**A** Does others' criticism of your drinking **A**nnoy you?
**G** Have you ever felt **G**uilty about drinking?
**E** Have you ever had an "**E**ye opener" to steady your nerves or get rid of a hangover?
 (*Positive response to any suggests problem drinking.*)

***Detecting Harmful Drinking*** (≥2 drinks/d for women, ≥3 drinks/d for men is potentially harmful):
May be missed by CAGE; ask
- How many days per week?
- How many drinks on those days?
- Maximum intake on any one day?

- What type (ie, beer, wine, or liquor)?
- What is in "a drink"?

### Aggravating Factors
***Alcohol and Aging:*** Higher blood levels per amount consumed due to decreased lean body mass and total body water; concomitant medications may interact with alcohol.
***Age-related Diseases:*** Cognitive impairment, HTN.

*Medications:* Many drug interactions, eg, APAP, antihypertensives, NSAIDs, sedatives, antidepressants.

**Management**
*Alcohol Guidelines for Moderate Drinking:* No more than 1 drink/d after age 65; 1 drink/d probably reduces cardiovascular and cerebrovascular risk.
*Psychosocial Interventions:*
• Problem drinking or alcohol misuse: Brief intervention; educate patient on effects of current drinking, point out current adverse effects.
• Alcohol dependence or abuse: Self-help groups (eg, Alcoholics Anonymous); professional (eg, psychodynamic, cognitive-behavioral, counseling, social support, family therapy, age-specific inpatient or outpatient).
• Drug therapy: Naltrexone *(Depade, REVIA, Trexan)* 25 mg × 2d, then 50 mg qd [T: 50]. Monitor liver enzymes; useful adjunct to psychosocial therapy; contraindicated in kidney failure; ~10% get nausea, headache (L, K).
• Acute alcohol withdrawal: See p 43.

**SMOKING CESSATION**
**Nonpharmacologic Therapy**
*What Health Providers Should Do:*
• **Ask** about tobacco use at every visit
• **Advise** all users to quit
• **Assess** willingness to quit
• **Assist** the patient with a quit plan, education, pharmacotherapy
*Making the Decision to Quit:*
Patients are more likely to stop smoking if they:
• Believe they could get a smoking-related disease
• Believe they can make an honest attempt at quitting
• Believe the benefits of quitting outweigh the benefits of continued smoking
• Know someone who has had health problems as a result of smoking
*Setting a Quit Date and Deciding on a Plan:*
• Pick a specific day within the next month (gives time to develop a plan).
• Will nicotine replacement therapy be used?
• Will the patient attend a smoking cessation class?
• On quit day, get rid of all cigarettes and related items.
*Managing Symptoms of Withdrawal:*
• **Physical:** Pharmacotherapy (**Table 9**) helps physical symptoms.
• Who should/should not receive pharmacotherapy?
  ○ Nicotine replacement:
    ▪ Improves quit rates in most patients
    ▪ Is contraindicated with recent MI, uncontrolled high BP, arrhythmias, severe angina, gastric ulcer
    ▪ May not be needed if patient smokes fewer than 10 cigarettes/d; if used, recommend lower dosages
  ○ Other agents (bupropion, etc):
    ▪ May be used if nicotine contraindicated
    ▪ Use in combination with nicotine if prior failure using nicotine alone

- **Psychological:**
  - Smoking is linked with many activities, and the link must be unlearned.
  - Avoid people and places where tempted to smoke.
  - Alter habits: 1) switch to juices or water instead of alcohol or coffee, 2) take a brisk walk instead of a coffee break, and 3) use oral substitutions such as sugarless gum or hard candy.
  - Three types of counseling and behavioral therapies are effective: 1) provide problem solving/skills training, 2) provide social support as part of treatment, and 3) provide social support outside of treatment.

*Maintaining Smoking Cessation:* Use the same methods that helped during withdrawal.

Source: Adapted from *Global Strategy for the Diagnosis, Management, and Prevention of Chronic Obstructive Pulmonary Disease, Global Initiative for Chronic Obstructive Lung Disease (GOLD)*. NHLBI/WHO Workshop Report, Executive Summary. National Institutes of Health, National Heart, Lung and Blood Institute. March 2001. NIH Publication No. 2701A (for full report, see http://www.goldcopd.com).

### Table 9. Pharmacotherapy for Tobacco Abuse

| Drug | Dosage | Formulations | Comments (Metabolism, Excretion) |
|---|---|---|---|
| **Tobacco Abuse** | | | |
| Bupropion* (*Wellbutrin SR, Zyban*) | 150 mg bid × 7–12 wk | SR: 100, 150 | Combined with nicotine replacement, doubles quit rate to 30% at 12 mo; contraindicated with seizure disorders (L) |
| **Nicotine Replacement**\*\* | | | |
| Transdermal patches† (eg, *Habitrol, NicoDerm*) | 21 mg/d × 4–8 wk§ 14 mg/d × 2–4 wk 7 mg/d × 2–4 wk | 7, 14, 21 | Apply to clean, nonhairy skin on upper torso, rotate sites; start 14 mg/d with cardiovascular disease or body wt <100 lb or if smoking <10 cigarettes/d (L) |
| (*Nicotrol*) | 15 mg/d × 8 wk§ 10 mg/d × 4–6 wk 5 mg/d × 4–6 wk | 5, 10, 15 | Gradually released over 16 h (L) |
| (*ProStep*) | 22 mg/d × 4–8 wk§ 11 mg/d × 4–8 wk | 11, 22 | Persons <100 lb start lower dose; reduce or D/C after 4–8 wk (L) |
| Polacrilex gum (*Nicorette*) | 9–12 pieces/d | 2, 4 | Chew 1 piece when urge to smoke; usual 10–12 d, max 30/d; 4 mg for smokers >21 cigarettes/d (L) |
| Nasal spray (*Nicotrol NS*) | 1 spr each nostril q 30–60 min | 0.5 mg/spr | Do not exceed 5 applications/h or 40 in 24 h (L) |
| Inhaler‡ (*Nicotrol Inhaler*) | 6–16 cartridges/d | 4 mg delivered/ cartridge | Max 16 cartridges/d with gradual reduction after 6–12 wk if needed (L) |

* Bupropion is FDA approved. Nortriptyline is an effective alternative. Hughes JR, Stead LF, Lancaster T. Antidepressants for smoking cessation. *Cochrane Database Syst Rev* 2002; 1:000031.
** Best used in combination with smoking cessation program; dyspepsia is most common drug-related adverse event.
† In patients receiving >600 mg cimetidine, reduce to next lower patch dose.
‡ Available by prescription only.
§ The next lower dose is less toxic and probably equally effective.

## WARFARIN THERAPY
### Prescribing Warfarin
- For anticoagulation in nonacute conditions, initiate therapy by giving warfarin (*Coumadin, Carfin, Sofarin*) 2– 5 mg/d as fixed dose [T: 1, 2, 2.5, 3, 4, 5, 6, 7.5, 10]; reduce dose if INR >2.5 on day 3.
- Half-life is 31–51 h; steady state is achieved on day 5–7 of fixed dose.
- Warfarin therapy is implicated in **many** adverse drug-drug interactions.
- The following drugs **increase** INR in conjunction with warfarin:

| | | |
|---|---|---|
| alcohol use (binge) | ASA (>3 g/d) | phenytoin |
| allopurinol | cimetidine | propoxyphene |
| amiodarone | clofibrate | SSRIs |
| androgens | corticosteroids | tamoxifen |
| antibiotics | NSAIDs | thyroid hormone |
| APAP (>1.3 g/d >1 wk; monitor INR) | omeprazole | vitamin E (≥400 IU) |

- The following drugs **decrease** INR in conjunction with warfarin:

| | | |
|---|---|---|
| alcohol use (moderate) | cholestyramine | sucralfate |
| barbiturates | estrogens | vitamin K |
| carbamazepine | rifampin | |

### Table 10. Indications for Anticoagulation in the Absence of Active Bleeding or Severe Bleeding Risk

| Condition | Target INR | Duration of Therapy |
|---|---|---|
| Hip or major knee surgery | 2.0–3.0 | 7–10 d or until patient is ambulatory |
| Idiopathic venous thromboembolism (includes PE) | 2.0–3.0 | First 3 mo |
| | 1.5–3.0 | 3 mo–indefinitely |
| Atrial fibrillation | 2.0–3.0 | Indefinitely |
| Mitral valvular heart disease with hx of systemic embolization or left atrial diameter >5.5 cm | 2.0–3.0 | Indefinitely |
| Cardiomyopathy with EF <25% | 2.0–3.0 | Indefinitely |
| Mechanical aortic valve with normal left atrial size and sinus rhythm | 2.0–3.0* | Indefinitely |
| Mechanical aortic valve with enlarged left atrium and/or atrial fibrillation | 2.5–3.5*[†] | Indefinitely |
| Mechanical mitral valve | 2.5–3.5*[†] | Indefinitely |
| Caged ball or caged disk valve | 2.5–3.5[‡] | Indefinitely |
| Bioprosthetic heart valve | 2.0–3.0 | 3 mo |
| Acute MI complicated by severe left ventricular dysfunction, HF, previous emboli, mural thrombus on echocardiography | 2.0–3.0 | 1–3 mo |

* If additional risk factors are present or if there is systemic embolism despite anticoagulation treatment, target INR is 2.5–3.5 and ASA 80–100 mg/d should be added.
† Alternative target INR 2.0–3.0 with addition of ASA 80–100 mg/d.
‡ With addition of ASA 80–100 mg/d.

## Cessation of Anticoagulation Before Surgery

• If INR is between 2.0 and 3.0, hold warfarin 4 doses before surgery; longer if INR >3.0.
• If patient has a mechanical valve, heparin should be used after warfarin is held before surgery.

### Table 11. Treatment of Warfarin Overdose

| INR | Clinical Situation | Action |
|---|---|---|
| ≥3.5 and <5.0 | No significant bleeding | Omit next warfarin dose and/or lower dose |
| ≥5.0 and <9.0 | No significant bleeding | Omit next 1–2 doses of warfarin and restart therapy at lower dose; alternatively, omit 1 dose and give vitamin K (VK) 1.0–2.5 mg po |
| ≥9.0 | No significant bleeding | D/C warfarin and give VK 3.0–5.0 mg po; give additional VK po if INR is not substantially reduced in 24–48 h. Restart warfarin at lower dose when INR is therapeutic. |
| ≥3.0 and <20.0 | Serious bleeding | D/C warfarin; give VK 3.0–10.0 mg by slow IV infusion, supplemented with fresh frozen plasma or prothrombin complex concentrate depending on urgency of situation; check INR q 6h; repeat VK q 12 h as needed |
| Any elevation | Life-threatening bleeding | D/C warfarin; give VK 10.0 mg by slow IV infusion, supplemented with prothrombin complex concentrate; repeat this treatment as needed |

Source: Data from American College of Chest Physicians Consensus Panel on Antithrombotic Therapy: Ansell J, Dalen J, Anderson D, et al. Managing oral anticoagulant therapy. In: Sixth ACCP Consensus Conference on Antithrombotic Therapy. *Chest.* 2001; 119(1 Suppl):22S–38S.

## ACUTE ANTICOAGULATION

### Table 12. Anticoagulants for DVT/PE Prophylaxis and Treatment

| Class, Agent | DVT/PE Prophylaxis Dosage By Condition Type | DVT/PE Treatment Dosage | Comments |
|---|---|---|---|
| **Heparin** | | | |
| Unfractionated heparin (*Hep-Lock*) | General surgery: 5000 U SC 2 h before and q 12 h after surgery | 5000 U/kg IV bolus followed by 15 mg/kg/h IV* | Bleeding, anemia, thrombocytopenia, hypertransaminasemia, urticaria (L, K) |
| **LMWH** | | | |
| Enoxaparin (*Lovenox*) | THA, HFX: 30 mg SC q 12 h or 40 mg SC qd KR: 30 mg SC q 12 h; AS: 40 mg SC qd | Outpatient treatment of DVT: 1 mg/kg SC q 12 h; inpatient treatment of DVT ± PE: 1 mg/kg SC q 12 h or 1.5 mg/kg SC qd* | Bleeding, anemia, hyperkalemia, hypertransaminasemia, thrombocytopenia, thrombocytosis, urticaria, angioedema (K) |

(cont.)

Table 12. Anticoagulants for DVT/PE Prophylaxis and Treatment (cont.)

| Class, Agent | DVT/PE Prophylaxis Dosage By Condition Type | DVT/PE Treatment Dosage | Comments |
|---|---|---|---|
| Dalteparin (*Fragmin*) | Low-risk THA: 2500–5000 U SC before surgery, 5000 U SC qd after surgery Abdominal surgery: 2500–5000 U SC before and after surgery | DVT: 100 U/kg SC q 12 h; also indicated for anticoagulation in acute coronary syndrome | Same (K) |
| Tinzaparin (*Innohep*) | NA | 175 anti-Xa IU/kg SC qd* | Same (K) |
| **Heparinoid** | | | |
| Danaparoid (*Orgaran*) | THA, HFX, HIT: 750 anti-Xa U SC bid | NA | Same as LMWH (K) |
| **Factor Xa Inhibitor** | | | |
| Fondaparinux (*Arixtra*) | THA, HFX, KR: 2.5 mg SC qd beginning 6–8 h after surgery | Weight <50 kg: 5 mg SC qd; Weight 50–100 kg: 7.5 mg SC qd; Weight >100 kg: 10 mg SC qd | Contraindicated if CrCl <30 mL/min (K) |
| **Direct Thrombin Inhibitors** | | | |
| Argatroban | HIT: 2 µg/kg/min IV infusion | HIT: 2 µg/kg/min IV infusion | ↓ dosage if hepatic impairment (L) |
| Lepirudin (*Refludan*) | HIT: 4 mg/kg bolus, then 0.15 mg/kg/h | HIT: 4 mg/kg bolus, then 0.15 mg/kg/h | ↓ bolus to 0.2 mg/kg if CrCl <60 |
| **Thrombolytics** | | | |
| Streptokinase (*Kabikinase, Streptase*) | NA | 250,000 U IV over 30 min, then 100,000 U/h for 24 h† | Risk of hemorrhage ↑ with age and higher BMI; HTN, hallucination, agitation, confusion, serum sickness (L) |

Note: THA = total hip arthroplasty (hip replacement); HFX = hip fracture surgery; KR = knee replacement; HIT = heparin-induced thrombocytopenia; NA = not applicable.
* Also indicated for anticoagulation in acute coronary syndrome (see **Table 14**).
† Dose in acute MI is 1.5 million U IV over 60 min.

# ANXIETY

## DIAGNOSIS
Anxiety disorders are less prevalent in elderly than in younger adults. New-onset anxiety in elderly persons is often secondary to physical illness, depression, medication adverse events, or withdrawal from drugs.

*DSM-IV* recognizes several anxiety disorders:
(*Italicized type indicates the most common anxiety disorders occurring in older persons.*)
- Acute stress disorder
- Agoraphobia without a history of panic
- *Generalized Anxiety Disorder (GAD)*
- *Anxiety disorder due to a general medical condition*
- Obsessive-compulsive disorder (OCD)
- Panic disorder, with or without agoraphobia
- Post-traumatic stress disorder
- Social phobia (social anxiety disorder)
- Specific phobia
- Substance-induced anxiety disorder

### *DSM-IV* Criteria for GAD
- Excessive anxiety and worry on more days than not for ≥6 mo, about a number of events or activities
- Difficulty controlling the worry
- Anxiety and worry associated with ≥3 of 6 symptoms:
  ○ restlessness or feeling keyed up or on edge
  ○ being easily fatigued
  ○ difficulty concentrating or mind going blank
  ○ irritability
  ○ muscle tension
  ○ sleep disturbance (difficulty falling or staying asleep, or restless unsatisfying sleep)
- Focus of anxiety and worry not confined to features of an Axis I disorder (primary psychiatric disorder); often, about routine life circumstances; may shift from one concern to another
- Anxiety, worry, or physical symptoms cause clinically significant distress or impairment in social, occupational, or other important areas of functioning
- Disturbance not due to the direct physiologic effects of a drug of abuse or a medication or to a medical condition; does not occur exclusively during a mood disorder, psychotic disorder, or a pervasive development disorder.

### *DSM-IV* Criteria for Panic Attack
Discrete period of intense fear or discomfort with ≥4 of the following (also, must peak within 10 min):
- Palpitations, rapid HR
- Sweating
- Feeling dizzy, unsteady, lightheaded, or faint
- Trembling or shaking
- Sensations of shortness of breath or smothering
- Choking feeling

- Chest pain or discomfort
- Nausea or abdominal distress
- Feeling dizzy, unsteady, lightheaded, or faint
- Feelings of unreality or being detached from self
- Fear of losing control or going crazy
- Fear of dying
- Paresthesias
- Chills or hot flushes

## Differential Diagnosis
- Panic disorder: recurrent, unexpected panic attacks
- Physical conditions producing anxiety
  - Cardiovascular: Arrhythmias, angina, MI, HF
  - Endocrine: Hyperthyroidism, hypoglycemia, pheochromocytoma
  - Neurologic: Movement disorders, temporal lobe epilepsy, AD, stroke
  - Respiratory: COPD, asthma, pulmonary embolism
- Medications producing anxiety
  - Caffeine
  - Corticosteroids
  - Nicotine
  - Psychotropics: Antidepressants, antipsychotics, stimulants
  - Sympathomimetics: Pseudoephedrine, $\beta$-agonists
  - Thyroid hormones: Overreplacement
- Withdrawal states: alcohol, sedatives, hypnotics, benzodiazepines
- Depression

## EVALUATION
- Past psychiatric hx
- Drug review: Prescribed, OTC, alcohol, caffeine
- Mental status evaluation
- Physical examination: Focus on signs and symptoms of anxiety (eg, tachycardia, hyperpnea, sweating, tremor)
- Laboratory tests: Consider CBC, blood glucose, TSH, $B_{12}$, ECG, oxygen saturation, drug and alcohol screening

## MANAGEMENT
### Nonpharmacologic
- Cognitive-behavior therapy may be useful for GAD, panic disorder, and OCD.
- May be effective alone but mostly used in conjunction with pharmacotherapy.
- Requires a cognitively intact, motivated patient.

### Pharmacologic
*Antidepressants Approved for Anxiety Disorders:* See **Table 27** for dosing.
- Obsessive-compulsive: fluoxetine, fluvoxamine, paroxetine, sertraline; secondary choices include $\beta$-blockers and atypical antipsychotics
- Panic: sertraline, paroxetine; secondary choices include $\beta$-blockers and atypical antipsychotics
- Social phobia: paroxetine, sertraline, venlafaxine XR
- Generalized anxiety: escitalopram, paroxetine, sertraline, venlafaxine XR
- Post-traumatic stress: paroxetine, sertraline

### Buspirone (BuSpar):

- Serotonin 1A partial agonist effective in GAD and anxiety symptoms accompanying general medical illness
- Not effective for acute anxiety, panic, or OCD
- May take 2–4 wk for therapeutic response
- Recommended geriatric dosage: 7.5–10 mg bid [T: 5, 10, 15, 30]
- No dependence, tolerance, withdrawal, CNS depression, or significant drug-drug interactions

### Benzodiazepines:

- Most often used for acute anxiety, GAD, panic, OCD
- Preferred: Intermediate–half-life drugs inactivated by direct conjugation in liver and therefore less affected by aging
- Avoid long-acting benzodiazepines (eg, flurazepam, diazepam, chlordiazepoxide); linked to cognitive impairment, falls, sedation, psychomotor impairment
- Problems: Dependence, tolerance, withdrawal, more so with short-acting benzodiazepines; seizure risk with alprazolam withdrawal
- Potentially fatal if combined with alcohol or other CNS depressants
- Only short-term (60–90 d) use recommended

Table 13. Benzodiazepines for Anxiety Recommended for Geriatric Patients

| Drug | Dosage | Formulations |
|---|---|---|
| Lorazepam (*Ativan*) | 0.5–2 mg in 2–3 divided doses | T: 0.5, 1, 2; S: 2 mg/mL; Inj: 2 mg/mL |
| Oxazepam (*Serax*) | 10–15 mg bid–tid | T: 10, 15, 30 |

# CARDIOVASCULAR DISEASES

## CORONARY ARTERY DISEASE
### Diagnostic Cardiac Tests
- Cardiac catheterization is the gold standard.
- Stress testing: The heart is stressed either through exercise (treadmill, stationary bicycle) or, if the patient cannot exercise or the ECG is markedly abnormal, with pharmacologic agents (dipyridamole, adenosine, dobutamine). Exercise stress tests can be performed with or without cardiac imaging, while pharmacologic stress tests always include imaging. Imaging can be accomplished by a nuclear isotope (eg, thallium) or echocardiography.

## Acute Myocardial Infarction
### Evaluation and Assessment
- Presentation frequently atypical—suspect MI with atypical chest pain; arm, jaw, or abdominal pain (with or without nausea); acute functional decline.
- As in younger persons, diagnosis is made by cardiac enzyme rises, with or without ECG changes. Serial enzyme measurements are necessary to exclude MI.
  - Both creatine kinase MB isoenzymes (CK-MB) and cardiac troponins T and I usually become elevated 4 h following myocardial injury.
  - CK-MB subforms are the most sensitive and specific test for detecting MI in the first 6 h, but troponin remains elevated longer.
  - Elevated troponin in the face of normal CK-MB can indicate increased risk of MI in the ensuing 6 mo.
  - Troponins are not useful for detecting reinfarction within first wk of an MI. CK-MB is the preferred marker for early reinfarction.
  - Both CK-MB and cardiac troponins can exhibit false-positive results that are due to subclinical ischemic myocardial injury or nonischemic myocardial injury.
- Risk factors for acute MI in older adults:

  *Strong:*
  - Previous MI or angina
  - Age
  - Diabetes mellitus
  - Hypertension
  - Smoking
  - Severe coronary artery calcification

  *Weak:*
  - Dyslipidemia (except in those with overt coronary disease)
  - Family hx
  - Obesity
  - Sedentary life style

### Management
- Acute MI management (give at initial presentation): For both ST segment elevation MI and acute coronary syndrome (unstable angina or non-ST segment elevation MI)
  - Bedrest with continuous ECG monitoring.
  - Oxygen to maintain saturation >90%.
  - ASA ± clopidogrel (*Plavix*) and an anticoagulant (see **Table 14**).
  - If catheterization with angioplasty/stent placement is planned, give a glycoprotein IIb/IIIa inhibitor (see **Table 14**).
  - β-Blockers given acutely and continued chronically unless systolic failure or pronounced bradycardia is present. Acute phase: Atenolol (*Tenormin*) 5 mg IV over 5

min and repeat in 10 min, or metoprolol (*Lopressor*) 5 mg IV q 5 min up to a total of 15 mg. Begin chronic phase within 1–2 h: atenolol 25–100 mg po qd or metoprolol 50–200 mg po bid.
○ Nitroglycerin is indicated acutely for persistent ischemia, hypertension, large anterior infarction, or HF. Begin at 5–10 μg/min IV and titrate to pain relief, SBP >90 mm Hg, or resolution of ECG abnormalities.
○ Morphine sulfate 1–5 mg IV if chest pain persists on nitroglycerin therapy.

#### Table 14. Antithrombotic Therapy in Acute Coronary Syndrome

| Class, Agent | Dosage | Indications in Acute Coronary Syndrome |
|---|---|---|
| **Antiplatelet Agents** | | |
| ASA | 162–325 mg po initially followed by 75–160 mg po qd | PACS, DACS, PCI, CABG |
| Clopidogrel (*Plavix*) | 300 mg po initially followed by 75 mg po qd | DACS, PCI* |
| **Anticoagulants** | | |
| Enoxaparin (*Lovenox*) | 30 mg IV bolus, followed by 1 mg/kg SC q 12 h | DACS |
| Dalteparin (*Fragmin*) | 120 IU/kg SC q 12 h | DACS |
| Heparin (*Hep-Lock*) | 60–70 U/kg (maximum 5000 U) IV bolus followed by 12–15 U/kg/h IV | PCI, CABG |
| **Glycoprotein IIb/IIIa Inhibitors** | | |
| Abciximab (*ReoPro*) | 0.25 mg/kg IV bolus followed by 0.125 μg/kg/min (maximum 10 μg/min) | PCI |
| Eptifibatide (*Integrilin*) | 180 μg/kg IV bolus followed by 2.0 μg/kg/min IV | PCI |
| Tirofiban (*Aggrastat*) | 0.4 μg/kg/min IV for 30 min, followed by 0.1 μg/kg/min | PCI |

Note: PACS = possible or suspected acute coronary syndrome; DACS = definite acute coronary syndrome; PCI = acute coronary syndrome with planned percutaneous cardiac intervention; CABG = acute coronary syndrome with emergent CABG a likely possibility
* Use clopidogrel in PACS if patient is allergic to ASA. In combination with ASA, clopidogrel causes increased risks of bleeding, so use carefully in elderly patients. Following an episode of acute coronary syndrome, ASA therapy should be lifelong, while clopidogrel should be given for 9–12 mo. Do not use clopidogrel if there is a reasonable possibility that patient will be undergoing CABG within the next 5 d.

• For Q-wave MI (chest pain <12 h, ≥1 mm ST-segment elevation), re-establishment of blood flow via PTCA, preferably with stent placement, or thrombolytic therapy is indicated.
• Thrombolytic therapy for Q-wave MI:
  ○ Age is not a contraindication.
  ○ Absolute contraindications (ACC/AHA):
    ■ Prior hemorrhagic stroke
    ■ Other stroke or intracerebral event in past yr
    ■ Active internal bleeding
    ■ Known malignant intracranial neoplasm
    ■ Aortic dissection
    ■ Structural cerebral vascular lesion (eg, arteriovenous malformation)
    ■ Significant closed head or facial trauma within 3 mo

○ Relative contraindications:
- BP >180/110 on presentation
- Hx of prior stroke >3 mo, dementia or known intracerebral pathology not covered in absolute contraindications
- Current therapeutic INR ≥3
- Known bleeding diathesis
- Recent (<3 wk) major surgery
- Prolonged (>10 min) or traumatic CPR
- Recent (<2–4 wk) trauma or internal bleeding
- Noncompressible vascular puncture
- Active peptic ulcer
- Hx of severe, chronic HTN
- For streptokinase or anistreplase, prior exposure (5 d–2 yr) or prior allergic reactions

- Emergent CABG is an alternative to PTCA or thrombolytic therapy.
- Subacute pharmacologic management (give during hospitalization): For both ST-segment elevation MI and acute coronary syndrome (unstable angina or non-Q-wave MI)
  ○ Patients with hematocrit ≤30 and who are not in HF should be transfused to achieve hematocrit >33.
  ○ ACE inhibitors should be started within first 24 h following MI with ST-segment elevation, particularly in cases with systolic dysfunction (see **Table 17**).
  ○ Warfarin therapy is indicated in post-MI patients with atrial fibrillation, left ventricular thrombosis, or large anterior infarction (see **Table 10**).
  ○ Lipid-lowering therapy (see Dyslipidemia, p 30) to achieve target levels (total cholesterol <160 mg/dL, LDL cholesterol <70–100 mg/dL, HDL cholesterol >45 mg/dL) should be initiated by the time of hospital discharge.
  ○ At time of discharge, prescribe rapid-acting nitrates prn: Sublingual nitroglycerin or nitroglycerin spray every 5 min for max of 3 doses in 15 min. See **Table 15**.
  ○ Longer-acting nitrates should be prescribed if symptomatic angina and treatment will be medical rather than surgical or angioplasty. May be combined with β-blockers or calcium channel blockers, or both. See **Table 15**.
  ○ Calcium channel blockers should be used cautiously for management of angina only in non-Q-wave infarctions without systolic dysfunction and a contraindication to β-blockers.

**Table 15. Nitrate Dosages and Formulations**

| Drug | Dosage | Formulations |
|---|---|---|
| **Oral** | | |
| Isosorbide dinitrate (*Isordil, Sorbitrate*) | 10–40 mg tid (6 h apart) | T: 5, 10, 20, 30, 40; CT: 5, 10 |
| Isosorbide dinitrate SR (*Isordil Tembids, Dilatrate SR*) | 40–80 mg bid–tid | T: 40 |
| Isosorbide mononitrate (*ISMO, Monoket*) | 20 mg bid (8 AM and 3 PM) | T: 10, 20 |
| Isosorbide mononitrate SR (*Imdur*) | start 30–60 mg qd; max 240 mg/d | T: 30, 60, 120 |
| Nitroglycerin (*Nitro-Bid*) | 2.5–9 mg bid–tid | T: 2.5, 6.5, 9 |

(cont.)

Table 15. Nitrate Dosages and Formulations (cont.)

| Drug | Dosage | Formulations |
|---|---|---|
| **Sublingual** | | |
| Isosorbide dinitrate (*Isordil, Sorbitrate*) | 1 tablet prn | T: 2.5, 5, 10 |
| Nitroglycerin (*Nitrostat*) | 0.4 mg prn | T: 0.15, 0.3, 0.4, 0.6 |
| **Oral spray** | | |
| Nitroglycerin (*Nitrolingual*) | 1–2 spr prn; max 3/15 min | 0.4 mg/spr |
| **Ointment** | | |
| Nitroglycerin 2% (*Nitro-Bid, Nitrol*) | start 0.5–4 inches q 4–8 h | 2% |
| **Transdermal** | | |
| Nitroglycerin | 1 Pch 12–14 h/d | (all in mg/h) |
| (*Deponit*) | | 0.2, 0.4 |
| (*Minitran*) | | 0.1, 0.2, 0.4, 0.6 |
| (*Nitrek*) | | 0.2, 0.4, 0.6 |
| (*Nitro-Dur*) | | 0.1, 0.2, 0.3, 0.4, 0.6, 0.8 |
| (*Nitrodisc*) | | 0.2, 0.3, 0.4 |
| (*Transderm-Nitro*) | | 0.1, 0.2, 0.4, 0.6, 0.8 |

## POST-MI AND CHRONIC STABLE ANGINA CARE
• Unless contraindicated, all patients should be on ASA, a $\beta$-blocker, and an ACE inhibitor.
• If $\beta$-blockers are contraindicated, use long-acting nitrates or long-acting calcium channel blockers for chronic angina.
• Use sublingual or spray nitroglycerin for acute angina.
• Treat hypertension; goal of <140/90 or <130/80 if HF, diabetes mellitus, or kidney failure is present.
• Treat dyslipidemia; goals of LDL <70–100 mg/dL and TG <150 mg/dL.
• Treat diabetes mellitus; see p 61 for target goals.
• Weight reduction in obese individuals; goal BMI <25 kg/m$^2$.
• Aerobic exercise; goal 30 min at least 3 times/wk.
• Smoking cessation.
• Use folic acid 1 mg po qd to treat homocysteinemia; goal homocysteine <10 µmoles/L.
• Increase consumption of oily fish (eg, white canned or fresh tuna, salmon, mackerel, herring) and foods rich in $\alpha$-linolenic acid (eg, flax-seed, canola, and soybean oils; flax seed; walnuts). Consider supplementation with fish oil capsules to achieve omega-3 fatty acid intake of 1 g/d.
• Strongly consider placement of implantable cardiac defibrillator in patients with LVEF ≤30% at least 1 mo after MI or 3 mo after CABG.

## HEART FAILURE (HF)
### Evaluation and Assessment
• All patients initially presenting with HF should have an echocardiogram to evaluate left ventricular function. An ejection fraction (EF) of <40% indicates systolic dysfunction. HF with an EF ≥40% indicates diastolic dysfunction.

- Other routine assessment tests: ECG, CXR, CBC, electrolytes, creatinine, albumin, LFTs, TSH, UA
- Measurement of plasma brain natriuretic peptide (BNP) can be helpful in diagnosing acute HF. A BNP >100 pg/mL strongly suggests decreased LV function or acute HF.
- Optional: Radionuclide ventriculography, which measures EF more precisely, provides a better evaluation of right ventricular function, and is more expensive than echocardiography.

**Table 16. Heart Failure Staging**

| Clinical Profile | ACC/AHA Staging | New York Heart Association Staging |
|---|---|---|
| Asymptomatic but at high risk for developing HF (eg, HTN, diabetes mellitus, CAD present) | Stage A | — |
| Asymptomatic with structural disease: LVH, left ventricular dysfunction, prior MI, or valvular disease | Stage B | Class I |
| Structural disease; currently asymptomatic but with hx of symptoms | Stage C | Class I |
| Structural disease; patient comfortable at rest but symptomatic on normal physical activity | Stage C | Class II |
| Structural disease; patient comfortable at rest but symptomatic on slight physical activity | Stage C | Class III |
| Structural disease; patient symptomatic at rest | Stage C | Class IV |
| Refractory symptoms at rest in hospitalized patient requiring specialized interventions or hospice care | Stage D | Class IV |

## Management*
### Nonpharmacologic:
- Exercise: Regular walking or cycling for NYHA Class I–III or AHA/ACC Stage A–C disability (See **Table 16**)
- Measure weight daily
- Salt restriction: 3 g sodium diet is reasonable goal; 2 g in severe HF

### Pharmacologic:
For information on drug dosages and adverse events not listed below, see **Table 20**. Clinicians should be aware that efficacy of different medications may vary significantly across racial and ethnic groups; eg, blacks may require higher doses of ACE inhibitors and β-blockers.

- Systolic dysfunction:
  - Diuretics if volume overload
  - ACE inhibitors to target levels (see **Table 17**)
  - Once volume status is stabilized, a β-blocker (metoprolol XL [*Toprol-XL*] 12.5–25 mg po qd initially, target 200 mg/d; or bisoprolol [*Zebeta*] 1.25 mg po qd initially, target 5 mg qd); or carvedilol (*Coreg*) 3.125 mg po bid initially, target 25 mg bid should be added for long-term HF management if there is no contraindication to β-blockers (do not add β-blockers in acutely ill patients).
  - Add low-dose digoxin (*Lanoxin*) [T: 0.125, 0.25; S: 0.05 mg/mL]; (*Lanoxicaps*) [T: 0.05, 0.1, 0.2], 0.125–0.375 mg qd (target serum levels 0.5–0.8 mg/dL) if HF is not controlled

on diuretics and ACE inhibitors. Digoxin may be less effective and even harmful in women.

○ Adding an aldosterone antagonist can reduce mortality. Use either spironolactone (*Aldactone*) 25 mg qd [T:25] in patients with NYHA Class III or IV failure or eplerenone (*Inspra*) 25–50 mg po qd [T:25, 50, 100] in patients with LVEF <40% who have had MI in the previous 2 wk. Monitor serum potassium carefully and avoid these drugs if Cr ≥2.5 mg/dL.

○ An angiotensin II receptor blocker is indicated in patients being treated with a diuretic, a β-blocker, and digoxin and who cannot receive an ACE inhibitor secondary to cough or angioedema (see **Table 17**).

○ Some clinicians recommend anticoagulating patients with EF <25% (see **Table 10**).

○ Calcium channel blockers, Class I antiarrhythmics, hydralazine, and nitroglycerin are not indicated.

• Diastolic dysfunction:
  ○ Diuretics should be used judiciously and only if there is volume overload.
  ○ There is no agreed-upon primary treatment of diastolic dysfunction. β-Blockers, ACE inhibitors, and/or nondihydropyridine calcium channel blockers may be of benefit.

*Source: Hunt SA, Baker DW, Chin MH, et al. ACC/AHA guidelines for the evaluation and management of chronic heart failure in the adult: executive summary: a report of the American College of Cardiology/American Heart Association Task Force on Practice Guidelines (Committee to Revise the 1995 Guidelines for Evaluation and Management of Heart Failure). *Circulation* 2001;104:2996–3007.

### Table 17. Target Doses of ACE Inhibitors and Angiotensin II Receptor Blockers in Patients with HF

| Agent | Starting Dose | Target Dose |
|---|---|---|
| **ACE Inhibitors** | | |
| Benazepril | 2.5 mg qd | 40 mg qd |
| Captopril | 12.5 mg bid | 50 mg tid |
| Enalapril | 2.5 mg qd | 10 mg bid |
| Fosinopril | 5 mg qd | 40 mg qd |
| Lisinopril | 2.5 mg qd | 20 mg qd |
| Moexipril | 3.75 mg qd | 15 mg qd |
| Perindopril | 4 mg qd | 8 mg qd |
| Quinapril | 5 mg qd | 40 mg qd |
| Ramipril | 1.25 mg qd | 10 mg qd |
| Trandolapril | 1 mg qd | 4 mg qd |
| **Angiotensin Receptor Blockers** | | |
| Candesartan | 4 mg qd | 32 mg qd |
| Eprosartan | 400 mg qd | 400 mg bid |
| Irbesartan | 75 mg qd | 150 mg qd |
| Losartan | 12.5 mg qd | 50 mg bid |
| Olmesartan | 20 mg qd | 40 mg qd |
| Telmisartan | 20 mg qd | 80 mg qd |
| Valsartan | 40 mg qd | 320 mg bid |

## DYSLIPIDEMIA

### Table 18. Treatment Indications for Dyslipidemia

| Risk Category | Conditions | LDL-Cholesterol Goal | Initiate Nonpharmacologic Management | Consider Drug Therapy (see Table 19) |
|---|---|---|---|---|
| Low | 0–1 risk factor* | <160 mg/dL | ≥160 mg/dL | ≥190 mg/dL; optional: 160–189 mg/dL |
| Moderate | 2+ risk factors; 10-yr CAD risk <10%[†] | <130 mg/dL | ≥130 mg/dL | ≥160 mg/dL |
| Moderately high | 2+ risk factors; 10-yr CAD risk 10–20%[†] | <130 mg/dL | ≥130 mg/dL | ≥130 mg/dL; optional: 100–129 mg/dL |
| High | CVD[‡], DM, or 10-yr CAD risk >20%[†] | <100 mg/dL | ≥100 mg/dL | ≥100 mg/dL |
| Very high | DM + CVD[‡]; acute coronary syndrome; multiple severe or poorly controlled risk factors | <100 mg/dL; optional: <70 mg/dL | ≥100 mg/dL | ≥100 mg/dL; optional: 70–99 mg/dL |

* Risk factors are cigarette smoking, HTN, HDL <40 mg/dL, family history of premature CAD, male age ≥45 yr, female age ≥55 yr.
† Calculation of 10-yr risk of CAD is available at http://www.nhlbi.nih.gov/guidelines/cholesterol/
‡ CVD (cardiovascular disease) is signified by CAD, angina, PAD, TIA, stroke, abdominal aortic aneurysm, or 10-yr CAD risk >20%.

### Management

**Nonpharmacologic:** A cholesterol-lowering diet should be considered initial therapy for dyslipidemia and should be used as follows:
• The patient should be at low risk for malnutrition.
• The diet should be nutritionally adequate, with sufficient total calories, protein, calcium, iron, and vitamins.
• The diet should be easily understood and affordable (a dietitian can be very helpful).
• Cholesterol-lowering margarines can lower LDL cholesterol by 10% to 15% (*Take Control* 1–2 tbsp/d; *Benecol* 3 servings of 1.5 tsp each/d).

**Pharmacologic:** Target drug treatment according to type of dyslipidemia.

### Table 19. Drug Regimens for Dyslipidemia

| Condition | Drug | Dosage | Formulations |
|---|---|---|---|
| Elevated LDL, normal TG | HMG-CoA reductase inhibitor* | | |
| | Atorvastatin (*Lipitor*) | 10–80 mg qd | T: 10, 20, 40, 80 |
| | Fluvastatin (*Lescol*) | 20–80 mg qd in PM, max 80 mg | C: 20, 40; T: ER 80 |
| | Lovastatin (*Mevacor, Altocor*) | 10–40 mg qd in PM or bid | T: 10, 20, 40 |
| | Pravastatin (*Pravachol*) | 10–40 mg qd | T: 10, 20, 40, 80 |
| | Rosuvastatin (*Crestor*) | 10–40 mg qd | T: 5, 10, 20, 40 |
| | Simvastatin (*Zocor*) | 5–80 mg qd in PM | T: 5, 10, 20, 40, 80 |

*(cont.)*

Table 19. Drug Regimens for Dyslipidemia (cont.)

| Condition | Drug | Dosage | Formulations |
|---|---|---|---|
| Elevated TG (>500 mg/dL) | Fenofibrate (*Tricor*) | 54–160 mg qd | T: 54, 160 |
| | Gemfibrozil (*Lopid*) | 300–600 mg po bid | T: 600 |
| Combined elevated LDL, low HDL, elevated TG | Fenofibrate, gemfibrozil, or HMG-CoA if TG <300 mg/dL | as above | as above |
| Alternative for any of above | Niacin† | 100 mg tid to start; increase to 500–1000 mg tid; extended release 150 mg qhs to start, increase to 2000 mg qhs as needed | T: 25, 50, 100, 250, 500, ER 150, 250, 500, 750, 1000; C: TR 125, 250, 400, 500 |
| Elevated LDL or combined with inadequate response to one agent | Lovastatin/niacin combination*† (*Advicor*) | 20 mg/500 mg qhs to start; increase to 40 mg/2000 mg as needed | T: 20/500, 20/750, 20/1000 |
| | Colesevelam (*WelChol*) | Monotherapy: 1850 mg po bid; combination therapy: 2500–3750 mg/d in single or divided doses | T: 625 |
| | Ezetimibe (*Zetia*) | 10 mg qd | T: 10 |
| | Ezetimibe/simvastatin combination (*Vytorin*) | 1 tab qd | T: 10/10, 10/20, 10/40, 10/80 |

* Baseline CPK and transaminases. Repeat CPK if symptoms of myopathy. Repeat transaminases at 3 mo, then periodically. Watch for myopathy at higher doses or when used with another antidyslipidemic drug.

† Monitor for flushing, pruritus, nausea, gastritis, ulcer. Dosage increases should be spaced 1 mo apart. ASA 325 mg po 30 min before first niacin dose of the day is quite effective in preventing adverse events.

## HYPERTENSION
### Definition, Classification
JNC 7 defines HTN as SBP >140 or DBP >90. In elderly persons, base treatment decisions primarily on the SBP level.

### Evaluation and Assessment
• Measure both standing and sitting BP after 5 min of rest.
• Base diagnosis on two or more readings at each of two or more visits. Once diagnosis is made, evaluation includes:
  ○ Assessment of cardiac risk factors: smoking, dyslipidemia, obesity, and diabetes mellitus are important in older adults.
  ○ Assessment of end-organ damage: LVH, angina, prior MI, prior coronary revascularization, HF, stroke or TIA, nephropathy, peripheral arterial disease, retinopathy.
  ○ Routine laboratory tests: CBC, UA, electrolytes, creatinine, fasting glucose, total cholesterol, HDL cholesterol, and ECG.

○ Think renal artery stenosis if sudden onset of HTN, sudden rise in BP in previously well-controlled HTN, or HTN despite treatment with three antihypertensives.

**Aggravating Factors**
Almost all are related to life style:
- Emotional stress
- Excessive alcohol intake
- Excessive salt intake
- Lack of aerobic exercise
- Low potassium intake
- Low calcium intake
- Nicotine
- Obesity

**Management**
(JNC 7 recommendations.) Target is <140/90 (130/80 in persons with diabetes or kidney disease). Lowering BP below 120/80 is not recommended. Particularly in patients with "white coat" HTN, home monitoring of BP with a properly calibrated machine can produce more reliable readings than office-based measurements.

*Nonpharmacologic:*
- Adequate calcium and magnesium intake as well as a low-fat diet are recommended for optimizing general health.
- Adequate dietary potassium intake; fruits and vegetables are the best sources.
- Aerobic exercise—30–45 min most days of the week—is recommended.
- Moderation of alcohol intake—limit to 1 oz of ethanol/d.
- Moderation of dietary sodium: watch for volume depletion with diuretic use. Goal: 2.4 g $Na^+$/d.
- Smoking cessation
- Weight reduction in obese persons: even a 10-lb weight loss can significantly lower BP. Goal: BMI (kg/m$^2$) <25.

*Pharmacologic:*
**Table 20** lists commonly used antihypertensives.
- Use antihypertensives carefully in patients with orthostatic BP drop.
- Base treatment decisions on standing BP.
- In the absence of coexisting conditions, a thiazide diuretic, a $\beta$-blocker, or an ACE inhibitor can be used as a first-line drug.
- In the presence of coexisting conditions, therapy should be individualized (see **Table 21**).
- Combination drugs for hypertension are listed in **Table 22**.
- Available dose formulations of oral potassium supplements: [T: (mEq) 6, 7, 8, 10, 20; S: (mEq/15 mL) 20, 40; powders (mEq/pk) l5, 20, 25]
- Follow-up BP measurements monthly until target BP is attained; visits may be q 3–6 mo if BP is stable at target goal.

*Hypertensive Emergencies and Urgencies:*
- Elevated BP alone without symptoms or target end-organ damage rarely requires emergent BP lowering.
- Conditions requiring emergent BP lowering include hypertensive encephalopathy, intracranial hemorrhage, unstable angina, acute MI, acute LV failure with pulmonary edema, dissecting aortic aneurysm.
- Most common initial treatment for emergent BP lowering is sodium nitroprusside (*Nipride*) 0.25–10 mg/kg/min as IV infusion.

• For nonemergent (ie, urgent) BP lowering, give a standard dose of a recommended antihypertensive orally (see **Table 20**) or an extra dose of the patient's usual oral antihypertensive.

**Table 20. Oral Antihypertensive Agents**

| Class, Drug | Geriatric Dosage Range, total mg/d (times/d) | Formulations | Comments (Metabolism, Excretion) |
|---|---|---|---|
| **Diuretics** | | | ↓ potassium, Na, magnesium levels; ↑ uric acid, calcium, cholesterol (mild), and glucose (mild) levels |
| *Thiazides* | | | |
| ✔ Chlorothiazide (*Diuril*) | 125–500 (1) | T: 250, 500 | |
| ✔ Chlorthalidone (*Hygroton*) | 12.5–25 (1) | T: 15, 25, 50, 100 | ↑ adverse events at >25 mg/d (L) |
| ✔ HCTZ (*Esidrix, HydroDIURIL, Oretic*) | 12.5–25 (1) | T: 25, 50, 100; S: 50 mg/mL; C: 12.5 | ↑ adverse events at >25 mg/d (L) |
| ✔ Indapamide (*Lozol*) | 0.625–2.5 (1) | T: 1.25, 2.5 | Less or no hypercholesterolemia (L) |
| ✔ Metolazone (*Mykrox*) | 0.25–0.5 (1) | T rapid: 0.5 | Monitor electrolytes carefully (L) |
| ✔ Metolazone (*Zaroxolyn*) | 2.5–5 (1) | T: 2.5, 5, 10 | Monitor electrolytes carefully (L) |
| ✔ Polythiazide (*Renese*) | 1–4 (1) | T: 1, 2, 4 | |
| *Loop diuretics* | | | |
| ♥ Bumetanide (*Bumex*) | 0.5–4 (1–3) | T: 0.5, 1, 2 | Short duration of action, no hypercalcemia (K) |
| ♥ Furosemide (*Lasix*) | 20–160 (1–2) | T: 20, 40, 80; S: 10, 40 mg/5 mL | Short duration of action, no hypercalcemia (K) |
| ♥ Torsemide (*Demadex*) | 2.5–50 (1–2) | T: 5, 10, 20, 100 | Short duration of action, no hypercalcemia (K) |
| *Potassium-sparing drugs* | | | |
| Amiloride (*Midamor*) | 2.5–10 (1) | T: 5 | (L, K) |
| Triamterene (*Dyrenium*) | 25–100 (1–2) | T: 50, 100 | (L, K) |
| *Aldosterone receptor-blockers* | | | |
| ♥ Eplerenone (*Inspra*) | 25–100 (1) | T: 25, 50, 100 | (L, K) |
| ♥ Spironolactone (*Aldactone*) | 12.5–50 (1–2) | T: 25, 50, 100 | Gynecomastia (L, K) |
| **Adrenergic Inhibitors** | | | |
| *α₁-Blockers* | | | Avoid as primary therapy for HTN unless patient has BPH |
| Doxazosin (*Cardura*) | 1–16 (1) | T: 1, 2, 4, 8 | (L) |
| Prazosin (*Minipress*) | 1–20 (2–3) | T: 1, 2, 5 | (L) |
| Terazosin (*Hytrin*) | 1–20 (1–2) | T: 1, 2, 5, 10; C: 1, 2, 5, 10 | (L, K) |

*(cont.)*

Note: Listing of adverse events is not exhaustive, and adverse events are for the class of drugs except where noted for individual drugs. ✔ = preferred for treating older persons; ♥ = useful in treating HF.

## Table 20. Oral Antihypertensive Agents (cont.)

| Class, Drug | Geriatric Dosage Range, total mg/d (times/d) | Formulations | Comments (Metabolism, Excretion) |
|---|---|---|---|
| Central $\alpha_2$-agonists and other centrally acting drugs | | | Sedation, dry mouth, bradycardia, withdrawal hypertension |
| Clonidine (*Catapres, Catapres-TTS*) | 0.1–1.2 (2–3) *or* 1 Pch/wk | T: 0.1, 0.2, 0.3; Pch: 0.1, 0.2, 0.3 mg/d | Continue oral for 1–2 d when converting to patch (L, K) |
| Guanfacine (*Tenex*) | 0.5–2 (1) | T: 1, 2 | (K) |
| Methyldopa (*Aldomet*) | 250–2500 (2) | T: 125, 250, 500; S: 250 mg/5 mL | (L, K) |
| Reserpine (*Serpasil*) | 0.05–0.25 (1) | T: 0.1, 0.25 | Depression, nasal congestion, activation of peptic ulcer (L, K) |
| β-Blockers | | | Bronchospasm, bradycardia, acute HF, may mask insulin-induced hypoglycemia; lipid solubility is a risk factor for delirium |
| ✔ Acebutolol (*Sectral*) | 200–800 (1) | C: 200, 400 | $\beta_1$, low lipid solubility, intrinsic sympathomimetic activity (L, K) |
| ✔ Atenolol (*Tenormin*) | 12.5–100 (1) | T: 25, 50, 100 | $\beta_1$, low lipid solubility (K) |
| ✔ Betaxolol (*Kerlone*) | 5–20 (1) | T: 10, 20 | $\beta_1$, low lipid solubility (L, K) |
| ✔♥ Bisoprolol (*Zebeta*) | 2.5–10 (1) | T: 5, 10 | $\beta_1$, low lipid solubility (L, K) |
| ✔ Carteolol (*Cartrol*) | 1.25–10 (1) | T: 2.5, 5 | $\beta_1$, low lipid solubility, intrinsic sympathomimetic activity (K) |
| ✔ Metoprolol (*Lopressor*) | 25–400 (2) | T: 25, 50, 100 | $\beta_1$, moderate lipid solubility (L) |
| ✔♥ Long-acting (*Toprol XL*) | 50–400 (1) | T: 25, 50, 100, 200 | (L) |
| Nadolol (*Corgard*) | 20–160 (1) | T: 20, 40, 80, 120, 160 | $\beta_1$, $\beta_2$, low lipid solubility (K) |
| Penbutolol (*Levatol*) | 10–40 (1) | T: 20 | $\beta_1$, $\beta_2$, high lipid solubility, intrinsic sympathomimetic activity, (L, K) |
| Pindolol (*Visken*) | 5–40 (2) | T: 5, 10 | $\beta_1$, $\beta_2$, moderate lipid solubility, intrinsic sympathomimetic activity (K) |
| Propranolol (*Inderal*) | 20–160 (2) | T: 10, 20, 40, 60, 80, 90; S: 4 mg/mL, 8 mg/mL, 80 mg/mL | $\beta_1$, $\beta_2$, high lipid solubility (L) |
| Long-acting (*Inderal LA, InnoPran XL*) | 60–180 (1) | C: 60, 80, 120, 160 | $\beta_1$, $\beta_2$, high lipid solubility (L) |
| Timolol (*Blocadren*) | 10–40 (2) | T: 5, 10, 20 | $\beta_1$, $\beta_2$, low to moderate lipid solubility (L, K) |
| Combined α- and β-blockers | | | Postural hypotension, bronchospasm |

*(cont.)*

Note: Listing of adverse events is not exhaustive, and adverse events are for the class of drugs except where noted for individual drugs. ✔ = preferred for treating older persons; ♥ = useful in treating HF.

**Table 20. Oral Antihypertensive Agents (cont.)**

| Class, Drug | Geriatric Dosage Range, total mg/d (times/d) | Formulations | Comments (Metabolism, Excretion) |
|---|---|---|---|
| ✔ ♥ Carvedilol (*Coreg*) | 3.125–25 (2) | T: 3.125, 6.25, 12.5, 25 | $\beta_1$, $\beta_2$, high lipid solubility (L) |
| ✔ Labetalol (*Normodyne, Trandate*) | 100–600 (2) | T: 100, 200, 300 | $\beta_1$, $\beta_2$, moderate lipid solubility (L, K) |
| **Direct Vasodilators** | | | Headaches, fluid retention, tachycardia |
| Hydralazine (*Apresoline*) | 25–100 (2–4) | T: 10, 25, 50, 100 | Lupus syndrome (L, K) |
| Minoxidil (*Loniten*) | 2.5–50 (1) | T: 2.5, 10 | Hirsutism (K) |
| **Calcium Antagonists** | | | |
| Nondihydropyridines | | | Conduction defects, worsening of systolic dysfunction, gingival hyperplasia |
| ✔ Diltiazem SR (*Cardizem CD, Cardizem SR, Dilacor XR, Tiazac*) | 120–360 (1–2) max 480 | C: 1/d: 120, 180, 240, 300, 360, 420; 2/d: 60, 90, 120; T: 30, 60, 90, 120, ER: 120, 180, 240 | Nausea, headache (L) |
| ✔ Verapamil SR (*Calan SR, Covera-HS, Isoptin SR, Verelan*) | 120–360 (1–2) | T: SR 120, 180, 240; C: SR 100, 120, 180, 200, 240, 300, 360; T: 40, 80, 120 | Constipation, bradycardia (L) |
| Dihydropyridines | | | Ankle edema, flushing, headache, gingival hypertrophy |
| ✔ Amlodipine (*Norvasc*) | 2.5–10 (1) | T: 2.5, 5, 10 | (L) |
| ✔ Felodipine (*Plendil*) | 2.5–20 (1) | T: 2.5, 5, 10 | (L) |
| ✔ Isradipine (*DynaCirc*) | 2.5–20 (2) | T: 2.5, 5 | (L) |
| ✔ Sustained release (*DynaCirc CR*) | 2.5–10 (1) | T: 5, 10 | (L) |
| ✔ Nicardipine (*Cardene*) | 60–120 (3) | C: 20, 30 | (L) |
| ✔ Sustained release (*Cardene SR*) | 60–120 (2) | T: 30, 45, 60 | (L) |
| ✔ Nifedipine SR (*Adalat CC, Procardia XL*) | 30–60 (1) | T: 30, 60, 90 | (L) |
| ✔ Nisoldipine (*Sular*) | 10–40 (1) | T: ER 10, 20, 30, 40 | (L) |
| **ACE Inhibitors*** | | | Cough (common), angioedema (rare), hyperkalemia, rash, loss of taste, leukopenia |
| ✔ ♥ Benazepril (*Lotensin*) | 2.5–40 (1–2) | T: 5, 10, 20, 40 | (L, K) |
| ✔ ♥ Captopril (*Capoten*) | 12.5–150 (2–3) | T: 12.5, 25, 50, 100 | (L, K) |
| ✔ ♥ Enalapril (*Vasotec*) | 2.5–40 (1–2) | T: 2.5, 5, 10, 20 | (L, K) |

*(cont.)*

Note: Listing of adverse events is not exhaustive, and adverse events are for the class of drugs except where noted for individual drugs. ✔ = preferred for treating older persons; ♥ = useful in treating HF.
* See **Table 17** for target doses in treating HF.

## Table 20. Oral Antihypertensive Agents (cont.)

| Class, Drug | Geriatric Dosage Range, total mg/d (times/d) | Formulations | Comments (Metabolism, Excretion) |
|---|---|---|---|
| ✔♥ Fosinopril (*Monopril*) | 5–40 (1–2) | T: 10, 20, 40 | (L, K) |
| ✔♥ Lisinopril (*Prinivil, Zestril*) | 2.5–40 (1) | T: 2.5, 5, 10, 20, 30, 40 | (K) |
| ✔♥ Moexipril (*Univasc*) | 3.75–30 (1) | T: 7.5, 15 | (L, K) |
| ✔♥ Perindopril (*Aceon*) | 4–8 (1–2) | T: 2, 4, 8 | (L, K) |
| ✔♥ Quinapril (*Accupril*) | 5–40 (1) | T: 5, 10, 20, 40 | (L, K) |
| ✔♥ Ramipril (*Altace*) | 1.25–20 (1) | T: 1.25, 2.5, 5, 10 | (L, K) |
| ✔♥ Trandolapril (*Mavik*) | 1–4 (1) | T: 1, 2, 4 | (L, K) |
| **Angiotensin II Receptor Blockers (ARBs)*** | | | Angioedema (very rare), hyperkalemia |
| ✔♥ Candesartan (*Atacand*) | 4–32 (1) | T: 4, 8, 16, 32 | (K) |
| ✔♥ Eprosartan (*Teveten*) | 400–800 (1–2) | T: 400, 600 | (biliary, K) |
| ✔♥ Irbesartan (*Avapro*) | 75–300 (1) | T: 75, 150, 300 | (L) |
| ✔♥ Losartan (*Cozaar*) | 12.5–100 (1–2) | T: 25, 50, 100 | (L, K) |
| ✔♥ Olmesartan (*Benicar*) | 20–40 (1) | T: 5, 20, 40 | (F, K) |
| ✔♥ Telmisartan (*Micardis*) | 20–80 (1) | T: 20, 40, 80 | (L) |
| ✔♥ Valsartan (*Diovan*) | 40–320 (1) | T: 80, 160, 320; C: 80, 160 | (L, K) |

Note: Listing of adverse events is not exhaustive, and adverse events are for the class of drugs except where noted for individual drugs. ✔ = preferred for treating older persons; ♥ = useful in treating HF.
* See **Table 17** for target doses in treating HF.
Source: Data in part from The seventh report of the Joint National Committee on Prevention, Detection, Evaluation, and Treatment of High Blood Pressure: The JNC 7 report. *JAMA.* 2003;289:2560–2572.

## Table 21. Choosing Antihypertensive Therapy on the Basis of Coexisting Conditions

| Condition | Appropriate For Use | Avoid or Contraindicated |
|---|---|---|
| Angina | β, D, non-D | |
| Atrial tachycardia and fibrillation | β, non-D | |
| Bronchospasm | | β, αβ |
| Diabetes mellitus | ACEI, ARB, β, T[†] | T[†] |
| Dyslipidemia | | β, T[‡] |
| Essential tremor | β | |
| HF | AA, ACEI, ARB, β, αβ, L | D, non-D* |
| Hyperthyroidism | β | |
| MI | β, AA, ACEI | non-D |
| Osteoporosis | T | |
| Prostatism (BPH) | α | |
| Renal insufficiency | AA, ACEI[§] | |

*(cont.)*

#### Table 21. Choosing Antihypertensive Therapy on the Basis of Coexisting Conditions (cont.)

| Condition | Appropriate For Use | Avoid or Contraindicated |
|---|---|---|
| Urge UI | D, non-D | L, T |

Note: AA = aldosterone antagonist; α = α-blocker; β = β-blocker; αβ = combined α- and β-blocker; ACEI = ACE inhibitor; ARB = angiotensin receptor blocker; D = dihydropyridine calcium antagonist; L = loop diuretic; non-D = nondihydropyridine calcium antagonist; L = loop diuretic; T = thiazide diuretic.
\* May be beneficial in HF caused by diastolic dysfunction.
† Low-dose diuretics are probably beneficial in type 2 diabetes; high-dose diuretics are relatively contraindicated in types 1 and 2.
‡ Low-dose diuretics have a minimal effect on lipids.
§ Use with great caution in renovascular disease.

#### Table 22. Combination Drugs for Hypertension

| Combination Type | Fixed-dose Combination, mg* | Trade Name |
|---|---|---|
| ACE inhibitors and calcium channel blockers | Amlodipine/benazepril hydrochloride (2.5/10, 5/10, 5/20, 10/20) | *Lotrel* |
| | Enalapril maleate/felodipine (5/5) | *Lexxel* |
| | Trandolapril/verapamil (2/180, 1/240, 2/240, 4/240) | *Tarka* |
| ACE inhibitors and diuretics | Benazepril/HCTZ (5/6.25, 10/12.5, 20/12.5, 20/25) | *Lotensin HCT* |
| | Captopril/HCTZ (25/15, 25/25, 50/15,50/25) | *Capozide* |
| | Enalapril maleate/HCTZ (5/12.5, 10/25) | *Vaseretic* |
| | Lisinopril/HCTZ (10/12.5, 20/25) | *Prinzide* |
| | Moexipril hydrochloride/HCTZ (7.5/12.5, 15/25) | *Uniretic* |
| | Quinapril hydrochloride/HCTZ (10/12.5, 20/12.5, 20/25) | *Accuretic* |
| Angiotensin-receptor blockers and diuretics | Candesartan cilexetil/HCTZ (16/12.5, 32/12.5) | *Atacand HCT* |
| | Eprosartan mesylate/HCTZ (600/12.5, 600/25) | *Teveten HCT* |
| | Irbesartan/HCTZ (75/12.5, 150/12.5, 300/12.5) | *Avalide* |
| | Losartan potassium/HCTZ (50/12.5, 100/25) | *Hyzaar* |
| | Telmisartan/HCTZ (40/12.5, 80/12.5) | *Micardis HCT* |
| | Valsartan/HCTZ (80/12.5, 160/12.5) | *Diovan HCT* |
| β-Blockers and diuretics | Atenolol/chlorthalidone (50/25, 100/25) | *Tenoretic* |
| | Bisoprolol fumarate/HCTZ (2.5/6.25, 5/6.25, 10/6.25) | *Ziac* |
| | Propranolol LA/HCTZ (40/25, 80/25) | *Inderide* |
| | Metoprolol tartrate/HCTZ (50/25, 100/25) | *Lopressor HCT* |
| | Nadolol/bendroflumethiazide (40/5, 80/5) | *Corzide* |
| | Timolol maleate/HCTZ (10/25) | *Timolide* |
| Centrally acting drug and diuretic | Methyldopa/HCTZ (250/15, 250/25, 500/30, 500/50) | *Aldoril* |
| | Reserpine/chlorothiazide (0.125/250, 0.25/500) | *Diupres* |
| | Reserpine/HCTZ (0.125/25, 0.125/50) | *Hydropres* |
| Diuretic and diuretic | Amiloride hydrochloride/HCTZ (5/50) | *Moduretic* |
| | Spironolactone/HCTZ (25/25, 50/50) | *Aldactazide* |
| | Triamterene/HCTZ (37.5/25, 50/25, 75/50) | *Dyazide, Maxzide* |

*Some drug combinations are available in multiple fixed doses. Each drug dose is reported in mg.
Source: The seventh report of the Joint National Committee on Prevention, Detection, Evaluation, and Treatment of High Blood Pressure: The JNC 7 report. *JAMA.* 2003;289:2560–2572.

## ATRIAL FIBRILLATION (AF)
### Evaluation and Assessment
*Causes:*
- Cardiac disease: Cardiac surgery, cardiomyopathy, HF, hypertensive heart disease, ischemic disease, pericarditis, valvular disease
- Noncardiac disease: Alcoholism, chronic pulmonary disease, infections, pulmonary emboli, thyrotoxicosis

*Standard testing:* ECG, CXR, CBC, electrolytes, creatinine, BUN, TSH, echocardiogram

### Management
- Correct precipitating cause.
- For both acute and chronic AF, the preferred management for most patients is rate control and anticoagulation rather than rhythm control.
  - Rate control (target <80 beats/min) can be achieved with atenolol, metoprolol, diltiazem, or verapamil, given IV (in cases of acute hemodynamic instability) or orally.
  - Digoxin can be used as a second-line agent for rate control.
  - Anticoagulation to INR 2.0–3.0 should be achieved with oral warfarin (see p 18) and continued indefinitely.
  - If anticoagulation is contraindicated, use ASA 325 mg po qd and continue indefinitely.
- Rhythm control via D/C (direct current) or pharmacologic cardioversion is an alternative treatment option in patients with unpleasant symptoms or decreased exercise tolerance on rate control therapy.
  - For D/C (direct current) cardioversion, two methods may be used:
    - Early cardioversion: perform transesophageal echocardiography to exclude intracardiac thrombus; if no thrombus, begin anticoagulation and cardiovert with 4 wk of post-cardioversion anticoagulation.
    - Delayed cardioversion: anticoagulate for 3 wk before cardioversion, followed by 4 wk of post-cardioversion anticoagulation.
  - For pharmacologic cardioversion and rhythm maintenance (recommended only if AF produces symptoms significantly impairing quality of life), the following agents may be tried: amiodarone, disopyramide, propafenone, and sotalol.
- D/C (direct current) cardioversion should be attempted in acute-onset AF with compromised cardiac output or angina.

## AORTIC STENOSIS (AS)
### Evaluation and Assessment
- Presence of symptoms—angina, syncope, HF (frequently diastolic dysfunction)—indicates severe disease and a life expectancy without surgery of <2 yr.
- Echocardiography is essential to measure aortic jet velocity (AJV) and aortic valve area (AVA).
  - Moderate AS is indicated by an AJV of 3.0–4.0 meters/sec and by an AVA of 1.0–1.5 cm$^2$.
  - Severe AS is indicated by an AJV >4.0 meters/sec and by an AVA <1.0 cm$^2$.

- For asymptomatic cases, echocardiography should be repeated annually for moderate AS and every 6–12 mo for severe AS.
- ECG and CXR should be obtained initially to look for conduction defects, LVH, and pulmonary congestion.

### Treatment

- Aortic valve replacement (AVR) surgery
  - Alleviates symptoms and improves ventricular functioning.
  - In most cases, perform AVR promptly *after* symptoms have appeared.
  - Consider risks and benefits of AVR on individual basis (see pp 156–158).
- There is no effective medical treatment. Avoid vasodilators if possible.

## PERIPHERAL ARTERIAL DISEASE (PAD)

Table 23. Classes of Peripheral Arterial Disease

| Class | ABI | Symptoms | Treatment |
|---|---|---|---|
| Normal | >0.9 | None | RFM |
| Mild | 0.8–0.9 | No limitation in walking distance | RFM, AT |
| Moderate to severe | 0.4–0.8 | Walking limited by claudication | RFM, AT, CRx |
| Severe to critical | <0.4 | Rest pain; ischemia on exam | RFM, AT, CRx, LS |

Note: ABI = ankle-brachial BP index; AT = antiplatelet therapy; CRx = claudication therapy; LS = limb salvage; RFM = risk factor modification.

### Treatment

*Risk Factor Modification:*
- Low-fat diet
- Exercise: walking program
- Smoking cessation
- Lipid-lowering therapy
- BP control
- Glycemic control in diabetic patients

*Antiplatelet Therapy:*
- ASA 325 mg qd
- Clopidogrel (*Plavix*) 75 mg qd [T: 75] if ASA failure or intolerant to ASA

*Claudication Treatment:*
- Walking program
- Drug therapy: cilostazol (*Pletal*) 100 mg bid (contraindicated in patients with HF) 1 h before or 2 h after meals [T: 50, 100]; pentoxifylline (*Trental*) 400 mg tid [T: 400]; conventional analgesics

*Limb Salvage:*
- Percutaneous angioplasty
- Bypass surgery

## SYNCOPE

### Table 24. Classification of Syncope

| Cause | Frequency (%) | Features | Increased Risk of Death |
|---|---|---|---|
| Vasovagal | 21 | Preceded by lightheadedness, nausea, diaphoresis; recovery gradual, frequently with fatigue | No |
| Cardiac | 10 | Little or no warning before blackout, rapid and complete recovery | Yes |
| Orthostatic | 9 | Lightheaded prodrome after standing, recovery gradual | No |
| Medication-induced | 7 | Lightheaded prodrome, recovery gradual | No |
| Seizure | 5 | No warning, may have neurologic deficits, slow recovery | Yes |
| Stroke/TIA | 4 | Little or no warning, neurologic deficits | Yes |
| Other causes | 8 | Preceded by cough, micturition, or specific situation | No |
| Unknown | 37 | Any of the above | Yes |

Source: Adapted from Soteriades ES, Evans JC, Larson MG, et al. Incidence and prognosis of syncope. *N Engl J Med* 2002;347:878–885.

### Evaluation
- Focus hx on events before, during, and after loss of consciousness; hx of cardiac disease (significantly worsens prognosis of syncope of all causes); careful medication review.
- Focus on cardiovascular and neurologic systems in physical examination.
- ECG and orthostatic BP/pulse check for all patients.
- Additional testing as suggested by initial evaluation:
  - Ambulatory ECG monitoring for further evaluation of arrhythmia
  - Stress testing to investigate ischemic heart disease
  - Echocardiography to investigate structural heart disease
  - Electrophysiologic studies in patients with prior MI and structural heart disease
  - Tilt-table testing for suspected vasovagal cause
  - Head imaging, electroencephalogram for suspected neurologic cause
  - If suspected orthostatic cause, evaluation for Parkinson's disease, autonomic neuropathy, diabetes mellitus, hypovolemia

### Management
- Patients with cardiac syncope require immediate hospitalization on telemetry; exclude MI and PE.
- Strongly consider hospital admission for patients with syncope due to neurologic or unknown causes, particularly if concurrent heart disease.
- Patients with syncope due to vasovagal, orthostatic, medication-induced, or other causes can usually be managed as outpatients, particularly if there is no hx of heart disease.
- Treatment is correction of underlying cause.

## IMPLANTABLE CARDIAC DEFIBRILLATOR (ICD) PLACEMENT
### Indications (consider life expectancy and comorbidities)
- Established:
  - Cardiac arrest due to ventricular fibrillation (VF) or ventricular tachycardia (VT)
  - Spontaneous sustained VT with structural heart disease
  - Spontaneous sustained VT without structural heart disease not alleviated by other treatments
  - Unexplained syncope with hemodynamically significant VF or VT inducible by electrophysiologic study when drug therapy is ineffective, not tolerated, or not preferred
  - Nonsustained VT, CAD, and inducible VF by electrophysiologic study that is not suppressed by Class I antiarrhythmic
  - LVEF ≤30% and CAD
- Less established:
  - ICD + biventricular pacing for advanced HF (NYHA Class III or IV) and QRS interval ≥120 millisec
  - LVEF ≤35% and nonischemic cardiomyopathy

### Contraindications
- Terminal illness with life expectancy <6 mo
- Unexplained syncope without inducible VT or VF and without structural heart disease
- VT or VF due to transient or easily reversible disorder
- End-stage HF (ACC/AHA Stage D) not awaiting cardiac transplant

### Complications
- Surgical: infection (1%–2%), hematoma, pneumothorax
- Device-related: lead dislodgement or malfunction, connection problems, inadequate defibrillation threshold
- Therapy-related: frequent shocks (appropriate or inappropriate), acceleration of VT, anxiety and other psychological stress

# DELIRIUM

## DIAGNOSIS
### Diagnostic Criteria—Adapted from *DSM-IV*
- Disturbed consciousness (ie, decreased attention, environmental awareness)
- Cognitive change (eg, memory deficit, disorientation, language disturbance), or perceptual disturbance (eg, visual illusions, hallucinations)
- Rapid onset (hours to days) and fluctuating daily course
- Evidence of a causal physical condition

### Risk Factors
- Dementia greatly increases risk for delirium.
- Advanced age, comorbid physical problems (especially sleep deprivation, immobility, dehydration, pain, sensory impairment).

### Evaluation
- Assume reversibility unless proven otherwise.
- Thoroughly review prescription and OTC medications.
- Exclude infection and other medical causes.
- Laboratory studies may include CBC, electrolytes, LFTs, renal function tests, serum albumin, serum calcium, serum glucose, UA, oxygen saturation, CXR, and ECG
- Confusion Assessment Method (CAM): BOTH acute onset and fluctuating course AND inattention AND EITHER disorganized thinking OR altered level of consciousness (Inouye S, *Ann Intern Med.* 1990;113:941–948).

## CAUSES
*(Italicized type indicates the most common causes in older persons.)*
### Drugs
- *Anticholinergics* (eg, diphenhydramine), TCAs, (eg, amitriptyline, imipramine), antipsychotics (eg, chlorpromazine, thioridazine)
- Anti-inflammatory agents, including prednisone
- Benzodiazepines or alcohol—acute toxicity or withdrawal
- Cardiovascular (eg, digitalis, antihypertensives)
- Diuretics
- GI (eg, cimetidine, ranitidine)
- Lithium
- Opioid analgesics (especially meperidine)

### Infections
*Respiratory, skin, urinary tract,* and others

### Metabolic Disorders
Acute blood loss, *dehydration, electrolyte imbalance,* end-organ failure (hepatic, renal), hyperglycemia, *hypoglycemia, hypoxia*

### Cardiovascular
Arrhythmia, *HF, MI,* shock

### Neurologic
CNS infections, head trauma, seizures, stroke, subdural hematoma, TIAs, tumors

### Miscellaneous
Fecal impaction, *postoperative state,* sleep deprivation, urinary retention

## MANAGEMENT
### Nonpharmacologic
• Identify and remove or treat underlying cause(s)
• Provide general supportive measures:
  ○ Environmental modifications
    ▪ communication to reorient to new surroundings
    ▪ objects that provide orientation (eg, calendar, clock)
    ▪ quiet, well-lit surroundings
    ▪ familiar faces (eg, family members) at bedside for reassurance
    ▪ sitters
  ○ Stimulating activities during daytime
    ▪ cognitive activities (eg, current events discussion, word games)
    ▪ ambulation, active range-of-motion exercises
  ○ Correction of sensory deficits
    ▪ eyeglasses
    ▪ adequate lighting
    ▪ magnifying lenses
    ▪ cerumen removal
    ▪ hearing aids
    ▪ portable amplification device
  ○ Measures to promote normal sleep
    ▪ warm milk at bedtime
    ▪ relaxation tapes
    ▪ back massage
    ▪ nighttime noise reduction
  ○ Prevention of dehydration: oral or parenteral supplementation if BUN/creatinine ratio >18
  ○ Physical restraints (only as last resort to maintain patient safety, eg, preventing patient from pulling out tubes or catheters)

### Pharmacologic
• For acute agitation or aggression accompanying delirium, use a high-potency antipsychotic such as haloperidol (*Haldol*) 0.5–2 mg po [T: 0.5, 1, 2, 5, 10, 20; S: 2 mg/mL] or IV or IM (twice as potent as po). May also be given as slow IV push; titrate upward as needed. Reevaluate every 30 min. Observe for development of EPS.
• Other IM antipsychotics are less valuable because of the following concerns:
  ○ Ziprasidone (*Geodon*): cardiac conduction delays
  ○ Risperidone IM (*Risperdal Consta*): not appropriate for acute treatment, only a small initial release of drug occurs.
  ○ Olanzapine IM (*Zyprexa*): anticholinergic and hypotensive effects
• Avoid low-potency antipsychotics such as chlorpromazine (*Thorazine*) or thioridazine (*Mellaril*) because of their anticholinergic and arrythmogenic properties (torsade de pointes). If patient is able to take drugs po, consider low dose of atypical antipsychotic (see **Table 73**).
• If delirium is secondary to alcohol or benzodiazepine withdrawal, use a benzodiazepine such as lorazepam (*Ativan*) in doses of 0.5–2 mg every 4–6 h. Because these agents themselves may cause delirium, gradual withdrawal and discontinuation are desirable. If delirium is secondary to alcohol, also use thiamine 100 mg qd (po, IM, or IV).

# DEMENTIA

## DEMENTIA SYNDROME
### Definition
Acquired decline in memory and in at least one other cognitive function (eg, language, visual-spatial, executive) sufficient to affect daily life in an alert person.

### Estimated Frequencies of Dementia Causes
• AD: 60% to 70%
• Other progressive disorders: 15% to 30% (eg, vascular, Lewy body)
• Completely reversible dementia (eg, drug toxicity, metabolic changes, thyroid disease, subdural hematoma, normal-pressure hydrocephalus): 2% to 5%

## DIAGNOSIS OF AD
• Dementia syndrome
• Gradual onset and continuing decline
• Not due to another physical, neurologic, or psychiatric condition or to medications
• Deficits not occurring exclusively during delirium

## PROGRESSION OF AD
### Mild Cognitive Impairment (preclinical)                    MMSE: 26–30
• Report by patient or informant of memory loss
• Delayed paragraph recall
• Cognition otherwise intact
• No functional impairment, normal ADL
• Mild construction, language, or executive dysfunction
• Some cases of mild cognitive impairment may not progress to AD

### Early, Mild Impairment (yr 1–3 from onset of symptoms)      MMSE: 22–28
• Disorientation for date
• Naming difficulties (anomia)
• Recent recall problems
• Mild difficulty copying figures
• Decreased insight
• Social withdrawal
• Irritability, mood change
• Problems managing finances

### Middle, Moderate Impairment (yr 2–8)                       MMSE: 10–21
• Disoriented to date, place
• Comprehension difficulties (aphasia)
• Impaired new learning
• Getting lost in familiar areas
• Impaired calculating skills
• Delusions, agitation, aggression
• Not cooking, shopping, banking
• Restless, anxious, depressed
• Problems with dressing, grooming

### Late, Severe Impairment (yr 6–12)                          MMSE: 0–9
• Nearly unintelligible verbal output
• Remote memory gone
• Unable to copy or write
• No longer grooming or dressing
• Incontinent
• Motor or verbal agitation

## NONCOGNITIVE SYMPTOMS
### Psychotic Symptoms (eg, Delusions, Hallucinations)
• Occur in about 20% of AD patients
• Delusions may be paranoid (eg, people stealing things, spouse unfaithful)
• Hallucinations (approximately 11% of patients) are more commonly visual

### Depressive Symptoms
• Occur in up to 40% of AD patients; may herald onset of AD
• May cause acceleration of decline if untreated
• Need to suspect if patient stops eating or withdraws

### Agitation or Aggression
• Occurs in up to 80% of patients with AD
• A leading cause of nursing-home admission
• Consider superimposed delirium or pain as a trigger

## RISK AND PROTECTIVE FACTORS FOR AD

| Definite Risks | Possible Risks | Possible Protections |
|---|---|---|
| Age | Other genes | Antioxidants (eg, |
| Family history | Head trauma | vitamin E, beta |
| Down syndrome | Lower educational level | carotene) |
| APOE-E4 | Depression | |

### Clinical Features Distinguishing AD and Other Types of Dementia
• AD: Memory, language, visual-spatial disturbances, indifference, delusions, agitation
• Frontotemporal dementia: Personality change, executive dysfunction, hyperorality, relative preservation of visual-spatial skills
• Lewy body dementia: visual hallucinations, delusions, EPS, fluctuating mental status, sensitivity to antipsychotic medications
• Vascular dementia: abrupt onset, stepwise deterioration, prominent aphasia, motor signs

## EVALUATION
Although completely reversible (eg, drug toxicity) dementia is rare, identifying and treating secondary physical conditions may improve function.

• Hx: Obtain from family or other informant
• Physical and neurologic examination
• Assess functional status
• Evaluate mental status for attention, immediate and delayed recall, remote memory, executive function, and depression. Screening tests may include Mini-Cog (p 204), number of animals named in 1 min, MMSE, GDS (p 206)

### Laboratory Testing
CBC, TSH, B$_{12}$, serum calcium, liver and kidney function tests, electrolytes, serologic test for syphilis (selectively); at this time genetic testing and commercial "Alzheimer blood tests" are not recommended for clinical use.

### Neuroimaging
The likelihood of detecting structural lesions is increased with:
• Onset age <60
• Focal (unexplained) neurologic signs or symptoms
• Abrupt onset or rapid decline (weeks to months)
• Predisposing conditions (eg, metastatic cancer or anticoagulants)
Neuroimaging may detect the 5% of patients with clinically significant structural lesions that would otherwise be missed.

### TREATMENT
Primary goals of treatment are to improve quality of life and maximize functional performance by enhancing cognition, mood, and behavior.

### General Treatment Principles
• Identify and treat comorbid physical illnesses (eg, HTN, diabetes mellitus)
• Avoid anticholinergic medications, eg, benztropine, diphenhydramine, hydroxyzine, oxybutynin, TCAs, clozapine, thioridazine
• Set realistic goals
• Limit prn psychotropic medication use
• Specify and quantify target behaviors
• Maximize and maintain functioning

### Nonpharmacologic Approaches
To improve function:
• Behavior modification, scheduled toileting, and prompted toileting (see p 86) for UI
• Graded assistance (as little help as possible to perform ADLs), practice, and positive reinforcement to increase independence
For problem behaviors:
• Music during meals, bathing
• Walking or light exercise
• Simulate family presence with video or audio tapes
• Pet therapy
• Speak at patient's comprehension level
• Bright light, white noise

### Pharmacologic Treatment of Cognitive Dysfunction in AD
• Patients with a diagnosis of mild or moderate AD should receive a cholinesterase inhibitor that will increase level of acetylcholine in brain (**Table 25**).
  ○ Controlled data show modest symptomatic benefit for cognition, mood, behavioral symptoms, and daily function of cholinergic drugs compared with placebo for 1 yr, and open trials demonstrate benefit for 3 yr.
  ○ Only 10–25% of patients taking cholinesterase inhibitors show clinical improvement, but 80% have less rapid decline.
  ○ Initial studies show benefits of these drugs for patients with Lewy body dementia and dementia with vascular risk factors.
  ○ Cholinergic therapy may attenuate noncognitive symptoms and delay nursing-home placement.

- ○ To evaluate response to stabilize:
  - Elicit caregiver observations of patient's behavior (alertness, initiative) and follow functional status (ADLs [p 204] and IADLs [p 205]).
  - Follow cognitive status (eg, improved or stabilized) by caregiver's report or serial ratings of cognition (eg, Mini-Cog, see p 204; MMSE).
- Memantine (*Namenda*) demonstrated modest efficacy compared with placebo in moderate to severe AD as monotherapy and when combined with donepezil (*Aricept*).
- Consider the antioxidant vitamin E at 1000 IU bid (shown to delay functional decline thought to occur from oxidative stress).
- *Ginkgo biloba* is not generally recommended because clinical trial results are not yet definitive, and preparations vary because such nutriceuticals are not regulated by the FDA (see **Table 8**).
- Estrogen replacement therapy in older women may increase risk of developing AD.

### Table 25. Cognitive Enhancers

| Drug | Formulations | Dosing (Metabolism) |
|---|---|---|
| Donepezil (*Aricept*)* | T: 5, 10; ODT: 5, 10;** S: 5 mg/mL | Start at 5 mg qd, increase to 10 mg qd after 1 mo (CYP2D6, 3A4) (L) |
| Galantamine (*Reminyl*)* | T: 4, 8, 12; S: 4 mg/mL | Start at 4 mg bid, increase to 8 mg bid after 4 wk; recommended dose 8 or 12 mg bid (CYP2D6, 3A4) (L) |
| Rivastigmine (*Exelon*)* | T: 1.5, 3, 4.5, 6 | Start at 1.5 mg bid and gradually titrate up to 6 mg bid as tolerated; retitrate if drug is stopped (K) |
| Memantine (*Namenda* [NMDA antagonist]) | T: 5, 10 | Start at 5 mg qd, increase by 5 mg at weekly intervals to maximum of 10 mg bid; reduce dose if kidney function impaired (K) |

* Cholinesterase inhibitors. Adverse events increase with higher dosing. Continue if improvement or stabilization occurs; stopping drugs can lead to rapid decline. Possible adverse events include nausea, vomiting, diarrhea, dyspepsia, anorexia, weight loss, leg cramps, bradycardia, insomnia, and agitation.

** ODT = oral disintegrating tablet.

### Treatment of Agitation
See also **Table 73**, Antipsychotic Medications.

### Table 26. Agitation Treatment Guidelines

| Symptom | Drug | Dosage | Formulations |
|---|---|---|---|
| Agitation in context of nonacute psychosis | Risperidone* (*Risperdal*) | 0.25–1.5 mg/d | T: 0.25, 0.5, 1, 2, 3, 4; S: 1 mg/mL |
| | Olanzapine (*Zyprexa*) (*Zydis*) | 2.5–10 mg/d | T: 2.5, 5, 7.5, 10, 15, 20 T: oral disintegrating 5, 10, 15, 20 |
| | Quetiapine (*Seroquel*) | 25–400 mg/d | T: 25, 100, 200, 300 |
| | Aripiprazole (*Abilify*) | 5–10 mg/d | T: 5, 10, 15, 20, 30 |
| Acute psychosis agitation if IM or IV is needed | Haloperidol (*Haldol*) | 0.5–2 mg/d** | T: 0.5, 1, 2, 5, 10, 20; S: 2 mg/mL; Inj |
| Agitation in context of depression | SSRI, eg, citalopram (*Celexa*) | 10–30 mg/d | T: 20, 40; S: 2 mg/mL |

(cont.)

Table 26. Agitation Treatment Guidelines (cont.)

| Symptom | Drug | Dosage | Formulations |
|---------|------|--------|--------------|
| Anxiety, mild to moderate irritability | Trazodone (Desyrel) | 50–100 mg/d[†] | T: 50, 100, 150, 300 |
| | Buspirone (BuSpar) | 30–60 mg/d[‡] | T: 5, 7.5, 10, 15, 30 |
| As a possible second-line treatment for significant agitation or aggression | Divalproex sodium (Depakote, Epival) | 500–1500 mg/d[§] | T: 125, 250, 500; S: syr 250 mg/mL; sprinkle capsule: 125 |
| | Carbamazepine (Tegretol) | 300–600 mg/d[§§] | T: 200; ChT: 100; S: sus 100/5 mL |
| | Olanzapine (Zyprexa IntraMuscular) | 2.5–5 mg IM | Inj |
| Sexual aggression, impulse-control symptoms in men | Atypical antipsychotic or divalproex | See dosages above | |
| | If no response, estrogen (Premarin) or | 0.625–1.25 mg/d | T: 0.3, 0.625, 0.9, 1.25, 2.5 |
| | medroxyprogesterone (Depo-Provera) | 100 mg IM/wk | Inj |

* Use with caution in patients with cerebrovascular disease or hypovolemia; may increase risk of cerebrovascular adverse events compared with placebo; similar comparative data not available for other atypical antipsychotics.
** May need to give higher doses in emergency situations; should be used for only short periods of time.
† May need to give higher daytime dosage and larger bedtime dosage; watch for sedation and orthostasis.
‡ Can be given bid; 2–4 wk for adequate trial.
§ Can monitor serum levels; usually well tolerated; check CBC, platelets for agranulocytosis, thrombocytopenia risk in older patients.
§§ Monitor serum levels; periodic CBCs, platelet counts secondary to agranulocytosis risk. Beware of drug-drug interactions.

## CAREGIVER ISSUES
• Over 50% develop depression.
• Physical illness, isolation, anxiety, and burnout are common.
• Intensive education and support of caregivers may delay institutionalization.
• Adult day care for patients and respite services may help.
• Alzheimer's Association offers support, education; chapters are located in major cities throughout US. (See p 226 for telephone, Web site.)
• Family Caregiver Alliance offers support, education, information for caregivers. (See p 226 for telephone, Web site.)

## ADDITIONAL REFERENCES
Doody RS, Stevens JC, Beck C, et al. Practice parameter: management of dementia (an evidence-based review): report of the Quality Standards Subcommittee of the American Academy of Neurology. Neurology 2001; 56(9):1154–1166.

Palmer K, Fratiglioni L, Winblad B. What is mild cognitive impairment? Variations in definitions and evolution of nondemented persons with cognitive impairment. Acta Neuro Scand. 2003;107(Suppl 179):14–20.

# DEPRESSION

## EVALUATION AND ASSESSMENT
Recognizing and diagnosing late-life depression can be difficult. Older patients may complain of lack of energy or other somatic symptoms, attribute symptoms to old age or other physical conditions, or fail to mention them to a health care professional.

### Medical Evaluation
TSH, $B_{12}$, calcium, LFTs, kidney function tests, electrolytes, UA, CBC

### *DSM-IV* Criteria for Major Depressive Episode (Abbreviated)
Five or more of the following symptoms have been present during the same 2-wk period and represent a change from previous functioning; at least one of the symptoms is either (1) depressed mood or (2) loss of interest or pleasure.

- Depressed mood
- Loss of interest or pleasure in activities
- Significant weight loss or gain (not intentional), or decrease or increase in appetite
- Insomnia or hypersomnia
- Psychomotor agitation or retardation
- Fatigue or loss of energy
- Feelings of worthlessness or excessive or inappropriate guilt
- Diminished ability to think or concentrate, or indecisiveness
- Recurrent thoughts of death, suicidal ideation, attempt, or plan

The *DSM-IV* criteria are not specific for older adults; cognitive symptoms may be more prominent. The GDS and other instruments are useful for screening and monitoring (see p 207).

## MANAGEMENT
Treatment should be individualized on the basis of hx, past response, and severity of illness as well as concurrent illnesses. Treatments may be combined.

### Nonpharmacologic
For mild to moderate depression or in combination with pharmacotherapy: cognitive-behavioral therapy, interpersonal therapy, problem-solving therapy.

### Pharmacologic
For mild, moderate, or severe depression: the duration of therapy should be at least 6–12 mo following remission for patients experiencing their first depressive episode. Most older patients with major depression require maintenance antidepressant therapy.

### Choosing an Antidepressant (see **Table 27** and list at bottom of p 51)
*First-line Therapy:* Consider an SSRI for most older patients, especially those with:
- Heart conduction defects or ischemic heart disease
- Prostatic hyperplasia
- Uncontrolled glaucoma

*Second-line Therapy:* Consider venlafaxine, mirtazapine, or bupropion

*Third-line Therapy:* Consider nortriptyline or desipramine for patients with:
- Severe melancholic depression

- Urge incontinence, use duloxetine (*Cymbalta*) or tolterodine (*Detrol*) and an SSRI if avoidance of central anticholinergic effects of a TCA is important (see **Table 41**)

Bupropion, T$_3$, methylphenidate, olanzapine, or risperidone may be useful augmentation to SSRI in cases of partial response. Quetiapine, olanzapine, or risperidone, or electroconvulsive therapy may be necessary for psychotic depression.

**Table 27. Antidepressants Used for Older Adults**

| Class, Drug | Initial Dosage | Usual Dosage | Formulations | Comments (Metabolism, Excretion) |
|---|---|---|---|---|
| **Selective Serotonin-Reuptake Inhibitors** | | | | Class adverse events (EPS, hyponatremia) (L, K [10%]) |
| Citalopram (*Celexa*) | 10–20 mg qam | 20–30 mg/d | T: 20, 40, 60; S: 5 mg/10 mL | |
| Escitalopram (*Lexapro*) | 10 mg/d | 10 mg/d | T: 10, 20 | |
| Fluoxetine (*Prozac*) | 5 mg qam | 5–60 mg/d | T: 10; C: 10, 20, 40; S: 20 mg/5 mL; C: SR 90 (weekly dose) | Long half-lives of parent and active metabolite may allow for less frequent dosing; may cause more insomnia than other SSRIs; CYP2D6, -2C9, -3A4 inhibitor (L) |
| Fluvoxamine (*Luvox*) | 25 mg qhs | 100–300 mg/d | T: 25, 50, 100 | Not approved as an antidepressant in US; CYP1A2, -3A4 inhibitor (L) |
| Paroxetine (*Paxil*) | 5 mg | 10–40 mg/d | T: 10, 20, 30, 40 | Helpful if anxiety symptoms are prominent; increased risk of withdrawal symptoms (dizziness); CYP2D6 inhibitor (L) |
| (*Paxil CR*) | 12.5 mg/d | — | T: ER 12.5, 25, 37.5; S: 10 mg/5 mL | Increase by 12.5 mg/d no faster than 1/wk (L) |
| Sertraline (*Zoloft*) | 25 mg qam | 50–200 mg/d | T: 25, 50, 100; S: 20 mg/mL | (L) |
| **Additional Medications** | | | | |
| Bupropion (*Wellbutrin*, *Zyban*) | 37.5–50 mg bid 100 mg (SR) qd or bid | 75–150 mg bid 100–150 mg (SR) bid | T: 75, 100, SR 100, 150 | Consider for SSRI, TCA nonresponders; safe in HF; may be stimulating; can lower seizure threshold (L) |
| Duloxetine (*Cymbalta*) | 20 mg qd | 20–30 mg bid | C: 20, 30, 60 | Most common side effects nausea, dry mouth, constipation, diarrhea, urinary hesitancy (L) |
| Methylphenidate (*Ritalin*) | 2.5–5 mg at 7 AM and noon | 5–10 mg at 7 AM and noon | T: 5, 10, 20 | Short-term treatment of depression or apathy in physically ill elderly; used as an adjunct (L) |
| Mirtazapine (*Remeron*) | 15 mg qhs | 15–45 mg/d | T: 15, 30, 45 | May increase appetite; sedating; oral disintegrating tablet (SolTab) available (L) |

*(cont.)*

Table 27. Antidepressants Used for Older Adults (cont.)

| Class, Drug | Initial Dosage | Usual Dosage | Formulations | Comments (Metabolism, Excretion) |
|---|---|---|---|---|
| Trazodone (*Desyrel*) | 25 mg qhs | 75–600 mg/d | T: 50, 100, 150, 300 | Sedation may limit dose; may be used as a hypnotic; ventricular irritability; priapism in men (L) |
| Venlafaxine (*Effexor*) | 25–50 mg bid | 75–225 mg/d | T: 25, 37.5, 50, 75, 100 | Low anticholinergic activity; minimal sedation and hypotension; may increase BP; may be useful when somatic pain present; EPS, withdrawal symptoms, hyponatremia (L) |
| (*Effexor XR*) | 75 mg qam | 75–225 mg/d | C: 37.5, 75, 150 | Same as above |
| **Tricyclic Antidepressants** | | | | |
| Desipramine (*Norpramin*) | 10–25 mg qhs | 50–150 mg/d | T: 10, 25, 50, 75, 100, 150 | Therapeutic serum level >115 ng/mL (L) |
| Nortriptyline (*Aventyl, Pamelor*) | 10–25 mg qhs | 75–150 mg/d | C: 10, 25, 50, 75; S: 10 mg/5 mL | Therapeutic window (50–150 ng/mL) (L) |
| **Monoamine Oxidase Inhibitors** | | | | Hypotension; drug, food interactions (K, L) |
| Isocarboxazid (*Marplan*) | 10 mg bid–tid | 10 mg tid | T: 10 | |
| Phenelzine (*Nardil*) | 15 mg qd | 15–60 mg/d | T: 15 | |
| Tranylcypromine (*Parnate*) | 10 mg bid | 20–40 mg/d | T: 10 | |

## Antidepressants to Avoid in Older Adults

- Amitriptyline (eg, *Elavil*): anticholinergic, sedating, hypotensive
- Amoxapine (*Asendin*): anticholinergic, sedating, hypotensive; also associated with EPS, tardive dyskinesia, and neuroleptic malignant syndrome
- Doxepin (eg, *Sinequan*): anticholinergic, sedating, hypotensive
- Imipramine (*Tofranil*): anticholinergic, sedating, hypotensive
- Maprotiline (*Ludiomil*): seizures and rashes
- Protriptyline (*Vivactil*): very anticholinergic; can be stimulating
- St. John's wort: decreases effects of digoxin and CYP3A4 substrates; efficacy questioned
- Trimipramine (*Surmontil*): anticholinergic, sedating, hypotensive

## Electroconvulsive Therapy

Generally safe and very effective.

***Indications:*** Severe depression when a rapid onset of response is necessary; when depression is resistant to drug therapy; for patients who are unable to tolerate antidepressants, have previous response to ECT, have psychotic depression, severe catatonia, or depression with Parkinson's disease.

***Complications:*** Temporary confusion, arrhythmias, aspiration, falls.

***Contraindications:***
- Increased intracranial pressure
- Intracranial tumor
- MI within 3 mo (relative)
- Stroke within 1 mo (relative)

Before ECT evaluation: CXR, ECG, serum electrolytes, and cardiac examination. Additional tests (eg, stress test, neuroimaging, EEG) are used selectively.

## BIPOLAR DISORDER

- 5%–19% of mood disorders in elderly persons.
- Usually begins in early adulthood, family hx.
- 10% may develop after age 50.
- A single manic episode is sufficient for a diagnosis if secondary causes are excluded.
- Late-onset mania may be secondary to head trauma, stroke, delirium, other neurologic disorders, alcohol abuse, or medications (eg, corticosteroids, L-dopa, thyroxine).
- Use olanzapine, quetiapine, risperidone for acute mania (see **Table 73**) and D/C antidepressants if taking.
- Initiate long-term treatment (**Table 28**) as soon as compliance with oral therapy is assured.

### Table 28. Long-term Treatment of Bipolar Disorders*

| Drug | Initial Dosage | Usual Dosage | Formulation | Comments |
|---|---|---|---|---|
| Lithium (*Eskalith, Eskalith CR, Lithobid*) | 150 mg/d | 300–900 mg/d Levels 0.4–0.8 mEq/L | C, T, L, XR | Risk of CNS toxicity; cognitive impairment; hypothyroidism; interactions with diuretics, ACE inhibitors, calcium-channel blockers, NSAIDS |
| Carbamazepine (*Tegretol, Tegretol XR*) | 100 mg bid | 800–1200 mg/d Levels 4–12 µg/L | T | Many drug interactions; may cause SIADH; risk of leukopenia, neutropenia, agranulocytosis, thrombocytopenia; monitor CBC; drowsiness, dizziness |
| Valproic acid (*Depacon, Depakene, Depakote*) | 125 mg bid | 750 mg/d divided doses Levels 50–125 µg/L | T | Can cause weight gain, tremor, several drug interactions; risk of hepatotoxicity, pancreatitis, neutropenia, thrombocytopenia; monitor LFTs and platelets |

*(cont.)*

| Table 28. Long-term Treatment of Bipolar Disorders* (cont.) | | | | |
|---|---|---|---|---|
| **Drug** | **Initial Dosage** | **Usual Dosage** | **Formulation** | **Comments** |
| Lamotrigine (*Lamictal*) | 25 mg/d | 100–200 mg/d | T | D/C if rash; interaction with valproate (when used together, begin at 25 mg qod, titrate to 25–100 mg bid); prolongs PR interval; somnolence, headache common |

* Limited evidence base in elderly persons. See www.mhmr.state.tx.us/centraloffice/medicaldirector/TMAPtoc.html. (See also **Table 60**.)

# DERMATOLOGIC CONDITIONS

## COMMON DERMATOLOGIC CONDITIONS

### Table 29. Dermatologic Conditions Common in Elderly Persons

| Condition | Areas Affected | Description |
|---|---|---|
| **Candidiasis** | Body folds | Erythema, pustules, or cheesy, whitish matter, satellite lesions |
| *Treatment:* See intertrigo, next; antifungal powders, p 56. | | |
| **Intertrigo** | Any place 2 skin surfaces rest against one another (eg, under the breasts) | Moist, erythematous with local superficial skin loss; satellite lesions due to candida |
| *Treatment:* Keep area dry; topical antifungals, absorbent pwd, 1% hydrocortisone or 0.1% triamcinolone crm bid × 1 or 2 d if inflamed. | | |
| **Neurodermatitis** | Any skin surfaces | Generalized, localized itching |
| *Treatment:* Mid- to higher-potency topical corticosteroids (**Table 32**); exclude other causes. | | |
| **Onychomycosis** | Nails | Thickening and discoloration |
| *Treatment:* Itraconazole (*Sporanox*)—toenails: 200 mg po qd × 3 mo or 200 mg po bid × 1 wk/mo × 3 mo; fingernails: 200 mg po bid × 1 wk/mo × 2 mo (L); fluconazole (*Diflucan*)—toenails: 150 or 300 mg po/wk × 6–12 mo; fingernails: 150 or 300 mg po/wk × 3–6 mo (L); terbinafine (*Lamisil*)—toenails: 250 mg po qd × 12 wk; fingernails: 250 mg qd × 6 wk. Obtain nail specimens for laboratory culturing to confirm diagnosis before prescribing itraconazole or terbinafine. | | |
| **Psoriasis** | All skin areas, nails (pitting) | Well-defined, erythematous plaques covered with silver scales; severity varies |
| *Treatment:* Topical corticosteroids, UV light, PUVA, methotrexate, cyclosporine, etretinate, sulfasalazine; anthralin preparations and tar + 1% to 4% salicylic acid; calcipotriene for nonfacial areas. | | |
| **Rosacea** | Face (nose, chin, cheeks, forehead) | Vascular and follicular dilation; mild to moderate |
| *Treatment:* Avoid triggers (stress, prolonged sun exposure and exercise, alcohol, hot drinks, spicy foods). Wear sun screen. | | |
| Topical: azelaic acid 15% gel bid (*Finacea*) or 20% crm bid (*Azelex, Finevin*); metronidazole 0.75% crm or gel bid (*MetroCream, MetroGel*) or 1% crm qd (*Noritate*); sodium sulfacetamide 10% + sulfa 5% qd (*Rosula* aqueous gel, *Clenia* crm, foaming wash), avoid if sulfa allergy or kidney disease (K). | | |
| Oral: tetracycline 500 mg bid–tid, doxycycline 100 mg qd, minocycline 100 mg bid, clarithromycin 250–500 mg bid. | | |
| **Scabies** | Interdigital webs, flexor aspects of wrists, axillary, umbilicus, nipples, genitals | Burrows, erythematous papules or nodules, dry or scaly skin, pruritus |
| *Treatment:* Can result in epidemics; treat all contacts and treat environment. Apply topical products from head to toe: Permethrin (*Elimite*) 5% crm, wash off after 8–14 h; 1% lindane (*K-well, Scabene*) crm, wash off after 8–12 h; oatmeal baths, topical corticosteroids, or emollient creams for symptom relief; ivermectin (*Stromectol*) 200 μg/kg po, may repeat once in 1 or 2 wk [T: 3, 6]. | | |
| **Seborrheic dermatitis** | Nasal labial folds, eyebrows, hairline, sideburns, posterior auricular and midchest | Greasy, yellow scales with or without erythematous base; common in Parkinson's disease and in debilitated patients |
| *Treatment:* Hydrocortisone 1% crm bid or triamcinolone 0.1% oint bid × 2 wk; scalp: shp (selenium sulfide, zinc, or tar); ketoconazole 2% crm for severe conditions when infection from *Pityrosporum orbiculare* is suspected. | | |

*(cont.)*

### Table 29. Dermatologic Conditions Common in Elderly Persons (cont.)

| Condition | Areas Affected | Description |
|---|---|---|
| **Skin maceration** | Any area constantly in contact with moisture, covered with occlusive dressing or bandage; skin folds, groin, buttocks | Erythema; abraded, excoriated skin; blisters; white and silver patches |

*Treatment:* Eliminate cause of moisture: toileting program for incontinence; condom catheter; indwelling catheter (reserve for most intractable conditions); fecal incontinence collector. Protect skin from moisture: clean gently with mild soap after each incontinent episode; apply moisture barrier (eg, *Vaseline, Proshield, Smooth and Cool, Calmoseptine*) to repel moisture; use disposable briefs that wick moisture from the skin; use linen incontinence pads when disposable briefs accentuate perineal dermatitis.

| | | |
|---|---|---|
| **Urticaria** | | |
| Hives | Skin surface | Uniform, red edematous plaques surrounded by white halos |

*Treatment:* Identify cause, oral $H_1$ antihistamines (see **Table 76**), oral glucocorticoids (eg, prednisone 40 mg qd), oral $H_2$ antihistamines, or doxepin (po or topical *Zonalon 5%*) for refractory cases.

| | | |
|---|---|---|
| Angioedema | Lips, eyelids, tongue, larynx, GI tract | Larger, deeper than hives |

*Treatment:* Oral $H_1$ antihistamines (see **Table 76**), oral glucocorticoids. Severe reactions: SC epinephrine 0.3 mL of a 1:1000 dilution (*EpiPen*).

| | | |
|---|---|---|
| Cholinergic | Skin surface | Round, red papular wheals |

*Treatment:* Oral $H_1$ antihistamines (see **Table 76**) 1 h before exercise. Hot shower may relieve itching.

| | | |
|---|---|---|
| **Xerosis** | All skin surfaces | Dull, rough, flaky, cracked; nummular |

*Treatment:* ↑ Humidity, apply emollient oint (eg, *Aquaphor*) or crm (eg, *Eucerin*) immediately after bathing; oatmeal baths; hydrocortisone 1% oint; avoid excess bathing and bath oils (falls).

### Table 30. Skin and Soft-Tissue Infections

| Condition | Areas Affected | Description |
|---|---|---|
| **Erysipelas** | Lower dermis and subcutaneous tissue, face and legs | Bright red, edematous, tender; unilateral distribution; orange peel appearance; well-demarcated border with vesicles and bullae |

*Treatment:* Penicillin; erythromycin or cephalosporin if penicillin allergy.

| **Cellulitis** | Lower dermis and subcutaneous soft tissue, commonly on the legs | Ill-defined erythema, pain, blisters and exudates |
|---|---|---|

*Treatment:* Antistaphylococcal penicillin, penicillin, or ampicillin × 10 d; erythromycin, 1st-generation cephalosporin, or tetracycline if penicillin allergy.

| **Impetigo** | Face around the nose and mouth | Very contagious; nonbullous and bullous variant; honey-colored crusts |
|---|---|---|

*Treatment:* Small, localized lesions; topical mupirocin 2% (*Bactroban*) × 7–10 d; widespread: oral antistaphylococcal penicillin, erythromycin, or a cephalosporin × 10 d.

| **Folliculitis** | Areas with coarse, short hair, ie, neck, beard, buttocks, thighs | Multiple small erythematous papules and pustules surrounding a hair |
|---|---|---|

*Treatment:* Mild localized cases can be treated with topical antibiotic: mupirocin 2%, erythromycin, or clindamycin; extensive or severe cases: oral antistaphylococcal penicillin, amoxicillin-clavulanic acid, or erythromycin.

## DERMATOLOGIC MEDICATIONS

### Table 31. Antifungal Medications

| Agent | Formulation | Dermatologic Indications | Dosing Frequency |
|---|---|---|---|
| **Topical Antifungals** | | | |
| Amphotericin B (*Fungizone*) | 3% crm, lot, or oint | Candidiasis | 2–4 times/d |
| Ciclopirox (*Loprox, Penlac*) | 0.77% crm, gel, lot, susp; 1% shp; 8% lacquer | *Tinea pedis, T cruris, T corpis, T versicolor;* candidiasis; scalp seborrhea; onychomycosis | 2 times/d; shp 3 times/wk; lacquer qhs |
| Clotrimazole* (*Cruex, Mycelex*, others) | 1% crm, sol | Candidiasis, dermatophytoses; superficial mycoses | 2 times/d |
| Econazole nitrate (*Spectazole*) | 1% crm | | |
| Ketoconazole (*Nizoral, Nizoral A-D**) | 2% crm, 1% shp | Candidiasis; *Tinea cruris, T corpis, T versicolor* | 1 or 2 times/d; shp 2 times/wk |
| Miconazole* (eg, *Micatin, Monistat-Derm*) | 2% crm, lot, pwd, spr, tinc | *Tinea cruris, T corpis, T pedis* | 2 times/d |
| Naftifine (*Naftin*) | 1% crm, gel | *Tinea cruris, T corpis, T pedis* | 2 times/d |
| Nystatin (*Mycostatin, Nilstat, Nystex*) | 100,000 units/g crm, oint, pwd | Mucocutaneous candidiasis | 2–3 times/d |
| Terbinafine (*Lamisil, LamisilAT**) | 1% crm, sol | *Tinea cruris, T corpis, T pedis, T versicolor* | 2 times/d |
| Tolnaftate* (*Absorbine Jr. Antifungal, Tinactin*, others) | 1% crm, gel, liq, pwd, spray | *Tinea cruris, T corpis, T pedis* | 2 times/d |
| **Oral Antifungals** | | | |
| Fluconazole (*Diflucan*) | T: 50, 100, 150, 200 S: 10, 40 mg/mL | | |
| Itraconazole (*Sporonax*) | C: 100 S: 100 mg/mL | | |
| Ketoconazole (*Nizoral*) | T: 200 | | |
| Terbinafine (*Lamisil*) | T: 250 | | |

*OTC

### Table 32. Topical Corticosteroids

| Name | Strength and Formulations | Frequency of Application |
|---|---|---|
| **Lowest Potency** | | |
| Dexamethasone phosphate (*Decaderm*) | 0.1% crm | qd–qid |
| Hydrocortisone acetate (*Hytone*) | 0.25%, 0.5%, 1%, 2.5% crm, oint | tid–qid |

*(cont.)*

## Table 32. Topical Corticosteroids (cont.)

| Name | Strength and Formulations | Frequency of Application |
|---|---|---|
| **Low Potency** | | |
| Alclometasone dipropionate (*Aclovate*) | 0.05% crm, oint | bid–tid |
| Betamethasone valerate (*Valisone*) | 0.1% lot | bid–qid |
| Desonide (*DesOwen, Tridesilon*) | 0.05% crm, lot, oint | bid–qid |
| Fluocinolone acetonide (*Synalar*) | 0.01% crm, sol | bid–qid |
| Triamcinolone acetonide (*Aristocort, Kenalog*) | 0.1% crm, 0.025% crm, lot, oint | bid–tid |
| **Mid-potency** | | |
| Betamethasone dipropionate (*Diprosone*) | 0.05% lot | bid–qid |
| Betamethasone valerate (*Valisone*) | 0.1% crm | bid–qid |
| Clocortolone pivalate (*Cloderm*) | 0.1% crm | qd–qid |
| Desoximetasone (*Topicort*) | 0.05% crm | bid |
| Fluocinolone acetonide (*Synalar*) | 0.025% crm, oint | bid–qid |
| Flurandrenolide (*Cordran*) | 0.05% crm, oint, lot | qd–bid |
| Fluticasone propionate (*Cutivate*) | 0.05% crm | bid |
| Hydrocortisone butyrate (*Locoid*) | 0.1% crm | qd–bid |
| Hydrocortisone valerate (*Westcort*) | 0.2% crm, oint | tid–qid |
| Mometasone furoate (*Elocon*) | 0.1% crm, lot | qd |
| Prednicarbate (*Dermatop*) | 0.1% crm, lot | bid |
| Triamcinolone acetonide (*Aristocort, Kenalog*) | 0.1% lot, oint | bid–tid |
| **High Potency** | | |
| Amcinonide (*Cyclocort*) | 0.1% crm, lot | bid–tid |
| Betamethasone dipropionate (*Diprosone*) | 0.05% crm | bid–qid |
| Betamethasone valerate (*Valisone*) | 0.1% oint | bid–qid |
| Diflorasone diacetate (*Florone, Maxiflor*) | 0.05% crm | bid–qid |
| Fluocinonide (*Lidex-E*) | 0.05% crm | bid–qid |
| Triamcinolone acetonide (*Aristocort, Kenalog*) | 0.5% crm, oint | bid–tid |
| **Higher Potency** | | |
| Amcinonide (*Cyclocort*) | 0.1% oint | bid–tid |
| Betamethasone dipropionate (*Diprolene AF*) | 0.05% augmented crm | bid–qid |
| Betamethasone dipropionate (*Diprosone*) | 0.05% oint | bid–qid |
| Desoximetasone (*Topicort*) | 0.25% crm, oint; 0.05% gel | bid |

*(cont.)*

### Table 32. Topical Corticosteroids (cont.)

| Name | Strength and Formulations | Frequency of Application |
|---|---|---|
| Diflorasone diacetate (*Florone, Maxiflor*) | 0.05% oint | bid–qid |
| Fluocinonide (*Lidex*) | 0.05% crm, oint, gel | bid–qid |
| Halcinonide (*Halog*) | 0.1% crm, oint, sol | qd–tid |
| Mometasone furoate (*Elocon*) | 0.1% oint | qd |
| **Super Potency** | | |
| Betamethasone dipropionate (*Diprolene*) | 0.05% oint | bid–qid |
| Clobetasol propionate (*Temovate*) | 0.05% crm, oint, sol, gel | bid |
| Diflorasone diacetate (*Psorcon*) | 0.05% optimized oint | qd–tid |
| Halobetasol propionate (*Ultravate*) | 0.05% crm, oint | bid |

# ENDOCRINE DISORDERS

## ADRENAL INSUFFICIENCY
### Common Causes
- Chronic glucocorticoid administration
- Pituitary tumors
- Tuberculosis
- Autoimmune

### Evaluation
- Basal plasma cortisol >15 µg/dL excludes adrenal insufficiency
- ACTH stimulation test: tetracosactin (*Synacthen Depot*) 250 µg IM or IV; peak value >19 µg/dL is normal

### Pharmacologic Therapy
For corticosteroid dose equivalencies, see **Table 33**.

### Management
Stress doses of corticosteroids for patients with severe illness, injury, or undergoing surgery: In emergency situations, do not wait for test results. Give hydrocortisone 100 mg IV q 8 h. For less severe stress, double or triple usual oral replacement dose and taper back to baseline as quickly as possible.

| | Approx Equivalent Dose (mg) | Relative Anti-Inflammatory Potency | Relative Mineralo-corticoid Potency | Biologic Half-Life (h) | |
|---|---|---|---|---|---|
| **Drug** | | | | | **Formulations** |
| Betamethasone (*Celestone*) | 0.6–0.75 | 20–30 | 0 | 36–54 | T: 0.6; S: 0.6 mg/5 mL |
| Cortisone (*Cortone*) | 25 | 0.8 | 2 | 8–12 | T: 5; S: 50 mg/mL |
| Dexamethasone (*Decadron, Dexone, Hexadrol*) | 0.75 | 20–30 | 0 | 36–54 | T: 0.25, 0.5, 0.75, 1, 1.5, 2, 4; S: elixir 0.5 mg/5 mL; Inj |
| Fludrocortisone (*Florinef*)* | NA | 10 | 4 | 12–36 | T: 0.1 |
| Hydrocortisone (*Cortef, Hydrocortone*) | 20 | 1 | 2 | 8–12 | T: 5, 10, 20; S: 10 mg/5 mL; Inj |
| Methylprednisolone (eg, *Medrol, Solu-Medrol, Depo-Medrol*) | 4 | 5 | 0 | 18–36 | T: 2, 4, 8, 16, 24, 32; Inj |
| Prednisolone (eg, *Delta-Cortef, Prelone Syr, Pediapred*) | 5 | 4 | 1 | 18–36 | S: 5 mg/5 mL; syr 5, 15 mg/5 mL |
| Prednisone (*Deltasone, Liquid Pred, Meticorten, Orasone*) | 5 | 4 | 1 | 18–36 | T: 1, 2.5, 5, 10, 20, 50; S: 5 mg/5 mL |
| Triamcinolone (eg, *Aristocort, Kenacort, Kenalog*) | 4 | 5 | 0 | 18–36 | T: 1, 2, 4, 8; S: syr 4 mg/5 mL |

Table 33. Corticosteroids

Note: NA = not available.
* Usually given for orthostatic hypotension 0.1 mg qd–tid.

## HYPOTHYROIDISM
### Common Causes
- Autoimmune (primary thyroid failure)
- Following therapy for hyperthyroidism
- Pituitary or hypothalamic disorders (secondary thyroid failure)
- Medications, especially amiodarone (rare after first 18 mo of therapy) and lithium

### Evaluation
TSH, free $T_4$

### Pharmacologic Therapy
- Thyroxine ($T_4$, levothyroxine [*Eltroxin, Levo-T, Levothroid, Levoxyl, Synthroid*]). Start at 25 µg and increase by 25-µg intervals q 4–6 wk [T: 25, 50, 75, 88, 100, 112, 125, 137, 150, 175, 200, 300 µg].
- Thyroxine and liothyronine ($T_3$) (*Thyrolar*). Start ¼ strength and increase [12.5/3.1 (¼ strength), 25/6.25 (½ strength), 50/12.5, 100/25, 150/37.5 µg].
- For myxedema coma: Load 400 µg IV or 100 µg q 6–8 h for 1 d, then 100 µg/d for 4 d; then start usual replacement regimen.
- To convert thyroid USP to thyroxine: 60 mg USP = 50 µg thyroxine.
- If patients are npo and must receive IV thyroxine, dose should be half usual po dose.

### Monitoring
In primary hypothyroidism, the goal of therapy is to maintain plasma TSH within the normal range. Further adjustments are made q 6–12 wk (12- to 25-µg increments) on basis of TSH levels until TSH is in normal range. Monitor TSH level at least q 12 mo (ATA) in patients on chronic thyroid replacement therapy. Following dose adjustment, recheck TSH in 6–12 wk.

## HYPERTHYROIDISM
### Common Causes
- Graves' disease
- Toxic nodule
- Toxic multinodular goiter
- Medications, especially amiodarone (can occur any time during therapy) and lithium

### Evaluation
TSH, free $T_4$. When indicated, $T_3$, thyroid autoantibodies, radioactive iodine uptake.

### Pharmacologic Therapy
- Radioactive iodine ablation is usual treatment of choice, but surgery or medical therapy (see Monitoring above) are options.
- Propylthiouracil (PTU): Start 100 po tid, then adjust up to 200 po tid as needed [T: 50].
- Methimazole (*Tapazole*): Start 5–20 mg po tid, then adjust [T: 5, 10].
- Adjunctive therapy with β-blockers (see **Table 20**) or calcium antagonists (see **Table 20**) may provide symptomatic improvement.

## DIABETES MELLITUS
### Definition and Classification (ADA)
Diabetes mellitus is a group of metabolic diseases characterized by hyperglycemia resulting from defects in insulin secretion, insulin action, or both.

*Type 1:* Caused by an absolute deficiency of insulin secretion.

*Type 2:* Caused by a combination of resistance to insulin action and an inadequate compensatory insulin secretory response.

*Criteria for Diagnosis:* One or more of the following:
- Symptoms of diabetes (eg, polyuria, polydipsia, unexplained weight loss) plus casual plasma glucose concentration ≥200 mg/dL
- Fasting (no caloric intake for ≥8 h) plasma glucose ≥126 mg/dL
- 2 h Plasma glucose ≥200 mg/dL during an oral glucose tolerance test (OGTT)

Diagnosis should be confirmed by reevaluating on a subsequent day.

*Pre-diabetes:* Either of the following:
- Impaired Fasting Glucose: Defined as fasting plasma glucose ≥110 and <126 mg/dL
- Impaired Glucose Tolerance: Abnormal casual plasma glucose concentration or response to OGTT but not meeting diagnostic criteria for diabetes

### Management
*Evaluate for Comorbid Conditions (AGS, ADA):* Depression (see p 49), polypharmacy (see p 9), cognitive impairment (see p 204), urinary incontinence (see p 85), falls (see p 65), pain (see p 141) (AGS), PAD (claudication history and assessment of pedal pulses) (see p 39) (ADA).

*Goals of Treatment (ADA, AGS):*
- Outpatient: Average preprandial capillary blood glucose 80–120 mg/dL, average bedtime capillary blood glucose 100–140 mg/dL, and HbA$_{1c}$ <7% (ADA); <8% if frail, life expectancy <5 yr, or high risk of hypoglycemia, polypharmacy, or drug interaction (AGS).
- Inpatient: ≤110 mg/dL in intensive-care units and preprandial in noncritical-care units; ≤180 mg/dL postprandial.

*Nonpharmacologic Interventions:*
- Individualized nutrition therapy (see p 114)
- Life style (eg, regular exercise, alcohol and smoking cessation)
- Patient and family education for self-management
- Self-monitoring of blood glucose
- High-fiber diet (25 g insoluble and 25 g soluble/d)

*Pharmacologic Interventions for Type 2:* Stepped therapy:
1. Monotherapy with a 2nd-generation sulfonylurea agent, metformin, α-glucosidase inhibitor, or thiazolidinedione (see **Table 34**)
2. Combination therapy with 2 or more agents with different actions
3. Add insulin hs or switch to insulin bid (see **Table 35**)
- Manage HTN (BP goal <130/80 mm Hg; also see HTN, p 31).
- Treat lipid disorders (see p 30); as CHD risk equivalent with target LDL <70 mg/dL if other risk factors are present (NHLBI), HDL >40 mg/dL, TG <150 mg/dL, as appropriate. If total cholesterol ≥135 mg/dL, statin therapy to reduce LDL by ~30% regardless of baseline LDL (ADA); statins should be used as primary prevention against macrovascular complications in patients with type 2 diabetes and other cardiovascular risk factors (ACP).

- ACE inhibitor or angiotensin II receptor blocker (ARB) if albuminuria, HTN, or another cardiovascular risk factor. Check kidney function within 1–2 wk of initiation of therapy, with each dose increase, and at least yearly.
- Daily ASA 75–162 mg.

**Table 34. Oral Agents for Treating Diabetes Mellitus**

| Drug | Dosage | Formulations | Comments (Metabolism) |
|---|---|---|---|
| **2nd-Generation Sulfonylureas** | | | Increase insulin secretion; lower HbA$_{1c}$ by 1.0%–2.0% |
| Glimepiride (*Amaryl*) | 4–8 mg once, begin 1–2 mg | T: 1, 2, 4 | Numerous drug interactions, long-acting (L, K) |
| Glipizide (generic or *Glucotrol*) | 2.5–40 mg once or divided | T: 5, 10 | Short-acting (L, K) |
| (*Glucotrol XL*) | 5–20 mg once | T: ER 2.5, 5, 10 | Long-acting (L, K) |
| Glyburide (generic or *DiaBeta, Micronase*) | 1.25–20 mg once or divided | T: 1.25, 2.5, 5 | Long-acting, risk of hypoglycemia (L, K) |
| Micronized glyburide (*Glynase*) | 1.5–12 mg once | T: 1.5, 3, 4.5, 6 | (L, K) |
| **α-Glucosidase Inhibitors** | | | Delay glucose absorption; lower HbA$_{1c}$ by 0.5%–1.0% |
| Acarbose (*Precose*) | 50–100 mg tid, just before meals, start with 25 mg | T: 25, 50, 100 | GI adverse events common, avoid if Cr >2 mg/dL, monitor LFTs (gut, K) |
| Miglitol (*Glyset*) | 25–100 mg tid, with 1st bite of meal; start with 25 mg qd | T: 25, 50, 100 | Same as acarbose but no need to monitor LFTs (L, K) |
| **Biguanides** | | | Decrease hepatic glucose production; lower HbA$_{1c}$ by 1.0%–2.0% |
| Metformin (*Glucophage*) | 500–2550 mg divided | T: 500, 850, 1000 | Avoid in patients >80 yr, Cr >1.5 in men, Cr >1.4 in women, HF, COPD, ↑ LFTs; hold before contrast radiologic studies; may cause weight loss (K) |
| (*Glucophage XR*) | 1500–2000 mg qd | T: ER 500 | |
| **Meglitinides** | | | Increase insulin secretion; lower HbA$_{1c}$ by 1.0%–2.0% |
| Nateglinide (*Starlix*) | 60–120 mg tid | T: 60, 120 | Give 30 min before meals |
| Repaglinide (*Prandin*) | 0.5 mg bid–qid if HbA$_{1c}$ <8% or previously untreated 1–2 mg bid–qid if HbA$_{1c}$ ≥8% or previously treated | T: 0.5, 1, 2 | Give 30 min before meals, adjust dose at wkly intervals; potential for drug interactions, caution in hepatic, renal insufficiency (L) |

*(cont.)*

## Table 34. Oral Agents for Treating Diabetes Mellitus (cont.)

| Drug | Dosage | Formulations | Comments (Metabolism) |
|------|--------|--------------|------------------------|
| **Thiazolidinediones** | | | Insulin resistance reducers; lower HbA$_{1c}$ by 0.5%–1.0%; ↑ risk of HF; avoid if NYHA Class III or IV cardiac status; D/C if any decline in cardiac status |
| Pioglitazone (*Actos*) | 15 or 30 mg qd; max 45 mg/d as monotherapy, 30 mg/d in combination therapy | T: 15, 30, 45 | Check LFTs at start, q 2 mo during 1st yr, then periodically; avoid if clinical evidence of liver disease or if serum ALT levels >2.5 upper limit of normal (L, K) |
| Rosiglitazone (*Avandia*) | 4 mg qd–bid | T: 2, 4, 8 | Check LFTs at start, q 2 mo during 1st yr, then periodically; avoid if clinical evidence of liver disease or if serum ALT levels >2.5 upper limit of normal (L, K) |
| **Combinations** | | | |
| Glipizide and metformin (*METAGLIP*) | 2.5/250 once; 20/2000 in 2 divided doses | T: 2.5/250, 2.5/500, 5/500 | Avoid in patients >80 yr, Cr >1.5 in men, Cr >1.4 in women; see individual drugs (L, K) |
| Glyburide and metformin (*Glucovance*) | 1.25/250 mg initially if previously untreated; 2.5/500 mg or 5/500 mg bid with meals; max 20/2000/d | T: 1.25/250, 2.5/500, 5/500 | Starting dose should not exceed total daily dose of either drug; see individual drugs (L, K) |
| Rosiglitazone and metformin (*Avandamet*) | 4/1000– 8/2000 in 2 divided doses | T: 1/500, 2/500, 4/500, 2/1000, 4/1000 | Avoid in patients >80 yr, Cr >1.5 in men, Cr >1.4 in women; see individual drugs (L, K) |

## Table 35. Insulin Preparations

| Preparations | Onset | Peak | Duration |
|--------------|-------|------|----------|
| Insulin lispro (*Humalog*) | 15 min | 0.5–1.5 h | 6–8 h |
| Insulin (eg, *Humulin, Novolin*)* | | | |
| Regular | 0.5–1 h | 2–3 h | 8–12 h |
| NPH | 1–1.5 h | 4–12 h | 24 h |
| Insulin aspart (*NovoLog*) | 30 min | 1–3 h | 3–5 h |
| Long-acting (*Ultralente*) | 4–8 h | 16–18 h | >36 h |
| Insulin glargine (*Lantus*)** | 1–2 h | — | 24 h |
| Insulin, zinc (*Lente*) | 1–2.5 h | 8–12 h | 18–24 h |
| Isophane insulin and regular insulin inj. (*Novolin 70/30*) | 0.5 h | 2–12 h | 24 h |

\* Also available as mixtures of NPH and regular in 50:50 proportions.
\*\* To convert from NPH dosing, give same number of units once a day. For patients taking NPH bid, decrease the total daily units by 20%, and titrate on basis of response. Starting dose in insulin-naive patients is 10 U once daily hs.

**Monitoring (ADA)**
- Weight, BP, and foot examination, including monofilament, palpation, and inspection, each visit
- HbA$_{1c}$ twice/yr in patients with stable glycemic control; quarterly, if poor control
- Annual comprehensive dilated eye and visual examinations by an ophthalmologist or optometrist who is experienced in management of diabetic retinopathy
- Lipid profiles every 1–2 yr depending on whether values are in normal range
- Annual (unless microalbuminuria has previously been demonstrated) test for microalbuminuria by measuring albumin/creatinine ratio in a random spot collection

# FALLS

## DEFINITION
An event that results in a person's inadvertently coming to rest on the ground or lower level with or without loss of consciousness or injury. Excludes falls from major intrinsic event (seizure, stroke, syncope) or overwhelming environmental hazard.

## ETIOLOGY
Typically multifactorial. Composed of intrinsic (eg, poor balance, weakness, chronic illness, visual or cognitive impairment), extrinsic (eg, polypharmacy), and environmental (eg, poor lighting, no safety equipment, loose carpets) factors. Commonly a nonspecific sign for one of many acute illnesses in older persons.

## EVALUATION
Exclude acute illness or underlying systemic or metabolic process (eg, infection, electrolyte imbalance as indicated by history, examination, and laboratory studies). See **Figure 3** for recommended assessment and management. See also p 138.
- Laboratory tests for persons at risk: CBC, serum electrolytes, BUN, Cr, glucose, $B_{12}$, thyroid function
- Bone densitometry in women with additional risk factors for osteoporotic fracture (see p 138)
- Imaging: neuroimaging if head injury or new, focal neurologic findings on examination or if a CNS process is suspected.
- Ambulatory cardiac monitoring rarely helpful.
- Arrhythmic evaluation only if clinical evidence of this diagnosis (eg, hx of cardiac events or abnormal ECG)

### History
- Circumstances of fall (eg, activity at time of fall, location, time)
- Associated symptoms (eg, lightheadedness, vertigo, syncope, weakness, confusion, palpitations)
- Relevant comorbid conditions (eg, prior stroke, parkinsonism, cardiac disease, seizure disorder, depression, anxiety, anemia, sensory deficit, glaucoma, cataracts, osteoporosis, cognitive impairment)
- Previous falls
- Medication review, including OTC medications and alcohol use; note recent changes in medications; note drugs that have hypotensive or psychoactive effects (see p 67)

### Physical
Look for:
- Vital signs: postural pulse and BP changes, fever, hypothermia
- Head and neck: visual impairment (especially poor acuity, reduced contrast sensitivity, decreased visual fields, cataracts), motion-induced imbalance (Dix-Hallpike test), bruit, nystagmus
- Musculoskeletal: arthritic changes, motion or joint limitations (especially lower extremity joint function), postural instability, skeletal deformities, podiatric problems

## Figure 3. Assessment and Management of Falls

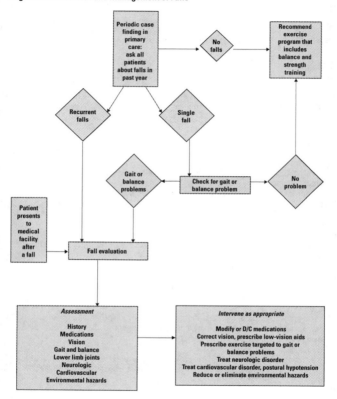

Sources: Adapted from American Geriatrics Society, British Geriatrics Society, and American Academy of Orthopaedic Surgeons Panel on Falls Prevention. Guideline for the prevention of falls in older persons. *J Amer Geriatr Soc.* 2001; 49(5):666, and Tinetti M. Preventing falls in elderly persons. *N Engl J Med* 2003;348(1):42–49.

- Neurologic: slower reflexes, altered proprioception, altered mental status, focal deficits, peripheral neuropathy, gait or balance disorders, muscle weakness (especially leg), instability, tremor, rigidity
- Cardiovascular: heart arrhythmias, cardiac valve dysfunction
- Other: fever; hypothermia

**Functional Assessment**
- Functional gait: observe patient rising from chair, walking (stride, length, velocity, symmetry), turning, sitting (Timed Get Up and Go test; see also POMA, p 208)
- Balance: Side-by-side, semi-tandem, and full tandem stance; Functional Reach test (see also POMA, p 208)
- Mobility: observe the patient's use of assistive device (cane, walker, or personal assistance), extent of ambulation, restraint use, footwear evaluation

Ask about person's ability to complete activities of daily living: bathing, dressing, transferring, continence.

**Medications Associated with Increased Fall Risk**
- Neuroleptics (especially phenothiazines)
- Sedatives, hypnotics (including benzodiazepines)
- Antidepressants (including MAOIs, SSRIs, TCAs)
- Antiarrhythmics (Class 1A)
- Anticonvulsants

**PREVENTION**
Goal is to minimize risk of falling without compromising mobility and functional independence.
- Fall risk assessment should be part of every routine primary health care visit (at least annually). Risk of falling significantly increases as number of risk factors increases.
- Assess for risk factors using a multidisciplinary approach, if appropriate, including physical and occupational therapy.
- Diagnose and treat underlying cause.
- Target interventions to risk factors (see **Table 36**). Correction of postural hypotension; review and elimination or dose reduction of medications; and interventions to improve balance, transfers, and gait are priority.
- Choose fall prevention programs that include more than one intervention. A structured, interdisciplinary approach should be used.
  ○ Establish tailored exercise programs targeted at older people without balance or gait difficulties that include balance and strength training.
  ○ Tai Chi classes should be offered to older people living in the community.
  ○ Counsel older patients or family members on multifactorial nature of most falls, specific risk factors, and measures to reduce the risk of falling, including exercise, safety-related skills and behaviors, and environmental hazard reduction.
  ○ Offer hip protectors to non-bedbound residents of nursing homes and others at high risk—available via http://www.hipprotector.com or http://www.hipsaver.com.
  ○ Recommend minimum supplementation of calcium (1200 mg/d) and vitamin D (400–800 IU).

• Focus on most common risk factors: Muscle weakness, history of falls, gait deficit, balance deficit, use of assistive devices, visual deficit, arthritis, impaired ADLs, depression, cognitive impairment, age >80 yr.

**Table 36. Preventing Falls: Selected Risk Factors and Suggested Interventions**

| Factors | Suggested Interventions |
|---|---|
| **Medication-related factors** | |
| Use of benzodiazepines, sedative-hypnotics, or antipsychotic | Consider agents with less risk for falls (eg, atypical antipsychotics such as olanzapine, risperidone, or quetiapine) |
| | Taper and D/C medications, as possible |
| | Address sleep problems with nonpharmacologic interventions (see p 190) |
| | Educate regarding appropriate use of medications and monitoring for adverse events |
| Recent change in dose *or* number of prescription medications *or* use of ≥4 prescription medications *or* use of other medications associated with fall risk | Review medication profile and modify, as possible |
| | Monitor response to medications and to dose changes |
| **Mobility-related factors** | |
| Presence of environmental hazards (eg, improper bed height, cluttered walking surfaces, lack of railings, poor lighting) | Improve lighting, especially at night |
| | Remove floor barriers (eg, loose carpeting) |
| | Replace existing furniture with safer furniture (eg, correct height, more stable) |
| | Install support structures (eg, railings, grab bars) |
| | Use nonslip bathmats |
| Impaired gait, balance, or transfer skills | Refer to PT for comprehensive evaluation and rehabilitation |
| | Gait training |
| | Balance or strengthening exercises |
| | Provide training in transfer skills |
| | Prescribe appropriate assistive devices |
| | Recommend protective hip padding |
| | Environmental changes (eg, grab bars, raised toilet seats) |
| | Recommend appropriate footwear |
| Impaired leg or arm strength or range of motion, or proprioception | Strengthening exercises (eg, use of resistive rubber bands, putty) |
| | Resistance training 2–3 times/wk to 10 repetitions with full range of motion, then increase resistance |
| | Tai Chi |
| | Physical therapy |

*(cont.)*

Table 36. Preventing Falls: Selected Risk Factors and Suggested Interventions (cont.)

| Factors | Suggested Interventions |
| --- | --- |
| **Medical factors** | |
| Parkinson's disease, osteoarthritis, depressive symptoms, impaired cognition, other conditions associated with increased falls | Optimize medical therapy |
| | Monitor for disease progression and impact on mobility and impairments |
| | Determine need for assistive devices |
| Postural hypotension: drop in SBP ≥20 mm Hg (or ≥20%) with or without symptoms, either immediately or within 2 min of standing | Review medications potentially contributing and adjust dosing or switch to less hypotensive agents; avoid vasodilators and diuretics if possible |
| | Educate on activities to decrease effect (eg, slow rising, ankle pumps, hand clenching, elevation of head of bed) and slow rising from recumbent or seated position |
| | Prescribe pressure stockings (eg, Jobst) |
| | Liberalize salt intake |
| | Caffeinated coffee (1 cup) or caffeine 100 mg with meals for postprandial hypotension |
| | Consider medication to increase pressure (if HTN, heart failure, and hypokalemia not serious): -fludrocortisone (*Florinef*) 0.1 mg qd–tid [T: 0.1] -midodrine (*ProAmatine*) 2.5–5 mg tid [T: 2.5, 5] |

# GASTROINTESTINAL DISEASES

**DYSPHAGIA**
See p 154.

## GASTROESOPHAGEAL REFLUX DISEASE (GERD)
### Definition
The retrograde movement of the gastric contents in the esophagus due to incompetent lower esophageal sphincter, transient relaxations of the sphincter, or compromise of other antireflux mechanisms.

### Evaluation and Assessment
Empiric treatment is appropriate when hx is typical for uncomplicated GERD.
- Endoscopy (if symptoms persist despite initial management, atypical presentation, or longstanding symptoms)
- 24-h pH monitoring

### Symptoms Suggesting Complicated GERD and Need For Evaluation
- Dysphagia
- Bleeding
- Weight loss
- Choking (acid causing cough, shortness of breath, or hoarseness)
- Chest pain

### Management
*Nonpharmacologic:*
- Antacids
- Avoid alcohol and fatty foods
- Avoid lying down 3 h after eating
- Avoid tight-fitting clothes
- Change diet (avoid pepper, spearmint, chocolate, spicy or acidic foods)
- Drink 6–8 oz water with all medications
- Elevate head of the bed (6–8 in)
- Lose weight (if overweight)
- Stop drugs that may promote reflux
- Stop smoking
- Consider surgery

*Pharmacologic:*

Table 37. Pharmacologic Management of GERD

| Drug | Initial Oral Dosage | Formulations (Excretion) |
|---|---|---|
| **Proton-Pump Inhibitors** | | |
| Esomeprazole (*Nexium*) | 20 mg qd × 4 wk | C: ER 20, 40 (L) |
| Lansoprazole (*Prevacid*) | 15 mg qd × 8 wk | C: ER 15, 30; granules for susp: 15, 30/packet (L) |
| Omeprazole (*Prilosec*) | 20 mg qd × 4–8 wk | C: ER 10, 20,* 40 (L) |
| Pantoprazole (*Protonix*) | 40 mg qd × 8 wk | T: enteric-coated, 20, 40; Inj (L) |
| Rabeprazole (*AcipHex*) | 20 mg qd × 4–8 wk; 20 mg qd maintenance, if needed | T: enteric-coated ER 20 (L) |
| **H2 Antagonists (for less severe GERD)** | | |
| Cimetidine (*Tagamet*) | 400 or 800 mg bid | S: 200 mg/20 mL, 300 mg/5 mL with alcohol 2.8%; T: 100, 200,* 300, 400, 800; Inj (K, L) |

*(cont.)*

#### Table 37. Pharmacologic Management of GERD (cont.)

| Drug | Initial Oral Dosage | Formulations (Excretion) |
|---|---|---|
| Famotidine (*Pepcid*) | 20 mg bid × 6 wk | S: oral sus 40 mg/5 mL; T: film-coated 10,* 20, 40, oral disintegrating 20, 40; C (gel): 10*; ChT: 10*; Inj (K) |
| Nizatidine (*Axid*) | 150 mg bid | C: 150, 300; T: 75 (K) |
| Ranitidine (*Zantac*) | 150 mg bid | Pk: gran, effervescent (EFFERdose) 150 mg; S: syr 15 mg/mL; T: 75,* 150, 300; T: effervescent (EFFERdose) 150; Inj (K, F) |
| **Mucosal Protective Agent** | | |
| Sucralfate (*Carafate*) | 1 g qid, 1h ac and hs | S: oral sus 1 g/10 mL; T: 1 g (F, K) |
| **Prokinetic Agents** | | |
| Bethanechol (*Urecholine*) | 25 mg qid | T: 5, 10, 25, 50 (unknown) |
| Metoclopramide† (*Reglan*) | 5 mg qid, ac, and hs | S: syr, sugar-free 5 mg/5 mL, conc 10 mg/mL; T: 5, 10; Inj (K, F) |

\* OTC strength.
† Risk of EPS high in persons aged >65 yr.
Source: Data from DeVault KR, Castell DO. Updated guidelines for the diagnosis and treatment of gastroesophageal reflux disease. *Am J Gastroenterol.* 1999;94:1430–1442.

## PEPTIC ULCER DISEASE
### Causes
*Helicobacter pylori* is the major cause. NSAIDs are the second most common cause.

### Diagnosis of *H pylori*
• Endoscopic examination      • Serology      • Urea breath test

### Initial Treatment Options
• Empiric anti-ulcer treatment for 6 wk
• Definitive diagnostic evaluation by endoscopy
• Noninvasive testing for *H pylori* and treatment with antibiotics for (+) patients (see **Table 38** for regimens)
• Review patient's chronic medications for drug interactions before selecting regimen; many potential drug interactions and adverse drug reactions.

#### Table 38. FDA-Approved Treatments for *H pylori*–Induced Ulcerations (all oral routes)

Lansoprazole 30 mg bid + amoxicillin 1 g bid + clarithromycin 500 mg tid × 10 (or 14) d

**or** Omeprazole 20 mg bid + clarithromycin 500 mg bid + amoxicillin 1 g bid × 10 d

**or** Lansoprazole 30 mg bid + clarithromycin 500 mg bid + amoxicillin 1 g bid × 10 d (*Prevpac*)

**or** Omeprazole 40 mg qd + clarithromycin 500 mg tid × 2 wk, then omeprazole 20 mg qd × 2 wk

**or** Lansoprazole 30 mg tid + amoxicillin 1 g bid × 2 wk (only for person allergic or intolerant to clarithromycin)

(cont.)

Table 38. FDA-Approved Treatments for *H pylori*–Induced Ulcerations (all oral routes) (cont.)

**or** Ranitidine bismuth citrate (RBC) 400 mg bid + clarithromycin 500 mg tid × 2 wk, then RBC 400 mg bid × 2 wk

**or** RBC 400 mg bid + clarithromycin 500 mg bid × 2 wk, then RBC 400 mg bid × 2 wk

**or** Bismuth subsalicylate (*Pepto-Bismol*) 525 mg qid (pc and hs) + metronidazole 250 mg qid + tetracycline 500 mg qid × 2 wk (*Helidac*) + H₂ receptor antagonist or proton-pump inhibitor as directed × 4 wk

Source: http://www.cdc.gov/ulcer/md.htm.
For additional, non-FDA approved regimens, see Howden CW, Hunt RH. Guidelines for the management of *Helicobacter pylori* infection. *Am J Gastroenterol* 1998;93:2330–2338, or http://www.acg.gi.org.

## Medications
Bismuth subsalicylate (*Pepto-Bismol*) [T: 324; ChT: 262; S: sus 262 mg/15 mL, 525 mg/15 mL]
***Antibiotics:*** (for complete information, see **Table 51**)
Amoxicillin (*Amoxil*) [C: 250, 500; ChT: 125, 250; S: oral sus 125 mg/5 mL, 250 mg/5 mL]
Clarithromycin (*Biaxin*) [T: film-coated 250, 500; S: oral sus 125 mg/5 mL, 250 mg/5 mL]
Metronidazole (*Flagyl*) [T: 250, 500, 750; C: 375]
Tetracycline (*Achromycin, Sumycin*) [T: 250, 500; S: oral sus 125 mg/5 mL]
***Proton-Pump Inhibitors:*** See **Table 37**.

## STRESS-ULCER PREVENTION IN HOSPITALIZED OLDER PERSONS

### Risk Factors (in order of prevalence in older persons)
• Hx of GI ulceration or bleed in the past year
• Sepsis
• Multiple organ failure
• Hypotension
• Respiratory failure requiring mechanical ventilation >48 h
• Kidney failure
• Major trauma, shock, or head injury
• Coagulopathy (platelets <50,000/μL, INR >1.5, or PTT >2 × control)
• Burns over >25% of body surface area
• Hepatic failure
• Intracranial hypertension
• Spinal cord injury
• Tetraplegia

### Prophylaxis
• H₂ antagonists (see **Table 37**)
• Proton-pump inhibitors (see **Table 37**)
• Sucralfate (see **Table 37**)
• Antacids
• Enteral feedings
Discontinue H₂ antagonists, proton-pump inhibitors, and other treatments for stress ulcer prevention before transfer or discharge.

**Key Points**
- Prophylaxis has not been shown to reduce mortality
- No one regimen has shown superior efficacy
- Choice of regimen depends on access to and function of GI tract and presence of nasogastric suction

## CONSTIPATION
### Definition
Infrequent (usually <3 times/wk), incomplete, or painful evacuation of feces.

### Drugs That Constipate
- Analgesics—opiates
- Antacids with aluminum or calcium
- Anticholinergic drugs
- Antidepressants, lithium
- Antihypertensives
- Antipsychotics
- Barium sulfate
- Bismuth
- Calcium channel blockers
- Diuretics
- Iron

### Conditions That Constipate
- Colon tumor or mechanical obstruction
- Dehydration
- Depression
- Diabetes mellitus
- Hypercalcemia
- Hypokalemia
- Hypothyroidism
- Immobility
- Low intake of fiber
- Panhypopituitarism
- Parkinson's disease
- Spinal cord injury
- Stroke
- Uremia

### Management of Chronic Constipation
**Step 1.** Stop all constipating medications, when possible.
**Step 2.** Increase dietary bran to 6–25 g/d, increase fluid intake to ≥1500 mL/d, and increase physical activity; or add bran supplements, provided fluid intake is ≥1500 mL/d.
**Step 3.** Add 70% sorbitol solution (15–30 mL qd or bid, max 150 mL/d).
**Step 4.** Add stimulant laxative (eg, senna, bisacodyl), 2–3 times/wk. (Alternative: Saline laxative, but avoid in renal insufficiency.)
**Step 5.** Use tap water enema or saline enema 2 times/wk.
**Step 6.** Use oil-retention enema for refractory constipation.

#### Table 39. Medications That May Relieve Constipation

| Medication | Onset of Action | Starting Dosage | Site and Mechanism of Action |
|---|---|---|---|
| Bisacodyl tablet (*Dulcolax*) | 6–10 h | 5–15 mg × 1 | Colon; increases peristalsis |
| Bisacodyl suppository (*Dulcolax*) | 0.25–1 h | 10 mg × 1 | Colon; increases peristalsis |
| Docusate (*Colace*) | 24–72 h | 100 mg qd–bid | Small and large intestine; detergent activity; facilitates admixture of fat and water to soften stool |

*(cont.)*

Table 39. Medications That May Relieve Constipation (cont.)

| Medication | Onset of Action | Starting Dosage | Site and Mechanism of Action |
|---|---|---|---|
| Lactulose (*Cephulac*)* | 24–48 h | 15–30 mL qd–bid | Colon; osmotic effect |
| Magnesium citrate (*Citroma*) | 0.5–3 h | 120–240 mL × 1 | Small and large intestine; attracts, retains water in intestinal lumen |
| Magnesium hydroxide (*Milk of Magnesia*) | 30 min–3 h | 30 mL qd–bid | Osmotic effect and increased peristalsis in colon |
| Methylcellulose (*Citrucel*), psyllium (*Metamucil*) | 12–24 h (up to 72 h) | 1–2 rounded tsp or packets qd–tid with water or juice | Small and large intestine; holds water in stool; mechanical distention |
| Polyethylene glycol (*MiraLax*)* | 48–96 h | 17 g pwd qd (~1 tbsp) dissolved in 8 oz water | GI tract; osmotic effect |
| Sodium phosphate/biphosphate emollient enema (*Fleet*) | 2–15 min | 1 4.5-oz enema × 1, repeat prn | Colon, osmotic effect; potential hyperphosphatemia in patients with renal insufficiency |
| Senna (*Senoket*) | 6–10 h | 2 tabs or 1 tsp qhs | Colon; direct action on intestine; stimulates myenteric plexus; alters water and electrolyte seceretion |
| Sorbitol 70% | 24–48 h | 15–30 mL qd–bid | Colon; delivers osmotically active molecules to colon |

*By prescription only.

## NAUSEA AND VOMITING
### Causes
- CNS disorders (eg, motion sickness, intracranial lesions)
- Drugs (eg, chemotherapy, NSAIDs, narcotic analgesics, antibiotics, digoxin)
- GI disorders (eg, mechanical obstruction; inflammation of stomach, intestine, or gallbladder; pseudo-obstruction, motility disorders, dyspepsia, diabetic gastroparesis)
- Infections (eg, viral or bacterial gastroenteritis, hepatitis, otitis, meningitis)
- Metabolic conditions (eg, uremia, acidosis, hyperparathyroidism, adrenal insufficiency)
- Psychiatric disorders

### Evaluation
- If patient is not seriously ill or dehydrated, can probably wait 24–48 h to see if symptoms resolve spontaneously.
- If patient is seriously ill, dehydrated, or has other signs of acute illness, hospitalize for further evaluation.
- If symptoms persist, evaluate according to suspected causes.

## Pharmacologic Management

Drugs that are useful in the management of nausea and vomiting are listed in **Table 40**.

| Table 40. Selected Antiemetics | | |
|---|---|---|
| **Drug** | **Formulations** | **Dosages (Metabolism)** |
| Dimenhydrinate* (*Dramamine*) | Inj; S: 12.5 mg/4 mL, 16.62 mg/5 mL; T: 50; ChT: 50 | Oral, IM IV: 50–100 mg q 4–6 h, not to exceed 400 mg/d (L) |
| Meclizine* (*Antivert*) | C: 25, 30; T: 12.5, 25, 50; ChT: 25; T: film-coated 25 | Motion sickness: 12.5–25 mg 1 h before travel, repeat dose q 12–24 h if needed; doses up to 50 mg may be needed; vertigo: 25–100 mg/d in divided doses (L) |
| Metoclopramide (*Reglan*) | Inj; S: oral conc 10 mg/mL, syr, sugar-free, 5 mg/5 mL; T: 5, 10 | Chemotherapy-induced emesis, IV: 1–2 mg/kg 30 min before chemotherapy and q 2–4 to q 4–6 h; postoperative nausea and vomiting: IM 5–10 mg near the end of surgery (K) |
| Prochlorperazine (*Compazine*) | C: ER: 10, 15, 30; Inj; Sp: 2.5, 5, 25; S: syr 5 mg/5 mL; T: 5, 10, 25 | Oral or IM: 5–10 mg 3–4 times/d, usual max, 40 mg/d; IV: 2.5–10 mg; max 10 mg/dose or 40 mg/d; may repeat dose q 3–4 h as needed; rectal: 25 mg bid (L) |

*Available OTC.
Note: All have potential CNS toxicity.

## DIARRHEA
### Causes
• Drugs (eg, antibiotics [see **Table 51**], laxatives, colchicine)
• Fecal impaction
• GI disorders (eg, irritable bowel syndrome, malabsorption, inflammatory bowel disease)
• Infections (eg, viral, bacterial, parasitic)
• Lactose intolerance

### Evaluation
• If patient is not seriously ill or dehydrated and there is no blood in the stool, can probably wait 48 h to see if symptoms resolve spontaneously.
• If patient is seriously ill, dehydrated, or has other signs of acute illness, hospitalize for further evaluation.
• If diarrhea persists, evaluate on the basis of the most likely causes.

## Pharmacologic Management

Drugs that are useful in the management of diarrhea are listed in **Table 41**.

| Table 41. Antidiarrheals | | |
|---|---|---|
| **Drug** | **Dosage (Metabolism)** | **Formulations** |
| ✔ Attapulgite* (*Kaopectate*) | 1200–1500 mg after each loose bowel movement or q 2 h; 15–30 mL up to 9 × /d, up to 9000 mg/24 h (not absorbed) | S: oral conc 600, 750 mg/15 mL; T: 750; ChT: 300, 600 |
| ✔ Bismuth subsalicylate* (*Pepto-Bismol*) | 2 tabs or 30 mL q 30 min to 1 h as needed up to 8 doses/24 h | S: 262 mg/15 mL, 525 mg/15 mL; T: 324; ChT: 262 |
| Diphenoxylate with atropine (*Lomotil*)† | 15–20 mg/d of diphenoxylate in 3–4 divided doses; maintenance 5–15 mg/d in 2–3 divided doses (L) | S: oral, diphenoxylate hydrochloride 2.5 mg + atropine sulfate 0.025 mg/5 mL; T: diphenoxylate hydrochloride 2.5 mg and atropine sulfate 0.025 mg |
| ✔ Loperamide* (*Imodium A-D*) | Initial: 4 mg followed by 2 mg after each loose stool, up to 16 mg/d (L) | Caplet, 2; C: 2; T: 2; S: oral, 1 mg/5 mL |

✔ = preferred for treating older persons.
* Available OTC.
† Anticholinergic, potentially CNS toxic.

## ANTIBIOTIC-ASSOCIATED DIARRHEA
(Antibiotic-associated pseudomembranous colitis, or AAPMC)

### Definition
A specific form of *Clostridium difficile* pseudomembranous colitis

### Risk Factors
Almost any oral or parenteral antibiotic and several antineoplastic agents, including cyclophosphamide, doxorubicin, fluorouracil, methotrexate.

### Presentation
- Abdominal pain, cramping
- Dehydration
- Diarrhea (can be bloody)
- Fecal leukocytes
- Fever (100–105°F)
- Hypoalbuminemia
- Hypovolemia
- Leukocytosis

Symptoms appear a few days after starting to 10 wk after discontinuing the offending agent.

### Diagnosis
- Isolation of *C difficile* or its toxin from symptomatic patient. Three negative stools are needed to exclude diagnosis.
- Lower endoscopy; however, lesions may be scattered.

**Treatment**
• D/C offending agent if possible.
• Metronidazole (*Flagyl*) 250 mg po qid or 500 mg po tid × 10 d or vancomycin 125–500 mg po qid × 10 d.
• Treat diarrhea with cholestyramine resin (eg, *Questran*) 4 g 1–6 ×/d to adsorb toxin.
• Avoid opiates or other agents that will slow GI motility.

**Recurrence**
Relapse seen in 10% to 20% of patients 1–4 wk after treatment (spore-producing organism). Re-treat with same regimen or use alternative.

# HEARING IMPAIRMENT

## DEFINITION
The most common sensory impairment in old age. To quantify hearing ability, the necessary intensity (decibel = dB) and frequency (Hertz) of the perceived pure-tone signal must be described.

## EVALUATION
### Screening
- Note problems during conversation
- Ask about hearing dysfunction
- Use a standardized questionnaire (see p 207)
- Test with handheld audioscope
- Use whisper test—stand behind patient 2 ft from ear, cover untested ear, fully exhale, whisper an easily answered question
- Refer patients who screen positive for audiologic evaluation

### Audiometry
- Documents the dB loss across frequencies
- Determines the pattern of loss (see Classification, below)
- Determines if loss is unilateral or bilateral **Note:** If speech discrimination is <50%, results with hearing aids may be poor.

### Aggravating Factors
- Sensorineural loss—medication ototoxicity (eg, aminoglycosides, loop diuretics, cisplatin), cerumen impaction (see p 79)
- Conductive loss—cerumen impaction, external otitis

## CLASSIFICATION
### Sensorineural Hearing Loss
Due to cochlear or retrocochlear pathology; both air and bone conduction thresholds are increased; causes: aging, eighth nerve damage from syphilis, viral meningitis, trauma, vascular events to eighth nerve or cortical tracts, acoustic neuroma, Ménière's disease.

### Conductive Hearing Loss
Occurs when sound transmission to inner ear is impaired; bone conduction better than air conduction; causes include: external or middle ear disorders, including otosclerosis; rheumatoid arthritis; Paget's disease.

### Central Auditory Processing Disorder
Loss of speech discrimination in excess of that from loss in hearing sensitivity; involves the CNS; occurs in dementia and infrequently with presbycusis.

### Presbycusis (Old-Age Hearing Loss, a Subtype of Sensorineural Loss):
- Mainly high-frequency loss
- Impaired speech discrimination
- Recruitment (an increase in sensation of loudness)
- Both bone and air conduction affected

## MANAGEMENT
### Remove Ear Wax
Fill ear canal with 5–10 gtt water and cover with cotton bid × 4 d or more. Liquid must stay in contact with ear for at least 15 min. Hearing may worsen as cerumen expands. Water is as effective as commercial preparations (eg, *Debrox, Cerumenex, Colace*). Use of any of the commercial preparations for more than 4 d may cause ear irritation.

#### Table 42. Effects and Rehabilitation of Hearing Loss, by Level of Loss

| Level of Loss | Difficulty Understanding | Need for Hearing Aid |
|---|---|---|
| 0–24 dB | None | None |
| 25–40 dB (mild) | Normal speech | In specific situations |
| 41–55 dB (moderate) | Loud speech | Frequent |
| 56–80 dB (severe) | Anything but amplified speech | For all communication |
| 81 dB or more (profound) | Even amplified speech | Plus speech reading, aural rehabilitation, sign language, or cochlear implants |

Source: Data in part from *A Report on Hearing Aids: User Perspectives and Concerns*. Washington, DC: American Association of Retired Persons; 1993:2.

### Hearing Devices
*Hearing Aids:* Appropriate for most hearing-impaired persons; enhance select frequencies; should be individualized for each ear. Amplification in both ears (binaural) achieves best speech understanding; unilateral aid may be appropriate if asymmetrical speech discrimination, if hearing aid care is challenging, or because of cost.

*Assistive Listening Devices:* Microphone placed close to sound source transmits to headphones or earpiece. Transmission is by wire or wireless (FM or infrared); these systems increase signal-to-noise ratio, which is useful for persons with central auditory processing disorder.

*Telephone Device for the Deaf (TDD):* Receiver is a keyboard that allows the hearing-impaired person to respond.

*Cochlear Implants:* Bypass the middle ear, directly innervate auditory nerve. Reserved for severe and profound hearing loss. Results after age 65 comparable to younger persons. Failure rate <1%, but patient selection important.

### Tips for Communication with Hearing-Impaired Persons
- Stand 2–3 ft away
- Have the person's attention
- Have the person seated in front of a wall, which will help reflect sound
- Use lower-pitched voice
- Speak slowly and distinctly; don't shout
- Rephrase rather than repeat
- Pause at the end of phrases or ideas

## TINNITUS
### Definition
The perception of sound in the absence of external acoustic stimulation; may be ringing, crackling, or whistling; may be continuous or intermittent

### Objective Tinnitus
Noise heard by both patient and examiner (rare); usually due to abnormal blood flow in or around ear (normal anatomic variants or a pathologic condition)

### Subjective Tinnitus
• Cannot be heard externally by others (common).
• Normal tinnitus lasts <5 min, < once/week.
• Pathologic tinnitus lasts >5 min, > weekly (usually in people with hearing loss).

### Evaluation
• Auscultate the head and neck near ear orbits, mastoids for objective tinnitus.
   ○ If pulsatile, obtain CT/MRA for vascular cause.
   ○ If continuous, obtain MRI looking for patulous Eustachian tube; other causes include palatal myoclonus, stapedial muscle spasm.
   ○ Refer to otolaryngology
• Examine ear canals for cerumen, otitis external or otitis interna; treat and reassess.
• Assess hearing (as above); unilateral hearing loss and tinnitus suggest acoustic neuroma; obtain MRI.
• Audiometry
   ○ Low- and high-tone loss supports Ménière's disease.
   ○ High-tone loss suggests presbycusis.
• Check medication list for drugs associated with tinnitus, eg, NSAIDs, ASA, antibiotics (especially erythromycin), loop diuretics (especially furosemide), chemotherapy, quinine.

### Treatment
• Objective tinnitus: refer to otolaryngology.
• Subjective tinnitus without distress:
   ○ Normal tinnitus: reassure patient.
   ○ Pathologic tinnitus: educate patient, encourage amplification for those with hearing impairment.
• Subjective tinnitus with distress:
   ○ Severe complaints about tinnitus are often a sign of depression
   ○ Evaluate for depression and treat (see page 49).

# HEMATOLOGIC DISORDERS

## ANEMIA
### Evaluation
- Some decrease in Hb with age is normal.
- Evaluate persons >65 when Hb <13.
- Evaluate if Hb falls >1 g/dL in 1 yr.
- Physical examination and laboratory tests to look for kidney or liver disease.
- Evaluate GI and GU source if iron deficient.
- Check WBC and peripheral blood smear, and pursue suspected causes as appropriate.
- Combined deficiencies are common in older people; reasonable to check $B_{12}$, folate, and iron in all cases.
- Check reticuloctye count and reticulocyte index.
  - Reticulocyte count/index high: adequate response, suspect blood loss or RBC destruction
  - Reticulocyte count/index normal or low, check MCV
    - MCV >100 $\mu m^3$/cell: see **Figure 4**
    - MCV <100 $\mu m^3$/cell: see **Figure 5**

## Common Anemias of Later Life: Diagnosis and Treatment
***Iron deficiency anemia:*** Usual laboratory values (Fe, TIBC, ferritin) less reliable in presence of other conditions (see **Figure 5**). Soluble transferrin receptors may help differentiate chronic disease anemia from iron deficiency; elevated receptors suggest iron deficiency.
***Chronic disease anemia:***
- Most common causes in elderly people are:
  - acute and chronic infection
  - chronic inflammation
  - malignancy
  - protein calorie malnutrition
  - unidentified chronic disease
- Laboratory tests: usually low iron, low or normal TIBC, high ferritin, low soluble transferrin receptor
- Type determines treatability:
  - "rheumatoid arthritis type" responds to erythropoietin at usual doses (see **Table 43**)
  - "cancer type" may respond to erythropoietin at high doses (see **Table 43**)
- Restoring Hb to higher levels improves quality of life, function, and possibly survival.
***Anemia of renal insufficiency:***
- Caused by decreased erythropoietin production; check epoetin level.
- Restoring Hb levels increases survival, quality of life, and cognitive function, and decreases hospitalization, LVH, and HF. Treatment is erythropoietin (see **Table 43**).
***Anemia of $B_{12}$ and folate deficiency:***
- Laboratory tests: anemia or pancytopenia, macrocytosis
- $B_{12}$ deficiency definite at levels <100 pg/mL, possible at levels of 100–300; check MMA or give trial of $B_{12}$ replacement (see **Figure 5**)
- Treatment: see **Table 43**

**Figure 4. Evaluation of Hypoproliferative Anemia with Elevated MCV**

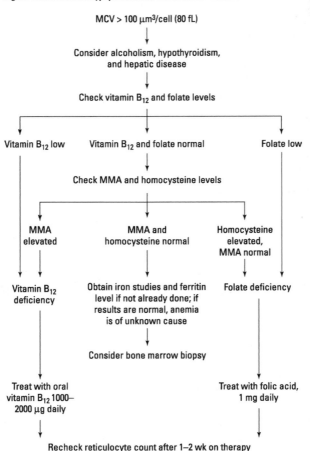

Source: Balducci L. Epidemiology of anemia in the elderly: Information on diagnostic evaluation. *J Amer Geriatr Soc* 2003; 51(3 Suppl):S2–9. Reprinted with permission.

**Figure 5. Evaluation of Hypoproliferative Anemia with Normal or Low MCV**

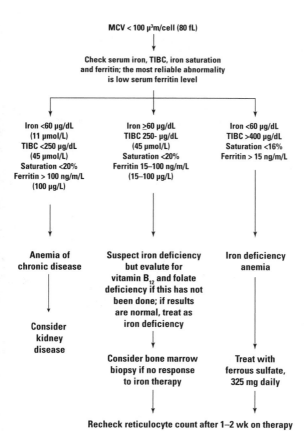

MCV < 100 µ³m/cell (80 fL)

Check serum iron, TIBC, iron saturation
and ferritin; the most reliable abnormality
is low serum ferritin level

Iron <60 µg/dL
(11 µmol/L)
TIBC <250 µg/dL
(45 µmol/L)
Saturation <20%
Ferritin > 100 ng/m/L
(100 µg/L)

Iron ≥60 µg/dL
TIBC 250- µg/dL
(45 µmol/L)
Saturation <20%
Ferritin 15–100 ng/m/L
(15–100 µg/L)

Iron <60 µg/dL
TIBC >400 µg/dL
Saturation <16%
Ferritin > 15 ng/m/L

**Anemia of
chronic disease**

**Consider
kidney
disease**

**Suspect iron deficiency
but evelute for
vitamin B$_{12}$ and folate
deficiency if this has not
been done; if results
are normal, treat as
iron deficiency**

**Consider bone marrow
biopsy if no response
to iron therapy**

**Iron deficiency
anemia**

**Treat with
ferrous sulfate,
325 mg daily**

**Recheck reticulocyte count after 1–2 wk on therapy**

Adapted from: Balducci L. Epidemiology of anemia in the elderly: Information on diagnostic evaluation. *J Amer Geriatr Soc* 2003; 51(3 Suppl):S2–9. Reprinted with permission.

### Anemia of unknown cause:
- Prevalence: 17% of all anemias after age 65
- May be age-related decline in hematopoietic reserve, low erythropoietin, and/or poor response to endogenous erythropoietin

### Pancytopenia:
- Unless due to $B_{12}$ deficiency, bone marrow aspirate is indicated
- Causes include cancer, fibrosis, myelodysplasia
- Aplastic anemia increases in prevalence with age; 50% respond to antithymocyte globulin and cyclosporine

| Table 43. Treatment of Anemias Associated with Deficiency | | |
|---|---|---|
| **Treatment** | **Formulation and Dosage** | **Comments** |
| Iron | Ferrous sulfate 325 mg po qd | Higher doses cause more GI adverse events |
| | Ferrous polysaccharide 150 mg po qd | Fewer GI adverse events |
| | Iron dextran: Dose (mL) = 0.0442 (desired Hb − observed Hb) × LBW (kg) + (0.26 × LBW). For LBW, see p 1. | For severe deficiency or poor absorption |
| | Administer test dose at 0.5 mL IM or IV sol (5 gtt/min). Wait 30–45 min. If tolerated, complete dose by slow IM injection ≤50 mg/min. By IV, dilute dose in 500 mL normal saline (45–60 mL/min). | |
| $B_{12}$ | 1000 µg IM every wk × 5, then 1000 µg IM every mo or 1000 µg po qd | Monitor $K^+$ in first wk of treatment |
| Folate | 1 mg po qd | |
| Erythropoietin | Epoetin alfa (*Epogen*) usual dose 50–150 U/kg SC every wk | Monitor BP, adjust dose based on response; Medicare pays for use in kidney failure and in anemia due to chemotherapy |
| | Darbepoetin alfa (*Aranesp*) 0.45 µg/kg every wk | See full prescribing information for titration |

# INCONTINENCE—URINARY AND FECAL

## URINARY INCONTINENCE (UI)
### General Information
UI is not a normal part of aging. It is a loss of urine control due to a combination of
- Genitourinary pathology
- Age-related changes
- Comorbid conditions
- Environmental obstacles

### Classification
*Reversible Causes of Incontinence (DRIP Mnemonic)*
**D**elirium
**R**estricted mobility (illness, injury, gait disorder, restraint)
**I**nfection (acute, symptomatic); **I**nflammation (atrophic vaginitis); **I**mpaction of stool
**P**olyuria (diabetes mellitus, caffeine intake, volume overload); **P**harmaceuticals (diuretics, autonomic agents, psychotropics)
*Established Incontinence*
- **Urge:** Detrusor muscle overactivity (uninhibited bladder contractions); small to large volume loss; may be idiopathic or associated with CNS lesions or bladder irritation from infection, stones, tumors; may be associated with impaired contractility and retention (detrusor hyperactivity with impaired contractility [DHIC]).
- **Stress:** Failure of sphincter mechanisms to remain closed during bladder filling (often due to insufficient pelvic support in women and trauma from prostate surgery in men); loss occurs with increased intra-abdominal pressure.
- **Overflow:** Impaired detrusor contractility or bladder outlet obstruction. Impaired contractility—chronic outlet obstruction, diabetes mellitus, vitamin $B_{12}$ deficiency, tabes dorsalis, alcoholism, or spinal disease. Outlet obstruction—in men, BPH, cancer, stricture; in women, prior incontinence surgery or large cystocele.
- **Mixed:** Combined urge and stress UI is common in older women.
- **Functional:** Inability or unwillingness to toilet because of physical, cognitive, psychologic, or environmental factors.
- **Other (rare):** Bladder-sphincter dyssynergia, fistulas, reduced detrusor compliance, recurrent cystitis.

### Risk Factors
- Age-related changes (BPH, atrophic urethritis)
- Constipation
- Dementia, depression, stroke, Parkinson's disease
- Detrusor overactivity and uninhibited contractions
- Fecal incontinence
- HF, nocturia, COPD, or chronic cough
- Increased postvoid residual or decreased bladder capacity
- Impaired ADLs
- Obesity

### Evaluation
*History*
- Precipitant urgency suggests detrusor overactivity.
- Loss with cough, laugh, or bend suggests stress.
- Continuous leakage suggests intrinsic sphincter insufficiency or overflow.
- Onset, frequency, volume, timing, precipitants (eg, caffeine, diuretics, alcohol, cough, medications).

### Physical Examination
- Functional status (eg, mobility, dexterity)
- Mental status
- Orthostatic BP, HR
- Findings:
  - Bladder distension
  - Cervical cord compression (interosseus muscle wasting, Hoffmann's or Babinski's signs)
  - Rectal mass or impaction
  - Sacral root integrity (anal sphincter tone, anal wink, perineal sensation)
  - Volume overload, edema

### Male GU
Prostate consistency; symmetry; for uncircumcised, check phimosis, paraphimosis, balanitis

### Female GU
Atrophic vaginitis (see p 201); pelvic support (see p 201)

### Testing
- **Voiding Record:** Record time and volume of incontinent, continent episodes; activities and time of sleep; knowing oral intake is sometimes helpful.
- **Standing Full Bladder Stress Test:** Relax perineum and cough once—immediate loss suggests stress, several seconds' delay suggests detrusor overactivity.
- **Postvoid Residual:** If >100 mL, repeat; still >100 mL suggests detrusor weakness, neuropathy, outlet obstruction, or DHIC.
- **Laboratory:** UA and urine C&S; glucose and calcium if polyuric; renal function tests and $B_{12}$ if urinary retention; urine cytology if hematuria or pain; PSA if cancer suspected.
- **Urodynamic Testing:** Not routinely indicated; indicated before corrective surgery, when diagnosis is unclear, or when empiric therapy fails.

### Management
In a stepped approach, treat all transient causes first (DRIP); avoid caffeine, alcohol, minimize evening intake of fluids.

### Nonpharmacologic Behavioral Therapy (First-Line Therapy)
- **Detrusor Instability:** Timed toileting—shortest interval to keep dry; urge control—when urgency occurs, sit or stand quietly, focus on letting urge pass, when no longer urgent walk slowly to the bathroom and void. When no incontinence for 2 d, increase voiding interval by 30–60 min until voiding every 3–4 h. Electrical stimulation often effective; refer to PT. Pelvic muscle exercises (see below).
- **Cognitively Impaired Persons:** Prompted toileting (ask if patient needs to void) at 2- to 3-h intervals during day; encourage patients to report continence status; praise patient when continent and responds to toileting.
- **Stress Incontinence:** Pelvic muscle (Kegel's) exercises—isolate pelvic muscles (avoid thigh, rectal, buttocks contraction); perform 3–10 sets of 10 contractions at max strength daily; progressively longer (up to 10-sec) contractions; follow up and encouragement necessary; consider biofeedback for training or have patient practice interrupting urine stream while voiding.
- **Pessaries:** May benefit women with vaginal or uterine prolapse who experience retention or stress UI.

- **Detrusor Hyperactivity with Impaired Contractility (DHIC):** Treat urge first; self-intermittent clean catheterization if needed.

### Nocturnal Frequency in the Absence of HF

- Two voidings per night is probably normal.
- Exclude sleep difficulties (see Sleep Disorders, p 190), then consider if the condition is due to excessive output or urinary tract dysfunction.
- All patients should restrict fluid intake after dinner.
- If there are frequent small-volume voidings, treat for detrusor hyperactivity or DHIC.
- If volume of most voidings is close to daytime voided volume (ie, bladder capacity), eg, 400 mL and 3 or more voidings per night, this is excessive fluid excretion.
  ○ If stasis edema is present, have patient wear pressure-graded stockings.
  ○ If no stasis edema, a potent, short-acting loop diuretic can be used in the early evening to induce a diuresis before bedtime, eg, bumetanide 0.5–1.5 mg titrated to achieve a brisk diuresis.

### Pharmacologic Therapy

Estrogen replacement benefits urge and possibly stress UI. Topical estrogens are effective; see **Table 84** for available preparations. See **Table 44** for other therapies.

#### Table 44. Drugs to Treat Urinary Incontinence, by Types

| $R_x$ by UI Type | Dosage | Formulations | Comments (Metabolism) |
|---|---|---|---|
| **Urge or Mixed UI\*** | | | |
| Hyoscyamine (*Anaspaz, Cystospaz, Levsin*) | 0.375–0.75 po q 12 h | SR: 0.375 | Prominent anticholinergic side effects; delirium, nervousness, insomnia (K) |
| Imipramine (*Tofranil*) | 10–25 mg tid | T: 10, 25, 50 | Dry mouth, blurry vision, ↑ intraocular pressure, delirium, constipation, plus postural ↓ BP, cardiac conduction disturbances (L) |
| ✔Oxybutynin (*Ditropan, Ditropan XL, Oxytrol*) | 2.5–5.0 mg bid-tid 5–20 mg qd 3.9 mg/d (apply patch 2 × /wk) | T: 5; S: 5 mg/5 mL SR: 5, 10, 15 transdermal 39 cm² patch | Dry mouth, blurry vision, ↑ intraocular pressure, delirium, constipation Pch: No more dry mouth than placebo; may irritate skin (L) |
| Propantheline (*Pro-Banthine*) | 15–30 mg (on empty stomach) | T: 15 | Dry mouth, blurry vision, ↑ intraocular pressure, delirium, constipation (L, K) |
| ✔ Tolterodine (*Detrol, Detrol LA*) | 2 mg bid 4 mg qd | T: 1, 2 C: ER 2, 4 | Dry mouth, dyspepsia, constipation, delirium (L) |
| Trospium (*Sanctura*) | 20 mg qd-bid (on empty stomach) | T: 20 | Dose once daily at hs in patients >75 yr old and in those with CrCl <30 mL. Dry mouth, constipation, dyspepsia, headache. Caution: narrow angle glaucoma, liver dysfunction. (L, K) |
| Darifenacin (*Enablex*) | 7.5–15 mg qd | T: 7.5, 15 | Dry mouth, constipation (L, CYP3A4 and CYP2D6) |

*(cont.)*

Table 44. Drugs to Treat Urinary Incontinence, by Types (cont.)

| R$_x$ by UI Type | Dosage | Formulations | Comments (Metabolism) |
|---|---|---|---|
| **Stress UI†** | | | |
| Pseudoephedrine (eg, *Sudafed*) | 15–30 mg tid | T: 30, 60; elixir 30 mg/5 mL | Headache, tachycardia, ↑ BP (L) |
| (*Sudafed XR*) | 120 mg qd, bid | SR: 120 | |

✔ = preferred in treating older people. For prostate obstruction UI, see benign prostatic hyperplasia, p 163.
* Drugs to treat urge or mixed UI: ↑ bladder capacity, ↓ involuntary contractions.
† Drugs to treat stress UI: ↑ urethral smooth muscle contraction.

## *Surgical Therapy*
- Consider for the 50% of women whose stress UI does not respond adequately to behavioral treatment and exercise.
- Urinary sphincter function has proximal, distal, and intrinsic components; a surgical approach addresses only one component.
  - Traditional surgery (retropubic colposuspension) addresses the proximal defect.
  - Periurethral injection improves intrinsic sphincter function.
  - Newer minimally invasive techniques (eg, tension-free vaginal tape) address the distal defect.
- At least two thirds of surgically treated patients should have substantial improvement or cure.

## Catheter Care
- Use catheter **only** for chronic urinary retention, nonhealing pressure ulcers in incontinent patients, and when requested by patients or families to promote comfort.
- Use closed drainage system only; avoid topical or systemic antibiotics or catheters treated with antibiotics. Silver alloy hydrogel catheters reduce UTI by 27% to 73%.
- Bacteriuria is universal; treat only if symptoms (ie, fever, inanition, anorexia, delirium), or if bacteriuria persists after catheter removal.
- How to culture from catheter: through the port, not from the bag.
- Replace catheter if symptomatic bacteriuria occurs, then culture urine.
- Nursing facility patients with catheters should be kept in separate rooms.
- For acute retention catheterize for 7–10 d, then do voiding trial after catheter removal, never clamping.
- **Replacing Catheters:** Routine replacement not necessary. Changing every 4–6 wk is reasonable to prevent blockage. Patients with recurrent blockage need increased fluid intake and dilute acetic acid bladder irrigation.

## FECAL INCONTINENCE (FI)
### Definition
Involuntary or inappropriate passing of feces that has an impact on social functioning or hygiene.

### Prevalence
Varies by setting. After age 65: 2% of community-dwelling, 14% of hospitalized, 54% of nursing-home residents (38% as a long-term problem).

**Risk Factors**
Constipation, age >80 yr, female sex (if younger than 80), UI, impaired mobility, dementia, neurologic disease.

**Age-related Factors**
Decreased strength of external sphincter and weak anal squeeze; possibly increased rectal compliance, decreased resting tone in internal anal sphincter, and impaired anal sensory function.

**Causes:** FI is commonly multifactorial.
- Overflow: from colonic fecal loading, causing continuous soiling.
- Loose stool: caused by drugs (eg, laxatives, antibiotics), neoplasm, colitis, lactose intolerance.
- Functional incontinence: associated with poor mobility.
- Dementia related: uninhibited rectal contraction, often have UI.
- Anorectal incontinence: weak external sphincter (surgery, multiparity, etc).
- Comorbidity: stroke, diabetes mellitus (autonomic neuropathy), sacral cord dysfunction.

**Evaluation**
*History*
- Description of FI (eg, diarrhea, hard stool, etc). Ask about usual bowel habit, change in habit, usual stool consistency.
- Ask about frequency, urgency, ability to delay, difficulty wiping, post-defecation soiling, ability to distinguish stool and flatus.
- Evacuation difficulties: straining, incomplete emptying, rectal prolapse or pain.
- Functional: communication of needs, need for assistance, toilet access.
- Other: bowel medications, other medications, UI, prior treatment (eg, pads).
*Examination*
- Abdomen for colonic distention
- Visual inspection of anus
- Check for prolapse while patient seated on commode
- Rectal examination for tone, volume, and consistency of stool; heme test
- Gait, mobility, dressing, hygiene, mental status
*Laboratory*
- TSH, electrolytes, calcium
*Bowel Investigations*
- Abdominal radiograph: may identify colonic loading in the presence of empty rectum
- Colonoscopy: only when pathology suspected (unexplained loose stool, bleeding, etc)
- Anorectal physiology tests: not generally needed for treatment, rarely alter plans even for surgery.

**Treatment:** Multiple interventions may be required.
*Main approach*
- Simulate the patient's usual bowel pattern.
- Use rectal evacuants to stimulate evacuation and to establish a bowel pattern.

- Use evacuants in the hierarchy: glycerine suppository, bisacodyl suppository, microenemas (eg, *Enemeez*, docusate 5 mL), phosphate or tap water enemas; digital stimulation for some patients.
- Use antidiarrheals to slow an overactive bowel or to enable planned evacuation with rectal preparations.

***Constipation*** (see p 73)

Often plays a role; evaluate (if needed) and treat

***Modify stool consistency*** to achieve soft, formed stool

- Loose stool: use fiber or loperamide titrated to effect, sometimes as little as qod.
- Hard stool; modify diet; fluids add osmotic agent ($MgSO_4$ or $MgOH$ are preferred). In poorly mobile people, bran and fiber may exacerbate constipation.

***Patient education***

- Respond promptly on urge to defecate.
- Use coffee to stimulate the gut.
- Position on toilet to facilitate rectal evacuation: back support, foot stool to achieve squat position.
- Exercise to improve bowel function.
- Those who are able may be taught rectal sphincter exercises (tighten rectal sphincter for 10 sec 50 times/d) using digital rectal examination or biofeedback.

***Rectal evacuation and toilet training***

- Bowel control is improved with regimens.
- Capitalize on the gastrocolic reflex.
- When no spontaneous bowel action, stimulate with suppositories or enemas (see above); those with incompetent sphincters may not retain usual enemas.
- Bed pans should not be used; bedside commodes are not as good as either toilets, sani-chairs, or shower chairs.

***Nursing-home residents and very disabled elderly persons:*** FI is most often due to colonic loading and overflow. Treat as follows:

- Daily enemas until no more results.
- Add a daily osmotic laxative (see **Table 39**) and follow bowel training (above).
- Stool transit can be stimulated with abdominal massage in direction of colonic transit.

***Other therapies***

- Manual evacuation may be appropriate in some patients.
- Skin care: Wet wipes better than dry; commercial preparations better than soap and water; toilet tongs and bottom wipers help those with shoulder disease.
- Surgery:
  ○ Full-thickness rectal prolapse usually requires surgery using a transanal approach in frail patients; full continence may not be restored.
  ○ Denervation of the sphincter can be repaired by placation of the puborectalis muscle to the anal canal, which increases the anorectal angle; long-term results are often unsatisfactory.
  ○ Division of the external anal sphincter (as may occur with childbirth) or anal fissure repair can be surgically repaired; short-term results are good, but long-term results are less satisfactory.
  ○ Selected patients have improved quality of life through creation of a stoma.

## PNEUMONIA
### Presentation
Can range from subtle signs such as lethargy, anorexia, dizziness, falls, and delirium to septic shock or adult respiratory distress syndrome. Pleuritic chest pain, dyspnea, productive cough, fever, chills, or rigors are not consistently present in older patients.

### Evaluation and Assessment
- Physical examination: Respiratory rate >20 breaths/min; low BP, chest sounds may be minimal, absent, or consistent with HF; temperature: 20% will be afebrile.
- CXR: Infiltrate may not be present on initial film if the patient is dehydrated.
- Sputum Gram's stain and culture (optional per ATS guidelines)
- CBC with differential: Up to 50% of patients have a normal white blood cell count, but 95% have a left shift.
- BUN, creatinine, electrolytes, glucose
- Blood culture × 2
- Oxygenation: arterial blood gas or oximetry
- Test for *Mycobacterium tuberculosis* with acid-fast bacilli strain and culture in selected patients.
- Test for *Legionella* spp in patients who are seriously ill without an alternative diagnosis, immunocompromised, nonresponsive to $\beta$-lactam antibiotics, have clinical features suggesting this diagnosis, or in outbreak setting. Urinary antigen testing is highly specific for serotype 1 but lacks specificity for other serotypes. Value and use vary by geographic region.
- Thoracentesis (if moderate to large effusion)

### Aggravating Factors
- Age-related changes in pulmonary reserve
- Alcoholism
- Altered mental status
- Comorbid conditions that alter gag reflexes or ciliary transport
- COPD or other lung disease
- Heart disease
- Malnutrition
- Medications: Immunosuppressants, sedatives, anticholinergic or other agents that dry secretions, agents that decrease gastric pH
- Nasogastric tubes

### Expected Organisms (in order of frequency of occurrence)

| *Community-Acquired:* | *Nursing-Home–Acquired:* | *Hospital-Acquired:* |
|---|---|---|
| *Streptococcus pneumoniae* | *S pneumoniae* | Gram-negative bacteria |
| Respiratory viruses | Gram-negative bacteria | Anaerobes |
| *Haemophilus influenzae* | *Staphylococcus aureus* | Gram-positive bacteria |
| Gram-negative bacteria | Anaerobes | Fungi |
| *Chlamydia pneumoniae* | *H influenzae* | |
| *Moraxella catarrhalis* | Group B streptococcus | |
| *Legionella* spp | *Chlamydia pneumoniae* | |
| *M tuberculosis* | | |
| Endemic fungi | | |

## Supportive Management
- Chest percussion
- Inhaled β-adrenergic agonists
- Mechanical ventilation (if indicated)
- Oxygen as indicated
- Rehydration

## Empiric Antibiotic Therapy (see Table 51)

| Table 45. Community-Acquired Pneumonia | |
|---|---|
| **Patient Type** | **Treatment Options** |
| Outpatient, previously healthy | |
| No recent antibiotic therapy | A macrolide* or doxycycline |
| Recent antibiotic therapy | A fluoroquinolone ** alone, **or** Azithromycin or clarithromycin plus amoxicillin 1 g po tid, **or** Azithromycin or clarithromycin plus amoxicillin-clavulanate 2 g po bid |
| Outpatient, with comorbidities | |
| No recent antibiotic therapy | Azithromycin or clarithromycin or a fluoroquinolone** alone |
| Recent antibiotic therapy | A fluoroquinolone** alone, **or** Azithromycin or clarithromycin plus amoxicillin, amoxicillin-clavulanate, cefpodoxime, cefprozil, or cefuroxime |
| Outpatient, suspected aspiration | Amoxicillin-clavulanate or clindamycin |
| Outpatient, influenza with bacterial superinfection | Amoxicillin, amoxicillin-clavulanate, cefpodoxime, cefprozil, or cefuroxime; **or** A fluoroquinolone** |
| Hospitalized patient | |
| No recent antibiotic therapy | A fluoroquinolone** alone, **or** Azithromycin or clarithromycin plus amoxicillin, amoxicillin-clavulanate, cefpodoxime, cefprozil, or cefuroxime |
| Recent antibiotic therapy | Azithromycin or clarithromycin plus amoxicillin, amoxicillin-clavulanate, cefpodoxime, cefprozil, or cefuroxime; **or** A fluoroquinolone** alone (base decision on previous antibiotic therapy) |
| Hospitalized patient, intensive care unit | |
| No concern about *Pseudomonas* | Cefotaxime, ceftriaxone, ampicillin-sulbactam, or ertapenem plus azithromycin or clarithromycin or a fluoroquinolone** |
| No concern about *Pseudomonas* but β-lactam allergy | A fluoroquinolone** with or without clindamycin |
| Concern about *Pseudomonas* | Antipseudomonal agent plus an aminoglycoside plus a fluoroquinolone** or a macrolide |

(cont.)

Table 45. **Community-Acquired Pneumonia (cont.)**

| Patient Type | Treatment Options |
|---|---|
| Concern about *Pseudomonas* and β-lactam allergy | Aztreonam plus levofloxacin; **or** Aztreonam plus moxifloxacin or gatifloxacin, with or without an aminoglycoside |
| Nursing-home patient | A fluoroquinolone** alone **or** Amoxicillin-clavulanate plus azithromycin or clarithromycin |

\* Macrolides: erythromycin, azithromycin, or clarithromycin.

\*\* Fluoroquinolones: moxifloxacin, gatifloxacin, levofloxacin, or gemifloxacin.

Source: Mandell LA, Bartlett JG, Dowell SF, et al. Update of practice guidelines for the management of community-acquired pneumonia in immunocompetent adults. *Clin Infect Dis* 2003;37:1405–1433.

***Nursing-Home Acquired (IV):*** [(1$^{st}$ or 2$^{nd}$ gen ceph or antipseudomonal β-lact) + AG] ± pen G, clinda, or vanco
***or*** 3$^{rd}$ or 4$^{th}$ gen ceph ± AG ± pen G, clinda, or vanco
***or*** antipseudomonal β-lact + AG
***or*** vanco + clinda + AG
For the oral route: see Community-Acquired (above) ± FLQ

***Hospital-Acquired (IV):*** [3$^{rd}$ or 4$^{th}$ gen ceph + clinda or pen G] ± AG
***or*** antipseudomonal β-lact + AG or other antipseudomonal agent
***or*** 1$^{st}$ or 2$^{nd}$ gen ceph + AG
***or*** vanco + clinda + AG
***or*** antipseudomonal β-lact + 2$^{nd}$ gen ceph
***or*** β-lact + antipseudomonal agent
For hospital- or nursing-home-acquired pneumonia, a macro, tetracycline, or FLQ may be added or substituted when *Legionella* spp or *Mycobacterium pneumonia* is suspected.

Note: AG = aminoglycoside; β-lact = β-lactam/β-lactamase inhibitor; ceph = cephalosporin; clinda = clindamycin; FLQ = fluoroquinolone; gen = generation; macro = macrolide; pen G = penicillin G; vanco = vancomycin.

Note: The empiric use of vancomycin should be reserved for patients with a serious allergy to β-lactam antibiotics or for patients from environments in which methicillin-resistant *S aureus* is known to be a problem pathogen. For all cases, antimicrobial therapy should be individualized once Gram's stain or culture results are known.

## URINARY TRACT INFECTION OR UROSEPSIS
### Definition
**Bacteriuria** is the presence of significant number of bacteria without reference to symptoms.

• **Symptomatic bacteriuria** usually has signs of dysuria and increased frequency of urination; fever, chills, nausea may be present; pyuria ($>10^5$ cfu/mL) supports the diagnosis of UTI.

• **Asymptomatic bacteriuria** is seen when the same organism(s) ($\geq 10^5$ cfu/mL) is found on 2 consecutive cultures in the absence of symptoms of a UTI; no treatment is necessary.

## Risk Factors
• Abnormalities in function or anatomy of the urinary tract
• Catheterization or recent instrumentation
• Comorbid conditions (eg, diabetes mellitus, BPH)
• Female gender
• Limited functional status

## Assessment and Evaluation
Choice is based on presenting symptoms and severity of illness.
• Urinalysis with culture (do not obtain specimen from catheter bag)
• Blood culture × 2
• BUN, creatinine, electrolytes
• CBC with differential

## Expected Organisms
***Noncatheterized Patients:*** Most common: *Escherichia coli*, *Proteus* spp, *Klebsiella* spp, *Providencia* spp, *Citrobacter* spp, *Enterobacter* spp, and *Pseudomonas aeruginosa* if recent antibiotic exposure, known colonization, or known institutional flora
***Nursing-Home–Catheterized Patients:*** *Enterobacter* spp and gram-negative bacteria

## Empiric Antibiotic Management
Duration should be at least 7–10 d.
***Community-Acquired or Nursing-Home–Acquired Cystitis or Uncomplicated UTI (Oral Route):*** TMP/SMZ DS, cephalexin, ampicillin, or amoxicillin. Amoxicillin/clavulanic acid should be reserved for patients with sulfa allergy and in settings where β-lactam resistance is known. Fluoroquinolones should be reserved for patients with allergies to sulpha, β-lactams, or in settings where resistance is known.
***Suspected Urosepsis (IV Route):*** Third-generation cephalosporin plus aminoglycoside, aztreonam, or fluoroquinolone ± aminoglycoside.

Vancomycin should be used in patients with severe β-lactam allergy.

## UTI Prophylaxis
Generally not recommended because it leads to antibiotic resistance

## HERPES ZOSTER ("SHINGLES")
### Definition
Cutaneous vesicular eruptions followed by radicular pain secondary to the recrudescence of varicella zoster virus.

### Clinical Manifestations
• An abrupt onset of pain along a specific dermatome (see **Figure 1**)
• Macular, erythematous rash after ~3 d which becomes vesicular and pustular (Tzanck cell test positive), crusts over and clears in 10–14 d

- Complications: post-herpetic neuralgia, visual loss or blindness if ophthalmic involvement

## Pharmacologic Management

When started within 72 h of the rash's appearance, antiviral therapy (see **Table 46**) decreases the severity and duration of the acute illness and possibly shortens the duration and reduces the risk of post-herpetic neuralgias. Corticosteroids may also decrease the risk and severity of post-herpetic neuralgias. (See p 136 for treatment of post-herpetic neuralgia.)

**Table 46. Antiviral Treatments for Herpes Zoster**

| Agent, Route | Dosage | Formulations | Comment |
|---|---|---|---|
| Acyclovir (*Zovirax*) | | | |
| Oral | 800 mg 5 ×/d for 7–10 d | T: 400, 800; C: 200; S: 200 mg/5 mL | Reduce dose when CrCl* <50 mL/min |
| IV** | 7.5–10 mg/kg q 8 h for 7–10 d | 500 mg/10 mL | |
| Famciclovir (*Famvir*) | | | |
| Oral | 500 mg q 8 h for 7 d | T: 125, 250, 500 | Reduce dose when CrCl* <60 mL/min |
| Valacyclovir[†] (*Valtrex*) | | | |
| Oral | 1000 mg q 8 h for 7 d | C: 500, 1000 | Reduce dose when CrCl* <50 mL/min |

\* The CrCl listed is the threshold below which the dose or frequency should be reduced. See alternative reference or the drug's package insert for detailed dosing guidelines.

\*\* Use IV for serious illness, ophthalmic infection, or patients who cannot take oral medication.

† Preferred to po acyclovir; prodrug of acyclovir with serum concentrations equal to IV.

## INFLUENZA

### Vaccine Prevention (ACIP Guidelines)

Yearly vaccination is recommended for all persons ≥65 years and all residents and staff of nursing homes, or residential or long-term-care facilities. Nursing-home residents admitted during the winter months after the completion of the vaccination program should be vaccinated at admission if they have not already been vaccinated. The influenza vaccine is contraindicated in persons with an anaphylactic hypersensitivity to eggs or any other component of the vaccine. Dose: 0.5 mL IM × 1 in the fall (Oct – Nov) for residents in the northern hemisphere.

### Pharmacologic Prophylaxis and Treatment with Antiviral Agents
#### Indications:

- Prevention (during an influenza outbreak): persons who are not vaccinated, are immunodeficient, or may spread the virus
- Prophylaxis: during 2 wk required to develop antibodies for persons vaccinated after an outbreak of influenza A
- Reduction of symptoms, duration of illness when started within the first 48 h of symptoms
- During epidemic outbreaks in nursing homes

***Duration:*** Treatment of symptoms: 3–5 d or for 24–48 h after symptoms resolve.
Prophylaxis during outbreak: Minimum 2 wk or until ~1 wk after end of outbreak.

### Table 47. Antiviral Treatment of Influenza

| Agent | Formulation | Dosage |
|---|---|---|
| Amantadine (*Symmetrel*) | C: 100 mg; S: 50 mg/5 mL | 100 mg po daily* |
| ✔ Oseltamivir (*Tamiflu*)** | C: 75 mg; S: 12 mg/mL | Treatment: 75 mg po bid × 5 d (75 mg po qd if CrCl 10–30 mL/min); not recommended if CrCl <10 mL/min |
| | | Prophylaxis: 75 mg po qd × ≥7 d up to 6 wk (75 mg po qod if CrCl 10–30 mL/min); not recommended if CrCl <10 mL/min |
| ✔ Rimantadine (*Flumadine*) | T: 100 mg; S: 50 mg/5 mL | 100 mg po qd for frail elderly and nursing-home residents |
| | | 200 mg po qd for other adults, including those ≥65 yr |
| | | Decrease dose to 100 mg if adverse events appear |
| Zanamivir (*Relenza*)**† | Inh: 5 mg/blister | 2 × 5–mg inhalations q 12 h × 5 d |
| | | Give doses on 1st d at least 2 h apart |

✔ = preferred for treating older persons.
 * Dose adjustments for kidney function, CrCl (mL/min): ≥30 = 100 mg daily; 20 – 29 = 200 mg 2 ×/wk; 10–19 = 100 mg 3 × /wk; <10 = 200 mg alternating with 100 mg q 7 d.
 ** Must be started within 2 d of symptom onset.
 † Do not use in patients with COPD or asthma.

## INFECTIOUS TUBERCULOSIS
Tuberculosis (TB) in elderly patients may be the reactivation of old disease or a new infection due to exposure to an infected individual. Treatment recommendations differ; if a new infection is suspected or the patient has risk factors for resistant organisms, then bacterial sensitivities must be determined.

### Risk or Reactivating Factors
• Chronic institutionalization
• Corticosteroid use
• Diabetes mellitus
• Malignancy
• Malnutrition
• Kidney failure

### Risk Factors for Resistant Organisms
• HIV infection
• Homelessness, institutionalization (other than a nursing home)
• IV drug abuse
• Origin from geographic regions with a high prevalence of resistance (New York, Mexico, Southeast Asia)
• Exposure to INH-resistant TB or history of failed chemotherapy
• Previous treatment for TB
• AFB-positive sputum smears after 2 mo of treatment
• Positive cultures after 4 mo of treatment

## Diagnosis

• PPD with booster 5-TU subdermal; read in 48–72 h; repeat in 1–2 wk if negative (see **Table 48** for interpretation of test results)
• CXR

## Treatment

*Latent Infection:* See **Table 48** and **Table 49.**

#### Table 48. Identification of Patients at High Risk of Developing TB Who Would Benefit from Treatment of Latent Infection

| Population | Minimum Induration Considered a Positive Test |
|---|---|
| Low risk: testing generally not indicated | 15 mm |
| Residents and employees of hospitals, nursing homes, and long-term facilities for elderly persons, residential facilities for AIDS patients, and homeless shelters | |
| Recent immigrants (<5 yr) from high-prevalence countries | 10 mm |
| Injection drug users | |
| Persons with silicosis; diabetes mellitus; chronic kidney failure; leukemia; lymphoma; carcinoma of the head, neck, or lung; weight loss of ≥10%; gastrectomy or jejunoileal bypass | |
| Recent contact with TB patients | |
| Fibrotic changes on CXR consistent with prior TB | |
| Immunosuppressed (receiving the equivalent of ≥15 mg/d of prednisone for ≥1 mo) or organ transplants | 5 mm |
| HIV-positive patients | |

#### Table 49. Treatment of Latent Tuberculosis

| Drug | Dosage and Duration |
|---|---|
| INH* | 5 mg/kg/d (max 300 mg/d) for 6 or 9 mo; or 15 mg/kg/d (max 900 mg/d) 2 × /wk with directly observed therapy (DOT) for 6 or 9 mo |
| RIF plus | 10 mg/kg/d (max 600 mg/d) |
| PZA† | 15–20 mg/kg/d (max 2 g/d) daily for 2 mo |
| **or** | |
| RIF plus | 10 mg/kg/d (max 600 mg/d) 2 × /wk with DOT for 2–3 mo |
| PZA† | 50 mg/kg/d (max 4 g/d) 2 × /wk with DOT for 2–3 mo |
| RIF | 10 mg/kg/d (max 600 mg/d) for 4 mo |

Note: INH = isoniazid; PZA = pyrazinamide; RIF = rifampin.

* The preferred treatment for patients not infected with HIV.

† Use the combination therapy with caution, as the 2-mo regimen has been associated with liver injury. Obtain a serum aminotransferase, and bilirubin at baseline and 2, 4, and 6 wk of treatment. For additional information, see *MMWR* 2001; 50(34):733–735 or http://www.atsjournal.org

Source: Data from: American Thoracic Society. Targeted tuberculin testing and treatment of latent tuberculosis. *Am J Respir Crit Care Med* 2000;161:S221–S247 (also available at http://www.atsjournal.org).

### Active Infection:

Initial treatment options for adults with active *Mycobacterium tuberculosis* infection in order of evidence-based preference are listed below. Daily observed therapy is preferred for all regimens. See http://www.cdc.gov/mmwr/preview/mmwrhtml/rr5211a1.htm for more information. (Note: EMB=ethambutol, INH=isoniazid, PZA=pyrazinamid, RIF=rifampin)

- INH, RIF, PZA, EMB daily × 8 wk or 5 d/wk × 8 wk, then INH + RIF daily × 18 wk or 5 d/wk × 18 wk.
- INH, RIF, PZA, EMB daily × 2 wk, then all agents 2 d/wk × 6 wk *or* INH, RIF, PZA, EMB 5 d/wk × 2 wk, then all agents 2 d/wk × 6 wk. Either regimen should be followed with INH + RIF 2 d/wk × 18 wk or 1 d/wk × 18 wk.
- INH, RIF, PZA, EMB 3 d/wk × 8 wk, then INH + RIF 3 d/wk × 18 wk.
- INH, RIF, PZA, EMB daily × 8 wk or 5 d/wk × 8 wk, then INH + RIF daily × 31 wk or 5 d/wk × 31 wk, or 2 d/wk × 31 wk.

#### Table 50. Dosing for Treatment Options for Active Tuberculosis

| Agent | Route | Daily | 2/Wk | 3/Wk |
|---|---|---|---|---|
| INH | po, IM | 5 mg/kg* | 15 mg/kg* | 15 mg/kg* |
| RIF | po, IM | 600 mg** | 600 mg** | 600 mg** |
| PZA | po | 1.5 g (<50 kg) | 2.0 g (<50 kg) | 2.0 g (<50 kg) |
| | | 2 g (51–74 kg) | 2.5 g (51–74 kg) | 2.5 g (51–74 kg) |
| | | 2.5 g (≥75 kg) | 3.0 g (≥75 kg) | 3.0 g (≥75 kg) |
| Ethambutol | po | 15–25 mg/kg† | 50 mg/kg | 30 mg/kg |
| Streptomycin | IM | 10 mg/kg | — | — |

\* Max: daily = 300 mg; 2/wk = 900 mg; 3/wk = 900 mg.
\*\* Max: daily = 600 mg; 2/wk = 600 mg; 3/wk = 600 mg.
† Max: daily = 2.5 g.

## ANTIBIOTICS

#### Table 51. Antibiotics

| Antimicrobial Class, *Subclass* | Route of Elimination (%) | Dosage | Adjust When CrCl* Is: (mL/min) | Formulations |
|---|---|---|---|---|
| *β–Lactams* *Penicillins* | | | | |
| Amoxicillin (*Amoxil*) | K (80) | po: 250 mg–1 g q 8 h | <50 | T: film coated 500, 875 C: 250, 500 ChT: 125, 200, 250, 400 S: 125, 200, 250, 400 mg/5 mL |
| Ampicillin | K (90) | po: 250–500 mg q 6 h IM/IV: 1–2 g q 4–6 h | <30 | C: 250, 500 S: 125, 250 mg/5 mL Inj |
| Penicillin G | K L (30) | IV: 3–5 × 10⁶ U q 4–6 h IM: 0.6–2.4 × 10⁶ U q 6–12 h | <30 | Inj procaine for IM |

*(cont.)*

Table 51. Antibiotics (cont.)

| Antimicrobial Class, *Subclass* | Route of Elimination (%) | Dosage | Adjust When CrCl* Is: (mL/min) | Formulations |
|---|---|---|---|---|
| Penicillin VK | K, L | po: 125–500 mg q 6 h | | T: 250, 500<br>S: 125, 250 mg/5 mL |
| *Antipseudomonal Penicillins* | | | | |
| Carbenicillin indanyl sodium (*Geocillin*) | K (80–99) | po: 382–764 mg q 6 h | <50 | T: 382 |
| Piperacillin (*Pipracil*) | K, F | IM: 1–2 g q 8–12 h<br>IV: 2–4 g q 6–8 h | <40 | Inj |
| Ticarcillin (*Ticar*) | K | IM, IV: 1–4 g q 4–6 h | <60 | Inj |
| *Antistaphylococcal Penicillins* | | | | |
| Dicloxacillin (*Dycill, Pathocil*) | K (56–70) | po: 125–500 mg q 6 h | NA | C: 125, 250, 500;<br>S: 62.5 mg/5 mL |
| Nafcillin | L | IM: 500 mg q 4–6 h<br>IV: 500 mg–2 g q 4–6 h | NA | Inj |
| Oxacillin (*Bactocill*) | K | po: 500 mg–1 g q 4–6 h<br><br>IM, IV: 250 mg–2 g<br>q 6–12 h | <10 | C: 250, 500<br>S: 250 mg/5 mL<br>Inj |
| *Monobactam (antipseudomonal)* | | | | |
| Aztreonam (*Azactam*) | K (70) | IM: 500 mg–1 g q 8–12 h<br>IV: 500 mg–2 g q 6–12 h | <30 | Inj |
| *Carbapenem (antipseudomonal)* | | | | |
| Ertapenem (*Invanz*) | K, F | IM, IV: 1 g q 24 h ×<br>3–14 d<br>IM × 7 d max<br>IV × 14 d max | <30 | Inj |
| Imipenem-Cilastatin (*Primaxin*) | K (70) | IM: 500 mg–1 g q 8–12 h<br>IV: 500 mg–2 g q 6–12 h | <70 | Inj |
| Meropenem (*Merrem IV*) | K (75), L (25) | IV: 1 g q 8 h | ≤50 | Inj |
| *Penicillinase-resistant Penicillins* | | | | |
| Amoxicillin–Clavulanate (*Augmentin*) | K | po: 250 mg q 8 h, 500 mg q 12 h, 875 mg q 12 h | <30 | T: 250, 500, 875<br>ChT: 125, 200, 250, 400<br>S: 125, 200, 250, 400 mg/5 mL |
| Ampicillin–Sulbactam (*Unasyn*) | K (85) | IM, IV: 1–2 g q 6–8 h | <30 | Inj |

*(cont.)*

Table 51. **Antibiotics (cont.)**

| Antimicrobial Class, *Subclass* | Route of Elimination (%) | Dosage | Adjust When CrCl* Is: (mL/min) | Formulations |
|---|---|---|---|---|
| *Penicillinase-resistant and Antipseudomonal Penicillins* | | | | |
| Piperacillin–Tazobactam (*Zosyn*) | K | IV: 3.375 g q 6 h | <40 | Inj |
| Ticarcillin–Clavulanate (*Timentin*) | K, L | IV: 3 g q 4–6 h | <60 | Inj |
| *First-Generation Cephalosporins* | | | | |
| Cefadroxil (*Duricef*) | K (90) | po: 500 mg–1 g q 12 h | <50 | C: 500; T: 1 g S: 125, 250, 500 mg/5 mL |
| Cefazolin (*Ancef, Kefzol*) | K (80–100) | IM, IV: 500 mg–2 g q 8 h | <55 | Inj |
| Cephalexin (*Keflex*) | K (80–100) | po: 250 mg–1 g q 6 h | <40 | C: 250, 500 T: 250, 500; 1 g S: 125, 250 mg/5 mL |
| Cephalothin (*Keflin*) | K (50–75) | IM, IV: 500 mg–2 g q 4–6 h | <50 | Inj |
| Cephapirin (*Cefadyl*) | K (60–85) | IM, IV: 1–3 g q 6 h | <10 | Inj |
| Cephradine (*Anspor*) | K (80–90) | po, IM, IV: 500 mg–2 g q 6 h | <20 | C: 250, 500 T: 1 g S: 125, 250 mg/5 mL Inj |
| *Second-Generation Cephalosporins* | | | | |
| Cefaclor (*Ceclor*) | K (80) | po: 250–500 mg q 8 h | <50 | C: 250, 500 S: 125, 187, 250, 375 mg/5 mL T: ER 375, 500 |
| Cefamandole (*Mandol*) | K | IM, IV: 1–3 g q 6 h | <80 | Inj |
| Cefmetazole (*Zefazone*) | K (85) | IV: 2 g q 6–12 h | <90 | Inj |
| Cefotetan (*Cefotan*) | K (80) | IM, IV: 1–3 g q 12 h or 1–2 g q 24 h (UTI) | <30 | Inj |
| Cefoxitin (*Mefoxin*) | K (85) | IM, IV: 1–2 g q 6–8 h | <50 | Inj |
| Cefprozil (*Cefzil*) | K (60–70) | po: 250–500 mg q 12–24 h | <30 | T: 250, 500 S: 125, 250 mg/5 mL |
| Cefuroxime axetil (*Ceftin*) | K (66–100) | po: 125–500 mg q 12 h<br><br>IM, IV: 750 mg–1.5 g q 6 h | | T: 125, 250, 500 S: 125, 150 mg/5 mL Inj |
| Loracarbef (*Lorabid*) | K | po: 200–400 mg q 12–24 h | <50 | C: 200, 400 S: 100, 200 mg/5 mL |

*(cont.)*

Table 51. **Antibiotics (cont.)**

| Antimicrobial Class, *Subclass* | Route of Elimination (%) | Dosage | Adjust When CrCl* Is: (mL/min) | Formulations |
|---|---|---|---|---|
| **Third-Generation Cephalosporins** | | | | |
| Cefdinir (*Omnicef*) | K | po: 300 mg bid or 600 qd × 10 d | <30 | C: 300 S: 125 mg/5 mL |
| Cefditoren (*Spectracef*) | K | po: 400 mg bid × 10 d (bronchitis) 400 mg bid × 14 d (pneumonia) 200 mg bid × 10 d (soft tissue/skin) | <50 | T: 200 |
| Cefixime (*Suprax*) | K (50) | po: 400 mg q 24 h | <60 | T: 200, 400 S: 100 mg/5 mL |
| Cefoperazone (*Cefobid*) | L, K (25) | IM, IV: 1–2 g q 12 h | Adjust in cirrhosis | Inj |
| Cefotaxime (*Claforan*) | K, L | IM, IV: 1–2 g q 6–12 h | <20 | Inj |
| Cefpodoxime (*Vantin*) | K (80) | po: 100–400 mg q 12 h | <30 | T: 100, 250 S: 50, 100 mg/5 mL |
| Ceftazidime (*Ceptaz, Fortaz*) | K | IM, IV: 500 mg–2 g q 8–12 h UTI: 250–500 mg q 12 h | <50 | Inj |
| Ceftibuten (*Cedax*) | K (65–70) | po: 400 mg q 24 h | <50 | C: 400 S: 100, 200 mg/5 mL |
| Ceftizoxime (*Cefizox*) | K (100) | IM, IV: 500 mg–2 g q 4–12 h | <80 | Inj |
| Ceftriaxone (*Rocephin*) | K (33–65) | IM, IV: 1–2 g q 12–24 h | NA | Inj |
| **Fourth-Generation Cephalosporins** | | | | |
| Cefepime (*Maxipime*) | K (85) | IV: 500 mg–2 g q 12 h | <60 | Inj |
| **Aminoglycosides** | | | | |
| Amikacin (*Amikin*) | K (95) | IM, IV: 15–20 mg/kg/d divided q 12–24 h; 15–20 mg/kg q 24–48 h | | Inj |
| Gentamicin (*Garamycin*) | K (95) | IM, IV: 2–5 mg/kg/d divided q 12–24 h; 5–7 mg/kg q 24–48 h | | Inj ophth sus, oint |
| Streptomycin | K (90) | IM, IV: 10 mg/kg/d not to exceed 750 mg/d | <50 | Inj |
| Tobramycin (*Nebcin*) | K (95) | IM, IV: 2–5 mg/kg/d divided q 12–24 h; 5–7 mg/kg q 24–48 h | | Inj ophth sus, oint |

*(cont.)*

Table 51. Antibiotics (cont.)

| Antimicrobial Class, *Subclass* | Route of Elimination (%) | Dosage | Adjust When CrCl* Is: (mL/min) | Formulations |
|---|---|---|---|---|
| **Macrolides** | | | | |
| Azithromycin (*Zithromax*) | L | po: 500 mg day 1, then 250 mg IV: 500 mg qd | NA | C: 250 S: 100, 200 mg/5 mL, 1 g (single-dose pk) T: 600 |
| Clarithromycin (*Biaxin, Biaxin XL*) | L, K (20–30) | po: 250–500 mg q 12 h ER: 1000 mg q 24 h | <30 | S: 125, 250 mg/5 mL T: 250, 500 ER: 500 |
| Dirithromycin (*Dynabac*) | L, F | po: 500 mg qd with food | NA | T: 250 |
| Erythromycin | L | po: Base: 333 mg q 8 h Estolate, stearate or base: 250–500 mg q 6–12 h Ethylsuccinate: 400–800 mg q 6–12 h IV: 15–20 mg/kg/d divided q 6 h | NA | Base: C, T: 250, 333, 500 Estolate: 250 S: 125, 250 mg/5 mL T: 500 Ethylsuccinate: S: 100, 200, 400 mg/5 mL T: 400 ChT: 200 Stearate: T: 250, 500 Inj |
| **Ketolide** | | | | |
| Telithromycin (*Ketek*) | L, K | po: 800 mg q 24 h × 5–10 d | <30 | T: 800 |
| **Quinolones** | | | | |
| Cinoxacin (*Cinobac*) | K (60) | po: 500 mg bid | <80 | C: 250, 500 |
| Ciprofloxacin (*Cipro*) | K (30–50), L, F (20–40) | po: 250–750 mg q 12 h ophth: see **Table 90** note IV: 200–400 mg q 12 h | po: <50 IV: <30 | T: 100, 250, 500, 750 S: 250 mg/5 mL, 500 mg/5 mL ophth sol: 3.5 mg/5 mL Inj |
| Enoxacin (*Penetrex*) | K, L (15–20) | po: 200 mg q 12 h × 7 d or 400 mg q 12 h × 14 d | ≤30 | T: 200, 400 |
| Gatifloxacin (*Tequin*) | K (95), F (5) | po, IV: 200 – 400 mg qd × 7–10 d | <40 | T: 200, 400 Inj |
| Gemifloxacin (*Factive*) | K, L, F | po: 320 mg qd | ≤40 | T: 320 mg |
| Levofloxacin (*Levaquin*) | K | po, IV: 250–500 mg q 24 h | <50 | T: 250, 500 |
| Lomefloxacin (*Maxaquin*) | K | po: 400 mg q 24 h | <40 | T: 400 |
| Moxifloxacin (*Avelox*) | L (~55), F (25), K (20) | po: 400 mg q 24 h | NA | T: 400 |

*(cont.)*

## Table 51. Antibiotics (cont.)

| Antimicrobial Class, *Subclass* | Route of Elimination (%) | Dosage | Adjust When CrCl* Is: (mL/min) | Formulations |
|---|---|---|---|---|
| Norfloxacin (*Noraxin*) | K (30), F (30) | po: 400 mg q 12 h ophth: see **Table 90** note | <30 | T: 400 ophth: 0.3% |
| Ofloxacin (*Roxin*) | K | po, IV: 200–400 mg q 12–24 h ophth: see **Table 90** note | <50 | T: 200, 300, 400 ophth: 0.3% Inj |
| Sparfloxacin (*Zagam*) | L | po: 400 mg day 1, then 200 mg q 24 h | <50 | T: 200 |
| Trovafloxacin (*Trovan*) | L | po, IV: 200 mg q 24 h × 10–14 d | NA | T: 100, 200 Inj |
| **Tetracyclines** | | | | |
| Doxycycline (eg, *Vibramycin*) | K (25), F (30) | po, IV: 100–200 mg/d given q 12–24 h | NA | C: 50, 100 T: 50, 100 S: 25 mg/5 mL, 50 mg/5 mL Inj |
| Minocycline (*Minocin*) | K | po, IV: 200 mg once, then 100 mg q 12 h | NA | C: 50, 100 S: 50 mg/5 mL Inj |
| Tetracycline | K (60) | po, IV: 250–500 mg q 6–12 h | NA | C: 100, 250, 500 T: 250, 500 S: 125 mg/5 mL ophth: oint, sus topical: oint, sol |
| **Other Antibiotics** | | | | |
| Chloramphenicol (*Chloromycetin*) | L (90) | po, IV: 50 mg/kg/d given q 6 h; max: 4 g/d | | C: 250 topical ophth Inj |
| Clindamycin (*Cleocin*) | L (90) | po: 150–450 mg q 6–8 h; max: 1.8 g/d IM, IV: 1.2–1.8 g/d given q 8–12 h; max: 3.6 g/d | NA | C: 75, 150, 300 S: 75 mg/5 mL crm, vaginal: 2% gel, topical: 1% Inj |
| Co-trimoxazole (TMP/SMZ, *Bactrim*) | K, L | Doses based on the trimethoprim component: po: 1 double-strength tab q 12 h. IV: sepsis: 20 TMP/kg/d given q 6 h | ≤50 | T: SMZ 400; TMP 80 double-strength: SMZ 800; TMP 160 S: SMZ 200; TMP 40 mg/5 mL Inj |
| Daptomycin (*Cubicin*) | K, L | IV: 4 mg/kg q 24 h × 7–14 d | <30 | Inj |

*(cont.)*

Table 51. **Antibiotics (cont.)**

| Antimicrobial Class, *Subclass* | Route of Elimination (%) | Dosage | Adjust When CrCl* Is: (mL/min) | Formulations |
|---|---|---|---|---|
| Linezolid (*Zyvox*) | L (65), K (30) | po: 400–600 mg q 12 h<br>IV: 600 mg q 12 h | NA | T: 400, 600<br>S: 100 mg/5 mL<br>Inj |
| Metronidazole (*Flagyl, MetraGel*) | L (30–60), K (20–40), F (6–15) | po: 250–750 mg q 6–8 h<br><br>Topical: Apply bid<br><br>Vaginal: 1 applicator full (375 mg) qhs or bid | ≤10 | T: 250, 500<br>ER: 750<br>C: 375<br>gel, topical: 0.75% (30 g)<br>gel, vaginal: 0.75% (70 g)<br>Inj |
| Nitrofurantoin (*Macrodantin*) | L (60), K (40) | po: 50–100 mg q 6 h | Do not use if <40 | C: 25, 50, 100<br>S: 25 mg/5 mL |
| Quinupristin/dalfopristin (*Synercid*) | L, B, F (75), K (15–19) | Vancomycin-resistant *E faecium*: IV: 7.5 mg/kg q 8 h<br>Complicated skin or skin structure infection: 7.5 mg/kg q 12 h | NA | Inj |
| Vancomycin (*Vancocin*) | K (80–90) | po: *C difficile*: 125–500 mg q 6–8 h<br>IV: 500 mg–1 g q 8–24 h<br>Peak: 20–40 µg/mL<br>Trough: 5–10 µg/mL | | C: 125, 250<br>Inj |
| **Antifungals** (*see also* Table 31) | | | | |
| Amphotericin B (*Fungizone*) | K | IV: test dose: 1 mg infused over 20–30 min; if tolerated, initial therapeutic dose is 0.25 mg/kg; the daily dose can be increased by 0.25-mg/kg increments on each subsequent day until the desired daily dose is reached<br>Maintenance dose: IV: 0.25–1 mg/kg/d or 1.5 mg/kg qod; do not exceed 1.5 mg/kg/d | ** | topical: crm, lot, oint 3%<br>Inj |
| Amphotericin B Lipid Complex (*Abelcet*) | K | 2.5–5 mg/kg/d as a single infusion | | Inj |

*(cont.)*

Table 51. Antibiotics (cont.)

| Antimicrobial Class, *Subclass* | Route of Elimination (%) | Dosage | Adjust When CrCl* Is: (mL/min) | Formulations |
|---|---|---|---|---|
| Amphotericin B Liposomal (*AmBisome*) | K | 3–5 mg/kg/d infused over 1–2 h | | Inj |
| Amphotericin B Colloidal Dispersion (*Amphotec*) | K | 3–4 mg/kg/d infused at 1 mg/kg/h; max dosage 7.5 mg/kg/d | | Inj |
| Caspofungin (*Cancidas*) | L | Initial: 70 mg infused over 1 h, then 50 mg/d over 1 h | — | Inj |
| Fluconazole (*Diflucan*) | K (80) | po, IV: first dose 50–400 mg, then 50–400 mg qd for 14 d–12 wk, depending on indication Vaginal candidiasis: 150 mg as a single dose | <50 | T: 50, 100, 150, 200 S: 10 and 40 mg/mL Inj |
| Flucytosine (*Ancobon*) | K (75–90) | po: 50–150 mg/kg/d divided q 6 h | <40 | C: 250, 500 |
| Griseofulvin (*Fulvicin P/G, Grifulvin V*) | L | po: Microsize: 500–1000 mg/d in single or divided doses Ultramicrosize: 330–375 mg/d in single or divided doses Duration based on indication | NA | Microsize: S: 125 mg/5 mL; T: 250, 500 Ultramicrosize: T: 125, 165, 250, 330 |
| Itraconazole (*Sporanox*) | L | po: 200–400 mg/d; doses >200 mg/d should be divided. Life-threatening infections: loading dose: 200 mg tid (600 mg/d) should be given for the first 3 d of therapy IV: 200 mg bid × 4 d, then 200 mg qd | <30 | C: 100 S: 100 mg/10 mL Inj |
| Ketoconazole (*Nizoral*) | L, F | po: 200–400 mg qd shp: 2/wk × 4 wk with at least 3 d between each shp Topical: apply qd–bid | NA | T: 200 shp: 2% crm: 2% |

*(cont.)*

## Table 51. Antibiotics (cont.)

| Antimicrobial Class, *Subclass* | Route of Elimination (%) | Dosage | Adjust When CrCl* Is: (mL/min) | Formulations |
|---|---|---|---|---|
| Miconazole (*Monistat IV*) | L, F | IT: 20 mg q 1–2 d<br>IV: initial: 200 mg, then 1.2–3.6 g/d divided q 8 h for up to 2 wk | NA | Inj |
| Terbinafine (*Lamisil*) | L, K | po: 250 mg/d × 6–12 wk for superficial mycoses; 250–500 mg/d for up to 16 mo<br>Topical: apply 1–2 times/d for a max of 4 wk | <50 | T: 250 mg<br>crm: 1%; topical S: 1% |
| Voriconazole (*VFEND*) | L | IV: loading dose 6 mg/kg q 12 h for 2 doses, then 4 mg/kg q 12 h<br>po: >40 kg: 200 mg q 12 h; ≤40 kg: 100 mg q 12 h<br>If on phenytoin, IV: 5 mg/kg q 12 h, and po: >40 kg: 400 mg q 12 h; ≤40 kg: 200 mg q 12 h | <50 (IV only) | Inj<br>T: 50, 200 mg |

Note: NA = not applicable.
 * The CrCl listed is the threshold below which the dose or frequency should be adjusted. See alternative reference or the drug package insert for detailed dosing guidelines.
 ** Adjust dose if decreased kidney function is due to the drug, or give every other day.

# KIDNEY DISORDERS

## ACUTE KIDNEY FAILURE
### Definition
An acute deterioration in kidney function defined by decreased urine output or increased values of renal function tests, or both

### Precipitating and Aggravating Factors
- Acute tubular necrosis due to hypoperfusion or nephrotoxins
- Medications (eg, aminoglycosides, radiocontrast materials, NSAIDs, ACE inhibitors)
- Multiple myeloma
- Obstruction (eg, BPH)
- Vascular disease (thromboembolic, atheroembolic)
- Volume depletion or redistribution of extracellular fluid (eg, cirrhosis, burns)

### Evaluation
- Review medication list
- Catheterize bladder, determine postvoid residual
- Perform UA
- Perform renal ultrasonography
- If patient not on diuretics, determine fractional excretion of sodium (FENa):

$$FENa = \left[ \frac{urine\ Na/plasma\ Na}{urine\ creatinine/plasma\ creatinine} \right] \times 100$$

(FENa < 1% indicates prerenal cause; FENa > 3% indicates acute tubular necrosis; FENa 1%–3% is nondiagnostic. Note that some older persons who have prerenal cause may have FENa ≥ 1% because of age-related changes in sodium excretion.)

If patient receiving diuretics, determine fractional excretion of urea (FEun):

$$FEun = \left[ \frac{urine\ urea\ nitrogen/BUN}{urine\ CR/plasma\ CR} \right] \times 100$$

(FEun ≤ 35% indicates prerenal azotemia; FEun > 50% indicates acute tubular necrosis; FEun 36%–50% is nondiagnostic.)

### Treatment
- D/C medications that are possible precipitants; avoid contrast dyes.
- If prerenal pattern, treat HF (see p 27) if present. Otherwise, volume repletion. Begin with fluid challenge 500–1000 mL over 30–60 min. If no response, give furosemide 100–400 mg IV.
- If obstructed, leave bladder catheter in place while evaluation and specific treatment are being implemented.
- If acute tubular necrosis, monitor weights daily, record intake and output, and monitor electrolytes frequently. Fluid replacement should be equal to urinary output plus other drainage plus 500 mL/d for insensible losses.
- Dialysis is indicated when severe hyperkalemia, acidosis, or volume overload cannot be managed with other therapies or when uremic symptoms (eg, pericarditis, coagulopathy, or encephalopathy) are present.

## CHRONIC KIDNEY FAILURE
### Evaluation
- Hx and physical examination: assess for diabetes mellitus, HTN, vascular disease, HF, NSAIDs, contrast dye exposure, angiographic procedures with possible cholesterol embolization, glomerulonephritis, myeloma, BPH or obstructive cancers, nephrotoxic drug exposure, hereditary kidney disease (eg, polycystic)
- Blood tests (CBC, comprehensive metabolic profile, cholesterol, ESR, SPEP, estimate CrCl (see p 1)
- If CrCl 15–59 mL/min, then measure iPTH; if iPTH >100 pg/mL, then measure 25 (OH) vitamin D
- Urinalysis and quantitative urine protein (protein: Cr ratio or 24-h urine for protein and Cr); urine immunoelectrophoresis, if indicated
- Renal ultrasound, consider Doppler to exclude renal artery stenosis

### Treatment
- Attempt to slow progression of kidney failure
  - Control BP (target <125/75 if proteinuria or increased Cr); most important
  - ACE inhibitor or ARB (see **Table 17**)
  - Diabetes control, $HbA_{1c}$ <7
  - Moderate dietary protein restriction, 1 g/kg/d (controversial)
  - Smoking cessation
  - Reduction of proteinuria to <1g/d, if possible
- Prevent and treat symptoms and complications
  - Treat hyperkalemia if present; restrict orange juice, bananas, potatoes, cantaloupe, honeydew, tomatoes; diuretics and oral bicarbonate can also be helpful.
  - Normalize serum calcium with calcium carbonate (500 mg elemental calcium qd to qid) or calcium citrate if patient is on proton-pump inhibitor or has achlorhydria; if hypocalcemia is refractory, consider calcitriol (*Rocaltrol*) 0.25 µg/d
  - Normalize serum phosphate with target goal ≤6 mg/dL; restrict dairy products and cola. When hyperphosphatemia is refractory, begin:
    - If calcium is low, calcium carbonate or calcium acetate with meals.
    - If serum calcium is normal or calcium supplementation is ineffective, sevelamer (*Renagel*) [T: 400, 800; C: 403].
      - If phosphate 6–7.5 mg/dL, 800 mg po tid with each meal.
      - If phosphate 7.5–9.0 mg/dL, 1200–1600 mg po tid with each meal.
      - If phosphate >9 mg/dL, 1600 mg po tid with each meal.
  - Treat vitamin D insufficiency
    - If GFR <30 mL/min, iPTH >100 pg/mL, and 25(OH) serum vitamin D is <30 ng/mL, then vitamin $D_2$ (ergocalciferol) 50,000 U po every mo for 6 mo
    - If iPTH remains >100 pg/mL, then oral vitamin D therapy with calcitriol at 0.25 µg/d
  - Correct metabolic acidosis if $HCO_3$ falls below 18–20 mEq/L with sodium bicarbonate 325–650 mg tid
  - Treat anemia with iron (if iron-deficient) or erythropoietin-darbopoetin (see **Table 43**)
  - Manage volume overload (see HF, p 27)
  - Prevent and treat cardiovascular disease (see p 24) with target LDL goal <100 mg/dL
  - Treat secondary hyperparathyroidism; elevated PTH can be treated with calcitriol as mentioned above.

- Immunize with *Pneumovax* and, before dialysis, hepatitis B vaccines if hepatitis B surface antigen and antibody are negative.
- Preparation for renal replacement therapy. Educate patients regarding options of hemodialysis, peritoneal dialysis, and kidney transplantation. Arteriovenous fistula access referral recommended at estimated GFR <25 mL/min. Patients can be listed for cadaveric kidney transplant at estimated GFR <20 mL/min.
- Dialysis is indicated when severe hyperkalemia, acidosis, or volume overload cannot be managed with other therapies or when uremic symptoms (eg, pericarditis, coagulopathy, or encephalopathy) are present.

## VOLUME DEPLETION (DEHYDRATION)
### Definition
Losses of sodium and water that may be isotonic (eg, loss of blood) or hypotonic (eg, nasogastric suctioning)

### Precipitating Factors
- Blood loss
- Diuretics
- GI losses
- Kidney or adrenal disease (eg, renal sodium wasting)
- Sequestration of fluid (eg, ileus, burns, peritonitis)
- Age-related changes (impaired thirst, sodium wasting due to hyporeninemic hypoaldosteronism, and free water wasting due to renal insensitivity to antidiuretic hormone)

### Evaluation
*Clinical symptoms:*
- Anorexia
- Nausea and vomiting
- Orthostatic lightheadedness
- Delirium
- Weakness

*Clinical signs:*
- Dry tongue and axillae
- Oliguria
- Orthostatic hypotension
- Elevated heart rate
- Weight loss

### Laboratory Tests
- Serum electrolytes
- Urine sodium (usually <10 mEq/L) and FENa (usually <1% but may be higher because of age-related sodium wasting)
- Serum BUN and creatinine (BUN/creatinine ratio often >20)

### Management
- Daily weight; monitor fluid losses and serum electrolytes, BUN, creatinine
- If mild, oral rehydration of 2–4 L of water/d and 4–8 g Na diet; if poor oral intake, give IV D5W1/2 NS with potassium as needed
- If hemodynamically unstable, give IV 0.9% saline 500 mL bolus and 200 mL/h until systolic BP ≥100 and no longer orthostatic. Then switch to D5W1/2 NS. Monitor closely in patients with a hx of HF.

## HYPERNATREMIA
### Causes
- Pure water loss:
  - insensible losses due to sweating and respiration
  - central (eg, post-traumatic, CNS tumors, meningitis) diabetes insipidus or nephrogenic (eg, hypercalcemia, lithium) diabetes insipidus
- Hypotonic sodium loss:
  - renal causes: osmotic diuresis (eg, due to hyperglycemia); postobstructive diuresis; polyuric phase of acute tubular necrosis
  - GI causes: vomiting and diarrhea, nasogastric drainage, osmotic cathartic agents (eg, lactulose)
- Hypertonic sodium gain (eg, treatment with hypertonic saline)
- Impaired thirst (eg, delirious or intubated) or access to water (eg, functionally dependent) may sustain hypernatremia

### Evaluation
- Measure intake and output.
- Obtain urine osmolality:
  - >800 mOsm/kg suggests extrarenal (if urine Na <25 mEq/L) or remote renal water loss or administration of hypertonic Na+ salt solutions (if urine Na >100 mEq/L).
  - <250 mOsm/kg and polyuria suggest diabetes insipidus.

### Treatment
- Treat underlying causes.
- Correct slowly over at least 48–72 h using oral (can use pure water), nasogastric (can use pure water), or IV (D5W, 1/2 or 1/4 NS) fluids; correct at rate of no more than 1 mmol/L/h if acute (eg, developing over hours) and at no more than 10 mmol/L/d if of longer duration.
- Correct with normal saline only in cases of severe volume depletion with hemodynamic compromise; once stable, switch to hypotonic solution.
- When repleting, use the following formula to estimate the effect of 1 L of any infusate on serum Na:

$$\text{Change in serum Na} = \frac{\text{infusate Na} - \text{serum Na}}{\text{total body water} + 1}$$

  Infusate Na (mmol/L): D5W = 0; 1/4 NS = 34; 1/2 NS = 77; NS = 154.
  Calculate total body water as a fraction of body weight (0.5 kg in older men and 0.45 kg in older women).
- Divide treatment goal (usually 10 mmol/L/d) by change in serum Na/L (from formula) to determine amount of solution to be given over 24 h.
- Compensate for any ongoing obligatory fluid losses, which are usually 1.0–1.5 L/d.
- Divide amount of solution for repletion plus amount for obligatory fluid losses by 24 to determine rate per h.

## HYPONATREMIA
### Causes
- With increased plasma osmolality: Hyperglycemia (1.6 mEq/L decrement for each 100 mg/dL increase in plasma glucose)
- With normal plasma osmolality (pseudohyponatremia): Severe hyperlipidemia, hyperproteinemia (eg, multiple myeloma)
- With decreased plasma osmolality:
  - With extracellular fluid (ECF) excess: Kidney failure, HF, hepatic cirrhosis, nephrotic syndrome
  - With decreased ECF volume: Renal loss from salt-losing nephropathies, diuretics, osmotic diuresis; extrarenal loss due to vomiting, diarrhea, skin losses, and third-spacing (usually urine Na <20 mEq/L, FENa <1%, and uric acid >4 mg/dL)
  - With normal ECF volume: Primary polydipsia (urine osmolarity <100 mOsm/kg), hypothyroidism, adrenal insufficiency, SIADH (urine Na >40 mEq/L and uric acid <4 mg/dL)

### Management
Treat underlying cause. Specific treatment only if symptomatic (eg, altered mental status, seizures) or severe acute hyponatremia (eg, <120 mEq/L):
- Goal is 0.5 mEq/L/h rise in Na (more rapid correction can result in central pontine myelinolysis); time (in hours) to correct = (140 − Na)/0.5 mEq/L/h.
- Calculate free water excess (liters) = (0.5 × current body weight in kg) × (1 − [Na/140]).
- Target rate of free water removal (L/h) = free water excess/time to correct.
- Replace urine output with 3% saline or isotonic saline.
- Monitor Na closely and taper treatment when >120 or symptoms resolve.

## SIADH
### Definition
Hypotonic hyponatremia (<280 mOsm/kg) with:
- Less than maximally dilute urine (usually >100 mOsm/kg)
- Elevated urine sodium (usually >40 mEq/L)
- Normal volume status
- Normal kidney, adrenal, and thyroid function

### Precipitating Factors, Causes
- Drugs (eg, SSRIs, venlafaxine, chlorpropamide, carbamazepine, NSAIDs, barbiturates)
- Neuropsychiatric factors (eg, neoplasm, subarachnoid hemorrhage, psychosis, meningitis)
- Postoperative state, especially if pain or nausea
- Pulmonary disease (eg, pneumonia, tuberculosis, acute asthma)
- Tumors (eg, lung, pancreas, thymus)

### Evaluation
- BUN, creatinine, serum cortisol, TSH
- CXR
- Review of medications
- Neurologic tests as indicated
- Urine sodium and osmolality

## Management

*Acute Treatment:* See hyponatremia management (p 111).

*Chronic Treatment:*
- D/C offending drug or treat precipitating illness.
- Restrict water to 1000–1500 mL/d.
- Liberalize salt intake.
- Demeclocycline (*Declomycin*) 150–300 mg bid [T: 150, 300] (may be nephrotoxic in patients with liver disease).

## HYPERKALEMIA

### Causes
- Kidney failure
- Addison's disease
- Hyporeninemic hypoaldosteronism
- Renal tubular acidosis
- Acidosis
- Diabetic hyperglycemia
- Hemolysis, tumor lysis, rhabdomyolysis
- Medications (potassium-sparing diuretics, ACE inhibitors, trimethoprim-sulfamethoxazole, β-blockers, NSAIDs, cyclosporine, tacrolimus, pentamidine, heparin, digoxin toxicity)
- Pseudohyperkalemia from extreme thrombocytosis or leukocytosis
- Transfusions of stored blood
- Constipation

### Evaluation
- ECG; peaked T waves typically occur when $K^+$ exceeds 6.5 mEq/L. Acute changes of $K^+$ are more likely than chronic elevations to cause ECG changes.

### Treatment

*Minor elevations*
- $K^+$ <6 mEq/L without ECG changes:
  - Low-potassium diet
  - Oral diuretics (eg, oral torsemide or bumetanide, combined oral loop and thiazide-like diuretics; metolazone is the most $K^+$ wasting); avoid hypovolemia
  - Oral $NaHCO_3$ (650–1300 mg bid)
  - Reduce or D/C medications that increase $K^+$
- $K^+$ 6–6.5 mEq/L without ECG changes: above treatments plus sodium polystyrene sulfonate (*SPS*, *Kayexelate*) 15–30 g po qd to qid, or prn as enema 30–50 g in 100 mL of dextrose; full effect takes 4–24 h
- $K^+$ 6.5 mEq/L with peaked T waves but no other ECG changes; hospitalization is a case-by-case decision based on acuteness of onset, cause, and other patient factors.

*Absolute indications for hospitalization*
- $K^+$ >8.0 mEq/L
- ECG changes other than peaked T waves (eg, prolonged PR, loss of P waves, widened QRS)
- Acute deterioration of kidney function

### Inpatient management of hyperkalemia

- Antagonism of cardiac effects of hyperkalemia (acute therapy)
- 10% calcium gluconate IV infused over 2–3 min (20–30 min if on digoxin) with ECG monitoring; effect lasts 30–60 min, may repeat if needed
- Reduction of serum $K^+$ by redistribution into cells (acute therapy)
  - Insulin (regular) 10 U in 500 mL of 10% dextrose over 30–60 min or bolus insulin (regular) 10 U IV followed by 50 mL of 50% dextrose
  - Albuterol 0.5 mg in 100 mL of 5% dextrose given over 10–15 min or nebulized 10–20 mg in 4 mL of normal saline over 10 min (should not be used as single agent)
  - Sodium bicarbonate use is controversial
- Removal of potassium from body (definitive therapy)
  - Diuretics (eg, oral torsemide or bumetanide, intravenous furosemide, combined oral loop and thiazide-like diuretics; metolazone is the most $K^+$ wasting). Avoid hypovolemia.
  - Fludrocortisone (*Florinef*) 0.1–0.3 mg/d
  - Sodium polystyrene sulfonate (*SPS, Kayexalate*) 15–30 g po qd to qid or pr as enema 30–50 g in 100 mL of dextrose; full effect takes 4–24 h
  - Dialysis

# MALNUTRITION

## DEFINITION
There is no uniformly accepted definition of malnutrition in older persons. Some commonly used definitions include the following:

### Community-Dwelling Men and Women
- Involuntary weight loss (eg, ≥10 lb over 6 months, ≥4% over 1 yr)
- Abnormal body mass index (eg, BMI >27; BMI <22)
- Hypoalbuminemia (eg, ≤3.8 g/dL)
- Hypocholesterolemia (eg, <160 mg/dL)
- Specific vitamin or micronutrient deficiencies (eg, vitamin $B_{12}$)

### Hospitalized Patients
- Dietary intake (eg, <50% of estimated needed caloric intake)
- Hypoalbuminemia (eg, <3.5 g/dL)
- Hypocholesterolemia (eg, <160 mg/dL)

### Nursing-Home Patients (Triggered by the Minimum Data Set)
- Weight loss of ≥5% in past 30 d; ≥10% in 180 d
- Dietary intake of <75% at most meals

## EVALUATION
### Multidimensional Assessment
In the absence of valid nutrition screening instruments, clinicians should focus on whether the following issues may be affecting nutritional status:
- Economic barriers to securing food
- Availability of sufficiently high-quality food
- Dental problems that prohibit ingesting high-quality food
- Medical illnesses that
  ○ interfere with digestion or absorption of food
  ○ increase nutritional requirements
  ○ require dietary restrictions (eg, low-sodium diet or npo)
- Functional disability that interferes with shopping, preparing meals, or feeding
- Food preferences or cultural beliefs that interfere with adequate food intake
- Poor appetite
- Depressive symptoms

### Anthropometrics
Weight on each visit and yearly height (see p 1)

### Biochemical Markers
***Serum Proteins:*** All may drop precipitously because of trauma, sepsis, or major infection.
- Albumin (half-life 18–20 d) has prognostic value in all settings.
- Transferrin (half-life 7 d)
- Prealbumin (half-life 48 h) may be valuable in monitoring nutritional recovery.

*Serum Cholesterol (Low or Falling Levels):* Has prognostic value in all settings but may not be nutritionally mediated.

## MANAGEMENT
### Calculating Basic Energy (Caloric) and Fluid Requirements
• WHO energy estimates for adults aged 60 yr and older:
○ Women (10.5) (weight in kg) + 596
○ Men (13.5) (weight in kg) + 487
• Harris-Benedict energy requirement equations:
○ Women 655 + (9.6) (weight in kg) + (1.7) (height in cm) − (4.7) (age in yr)
○ Men 66 + (13.7) (weight in kg) + (5.0) (height in cm) − (6.8) (age in yr)
Depending on activity and physiologic stress levels, these basic requirements may need to be increased (eg, 25% for sedentary or mild, 50% for moderate, and 100% for intense or severe activity or stress).
• Fluid requirements for older persons without heart or kidney disease are approximately 30 mL/kg of body weight/d.

### Appetite Stimulants
• No drugs are FDA approved for weight loss in older persons.
• Dronabinol and megestrol acetate have been effective in promoting weight gain in younger adults with specific conditions (eg, AIDS, cancer).
• A minority of patients receiving mirtazapine report appetite stimulation and weight gain.
• All drugs used for appetite have substantial potential adverse events.

### Nutritional Supplements
Protein and energy supplements in older persons at risk of malnutrition appear to have benefits on weight gain and mortality, and shorten length of stay in hospitalized patients.
Many formulas are available (see **Table 52**). Read the content labels and choose on the basis of calories/mL, protein, fiber, lactose, and fluid load.
• Oral: Many (eg, *Carnation Instant Breakfast, Health Shake*) are milk-based and provide approximately 1.0–1.5 calories/mL.
• Enteral: Commercial preparations have between 0.5 and 2.0 calories/mL; most contain no milk (lactose) products. For patients who need fluid restriction, the higher concentrated formulas may be valuable, but they may cause diarrhea. Because of reduced kidney function with aging, some recommend that protein should contribute no more than 20% of the formula's total calories. If formula is sole source of nutrition, consider one that contains fiber (25 g/d is optimal).

### Table 52. Examples of Lactose-free Oral and Enteral Products

| Product | Kcal/mL | mOsm | Protein (g/L) | Water (mL/L) | Na (mEq/L) | K (mEq/L) | Fiber (g/L) |
|---|---|---|---|---|---|---|---|
| **Oral—low residue** | | | | | | | |
| *Boost Basic* | 1.06 | 650 | 37.0 | 850 | 37.0 | 41.0 | 0 |
| *Boost Plus* | 1.50 | 670 | 61.0 | 780 | 37.0 | 38.0 | <1 |

*(cont.)*

**Table 52. Examples of Lactose-free Oral and Enteral Products (cont.)**

| Product | Kcal/mL | mOsm | Protein (g/L) | Water (mL/L) | Na (mEq/L) | K (mEq/L) | Fiber (g/L) |
|---|---|---|---|---|---|---|---|
| *Ensure* | 1.06 | 470 | 37.3 | 845 | 37.0 | 40.0 | 0 |
| *Ensure Plus* | 1.50 | 690 | 54.9 | 769 | 46.0 | 40.0 | 0 |
| *Nu Basics* | 1.00 | 480 | 35.0 | 842 | 38.0 | 32.0 | 0 |
| *Nu Basics Plus* | 1.50 | 620 | 42.4 | 776 | 50.8 | 48.0 | 0 |
| **Oral—low volume** (packaged as 45 mL supplements; nutrients are provided per serving) | | | | | | | |
| *Resource Benecalorie* | 330 | NA | 7.0 | 0 | 15.0 | 0 | 0 |
| *Epulor* | 320 | 418 | 4.0 | 0 | 10.0 | 0 | 0 |
| **Oral—high fiber** (can also be given enterally) | | | | | | | |
| *Boost with Fiber* | 1.00 | 480 | 43.0 | 850 | 31.0 | 41.0 | 12.0 |
| *Ensure Fiber with FOS* | 1.06 | 500 | 36.0 | 780 | 37.0 | 40.0 | 12.0 |
| **Oral—clear liquid** | | | | | | | |
| *CitriSource* | 0.76 | 700 | 37.0 | 876 | 10.0 | 1.6 | 0 |
| *Resource* | 1.06 | 430 | 33.0 | 842 | 24.0 | 1.3 | 0 |
| **Oral—diabetes formulations** | | | | | | | |
| *ChoiceDM beverage* | 0.93 | 400 | 39.0 | 850 | 37.0 | 46.5 | 11 |
| *Glucerna shake* | 0.93 | 530 | 40.0 | 800 | 37.0 | 43.0 | 12 |
| *Enlive* | 1.25 | 671 | 40.0 | 764 | 11.6 | 4.1 | 0 |
| **Enteral—diabetes formulations** | | | | | | | |
| *ChoiceDM TF* | 1.06 | 300 | 45.0 | 850 | 37.0 | 47.0 | 14.4 |
| *Glucerna* | 1.00 | 355 | 41.8 | 853 | 40.5 | 40.2 | 14.4 |
| **Enteral—low residue** | | | | | | | |
| *Isocal* | 1.06 | 270 | 34.0 | 850 | 23.0 | 34.0 | 0 |
| *Osmolite* | 1.06 | 300 | 37.2 | 841 | 28.0 | 26.0 | 0 |
| *Nutren 1.0* | 1.00 | 315 | 40.0 | 852 | 38.1 | 32.0 | 0 |
| **Enteral—low volume** | | | | | | | |
| *Deliver* | 2.00 | 640 | 75.0 | 710 | 35.0 | 43.0 | 0 |
| *Nutren 2.0* | 2.00 | 745 | 80.0 | 700 | 56.5 | 49.2 | 0 |
| *TwoCal HN* | 2.00 | 730 | 83.5 | 701 | 63.5 | 62.7 | 0 |
| **Enteral—high fiber** | | | | | | | |
| *Jevity* | 1.06 | 310 | 44.4 | 830 | 40.0 | 40.0 | 14.4 |
| *Ultracal* | 1.06 | 310 | 44.0 | 850 | 40.0 | 41.0 | 14.4 |
| *Nutren 1.0 with fiber* | 1.00 | 320 | 40.0 | 840 | 38.1 | 32.0 | 14.0 |

NA = not available

## Important Drug-Enteral Interactions
• Soybean formulas increase fecal elimination of thyroxine; time administration of thyroxine and enteral nutrition as far apart as possible.
• Enteral feedings reduce absorption of phenytoin; administer phenytoin at least 2 h following a feeding and delay feeding at least 2 h after phenytoin is administered; monitor levels and adjust doses, as necessary.

• Check with pharmacy about suitability and best way to administer sustained-release, enteric-coated, and micro-encapsulated products (eg, omeprazole, lansoprazole, diltiazem, fluoxetine, verapamil).

## Tips for Successful Tube Feeding
• Gastrostomy tube feeding may be either intermittent or continuous.
• Jejunostomy tube feedings must be continuous.
• Continuous tube feeding is associated with less frequent diarrhea but with higher rates of tube clogging.
• To prevent clogging and to provide additional free water, flushing with at least 30–60 mL of water 4–6 times a day is recommended. Sometimes sugar-free carbonated beverages, cranberry juice, or meat tenderizer can restore patency to clogged tubes.
• Diarrhea, which occurs in 5%–30% of persons receiving enteral feeding, may be related to the osmolality of the formula, the rate of delivery, high sorbitol content in liquid medications (eg, APAP, lithium, oxybutynin, furosemide), or other patient-related factors such as antibiotic use or impaired absorption.
• To help prevent aspiration, maintain a 30-degree elevation of the head of the bed during continuous feeding and for at least 2 h after bolus feedings.
• Do not administer bulk-forming laxatives (eg, methylcellulose or psyllium) through feeding tubes.
• Check gastric residual volume before each bolus feeding and hold feeding for at least 1 h if residual is more than half of previous feeding volume. Metoclopramide (*Reglan*) 5–10 mg [5 mg/5 mL] qid may be useful for high gastric residual volume problems once mechanical obstruction has been excluded.

## Parenteral Nutrition
Indicated in those with digestive dysfunction precluding enteral feeding. Delivers protein as amino acids, carbohydrate as dextrose, and fat as lipid emulsions.
*Peripheral Parenteral Nutrition:* For short-term use. Requires rotation of peripheral IV site every 72 h. Solution osmolarity of less than 900 mOsm/L is recommended to reduce risk of phlebitis (see **Table 53**).
*Total Parenteral Nutrition:* Must be administered through a central catheter, which may be inserted peripherally.

| Table 53. Caloric Value and Osmolarity of Parenteral Solutions | | |
|---|---|---|
| **Solution** | **Caloric Value (Kcal/L)** | **Osmolarity (mOsm/L)** |
| Dextrose (%) | | |
| 5 | 170 | 250 |
| 10 | 340 | 500 |
| 20 | 680 | 1000 |
| Lipid emulsions (%) | | |
| 10 | 1100 | 230 |
| 20 | 2200 | 330–340 |

## SHOULDER PAIN: DIFFERENTIAL DIAGNOSIS AND TREATMENT

### Rotator Cuff Tendinitis, Subacromial Bursitis, or Rotator Tendon Impingement on Clavicle

Dull ache radiating to upper arm. Painful arc (on abduction 60–120 degrees and external rotation) is characteristic. Also can be distinguished by applying resistance against active range of motion while immobilizing the neck with hand.

***Treatment:*** Identify and eliminate provocative, repetitive injury (eg, avoid overhead reaching). A brief period of rest and immobilization with a sling may be helpful. Pain control with APAP or NSAIDs (**Table 54**), home exercises or PT (especially assisted range of motion and wall walking), and corticosteroid injections may be useful.

### Rotator Cuff Tears

Mild to complete; characterized by diminished shoulder movement. If severe, patients do not have full range of active or passive motion. The "drop arm" sign (the inability to maintain the arm in an abducted 90-degree position) indicates supraspinatus and infraspinatus tear. Weakness of external rotation (elbows flexed, thumbs up with examiner's hands outside patient's elbows; patient is asked to resist inward pressure) is common. MRI establishes diagnosis.

***Treatment:*** If due to injury, a brief period of rest and immobilization with a sling may be helpful. Pain control with APAP or NSAIDs (**Table 54**), home exercises or PT (especially assisted range of motion and wall walking) may be useful. If no improvement after 6–8 wk of conservative measures, consider surgical repair.

### Bicipital Tendinitis

Pain felt on anterior lateral aspect of shoulder, tenderness in the groove between greater and lesser tuberosities of the humerus. Pain is produced on resisted flexion of shoulder, flexion of the elbow, or supination (external rotation) of the hand and wrist with the elbow flexed at the side.

***Treatment:*** Identify and eliminate provocative, repetitive activities (eg, avoid overhead reaching). A period of rest (at least 7 d with no lifting) and corticosteroid injections are major components of therapy. After rest period, PT should focus on stretching biceps tendon (eg, putting arm on doorframe and hyperextending shoulder, with some external rotation).

### Frozen Shoulder (Adhesive Capsulitis)

Loss of passive external (lateral) rotation, abduction, and internal rotation of the shoulder to less than 90 degrees. Usually follows three phases: painful (freezing) phase lasting wks to a few mo; adhesive (stiffening) phase lasting 4–12 mo; resolution phase lasting 6–24 mo.

***Treatment:*** Avoid rest and begin PT and home exercises for stretching the arm inflexion, horizontal adduction, and internal and external rotation. Corticosteroid injections may reduce pain and permit more aggressive PT. Consider surgical manipulation under anesthesia or arthroscopic dilation of capsule.

## BACK PAIN: DIFFERENTIAL DIAGNOSIS AND TREATMENT

### Acute Lumbar Strain (Low Back Pain Syndrome)

Acute pain frequently precipitated by heavy lifting or exercise. Pain may be central or more prominent on one side and may radiate to sacroiliac region and buttocks. Pain is aggravated by motion, standing, and prolonged sitting, and relieved by rest. Sciatic pain may be present even when neurologic examination is normal.

*Treatment:* Most can continue normal activities. If a patient obtains symptomatic relief from bed rest, generally 1–2 d lying in a semi-Fowler position or on side with the hips and knees flexed with pillow between legs will suffice. Treat muscle spasm with the application of ice, preferably in a massage over the muscles in spasm. APAP or NSAIDs (**Table 54**) can be used to control pain. As pain diminishes, encourage patient to begin isometric abdominal and lower-extremity exercises. Symptoms often recur. Education on back posture, lifting precautions, and abdominal muscle strengthening may help prevent recurrences.

### Acute Disk Herniation

Over 90% of cases occur at L4–L5 or L5–S1 levels, resulting in unilateral impairment of ankle reflex, toe and ankle dorsiflexion, and pain (commonly sciatic) on straight leg raising (can be tested from sitting position by leg extension). Pain is acute in onset and varies considerably with changes in position.

*Treatment:* Initially same as acute lumbar strain (above). If unresponsive, administer epidural injection of a combination of a long-acting corticosteroid with an epidural anesthetic. Consider surgery if recurrence or persistence with neurologic signs beyond 6–8 wk after conservative treatment. The value of epidural injections and surgery for pain without neurologic signs is controversial. (See **Table 2** and **Table 3**.)

### Osteoarthritis and Chronic Disk Degeneration

Characterized by aching pain aggravated by motion and relieved by rest. Occasionally, hypertrophic spurring in a facet joint may cause unilateral radiculopathy with sciatica.

*Treatment:* Identify and eliminate provocative activities. Education on back posture, lifting precautions, and abdominal muscle strengthening. APAP or NSAIDs (**Table 54**). Corticosteroid injections may be useful. Consider opioids and other pain treatment modalities for chronic refractory pain (see p 144).

### Unstable Lumbar Spine

Severe, sudden, short-lasting, frequently recurrent pain often brought on by sudden, unguarded movements. Pain is reproduced upon moving from the flexed to the erect position. Pain is usually relieved by lying supine or on side. Impingement on nerve roots by spurs from facet joints or herniated disks can cause similar complaints, although symptoms in these conditions usually worsen as time passes. Symptoms can mimic disk herniation or degeneration, or osteoarthritis. Lumbar flexion x-rays can be diagnostic.

*Treatment:* Surgery only in severe cases.

### Lumbar Spinal Stenosis

Symptoms increase on spinal extension (eg, with prolonged standing, walking downhill, lying prone) and decrease with spinal flexion (eg, sitting, bending forward while walking, lying in the flexed position). Only symptom may be fatigue or pain in legs when walking (pseudo-claudication). May have immobility of lumbar spine, pain with straight leg raises, weakness of muscles innervated by L4 through S1 (see **Table 3**). Over 4 yr, 15% improve, 15% deteriorate, and 70% remain stable.

*Treatment:* APAP or NSAIDs (**Table 54**) and exercises to reduce lumbar lordosis are sometimes beneficial. Corticosteroid injections may be useful. Surgical intervention is more effective than conservative treatment in relieving moderate or severe symptoms; however, recurrence of pain several years after surgery is common.

### Vertebral Compression Fracture

Immediate onset of severe pain; worse with sitting or standing; sometimes relieved by lying down.

*Treatment:* See Osteoporosis, p 138. Bed rest, analgesia, and mobilization as tolerated. Calcitonin may provide symptomatic improvement. May require hospitalization to control symptoms. Percutaneous vertebroplasty or kyphoplasty may be effective for pain relief in refractory cases.

### Nonrheumatic Pain (eg, Tumors, Aneurysms)

Gradual onset, steadily expanding, often unrelated to position and not relieved by lying down. Night pain when lying down is characteristic. Upper motor neuron signs may be present. Involvement is usually in thoracic and upper lumbar spine.

## HIP PAIN: DIFFERENTIAL DIAGNOSIS AND TREATMENT

### Trochanteric Bursitis

Pain in lateral aspect of the hip that usually worsens when patient sits on a hard chair, lies on the affected side, or rises from a chair or bed; pain may improve with walking. Local tenderness over greater trochanter is often present, and pain is often reproduced on resisted abduction of the leg or internal rotation of the hip. However, trochanteric bursitis does not produce limited range of motion, pain on range of motion, pain in the groin, or radicular signs.

*Treatment:* Identify and eliminate provocative activities. Check for leg length discrepancy, prescribe orthotics if appropriate. Injection of a combination of a long-acting corticosteroid with an anesthetic is most effective treatment.

### Osteoarthritis

"Boring" quality pain in the hip, often in the groin, and sometimes referred to the back or knee with stiffness after rest. Passive motion is restricted in all directions if disease is fairly advanced. In early disease, pain in the groin on internal rotation of the hip is characteristic.

*Treatment:* See also Osteoarthritis, p 122. Elective total hip replacement is indicated for patients who have radiographic evidence of joint damage and moderate to severe persistent pain or disability, or both, that is not substantially relieved by an extended course of nonsurgical management.

National Institutes of Health Consensus Development Conference Statement September 12–14, 1994 (reviewed 1998).

### Hip Fracture
Sudden onset, usually after a fall, with inability to walk or bear weight, frequently radiating to groin or knee.
*Treatment:* Treatment is surgical with open reduction and internal fixation, hemiarthroplasty, or total hip replacement, depending on site of fracture and amount of displacement. For patients who were nonambulatory prior to the fracture, conservative management is an option.

### Nonrheumatic Pain
Referred pain from viscera, radicular pain from the lower spine, avascular necrosis, Paget's disease, metastasis.

## CARPAL TUNNEL SYNDROME
### Definition
Painful tingling or hypoesthesia, or both, in one or both hands in distribution innervated by median nerve

### Causes
- Repetitive activities
- Diabetes mellitus
- Thyroid disease
- Amyloidosis
- Rheumatoid arthritis
- Space-occupying lesions (eg, lymphoma)
- Trauma (eg, Colles' fracture)

### Evaluation and Assessment
*Physical Examination:*
- Decreased sensation in palm, thumb, index finger, middle finger, and thumb side of ring finger
- Weak handgrip
- Tapping over the median nerve at the wrist causes pain to shoot from wrist to hand (Tinel's sign)
- Acute flexion of wrist for 60 sec (Phalen's test) should also result in pain
*Laboratory Studies:*
- Fasting glucose
- TSH
- Nerve conduction velocity testing confirms diagnosis

### Treatment
*Nonpharmacologic:*
- Redesign work or leisure processes to avoid repetitive movements
- Splinting in neutral position, especially at night
- Surgery (more effective than splinting)
*Pharmacologic:*
- Injectable corticosteroids, eg, methylprednisolone 15 mg (more effective than oral)
- Oral corticosteroids, eg, prednisone 20 mg/d for 1 wk followed by 10 mg/d for a second wk

## OSTEOARTHRITIS
### Nonpharmacologic Approaches
- Superficial heat: Hot packs, heating pads, paraffin, or hot water bottles (moist heat is better).
- Deep heat: Microwave, shortwave diathermy, or ultrasound.
- Biofeedback and transcutaneous electrical nerve stimulation.
- Exercise (especially water-based), PT, OT: Strengthening, stretching, range of motion, functional activities.
- Weight loss: Especially for low back, hip, and knee arthritis.
- Splinting: Avoid splinting for long periods of time (eg, >6 wk) because periarticular muscle weakness and wasting may occur. Bracing (eg, neoprene sleeves over the knee) to correct malalignment is often helpful.
- Assistive devices: Cane should be used in the hand contralateral to the affected knee or hip.
- Surgical intervention (eg, debridement, meniscal repair, prosthetic joint replacement).

### Pharmacologic Intervention (See Figure 6.)
*Topical Analgesics:*  Liniment, capsaicin cream.
*Intra-articular Injections:*
- Corticosteroids: May be particularly effective if monoarticular symptoms (eg, methylprednisolone acetate, triamcinolone acetonide, and triamcinolone hexacetonide) 20–40 mg for large joints (eg, knee, ankle, shoulder), 10–20 mg for wrists and elbows, and 5–15 mg for small joints of hands and feet; often mixed with lidocaine 1% or its equivalent (in equal volume with corticosteroids) for immediate relief.
- Hyaluronan: Sodium hyaluronate (*Hyalgan*) injections weekly for 5 wk or hylan G-F 20 (*Synvisc*) 3 injections 1 wk apart for knee osteoarthritis.
*Nutriceuticals:*  Glucosamine (500 mg tid) or chondroitin (400 mg tid), or both, have been effective for some patients. Combination tablets and timed-release formulations (1500 mg and 1200 mg, respectively) are available. Clinical trials in the United States are in process.
*NSAIDs:*  Often provide pain relief but have higher rates of adverse events (see **Table 54**). Misoprostol (*Cytotec*) 100–200 mg qid with food [T: 100, 200] or a proton-pump inhibitor (see **Table 37**) may be valuable prophylaxis against NSAID-induced ulcers in high-risk patients. Selective COX-2 inhibitors have lower likelihood of causing gastroduodenal ulcers than nonselective NSAIDs. All may increase INR in patients receiving warfarin.
*Oral Analgesics:*  Eg, tramadol, other opioids (see **Table 65**).

**Figure 6. Pharmacologic Management of Osteoarthritis\***

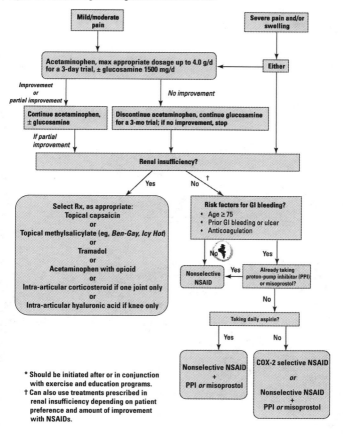

\* Should be initiated after or in conjunction with exercise and education programs.
† Can also use treatments prescribed in renal insufficiency depending on patient preference and amount of improvement with NSAIDs.

Source: Adapted from original material courtesy of Catherine MacLean, MD, PhD. Reprinted with permission.

Table 54. APAP and NSAIDs

| Class, Drug | Usual Dosage for Arthritis | Formulations | Comments (Metabolism, Excretion) |
|---|---|---|---|
| ✔APAP (*Tylenol*) | 650 mg q 4–6 h | T: 80, 325, 500, 650; C: 160, 325, 500; S: elixir 120/5 mL, 160/5 mL, 167/5 mL; 325/5 mL; S: 160/5 mL, 500/15 mL; Sp: 120, 325, 600 | Drug of choice for chronic musculoskeletal conditions; no anti-inflammatory properties; hepatotoxic above 4 g/d; at high doses (≥2g/d) may increase INR in patients receiving warfarin; reduce dose 50%–75% if liver or kidney disease or if harmful or hazardous drinking (L, K) |
| Extended release (*Tylenol ER*) | 1300 mg tid | ER: 650 | |
| ASA | 650 mg q 4–6 h | T: 81, 325, 500, 650, 975; Sp: 120, 200, 300, 600 | (K) |
| Extended release (*Ext Release Bayer 8 Hour,* *ZORprin*) | 1300 mg tid or 1600–3200 mg bid | CR: 650, 800 | |
| Enteric-coated* | 1000 mg qid | T: 81, 162, 325, 500, 650, 975 | |
| **Nonacetylated Salicylates** | | | Do not inhibit platelet aggregation; fewer GI and renal adverse events; no reaction in ASA-sensitive patients |
| ✔Choline magnesium salicylate (*Tricosal, Trilisate, CMT*) | 3 g/d in 1, 2, or 3 doses | T: 500, 750, 1000; S: 500 mg/5mL | (K) |
| ✔Choline salicylate (*Arthropan*) | 4.8–7.2 g/d divided | S: 870 mg/5 mL | (L, K) |
| ✔Magnesium salicylate* (eg, *Backache, Doan's, Mobigesic, Momentum*) | 650 mg q 4 h, max 3600–4800/d in 3–4 divided doses; 1090 mg tid | T: 325, 377, 580; C: 467 | Avoid in kidney failure |
| ✔Salsalate (eg, *Disalcid, Mono-Gesic, Salflex*) | 1500 mg to 4 g/d in 2 or 3 doses | T: 500, 750; C: 500 | (K) |
| ✔Sodium salicylate* | 325–650 mg q 4 h | T: 325, 650 | |
| **Nonselective NSAIDs** | | | |
| Diclofenac (*Cataflam, Voltaren, Voltaren-XR*) | 50–150 mg/d in 2 or 3 doses | T: 50, enteric coated 25, 50, 75, ER 100 | (L) |

*(cont.)*

## Table 54. APAP and NSAIDs (cont.)

| Class, Drug | Usual Dosage for Arthritis | Formulations | Comments (Metabolism, Excretion) |
|---|---|---|---|
| ✓Extended release 50 mg with 200 µg misoprostol (*Arthrotec 50*); 75 mg with 200 µg misoprostol (*Arthrotec 75*) | 100 mg/d | T: 100 | (L) |
| Diflunisal (*Dolobid*) | 500–1000 mg/d in 2 doses | T: 250, 500 | (K) |
| ✓Etodolac (*Lodine*) | 200–400 mg tid–qid | T: 400, 500; ER 400, 500, 600; | Fewer GI adverse events (L) |
| (*Lodine XL*) | 400–1000 mg/d | C: 200, 300 | |
| Fenoprofen (*Nalfon*) | 200–600 mg tid–qid | C: 200, 300; T: 600 | Higher risk of GI adverse events (L) |
| Flurbiprofen (*Ansaid*) | 200–300 mg/d in 2, 3, or 4 doses | T: 50, 100 | (L) |
| ✓Ibuprofen (eg, *Advil, Motrin, Nuprin*)** | 1200–3200 mg/d in 3 or 4 doses | T: 100, 200, 300, 400, 600, 800; ChT: 50, 100; S: 100 mg/5 mL | Fewer GI adverse events (L) |
| Indomethacin (*Indochron, Indocin*) | 25–50 mg bid–tid | C: 25, 50; Sp: 50; S: 25 mg/5 mL; Inj | High risk of GI adverse events; increased risk of CNS adverse events (L) |
| Extended release (*Indocin SR*) | 75 mg/d or bid | C: 75 | Increased risk of CNS adverse events (L) |
| ✓Ketoprofen (*Actron, Orudis*) | 50–75 mg tid | T: 12.5; C: 25, 50, 75 | (L) |
| Sustained release (*Actron 200,** Oruvail*) | 200 mg/d | C: 100, 150, 200 | (L) |
| Ketorolac (*Toradol*) | 10 mg q 4–6 h, 15 mg IM or IV q 6 h | T: 10; Inj | Duration of use should be limited to 5 d (K) |
| Meclofenamate sodium | 200–400 mg/d in 3 or 4 doses | C: 50, 100 | High incidence of diarrhea (L) |
| Mefenamic acid (*Ponstel*) | 50–100 mg tid–qid | T: 50, 100 | (L) |
| | 250 mg qid | T: 250 | |
| Meloxicam (*Mobic*) | 7.5–15 mg/d | T: 7.5, 15 | Has some COX-2 selectivity (L) |
| ✓Nabumetone (*Relafen*) | 500–1000 mg bid | T: 500, 750 | Fewer GI adverse events (L) |
| ✓Naproxen (*Aleve,** Naprosyn*) | 200–500 mg bid–tid | T: 220, 275, 375, 500; S: 125 mg/5 mL | (L) |
| Delayed release (*EC-Naprosyn*) | 375–500 mg bid | T: 375, 500 | (L) |
| Extended release (*Naprelan*) | 750–1000 mg daily | T: 375, 500, 750 | (L) |

(cont.)

#### Table 54. APAP and NSAIDs (cont.)

| Class, Drug | Usual Dosage for Arthritis | Formulations | Comments (Metabolism, Excretion) |
|---|---|---|---|
| Naproxen sodium (*Anaprox*) | 275 mg or 550 mg bid | T: 275, 550 | (L) |
| ✔Oxaprozin (*Daypro*) | 1200 mg/d | C: 600 | (L) |
| Piroxicam (*Feldene*) | 10 mg/d | T: 10, 20 | Can cause delirium (L) |
| Sulindac (*Clinoril*) | 150–200 mg bid | T: 150, 200 | May have higher rate of renal impairment (L) |
| Tolmetin (*Tolectin*) | 600–1800 mg/d in 3 or 4 doses | T: 200, 600; C: 400 | (L) |
| **Selective COX-2 Inhibitors** | | | Less GI ulceration; do not inhibit platelets; may increase INR if taking warfarin; avoid if moderate or severe hepatic insufficiency; may induce renal impairment |
| ✔Celecoxib (*Celebrex*) | 100–200 mg bid | C: 100, 200 | Contraindicated if allergic to sulfonamides (L) |
| ✔Valdecoxib (*Bextra*) | 10 mg once/d | T: 10, 20 | Contraindicated if allergic to sulfonamides (L) |

✔ = preferred for treating older persons.
  * Also available without prescription in a lower tablet strength.
 ** Available without a prescription.

## GOUT
### Definition
Urate crystal disease that may be expressed as acute gouty arthritis, usually in a single joint of foot, ankle, knee, or olecranon bursa; or chronic arthritis.

### Precipitating Factors
- Alcohol, heavy ingestion
- Allopurinol, stopping or starting
- Binge eating
- Dehydration
- Diuretics
- Fasting
- Infection
- Serum uric acid levels, any change up or down
- Surgery

### Evaluation of Acute Gouty Arthritis
Joint aspiration to remove crystals and microscopic examination to establish diagnosis; serum uric acid (can be normal during flare).

### Management
***Treatment of Acute Gouty Flare:*** Experts differ regarding order of choices:
- Intra-articular injections (see p 122)
- NSAIDs (see **Table 54**)
- Colchicine (more toxic in older persons; more effective if given within 24 hr of symptom onset)

○ Oral 0.5–0.6 mg (1 tablet) q 1–2 h until symptoms abate, GI toxicity occurs, or maximum dose of 6 mg/24-h period has been given.
○ IV 1–2 mg in 10–20 mL NS given over 3–5 min
  ▪ may repeat the following day
  ▪ contraindicated in patients who have had recent oral colchicine
  ▪ avoid in patients with kidney or liver disease
  ▪ potential for severe bone marrow toxicity
• Prednisone 20–40 mg po qd until response, then rapid taper
• ACTH 75 IU SC or cosyntropin (*Cortrosyn*) 75 μg SC; may repeat daily for 3 d
**Treatment of Hyperuricemia Following Acute Flare:** Colchicine 0.5–0.6 mg/d for 2–4 wk before beginning any treatment in **Table 55** and continued until serum uric acid has returned to normal.

**Table 55. Medications Useful in Managing Chronic Gout**

| Drug | Usual Dosage | Formulations | Comments (Metabolism, Excretion) |
|---|---|---|---|
| ✔Allopurinol (*Zyloprim, Lopurin*) | 100–200 mg qd | T: 100, 300 | Do not initiate during flare; reduce dose in renal or hepatic impairment; increase dose by 100 mg every 2–4 wk to normalize serum urate level; monitor CBC; rash is common (K) |
| Colchicine* | 0.5–0.6 mg | T: 0.5, 0.6; Inj | Follow CBC (L) |
| Probenecid* (*Benemid*) | 500–1500 mg in 2–3 divided doses | T: 500 | Adjust dose to normalize serum urate level or increase urine urate excretion; inhibits platelet function; may not be effective if renal impairment (K, L) |
| Sulfinpyrazone (*Anturane*) | 50 mg po bid to 100 mg qid | T: 100; C: 200 | Inhibits platelet function (K) |

✔ = preferred for treating older persons.
*Probenecid (500 mg) and colchicine (0.5 mg) combinations (*ColBenemid, Col-Probenecid, Proben-C*) are available.

## PSEUDOGOUT
### Definition
Crystal-induced arthritis (especially affecting wrists and knees) associated with calcium pyrophosphate.

### Risk Factors
• Advanced osteoarthritis
• Diabetes mellitus
• Gout
• Hemochromatosis
• Hypercalcemia
• Hyperparathyroidism
• Hypomagnesemia
• Hypophosphatemia
• Hypothyroidism
• Neuropathic joints
• Older age

### Precipitating Factors
• Acute illness  • Dehydration  • Minor trauma  • Surgery

### Evaluation of Acute Arthritis
Joint aspiration and microscopic examination to establish diagnosis; x-ray indicating chondrocalcinosis (best seen in wrists, knees, shoulder, symphysis pubis).

### Management of Acute Flare
See Gout, management (p 126). Colchicine is less effective in pseudogout.

## POLYMYALGIA RHEUMATICA, GIANT CELL (TEMPORAL) ARTERITIS
### Definitions
*Polymyalgia Rheumatica (PMR):* Proximal limb and girdle stiffness without tenderness but with constitutional symptoms (eg, fatigue, malaise) and elevated sedimentation rate, often ≥100, and C-reactive protein (CRP); consider ultrasound.
*Giant Cell (Temporal) Arteritis (GCA):* Medium to large vessel vasculitis that presents with symptoms of PMR, headache, scalp tenderness, jaw or tongue claudication, visual disturbances, TIA or stroke, and elevated sedimentation rate and CRP.

### Diagnosis and Management
- PMR is a clinical diagnosis supported by an increased sedimentation rate. Management is low-dose (eg, 5–20 mg/d) prednisone or its equivalent. Consider adding methotrexate po 10 mg/wk and folate 5–7.5 mg/d, which may have a steroid-sparing effect. After 2–4 wk, begin gradual taper to lowest dose that will control symptoms and CRP or sedimentation rate. Some patients with milder symptoms may respond to NSAIDs alone. Follow symptoms and CRP or sedimentation rate. Maintain therapy for at least 1 yr to prevent relapse. Consider osteoporosis prevention medication (see p 139).
- GCA is confirmed by temporal artery biopsy, but treatment should not wait for pathologic diagnosis. Begin prednisone (1.0–1.5 mg/kg/d) or its equivalent while biopsy and pathology are pending. Maintain therapy for at least 1 yr to prevent relapse. Consider osteoporosis prevention medication (see p 139).

# NEUROLOGIC DISORDERS

## TREMORS

**Table 56. Classification of Tremors**

| Type | Hz | Associated Conditions | Features | Treatment |
|------|-----|----------------------|----------|-----------|
| Cerebellar | 3–5 | Cerebellar disease | Present only during movement; ↑ with intention; ↑ amplitude as target is approached | Symptomatic management |
| Essential | 4–12 | Familial in 50% of cases | Varying amplitude; common in upper extremities, head, neck; ↑ with antigravity movements, intention, stress, medications | Long-acting propranolol or atenolol (see **Table 20**); or primidone (*Mysoline*) 100 mg qhs start, titrate to 0.5–1.0 g/d in 3–4 divided doses [T: 50, 250; S: 250 mg/5 mL]; or gabapentin (see **Table 60**) |
| Parkinson's | 3–7 | Parkinson's disease, parkinsonism | "Pill rolling;" present at rest; ↑ with emotional stress or when examiner calls attention to it; commonly asymmetric | See Parkinson's disease (p 132) |
| Physiologic | 8–12 | Normal | Low amplitude; ↑ with stress, anxiety, emotional upset, lack of sleep, fatigue, toxins, medications | Treatment of exacerbating factor |

## DIZZINESS

**Table 57. Classification of Dizziness**

| Primary Symptom | Features | Duration | Diagnosis | Management |
|-----------------|----------|----------|-----------|------------|
| Dizziness | Lightheadedness 1–30 min after standing | Seconds to minutes (E) | Orthostatic hypotension | See **Table 36** |
| | Impairment in >1 of the following: vision, vestibular function, spinal proprioception, cerebellum, lower-extremity peripheral nerves | Occurs with ambulation (C) | Multiple sensory impairments | Correct or maximize sensory deficits; PT for balance and strength training |
| | Unsteady gait with short steps; ↑ reflexes and/or tone | Occurs with ambulation (C) | Ischemic cerebral disease | Aspirin; modification of vascular risk factors; PT |
| | Provoked by head or neck movement; reduced neck range of motion | Seconds to minutes (E) | Cervical spondylosis | Behavior modification; reduce cervical spasm and inflammation |

*(cont.)*

## Table 57. Classification of Dizziness (cont.)

| Primary Symptom | Features | Duration | Diagnosis | Management |
|---|---|---|---|---|
| Drop attacks | Provoked by head or neck movement, reduced vertebral artery flow seen on Doppler or angiography | Seconds to minutes (E) | Postural impingement of vertebral artery | Behavior modification |
| Vertigo | Brought on by position change, positive Dix-Hallpike test | Seconds to minutes (E) | Benign paroxysmal positional vertigo | Epley's maneuver to reposition crystalline debris; exercises provoking symptoms may be of help |
| | Acute onset, nonpositional | Days | Labyrinthitis (vestibular neuronitis) | Methylprednisolone, 100 mg po qd × 3 d with subsequent gradual taper over 3 wk to improve vestibular function recovery; meclizine (**Table 40**) for acute symptom relief |
| | Low-frequency sensorineural hearing loss and tinnitus | Minutes to hours (E) | Ménière's disease | Meclizine for acute symptom relief; diuretics and/or salt restriction for prophylaxis |
| | Vascular disease risk factors, cranial nerve abnormalities | 10 min to several hours (E) | TIAs | Aspirin; modification of vascular risk factors |

Note: C = chronic; E = episodic.
Source: Data from Colledge NR, Barr-Hamilton RM, Lewis SJ, et al. Evaluation of investigations to diagnose the causes of dizziness in elderly people: a community based controlled study. *BMJ*. 1996;313(7060):788–792.

## MANAGEMENT OF ACUTE STROKE
### Attempt to Diagnose Cause
***Examination:***
- Cardiac (murmurs, arrhythmias, enlargement)
- Neurologic (serial examinations)
- Optic fundi
- Vascular (carotids and other peripheral pulses)

***Tests:***
- ABG
- Brain imaging
- BUN
- CBC
- LFTs
- Creatinine
- ECG
- Glucose
- Electrolytes
- ESR
- PT/PTT/INR

Transesophageal echocardiography is preferred over transthoracic echocardiography for detection of cardiogenic emboli. Carotid duplex and transcranial Doppler studies can detect carotid and vertebrobasilar embolic sources, respectively. Magnetic resonance angiography is indicated if one is considering emergent thrombolytic therapy to reverse stroke progression within 6 h of onset of symptoms (thrombolytic therapy is of unproven benefit in older adults).

### Provide Supportive Care
- Do not lower BP if SBP <220 or if DBP <120; higher BP should be lowered *gently*.
- Correct metabolic and hydration imbalances.
- Detect and treat coronary ischemia, HF, arrhythmias.
- Monitor and treat for hypoxia and hyperthermia.
- Monitor for depression.
- Refer to rehabilitation when medically stable.

### Halt or Reverse Progression
*Acute Noncardioembolic Stroke, Progressing Stroke, Crescendo TIAs, or TIA:* Use ASA, 160–325 mg/d, begun within 48 h of onset. The benefit of emergent thrombolytic therapy is unproven in older adults and should be considered on a case-by-case basis. Anticoagulants are not recommended.
*Cardioembolic Stroke:* Wait at least 48 h after symptom onset to begin anticoagulation. (See also p 18.)
*Hemorrhagic Stroke:* Supportive care.

## STROKE PREVENTION
### Risk Factor Modification
- Stop smoking
- Reduce SBP (goal <140 mm Hg)
- Lower serum LDL (goal <130 mg/dL; <100 mg/dL for those with prior stroke, TIA, CAD, diabetes mellitus)
- Start anticoagulation or antiplatelet therapy for atrial fibrillation (see p 18)

### Antiplatelet Therapy for Patients With Prior TIA or Stroke
- First line is ASA 81–325 mg qd.
- Clopidogrel (*Plavix*) 75 mg qd [T: 75] if intolerant to ASA or ASA failure.
- Ticlopidine (*Ticlid*) 250 mg bid [T: 250]; monitor CBC and differential.
- Addition of dipyridamole (*Persantine*) 200–400 mg/d in 3–4 divided doses [T: 25, 50, 75] to ASA may provide additional benefit, or can be tried in cases of ASA or clopidogrel failure. A combination form of ASA (25 mg) and long-acting dipyridamole (200 mg) (*Aggrenox*) 1 tablet bid is available.
- In the absence of atrial fibrillation, warfarin therapy is no more effective than ASA in preventing strokes.

**Table 58. Treatment Options for Carotid Stenosis**

| Presentation | % Stenosis | Preferred R$_x$ | Comments |
|---|---|---|---|
| Prior TIA or stroke | ≥70 | CE | CE superior to medical therapy only if patient is reasonable surgical risk and facility has track record of low complication rate for CE (<5%) |
| Prior TIA or stroke | 50–69 | CE or MM | Serial carotid Doppler testing may identify rapidly developing plaques |
| Prior TIA or stroke | <50 | MM | CE of no proven benefit in this situation |
| Asymptomatic | ≥80 | CE or MM | CE should be considered only for the most healthy |
| Asymptomatic | <80 | MM | CE of no proven benefit in this situation |

Note: CE = carotid endarterectomy; MM = medical management.

## PARKINSON'S DISEASE
### Parkinson's Disease Diagnosis Requires:
- Bradykinesia, eg,
  - Slowness of initiation of voluntary movements (eg, glue-footedness during gait initiation)
  - Reduced speed and amplitude of repetitive movements (eg, tapping index finger and thumb together)
  - Difficulty switching from one motor program to another (eg, multiple steps to turn during gait testing)
- **and** one or more of the following:
  - Muscular rigidity (eg, cogwheeling)
  - 4–6 Hz resting tremor
  - Impaired righting reflex (eg, retropulsed during sternal nudge)

### Nonpharmacologic Management
- Patient education is essential, and support groups are often helpful; see p 226 for telephone numbers, Web sites.
- Monitor for orthostatic hypotension (see **Table 36** for management).
- Exercise program
- Surgical therapies can be considered for disabling symptoms refractory to medical therapy. Tremor can be improved by thalamotomy or thalamic stimulation (fewer adverse events). Dyskinesias can be treated by pallidotomy or pallidal and subthalamic stimulation.

### Pharmacologic Treatment (see **Table 59**)
- Begin treatment when symptoms interfere with function.
- Start at low dose and titrate upward gradually.
- Monitor orthostatic BP during titration of medications.

### Table 59. Drugs for Parkinson's Disease

| Class, Drug | Initial Dose | Formulations | Comments (Metabolism, Excretion) |
|---|---|---|---|
| **Dopamine** | | | |
| ✔ Levodopa-carbidopa* (*Sinemet*) | 1/2 tab of 25/100 qd or bid | T: 10/100, 25/100, 25/250 | Mainstay of PD therapy; increase dose by 1/2–1 tab q 1–2 wk to achieve minimal target dose of 1 tab tid; then titrate gradually upward as needed; watch for GI adverse events, orthostatic hypotension, confusion (L) |
| ✔ Sustained-release levodopa-carbidopa* (*Sinemet CR*) | 1 tab qd | T: 25/100, 50/200 | Useful at daily dopamine requirement ≥300 mg; slower absorption than levodopa-carbidopa; can improve motor fluctuations (L) |
| **Dopamine agonists** | | | More CNS adverse events than dopamine |
| Bromocriptine (*Parlodel*) | 1.25 mg qd or bid | T: 2.5; C: 5 | Increase by 1.25-mg increments every 2–5 d, titrating to effective dose (10–30 mg/d); very expensive (L) |
| Pergolide (*Permax*) | 0.05 mg qd | T: 0.05, 0.25, 1 | Increase by 0.05 mg q 2–3 d, titrating to effective dose (1–3 mg/d); expensive (K) |
| ✔ Pramipexole* (*Mirapex*) | 0.125 qd | T: 0.125, 0.25, 0.5, 1, 1.5 | Increase gradually to effective dose (0.5–1.5 mg tid) (K) |
| ✔ Ropinirole* (*Requip*) | 0.25 mg qd | T: 0.25, 0.5, 1, 2, 3, 4, 5 | Increase gradually to effective dose (up to 1–8 mg tid) (L) |
| **Catechol *O*-methyl-transferase (COMT) inhibitors** | | | Adjunctive therapy with L-dopa |
| ✔ Tolcapone (*Tasmar*) | 100 mg tid | T: 100, 200 | Monitor LFT q 6 mo (L, K) |
| ✔ Entacapone (*Comtan*) | 200 mg with each L-dopa dose | T: 200 | Watch for nausea, orthostatic hypotension (L) |
| **Anticholinergics** | | | |
| Benztropine (*Cogentin*) | 0.5 mg po qd | T: 0.5, 1, 2 | Can cause confusion and delirium; helpful for drooling (L, K) |
| Trihexyphenidyl (*Artane, Trihexy*) | 1 mg qd | T: 2, 5; S: 2 mg/5 mL | Same as above (L, K) |
| **Dopamine reuptake inhibitor** | | | |
| Amantadine (*Symmetrel*) | 100 mg qd–bid | T: 100; C: 100; S: 50 mg/5 mL | Useful in early and late PD; watch closely for CNS adverse events; do not D/C abruptly (K) |
| **MAO B inhibitor** | | | |
| Selegiline (*Carbex, Eldepryl*) | 5 mg bid qam and noon | T: 5 | Symptomatic benefit; not proved to be neuroprotective; expensive (L, K) |

✔ = preferred for treating older persons
* = first-line therapy; PD = Parkinson's disease.

## SEIZURES
### Classification
- Generalized: All areas of brain affected with alteration in consciousness.
- Partial: Focal brain area affected, not necessarily with alteration in consciousness; can progress to generalized type.

### Evaluation, Assessment
*Initial:*
- History: Neurologic disorders, trauma, drug and alcohol use
- Physical examination: General, with careful neurologic
- Routine tests: BUN, calcium, CBC, creatinine, ECG, EEG, electrolytes, glucose, head CT, LFT, magnesium
- Tests as indicated: Head MRI, lumbar puncture, oxygen saturation, urine toxic or drug screen

*Common Causes:*
- Advanced dementia
- CNS infection
- Drug or alcohol withdrawal
- Idiopathic causes
- Metabolic disorders
- Prior stroke (most common)
- Toxins
- Trauma
- Tumor

### Management
- Treat underlying causes.
- Institute antiepileptic therapy (see **Table 60**). Virtually all antiepileptics can cause sedation and ataxia.

**Table 60. Antiepileptic Therapy in Elderly Patients**

| Drug | Dosage (mg) | Target Blood Level (µg/mL) | Formulations | Comments (Metabolism, Excretion) |
|---|---|---|---|---|
| Carbamazepine (*Tegretol*) (*Tegretol XR*) | 200–600 bid | 4–12 | T: 200; ChT: 100; S: 100/5 mL; T: 100, 200, 400; C: CR 200, 300 | Many drug interactions; mood stabilizer; may cause SIADH, thrombocytopenia, leukopenia (L, K) |
| Gabapentin (*Neurontin*) | 300–600 tid | NA | C: 100, 300, 400; T: 600, 800; S: 250/5 mL | Used as adjunct to other agents; adjust dose on basis of CrCl (K) |
| Lamotrigine (*Lamictal*) | 100–300 bid | 2–4 | T: 25, 100, 150, 200; ChT: 2, 5, 25 | Prolongs PR interval; risk of severe rash; when used with valproic acid, begin at 25 mg qod, titrate to 25–100 mg bid (L, K) |
| Levetiracetam (*Keppra*) | 500–1500 q 12 h | NA | T: 250, 500, 750 | Reduce dose in renal impairment: CrCl 30–50: 250–750 q 12 h CrCl 10–30: 250–500 q 12 h CrCl <10: 500–1000 q 24 h |
| Oxcarbazepine (*Trileptal*) | 300–1200 bid | NA | T: 150, 300, 600; ChT: 2, 5, 25; S: 300/5 mL | Can cause hyponatremia (L) |

*(cont.)*

## Table 60. Antiepileptic Therapy in Elderly Patients (cont.)

| Drug | Dosage (mg) | Target Blood Level (µg/mL) | Formulations | Comments (Metabolism, Excretion) |
|---|---|---|---|---|
| Phenobarbital (*Luminal*) | 30–60 bid-tid | 20–40 | T: 15, 16, 30, 32, 60, 100; S: 20/5 mL | Many drug interactions; not recommended for use in elderly patients (L) |
| Phenytoin (*Dilantin*) | 200–300 qd | 5–20* | C: 30, 100; ChT: 50; S: 125/5 mL | Many drug interactions; exhibits nonlinear pharmacokinetics (L) |
| Tiagabine (*Gabitril Filmtabs*) | 2–12 bid-tid | NA | T: 2, 4, 12, 16, 20 | Adverse-event profile in elderly patients less well described (L) |
| Topiramate (*Topamax*) | 25–100 qd-bid | NA | T: 25, 100, 200; C, sprinkle: 15, 25 | May affect cognitive functioning at high doses (L, K) |
| Valproic acid (*Depacon, Depakene, Depakote*) | 250–750 bid-tid | 50–100 | T: ER 125, 250, 500; C: 125, 250; S: 250/5 mL | Can cause weight gain, tremor, hair loss; several drug interactions; mood stabilizer; monitor LFTs and platelets; SR preparation (*Depakote ER*) also available [T: 500] (L) |
| Zonisamide (*Zonegran*) | 100–400 qd | NA | C: 100 | Anorexia; contraindicated in patients with sulfonamide allergy |

Note: NA = not available.
* Phenytoin is extensively bound to plasma albumin. In cases of hypoalbuminemia or marked renal insufficiency, calculate adjusted phenytoin concentration (C):

$$C_{adjusted} = \frac{C_{observed} (\mu g/mL)}{0.2 \times albumin\ (g/dL) + 0.1}$$

If creatinine clearance <10 mL/min, use:

$$C_{adjusted} = \frac{C_{observed} (\mu g/mL)}{0.1 \times albumin\ (g/dL) + 0.1}$$

Obtaining a free phenytoin level is an alternate method for monitoring phenytoin in cases of hypoalbuminemia or marked renal insufficiency.

## APHASIA

### Table 61. Aphasias in Which Repetition Is Impaired

| Type | Fluency | Auditory Comprehension | Associated Neurologic Deficits | Comments |
|---|---|---|---|---|
| Broca's | − | + | Right hemiparesis | Patient aware of deficit; high rate of associated depression; message board helpful for communication |
| Wernicke's | + | − | Often none | Patient frequently unaware of deficit; speech content usually unintelligible; therapy often focuses on visually based communication |

(cont.)

**Table 61. Aphasias in Which Repetition Is Impaired (cont.)**

| Type | Fluency | Auditory Comprehension | Associated Neurologic Deficits | Comments |
|------|---------|------------------------|-------------------------------|----------|
| Conduction | + | + | Occasional right facial weakness | Patient usually aware of the deficit; speech content usually intelligible |
| Global | − | − | Right hemiplegia with right field cut | Most commonly due to left middle cerebral artery thrombosis, which, if this is the cause, carries a poor prognosis for meaningful speech recovery |

Note: + = present; − = absent

## PERIPHERAL NEUROPATHY
### Diagnosis
See **Figure 7**.

### Treatment
***Prevention of Complications:***
- Protect distal extremities from trauma—appropriate shoe size, daily foot inspections, good skin care, avoidance of barefoot walking.
- Maintain tight glycemic control in diabetic neuropathy.

***Treatment of Painful Neuropathy:*** Start at low dose, increase as needed and tolerated:
- Nortriptyline (*Aventyl, Pamelor*) 10–100 mg qhs [T: 10, 25, 50, 75]; desipramine (*Norpramin*) 10–75 mg qam [T: 10, 25, 50, 75]
- Gabapentin (*Neurontin*) can begin 100–200 mg qhs but may need up to 100–600 mg tid [C: 100, 300, 400; T: 600, 800; S: 250/5 mL]
- Other oral agents that may be effective include:
  - Carbamazepine (*Tegretol*) 200–400 mg tid [T: 200; ChT: 100; S: 100 mg/5 mL]; (*Tegretol XR*) 200 mg bid [T: 100, 200, 400; C: CR 200, 300]
  - Duloxetine (*Cymbalta*) 60 mg qd [C: 20, 30, 60]
  - SSRIs (**Table 27**) have not been shown to be as effective as tricyclics
  - Lamotrigine (*Lamictal*, see **Table 60**) 400–600 mg/d
  - Opioids (**Table 65**); watch for adverse events of itching, mood changes, weakness, confusion
  - Tramadol (*Ultram*, see **Table 65**) 200–400 mg/d
- Topical agents that may be effective include:
  - Capsaicin cream (eg, *Zostrix*) 0.075% applied tid–qid [0.025%, 0.075%]
  - Transcutaneous electrical nerve stimulation
  - Lidocaine 5% patches (*Lidoderm*) 1–3 patches covering the affected area up to 12 h/d [700 mg patch]

**Figure 7. Diagnosis of Peripheral Neuropathy**

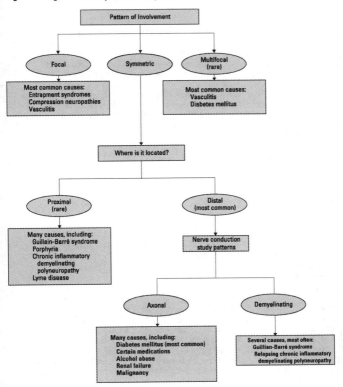

Source: Data from Poncelet AN. An algorithm for the evaluation of peripheral neuropathy. *Am Fam Phys.* 1998;57(4):755–764.

# OSTEOPOROSIS

## COMMONLY USED DEFINITIONS
- Established osteoporosis: occurrence of a minimal trauma fracture of any bone (WHO).
- Osteoporosis: a skeletal disorder characterized by compromised bone strength (bone density and bone quality) predisposing to an increased risk of fracture: NIH Consensus Development Panel. Osteoporosis prevention, diagnosis, and therapy. *JAMA* 2001; 285 (6):785–795.
- Osteoporosis: BMD 2.5 SD or more below that of younger normal individuals (T score) (WHO). Some experts prefer to use Z score, which compares an individual with a population adjusted for age, sex, and race. For each SD decrement in BMD, hip fracture risk increases about 2-fold; for each SD increment in BMD, hip fracture risk is about halved.

## RISK FACTORS FOR OSTEOPOROTIC FRACTURE
- Previous fracture as adult
- Dementia
- Depression
- Low calcium intake
- Impaired vision
- Low physical activity
- Fracture in 1st-degree relative
- Frailty
- Alcoholism
- Female sex
- Weight <127 lb if female
- Cigarette smoking
- Early menopause (<45 yr)
- Recurrent falls

## TOXINS AND MEDICATIONS THAT CAN CAUSE OR AGGRAVATE OSTEOPOROSIS
- Alcohol (>2 drinks/d)
- Anticonvulsants
- Corticosteroids
- Heparin
- Lithium
- Phenytoin
- Smoking
- Thyroxine (if overreplaced or in suppressive doses)

## EVALUATION
Some experts recommend excluding secondary causes (serum PTH, TSH, calcium, phosphorus, albumin, alkaline phosphatase, bioavailable testosterone in men, kidney and liver function tests, CBC, UA, electrolytes, protein electrophoresis). Less consensus on: vitamin D levels, 24-h urinary calcium excretion, cortisol, antibodies associated with gluten-enteropathy; BMD test only if results could influence treatment or to establish baseline (see screening p 159). The value of monitoring BMD in persons already receiving treatment is unproven.

## MANAGEMENT
### Universal Recommendations
- Calcium 1200 mg/d*
- Vitamin D 400–800 IU
- Avoid tobacco
- Weight-bearing exercise
- Falls prevention
- No more than moderate alcohol use

\* For most patients, calcium carbonate is sufficient and least expensive. For patients on proton-pump inhibitors (see **Table 37**) or who have achlorhydria, calcium citrate should be used.

## Pharmacologic Prevention

- Most organizations have recommended initiating pharmacologic management in women with BMD T scores below −2 in the absence of risk factors and in women with T scores below −1.5 if other risk factors are present.
- Regimens:
  - Bisphosphonates
    - Alendronate (*Fosamax*) 5 mg/d or 35 mg/wk [T: 5, 10, 35, 40, 70; 70 sol] (must be taken fasting with water; patient must remain upright and npo for at least 30 min after taking; do not use if CrCl < 35 mL/min; relatively contraindicated in GERD) **or**
    - Risedronate (*Actonel*) 35 mg/wk or 5 mg/d [T: 5, 30, 35] (must be taken fasting or at least 2 h after evening meal; patient must remain upright and npo for 30 min after taking; do not use if CrCl < 30 mL/min) **or**
  - Raloxifene (*Evista*) 60 mg/d [T: 60] **or**
  - Estrogen in selected patients (see **Table 93** for dosing).

## Nonpharmacologic Treatment

Vertebroplasty (injection of bone cement into a collapsed vertebra) or kyphoplasty (inflation of a balloon tamp before cement injection) has improved pain and function acutely in case studies and nonrandomized controlled studies; long-term benefits for pain, function, and vertebral height are uncertain.

## Pharmacologic Treatment Regimens for Those with Prior Osteoporotic Fractures

- Bisphosphonates
  - Alendronate (*Fosamax*) 10 mg/d or 70 mg/wk [T: 5, 10, 35, 40, 70; 70 sol] (must be taken fasting with water; patient must remain upright and npo for at least 30 min after taking; do not use if CrCl < 35 mL/min; relatively contraindicated in GERD) **or**
  - Risedronate (*Actonel*) 35 mg/wk or 5 mg/d [T: 5, 30, 35] (must be taken fasting or at least 2 h after evening meal; patient must remain upright and npo for 30 min after taking; do not use if CrCl < 30 mL/min) **or**
- Raloxifene (*Evista*) 60 mg/d [T: 60] **or**
- Calcitonin (*Calcimar, Cibacalcin, Miacalcin, Osteocalcin, Salmonine*) 100 IU/d SC [Inj: human (*Cibacalcin*) 0.5 mg/vial; salmon 200 units/mL) or 200 IU (*Miacalcin*) [200 units/activation] (intranasally, alternate nostrils every other day). May also be helpful for analgesic effect in patients with acute vertebral fracture (see also p 120) **or**
- Estrogen in selected patients (see **Table 93** for dosing).
- Teriparatide (*Forteo*) 20 µg/d for up to 24 mo [Inj 3 mL, 28-dose disposable pen device] for high-risk patients; contraindicated in patients with Paget's disease or prior skeletal radiation therapy (L, K).

---

**Table 62. Bone Outcomes of Drugs for Osteoporosis Based on Randomized Clinical Trials***

| Drug | Spine BMD and Fracture | Hip BMD | Hip Fracture | All Nonspinal Fractures |
|------|------------------------|---------|--------------|-------------------------|
| Estrogen** | improved | improved | reduced | no effect |
| Raloxifene | improved | improved | no data | no effect |
| Alendronate | improved | improved | reduced | reduced |
| Risedronate | improved | improved | reduced | reduced |
| Calcitonin (nasal) | improved | no effect | no effect | no effect |
| Teriparatide | improved | improved | no data | reduced |

\* The populations studied, sample sizes of individual studies, and duration of follow-up vary considerably; hence, this summary must be interpreted cautiously. Moreover, several randomized clinical trials are currently in progress and new findings may appear.
\*\* The least expensive of the drugs listed.

---

**Table 63. Effects on Other Outcomes, Level of Evidence,* and Risks of Drugs for Osteoporosis**

| Drug | CHD Risk Factors | CHD Prevention | CHD Treatment | Breast Cancer | Deep-Vein Thrombosis | Other |
|------|------------------|----------------|---------------|---------------|----------------------|-------|
| Estrogen** | improved–R | ↑ risk–R | no effect–R | ↑ risk–R | ↑ risk–R | ↑ vaginal bleeding, stroke, PE<br>↓ colorectal cancer–R |
| Raloxifene | improved–R | ↓ risk–R | ↓ risk–R | ↓ risk–R | ↑ risk–R | ↑ hot flushes–R |
| Alendronate | no data | no data | no data | no data | no data | esophagitis |
| Risedronate | no data | no data | no data | no data | no data | |
| Calcitonin (nasal) | no data | no data | no data | no data | no data | rhinitis in 10%–12% |

\* The populations studied, sample sizes of individual studies, and duration of follow-up vary considerably; hence, this summary must be interpreted cautiously. Moreover, several randomized clinical trials are currently in progress and new findings may appear.
\*\* In the Women's Health Initiative estrogen-alone trial, only stroke and pulmonary embolism risk were increased.
† Reduced risk demonstrated for high-risk women only.
Note: CHD = coronary heart disease; R = randomized clinical trial.

# PAIN

## DEFINITION
An unpleasant sensory and emotional experience associated with actual or potential tissue damage (International Association for Study of Pain taxonomy)

### Acute Pain
Distinct onset, usually evident pathology, short duration; common causes: postsurgical pain, trauma

### Persistent Pain
Pain due to ongoing nociceptive, neuropathic, or mixed pathophysiologic processes, often associated with functional and psychologic impairment, can fluctuate in character and intensity over time; common causes: arthritis, cancer, claudication, leg cramps, neuropathy, radiculopathy, low back pain, myofascial pain syndromes

## EVALUATION
### Key Points, Approach
- Perform comprehensive evaluation of cause of pain, pain characteristics, and impact of physical and psychosocial function.
- Assume patient's report is the most reliable evidence of pain intensity.
- Assess for pain on each presentation (older adults may be reluctant to report pain).
- Use synonyms for pain (eg, burning, aching, soreness, discomfort).
- Use a standard pain scale (see p 212); adapt for sensory impairments (eg, large print, written versus spoken).
- Assess cognitively impaired patients by:
  - Using simple tools or questions with yes/no answers.
  - Noting increased vocalizations (eg, moaning, groaning, crying).
  - Observing behaviors (eg, grimacing, irritability, failure to move an extremity, guarding).
  - Asking caregiver about recent changes in function, gait, behavior patterns, mood.
- Use a screening approach to recognize potential pain problems in nonverbal, cognitively impaired elders (see **Figure 8**).
- Reassess regularly for improvement, deterioration, complications; keep log.
- Refer for comprehensive multidisciplinary evaluation for complex pain problem.
- Document evaluation, plan of care, and monitoring of treatment effects on pain and function.

### History and Physical
- Focus on a complete examination of pain source, with emphasis on musculoskeletal and neurologic systems.
- Distinguish new illness from chronic condition.
- Analgesic history: effectiveness and adverse events, current and previous prescription drugs, OTC drugs, "natural" remedies.
- Assess effectiveness of prior nondrug treatments.
- Laboratory and diagnostic tests: to establish etiologic diagnosis.

## Figure 8. Pain Assessment in Elders with Severe Cognitive Impairment

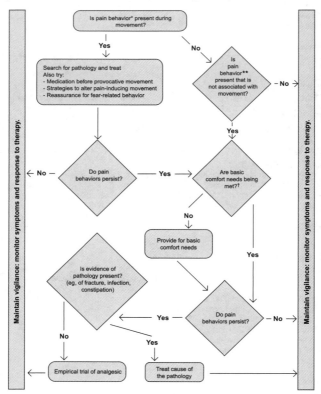

* Eg, grimacing, guarding, combativeness, groaning with movement; resisting care.
** Eg, agitation, fidgeting, sleep disturbance, diminished appetite, irritability, reclusiveness, disruptive behavior, rigidity, rapid blinking.
† Eg, toileting, thirst, hunger, visual or hearing impairment.

Sources: Data from American Geriatrics Society. The management of persistent pain in older persons. *J Amer Geriatr Soc* 2002; 50 (6, Suppl: S205–S240); and Weiner D, Herr K, Rudy T, eds. Persistent Pain in Older Adults: An Interdisciplinary Guide for Treatment, 2002, Copyright Springer Publishing Company, Inc., New York 10036.

## Characteristics of Pain Complaint

**P**rovocative (aggravating) and **P**alliative (relieving) factors
**Q**uality (eg, burning, stabbing, dull, throbbing)
**R**egion (eg, pain map)
**S**everity (eg, scale of 0 for no pain to 10 for worst pain possible; see p 212)
**T**iming (eg, when pain occurs, frequency and duration)

## Psychosocial Assessment

Depression (see p 206 for screen), anxiety, mental status (see p 204 for screen). Impact on family or significant other. Enabling behaviors by others (eg, oversolicitousness, codependency, reinforcing debility)

## Assess for Risk of Addiction with Opioid Use

- Addiction is rare in those without prior hx of substance abuse.
- Risk factors include men who exceed 4 drinks/d or 16 drinks/wk; women who exceed 3 drinks/d or 12 drinks/wk; admission to marijuana or hashish use in the past year; hx of alcohol abuse, drug abuse, or significant psychiatric illness; or a personal hx of previous physical, sexual, or emotional abuse.
- Record any suspicious drug-seeking or other aberrant behaviors observed or reported by others, along with action(s) taken.
- Document evaluation process, rationale for long-term opioid therapy, and periodic review of patient status.

## Functional Assessment

ADLs, impact on activities (see pp 204–206, for screens) and quality of life.

## Brief Pain Inventory

Use for comprehensive assessment of pain and its impact (see p 214).

## PAIN MANAGEMENT

Goal: To find optimal balance in pain relief, functional improvement, and side effects.

### Acute Pain and Short-Term Management

- Use fixed schedule of APAP, NSAIDs (consider nonselective versus COX-2 inhibitors depending on risk factors and comorbidities, see **Figure 6**), or opioids.
- Include nonpharmacologic strategies (eg, relaxation, heat or cold).
- For severe pain, consider patient-controlled analgesic pump.
- Patient-controlled analgesia (PCA)
  - Indications
    - Acute pain such as postoperative pain, trauma, acute changes in cancer pain, sickle cell crisis
    - Persistent pain in patients npo
    - Ability to understand PCA instructions
  - Dosing strategies (see **Table 64**)
    - Titrate up PCA dose 25–50% if pain still not well controlled after 12 h
    - Unless patient is awakened by pain during sleep, continuous opioid infusions not recommended because of increased risk of drug accumulation and toxicity.

- If basal rate used, hourly monitoring of sedation and respiratory status is warranted.
- D/C PCA when patient able to take oral analgesics or unable to self medicate due to altered mental status or physical limitations.

**Table 64. Typical Initial Dosing of PCA for Opioid-naive Elders with Severe Pain**

| Drug (usual concentration) | Usual Dose | Usual Lockout (min) |
|---|---|---|
| Morphine (1 mg/mL) | 2.5–5 mg | 5–10 |
| Hydromorphone (0.2 mg/mL) | 0.1–0.3 mg | 5–10 |

## Persistent Pain
- Use multidisciplinary assessment and treatment.
- Educate patient for self-management and coping.
- Combine drug and nondrug strategies.
- Anticipate and attend to depression and anxiety.
- Provide instruction in self-conditioning, strengthening, flexibility, stretching (all per patient's ability).

## Nonpharmacologic Treatment
- Educate patient and caregiver.
  ○ Explain difference between addiction, physical dependence, and tolerance.
  ○ http://www.ampainsoc.org/advocacy/opioids2.htm
- Emphasize self-administered therapies (eg, heat, cold, massage, liniments and topical agents).
- Prescribe exercise, especially for persistent pain (see p 162).
- Add therapy conducted by professionals (eg, distraction, relaxation techniques, music therapy, coping skills, biofeedback, imagery, hypnosis) as needed.
- When appropriate, obtain:
  ○ Rehabilitation medicine consult (OT, PT) for mechanical devices to minimize pain and facilitate activity (eg, splints), transcutaneous electrical nerve stimulation, range-of-motion and ADL programs.
  ○ Psychiatric pain management consult for somatization or severe mood or personality disorder.
  ○ Anesthesia pain management consult for possible interventional therapy (eg, neuroaxial analgesia, injection therapy, neuromodulation) when more conservative approaches are ineffective.
  ○ Pain or chemical dependency specialist referral for management of at-risk patients and ongoing chemical dependency, "chemical coping," aberrant drug-related behaviors, and drug withdrawal.

## Pharmacologic Treatment
### Selection of Agent(s):
- Base initial choice of analgesic on the severity and type of pain; consider cost, availability, patient preference, comorbidity, and impairments (see Osteoarthritis, **Figure 6**):
  ○ Consider nonopioids for mild pain (rating 1–3) (see **Table 54**).

- ○ Consider low-dose combination agents (see **Table 65**) for mild to moderate pain (rating 4–6).
- ○ Consider potent and titratable opioid agonists (see **Table 65**) for more severe pain (rating 7–10).
- ○ Consider adjuvant drugs (see **Table 67**) alone or in conjunction with opioids or nonopioids for neuropathic pain and other selected chronic conditions.
- ○ Select lowest adverse-event profile agents.
- Select least invasive route (usually oral) and fast-onset, short-acting analgesics for episodic or breakthrough pain.
- Use long-acting or sustained-release analgesics for continuous pain.
- Avoid long-term, nonselective NSAID use for chronic conditions.
- Consider COX-2 inhibitors for patients who would benefit from anti-inflammatory drug therapy on a continuous, long-term basis.
- Consider fixed-dose combinations (eg, APAP and hydrocodone or tramadol) for mild to moderate pain; do not exceed maximum dose for nonopioid.
- Avoid using multiple opioids or nonopioids when possible.
- Drugs with long half-life or depot effects (eg, methadone, levorphanol, transdermal fentanyl) need to be used and titrated cautiously, with close supervision of effects; duration of effect may exceed usual dose intervals because of reductions in metabolism and clearance.
- Methadone is an option if other long-acting agents are not affordable but should be used with caution and only with sufficient expertise and monitoring ability (see **Table 66**).

### Adjustment of Dosage:
- Begin with lowest dose possible, increasing slowly.
- Titrate dose on basis of persistent need for and use of medications for breakthrough pain. If using 3 or more doses of breakthrough pain medication per day, consider increased dose of sustained-release medication.
- Dose to therapeutic ceiling of nonopioid or NSAID if adverse events permit.
- Increase opioid dose until pain relief achieved or adverse events unmanageable before changing drugs (there is no max dose or analgesic ceiling with opioids).
- Use morphine equivalents as a common denominator for all dose conversions to avoid errors.
- When changing opioids, decrease equianalgesic dose by 25%–50% because of incomplete cross-tolerance.
- Administer around-the-clock for continuous pain.
- Reassess, re-examine, and readjust therapy frequently until pain is relieved.

### Management of Adverse Events:
- Anticipate, prevent, and vigorously treat adverse events; expect older patients to be more sensitive to adverse events.
- Warn patient about risk of sedation with opioids and that gradual resolution occurs within a week.
- Warn about risk of APAP toxicity and importance of including all OTC products with APAP in daily total (not to exceed 4 g/d).
- Begin prophylactic, osmotic or stimulant laxative when initiating opioid therapy (see **Table 39**); if patient taking sufficient fluids, cautiously increase fiber or psyllium; titrate laxative dose up with opiate dose. (See also p 73 for stepped approach.)

- Monitor for sedation, delirium, urinary retention, constipation, respiratory depression, and nausea; tolerance develops to mild sedation, nausea, and impaired cognitive function.
- On long-term NSAID use, monitor periodically for GI blood loss, renal insufficiency, and other drug-drug and drug-disease interactions.
- Avoid the following drugs: carisoprodol, chlorzoxazone, cyclobenzaprine, indomethacin, meperidine, metaxalone, methocarbamol, nalbuphine, pentazocine, propoxyphene (see also p 223 for CMS criteria regarding inappropriate drug use).

### Table 65. Opioid Analgesic Drugs

| Class, Drug | MS Equiv* (Route) | Starting Oral Dosage in Opioid-Naive Patients | Formulations | Indication for Pain** |
|---|---|---|---|---|
| **Short-Acting** | | | | |
| Codeine | 200 mg (po) | 15 mg q 4–6 h | T: 15, 30, 60; S: 15/5 mL; Inj | A |
| Codeine & APAP† | 200 mg (po) | 1–2 15/325 tabs q 4–6 h; if 1 tab used, add 325 mg APAP | T: 15/325, 30/325, 60/325, 30/500, 30/650, 7.5/300, 15/300, 30/300, 60/300; S: 12/120/5 mL | A |
| Hydrocodone & APAP† (eg, *Lorcet, Lortab, Vicodin*) | 30 mg | 5–10 mg q 4–6 h | T: 10/325, 5/400, 7.5/400, 10/400, 2.5/500, 5/500, 7.5/500, 10/500, 7.5/650, 7.5/750, 10/650, 10/660; C: 5/500; S: 2.5/167/5 mL (contains 7% alcohol) | A |
| Hydrocodone & ASA (eg, *Lortab ASA*) | 30 mg | 5/500 | T: 5/500 | A |
| Hydrocodone & ibuprofen (eg, *Vicoprofen*) | 30 mg | 7.5/200 | T: 7.5/200 | A |
| Oxycodone (*Oxy IR, Roxicodone*) | 20–30 mg (po) | 5 mg q 3–4 h | T: 5, 15, 30; C: 5; S: 5 mg/mL, 20 mg/mL | A |
| Oxycodone & APAP† (*Percocet, Tylox*) | 20 mg (po) | 2.5–5 mg oxycodone q 6 h | T: 2.5/325, 5/325, 5/500, 7.5/325, 7.5/500, 10/325, 10/650; C: 5/500; S: 5/325/5 mL | A |
| Oxycodone & ASA (*Percodan*) | 20 mg (po) | 2.25–4.5 mg oxycodone q 6 h | T: 2.25/325, 4.5/325 | A |
| Morphine (*MSIR, Astramorph PF, Duramorph, Infumorph, Roxanol, OMS Concentrate, MS/L, RMS, MS/S*) | 30 mg (po), 10 mg (IV, IM, SC) | 5 mg (po), 1–2 mg (IV) q 4–6 h | C: 15, 30; soluble T: 15, 30; S: 10 mg/5 mL, 20 mg/5 mL, 100 mg/5 mL, 4 mg/mL, 20 mg/mL; Sp: 5, 10, 20, 30; Inj | B |
| Hydromorphone (*Dilaudid, Hydrostat*) | 7.5 mg (po), 1.5 mg (IV, IM, SC), 6 mg (rectal) | 2 mg q 3–4 h | T: 2, 4, 8; S: 5 mg/5 mL; Sp: 3; Inj | B |

*(cont.)*

Table 65. Opioid Analgesic Drugs (cont.)

| Class, Drug | MS Equiv* (Route) | Starting Oral Dosage in Opioid-Naive Patients | Formulations | Indication for Pain** |
|---|---|---|---|---|
| Oxymorphone (*Numorphan*) | 1 mg (IV, IM, SC), 10 mg (rectal) | 0.5 mg IM, IV, SC q 4–6 h | Sp: 5; Inj | B |
| Fentanyl (*Actiq*) | NA | suck on 200 µg loz over 15 min, effect begins within 10 min | loz on a stick: 200, 400, 600, 800, 1200, 1600 µg | B |
| Tramadol (*Ultram*) | 150–300 mg | 25–50 mg q 4–6 h; not >300 for age 75+ | T: 50 | B |
| Tramadol & APAP† (*Ultracet*) | 37.5/325 mg | 2 tabs po q 4–6 h pain; max 8 tabs/d‡ | T: 50 | B |
| **Long-Acting** | | | | |
| ER Morphine (*MS Contin, Kadian, Oramorph SR, Avinza*) | 30 mg (po) *MS Contin, Kadian, Oramorph SR,* 60 mg (po) *Avinza* | 20–30 mg q 24 h, 15 mg q 12 h (*MS Contin* CR and XR tabs), 20 mg q 24 h (*Kadian* SR caps), 15 mg q 24 h (*Oramorph SR*), 30 mg q 24 h (*Avinza* caps) | T: CR 15, 30, 60, 100, 200, XR 15, 30, 60; C: SR 5, 20, 30, 60, 100; C: 30, 60, 90, 120; T: SR 15, 30, 60, 100 (tab must be swallowed whole) | B |
| ER Oxycodone (*OxyContin*) | 20–30 mg (po) | 20 mg q 24 h, 10 mg q 12 h | T: CR 10, 20, 40, 80, 160 | B |
| Hydromorphone HCl ER (*Palladone*) | 7.5 mg (po) | 12 mg q 24 h | C: 12, 16, 24, 32 | B |
| Transdermal fentanyl§ (*Duragesic*) | NA (see package insert) | 25 µg/h or higher (if able to tolerate 50 mg oral morphine equiv/24 h) | 25 µg/h (10 cm²), 50 µg/h (20 cm²), 75 µg/h (30 cm²), 100 µg/h (40 cm²) | B |

* MS Equiv = morphine sulphate (MS) equivalent dose: morphine equivalency = dose of opioid equivalent to 10 mg of parenteral morphine or 30 mg of oral morphine with chronic dosing. The parenteral:oral ratio is greater (1:6) during acute dosing, ie, 10 mg IM MS = 60 mg po MS. NA = not applicable.
** A = mild to moderate pain; B = moderate to severe pain.
† Caution: total APAP dose should not exceed 4 g/d.
‡ Treatment not to exceed 5 d; if CrCl <30 mL/min, max is 2 tab q 12 h, not to exceed 5 d.
§ Caution: Active ingredient accumulates in subcutaneous fat, thus duration of action may be >17 h. Do not use in opioid-naïve patients. Do not apply heat to patch. Not recommended for treatment of acute pain.

## Methadone Prescribing and Monitoring
- Relative potency of methadone is highly variable in patients already tolerant to other opioids.
- Reduce equianalgesic dose by 75% to 90% and provide immediate-release, short-acting opioid supplementation for rescue analgesia if conversion leads to underdosing.
- Dosing intervals start at q 4–6 h and may be increased over time to q 6–12 h.
- Do not increase dose more frequently than every 4 d.

- Assure patient has reliable caregiver (educated with patient) to monitor for mental status changes, especially progressive sedation. If observed, hold dose and contact health care provider.
- Follow-up after initial treatment and titration or dose conversion by telephone in 3–5 d; office visit in 1–2 wk.
- Do baseline ECG (if not within last year) to monitor for $QT_C$ prolongation.

### Table 66. Daily Oral Morphine Dose Equivalents and Conversion to Oral Methadone

| Daily Oral Morphine Dose Equivalents | Conversion Ratio of Oral Morphine to Oral Methadone |
|---|---|
| < 100 mg | 3:1 (ie, 3 mg morphine:1 mg methadone) |
| 101–300 mg | 5:1 |
| 301–600 mg | 10:1 |
| 601–800 mg | 12:1 |
| 801–1000 mg | 15:1 |
| >1001 mg | 20:1 |

Adapted from Gazelle G, Fine PG. Methadone for pain: #75. *J Palliative Med* 2004;7(2):303–304.

### Table 67. Adjuvant Drugs for Pain Relief in Older Patients

| Class, Drug | Formulations | Starting Dosage | Comments |
|---|---|---|---|
| **Anticonvulsants** (see **Table 60** and p 136) | | | If one does not work, try another |
| **Antidepressants** (see **Table 27**) | | | Use low-dose desipramine or nortryptiline; data on SSRIs lacking |
| Duloxetine (*Cymbalta*) | C: 20, 30, 60 | 60 mg q 24 h | For management of pain associated with diabetic peripheral neuropathy; most common adverse effects: nausea, dry mouth, constipation, diarrhea, urinary hesitancy |
| **Corticosteroids** (see **Table 32**) | | | Low-dose medical management may be helpful in inflammatory conditions |
| **Counterirritants** | | | |
| ✔Camphor-menthol-phenol (*Sarna*)* | lot: camphor 5%, menthol 5%, phenol 5% | prn | May be effective for arthritic pain, but effect limited when pain affects multiple joints; can cause skin injury, especially if used with heat or occlusive dressing |

*(cont.)*

Table 67. Adjuvant Drugs for Pain Relief in Older Patients (cont.)

| Class, Drug | Formulations | Starting Dosage | Comments |
|---|---|---|---|
| ✔Camphor and phenol (*Campho-Phenique*)* | S: camphor 5%, phenol 4.7% | prn | |
| ✔Methylsalicylate and menthol | | | |
| (*Ben-Gay* oint,* *Icy Hot* crm*) | methylsalicylate 18.3%, menthol 16% | 3–4 × /d | Apply to affected area |
| (*Ben-Gay* extra strength crm*) | methylsalicylate 30%, menthol 10% | 3–4 × /d | Apply to affected area |
| ✔Trolamine salicylate (*Aspercreme* rub*) | trolamine salicylate 10% | ≤4 × /d | Apply to affected area |
| **Other** | | | |
| Baclofen (*Lioresal*) | T: 10, 20; Inj | 2.5–5 mg 2–3 × /d | Probably increased sensitivity and decreased clearance; monitor for weakness, urinary dysfunction; avoid abrupt discontinuation because of CNS irritability |
| ✔Capsaicin (eg, *Capsin, Capzasin, No Pain-HP, R-Gel, Zostrix*) | crm, lot, gel, roll-on: 0.025%, 0.075% | 3–4 × /d | Renders skin and joints insensitive by depleting and preventing reaccumulation of substance P in peripheral sensory neurons; may cause burning sensation up to 2 wk; instruct patient to wash hands after application to prevent eye contact; do not apply to open or broken skin |
| ✔Lidocaine (*Lidoderm*) | transdermal Pch 5% | 12 h on/12 h off | Apply over affected area; used for neuropathic pain, may be helpful for low back pain, osteoarthritis |

✔ = preferred for treating older persons.
* Available OTC.
Note: Various adjuvant classes are useful for the treatment of neuropathic pain. TCAs are often helpful for migraine or tension headaches and arthritic conditions. Baclofen is particularly useful for muscle-related problems, such as spasms.

# PALLIATIVE AND END-OF-LIFE CARE

## DEFINITION
"Palliative care is an approach to care which improves quality of life of patients and their families facing life-threatening illnesses, through the prevention and relief of suffering by means of early identification and impeccable assessment and treatment of pain and other problems, physical, psychosocial, and spiritual." (WHO, 2002)

## PRINCIPLES
• Support, educate, and treat both patient and family.
• Address physical, psychologic, social, and spiritual needs.
• Use multidisciplinary team (physicians, nurses, social workers, chaplain, pharmacist, physical and occupational therapists, dietitian, family and caregivers, volunteers).
• Focus on symptom management, comfort, meeting goals, completion of "life business," healing relationships, and bereavement.
• Make care available 24 h/d, 7 d/wk.
• Educate, plan, and document advance directives; health care proxy; family awareness of decisions.
• Coordinate care among various providers. Help integrate potentially curative, disease-modifying, and palliative therapies.
• Offer bereavement support.
• Provide therapeutic environment (palliation can be given in any location).
• Advocate comprehensive palliative care for all dying patients.

## QUALITY OF LIFE
Ways to help patient and family enhance quality of life at the end of life:
• Communicate, listen
• Teach stress management, coping
• Use all available resources
• Support decision making
• Encourage conflict resolution
• Help complete unfinished business
• Urge focus on nonillness-related affairs
• Urge a focus on one day at a time
• Help anticipate grief, losses
• Help focus on attainable goals
• Encourage spiritual practices
• Promote physical, psychologic comfort

## END-OF-LIFE DECISIONS
Follow principles involved in informed decision making (see **Figure 2**).

### Hospice Referral
• Patients, families, or other health care provides can refer, but a physician's certification of limited life expectancy* is required for admission to a hospice program (see **Table 68**).
• Referral is appropriate when curative treatment is no longer indicated (ie, ineffective, too burdensome adverse events) and life is limited to months.
• Hospice must be accepted by the patient or family, or both, and can be rescinded at any time.

- Hospice provides palliative medications, durable medical supplies and equipment, team member visits as needed and desired by patient and family (physician, nurses, home health aide, social worker, chaplain) and volunteer services.
- Optimal hospice care requires adequate time in the program; referral when death is imminent does not take full advantage of hospice care.
- Hospice care is usually delivered in patient's home, but it can be delivered in a nursing home or residential care facility (long-term care, assisted living) or in an inpatient setting (hospice-specific or contracted facility) if acuity or social circumstances warrant.

* Prognosis of ≤6 mo for most hospice programs, and is a requirement for the Medicare Hospice Benefit and Medicaid programs.

### Table 68. Typical Trajectory and Hospice Eligibility for Selected Diseases

| Disease | Typical Determinants for Hospice Eligibility* |
|---|---|
| Cancer | Clinical findings of malignancy with widespread, aggressive, or progressive disease evidenced by increasing symptoms, worsening laboratory values, and/or evidence of metastatic disease<br>Impaired performance status with a Palliative Performance Scale (PPS)† value of ≤70%<br>Refuses further curative therapy or continues to decline in spite of definitive therapy |
| Dementia | FAST Scale† Stage 7 (loss of speech, locomotion, and consciousness) **and**<br>Comorbid or secondary conditions that contribute to structural or functional impairments suggesting a prognosis of ≤6 mo |
| Failure to thrive | BMI (kg/m²) <22<br>Karnofsky† or PPS value <40% |
| End-stage heart disease | Optimally treated with diuretics and vasodilators, which may include ACE inhibitors or combination of hydralazine and nitrates **or** has angina pectoris at rest, resistant to standard nitrate treatment and is either not candidate for or declines invasive procedures **and**<br>Significant symptoms of recurrent HF at rest and classified as NYHA Class IV (ie, unable to carry on any physical activity without symptoms, symptoms present at rest; symptoms increase if any physical activity is undertaken)<br>Additional support needed for treatment-resistant symptomatic supraventricular or ventricular arrhythmia, history of cardiac arrest or resuscitation or unexplained syncope, brain embolism of cardiac origin, concomitant HIV disease, documented ejection fraction of ≤20% |
| End-stage pulmonary disease | Disabling dyspnea at rest, poorly or unresponsive to bronchodilators, resulting in decreased functional capacity, eg, bed to chair existence, fatigue, and cough (documentation of FEV₁, after bronchodilator, <30% of predicted is objective evidence for disabling dyspnea, but is not necessary to obtain) **and**<br>Progression of end-stage pulmonary disease, as evidenced by *prior* increased visits to emergency department or *prior* hospitalization for pulmonary infections and/or respiratory failure (documentation of serial decrease of FEV₁ >40 mL/yr is objective evidence for disease progression, but is not necessary to obtain) **and**<br>Hypoxemia at rest on room air, as evidenced by pO₂ ≤55 mm Hg or O₂ sat ≤88% or hypercapnia, as evidenced by pCO₂ ≥50 mm Hg<br>Additional support needed for cor pulmonale and right heart failure secondary to pulmonary disease, unintentional progressive weight loss of >10% of body weight over preceeding 6 mo, resting tachycardia >100 beats/min |

(cont.)

Table 68. Typical Trajectory and Hospice Eligibility for Selected Diseases (cont.)

| Disease | Typical Determinants for Hospice Eligibility* |
|---|---|
| Acute renal failure | Not seeking dialysis or renal transplant<br>CrCl <10 mL/min (<15 mL/min for diabetes)<br>Serum creatinine >8.0 mg/dL (>6.0 mg/dL for diabetes)<br>Additional support needed for comorbid conditions such as malignancy, chronic lung disease (eg, mechanical ventilation), advanced cardiac disease, advanced liver disease |
| Chronic renal failure | Not seeking dailysis or renal transplant<br>CrCl <10 mL/min (<15 mL/min for diabetes)<br>Serum creatinine >8.0 mg/dL (>6.0 mg/dL for diabetes)<br>Additional support needed for following signs and symptoms of renal failure: uremia, oliguria (<400 mL/day), intractable hyperkalemia (>7.0) not responsive to treatment, uremic pericarditis, hepatorenal syndrome |

* May vary based on fiscal intermediary; additional supportive indications available for most diagnoses. Adapted from Palmetto GBA (http://www.palmettogba.com)

† Scales: Palliative Performance Scale, see p 216; FAST scale, see p 217; Karnofsky Scale, see p 216.

## Advance Directives
Designed to respect patient's autonomy and determine his/her wishes about future life-sustaining medical treatment if unable to indicate wishes.

### Oral Statements
- Conversations with relatives, friends, clinicians are most common form; should be thoroughly documented in medical record for later reference.
- Properly verified oral statements carry same ethical and legal weight as those recorded in writing.

### Instructional Advance Directives (DNR Orders, Living Wills)
- Written instructions regarding the initiation, continuation, withholding, or withdrawal of particular forms of life-sustaining medical treatment.
- May be revoked or altered at any time by the patient.
- Clinicians who comply with such directives are provided legal immunity for such actions.

### Durable Power of Attorney for Health Care or Health Care Proxy
A written document that enables a capable person to appoint someone else to make future medical treatment choices for him or her in the event of decisional incapacity (see Figure 2).

### Key Interventions, Treatment Decisions to Include in Advance Directives
- Resuscitation procedures
- Mechanical respiration
- Chemotherapy, radiation therapy
- Dialysis
- Simple diagnostic tests
- Pain control
- Blood products, transfusions
- Intentional deep sedation

## Withholding or Withdrawing Therapy
- There is no ethical or legal difference between withholding an intervention (not starting it) and withdrawing life-sustaining medical treatment (stopping it after it has been started).
- Beginning a treatment does not preclude stopping it later; a time-limited trial may be appropriate.

- Palliative care should not be limited, even if life-sustaining treatments are withdrawn or withheld.
- Decisions on artificial feeding should be based on the same criteria applied to ventilators and other medical treatment.

**Euthanasia**
- Active euthanasia: direct intervention, such as lethal injection, intended to hasten a patient's death; a criminal act of homicide.
- Passive euthanasia: withdrawal or withholding of unwanted or unduly burdensome life-sustaining treatment; appropriate in certain circumstances.
- Assisted suicide: the patient's intentional, willful ending of his/her own life with the assistance of another; a criminal offense in most states.

## MANAGEMENT OF COMMON END-OF-LIFE SYMPTOMS
### Pain
- The most distressing symptom for patients and caregivers.
- If intent is to relieve suffering, the risk that sufficient medication appropriately titrated will produce an unintended effect (hastening death) is morally acceptable (double effect).
- Primary goal: to alleviate suffering at end of life. See Pain (p 141) for assessment and interventions.
- Alternate routes may be needed, eg, transdermal, transmucosal, rectal, vaginal, topical, epidural, and intrathecal.
- Recommend expert pain management consult if pain not adequately relieved with standard analgesic guidelines and interventions.
- Additional treatment may include:
  ○ radionuclides and bisphosphonates (for metastatic bone pain).
  ○ treatments (eg, radiotherapy, chemotherapy) directed at source of pain.
- Pain crisis: Sedation at end of life for intractable pain and suffering is an important option to discuss with patients. Ketamine (*Ketalar*) 0.1 mg/kg IV bolus. Repeat as needed q 5 min. Follow with infusion of 0.015 mg/kg/min IV (SC if IV access not available at 0.3–0.5 mg/kg). Decrease opioid dose by 50%. A benzodiazepine may be useful. Observe for problems with increased secretions and treat (see p 155).

### Weakness, Fatigue
*Nonpharmacologic:*
- Modify environment to decrease energy expenditure (eg, placement of phone, bedside commode, and drinks).
- Adjust room temperature to patient's comfort.
- Teach energy-conserving techniques (eg, reordering tasks—eating first, resting, then bathing).
- Modify daily procedures (eg, sitting while showering, not standing).
*Pharmacologic:*
- Treat remediable causes such as pain, medication toxicity, insomnia, anemia, and depression.
- Consider psychostimulants (eg, dextroamphetamine [*Dexedrine*] 2.5 mg po qam or bid, methylphenidate [*Ritalin*] 5–10 mg po qam or bid, or modafinil [*Provigil*] 200 mg qam); monitor for signs of psychosis, agitation, or sleep disturbance.

## Dysphagia
### Nonpharmacologic:
- Feed small, frequent amounts of pureed or soft foods.
- Avoid spicy, salty, acidic, sticky, and extremely hot or cold foods.
- Keep head of bed elevated for 30 min after eating.
- Instruct patient to wear dentures and to chew thoroughly.
- Use suction machine when necessary.

### Pharmacologic:
- For painful mucositis: 1:2:8 mixture of diphenhydramine elixir: lidocaine [2%–4%]: magnesium-aluminum hydroxide (eg, *Maalox*) as a swish-and-swallow suspension before meals.
- For candidiasis: clotrimazole 10 mg troches, 5 doses/d, **or** fluconazole 150 mg po followed by 100 mg po qd × 5 d.
- For severe halitosis: antimicrobial mouthwash; fastidious oral and dental care; treat putative respiratory tract infection with broad-spectrum antibiotics.

## Dyspnea
### Nonpharmacologic:
- Teach positions to facilitate breathing, elevate head of bed.
- Teach relaxation techniques.
- Eliminate smoke and allergens.
- Assure brisk air circulation (facial breeze) with a room fan; oxygen is indicated only for symptomatic hypoxemia (ie, $SaO_2$ <90% by pulse oximetry).

### Pharmacologic:
- Opioids: oral morphine concentration (20 mg/mL): 1/4 to 1/2 mL sl/po; repeat in 10–15 min prn); nebulized morphine 2.5 mg in 2–4 mL NS **or** fentanyl 25–50 μg in 2–4 mL NS; **or** IV morphine 1 mg or equivalent opioid q 5–10 min.
- Bronchodilators (see **Table 80**).
- Diuretics, if evidence of volume overload (see **Table 20**).
- Anxiolytics (eg, lorazepam po/sl/SC 0.5–2 mg q 2–4 h or prn); titrate slowly to effect.

## Constipation
Most common cause: adverse effects of opioids, medications with anticholinergic adverse effects (see **Table 39**). Use stimulant or osmotic laxative.

## Bowel Obstruction
### Indications for Radiographic Evaluation:
- To differentiate between constipation and mechanical obstruction
- To confirm the obstruction, determine site and nature if surgery is being considered
### Nonpharmacologic Management:
- Nasogastric intubation: only if surgery is being considered, for high-level obstructions, and poor response to pharmacotherapy
- Percutaneous venting gastrostomy: for high-level obstructions and profuse vomiting not responsive to antiemetics
- Palliative surgery
- Hydration: IV or hypodermoclysis

*Pharmacologic Management (aimed at specific symptoms):*
- Nausea and vomiting: haloperidol (*Haldol*) po, IM 0.5–5 mg (≤10 mg) q 4–8 h prn; ondansetron (*Zofran*) IV (over 2–5 min) 4 mg q 12 h, po 8 mg q 12 h (L) [Inj; T: 4, 8, 24; S: 4 mg/5 mL], but costly; see also **Table 40**.
- Spasm, pain, and vomiting: scopolamine IM, IV, SC 0.3–0.65 mg q 4–6 h prn; oral 0.4–0.8 mg q 4–8 h prn; transdermal 2.5 cm² patch applied behind the ear q 3 d (L) [Inj; T: 0.4; patch 1.5 mg] or hyoscyamine (*Levsin/SL*) sublingual [T: 0.125; S: 0.125 mg/mL] 0.125–0.25 tid–qid.
- Diarrhea and excessive secretions: loperamide (*Imodium A-D*) see **Table 41**; octreotide (*Sandostatin*) SC 0.15–0.3 mg q 12 h (L) [Inj], very expensive.
- Pain: see **Table 65**.
- Inflammation due to malignant obstruction: dexamethasone (*Decadron*) oral: 4 mg qid × 5–7 d.

## Excessive Secretions
*Nonpharmacologic:* Positioning and suctioning, as needed
*Pharmacologic:* Glycopyrrolate 0.1–0.4 mg IV/SC q 4 h prn *or* scopolomine 0.3–0.6 mg SC prn *or* transdermal scopolomine patch q 72 h *or* atropine 0.3–0.5 mg SC, sublingual, nebulized q 4 h prn

## Cough
See Respiratory Diseases (p 167).

## Nausea, Vomiting
See Gastrointestinal Diseases (p 70).

## Malnutrition, Dehydration
See also Malnutrition (p 114).
*Nonpharmacologic:*
- Educate patient and family on effects of disease progression resulting in lack of appetite and weight loss.
- Promote interest, enjoyment in meals (eg, alcoholic beverage if desired, involve patient in meal planning, small frequent feedings, cold or semi-frozen nutritional drinks).
- Good oral care is important.
*Pharmacologic:*
- Corticosteroids: Dexamethasone 1–2 mg po tid; methylprednisolone 1–2 mg po bid; prednisone 5 mg po tid.
- Hormone therapy: Megestrol acetate 200–800 mg qd.

## Altered Mental Status, Delirium
See Delirium (p 42).

## Anxiety, Depression
- Provide opportunity to discuss feelings, fears, existential concerns
- Referral to appropriate team members (spiritual, nursing)
- Medicate (see Anxiety, p 21, and Depression, p 49).

Source: Fine P. *Hospice Companion—Processes to Optimize Care During the Last Phase of Life.* 2d ed. Scottsdale, AZ: VistaCare, Inc.; 2000.

**PREOPERATIVE CARE**
**Cardiac Risk Assessment**

**Figure 9. Reducing Cardiac Risk in Noncardiac Surgery**

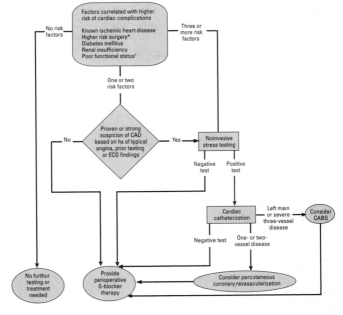

\* Intraperitoneal, intrathoracic, or suprainguinal vascular procedures
† Inability to walk 4 blocks or climb 2 flights of stairs
Source: Adapted from Fleisher LA, Eagle KA. Lowering cardiac risk in noncardiac surgery. *N Engl J Med* 2001;
345:1677–1682. Copyright © 2001, Massachusetts Medical Society. All rights reserved. Adapted with permission 2003.

**Pulmonary Risk Assessment**
Assessing the patient for risk of pulmonary complications (respiratory failure,
pneumonia, atelectasis) includes the following risk factors:
*Smoking:* To lower risk, patients should quit at least 8 wk before surgery.
*COPD:* Bronchodilators, physical therapy, antibiotics, and corticosteroids given
preoperatively can reduce risk.

*ASA Class:*  III—severe systemic disease; IV—life-threatening systemic disease;
V—moribund.
*Surgical Site:*  Upper abdominal, thoracic, >3-h surgeries pose the greatest increased
risk.

Note: Routine spirometry has not been shown to be useful in risk assessment.

## Other Assessments
*Anticoagulation Status:*  See pp 18–20.
*Cognitive Status:*  Unrecognized dementia is a risk factor for postoperative delirium.
Measure preoperative cognitive status with Mini-Cog (see p 204) or MMSE.
*Nutritional Status:*  Poor nutritional status can impair wound healing. Measure height,
weight, serum albumin.
*Routine Laboratory Tests:*  Recommended: Hb and hematocrit, electrolytes, creatinine,
BUN, ECG, CXR, albumin. Optional: CBC, platelets, ABG, PT, PTT.
*Cataract Surgery:*  Routine laboratory testing or cardiopulmonary risk assessment is
unneccessary for cataract surgery performed under local anesthesia.
*Advance Directives:*  Establish or update.

## PERIOPERATIVE MANAGEMENT
### β-Blocker Use
For patients at risk for cardiac complications (see **Figure 9**), begin β-blocker agent (eg,
atenolol or bisoprolol) po 1–2 wk before surgery to achieve heart rate <70 beats/min.
Continue therapy until 2 wk after surgery, with a goal of <80 beats/min in the
postoperative period. Withhold β-blockers if heart rate is <55 beats/min; SBP <100; or
the patient has asthma, decompensated HF, or third degree heart block.

### Endocarditis Prophylaxis
Depends on cardiac condition and type of procedure (see pp 160–161).

### DVT Prophylaxis (see **Table 12**)

### Common Problems to Monitor
- Confusion: see p 42
- Intra- and postoperative coronary
  events: postoperative ECG to check
- Malnutrition: see p 114
- Pain: see p 141
- Polypharmacy: review medications daily
- Pulmonary complications: minimized by
  incentive spirometry, coughing, early
  ambulation
- Rehabilitation: encourage early mobility
- Skin breakdown: see p 180

## DISCHARGE PLANNING
- Ideally, all team members should participate in discharge planning, beginning early in
  the hospitalization.
- Physician/general practitioner should provide discharge summary and orders,
  including medications.
- Site of care after discharge should be warranted by patient's needs (see **Table 69**).
- See also Housing Alternatives, p 5.

| Table 69. Sites of Post-Hospital Care | | |
|---|---|---|
| **Site** | **Requirements** | **Funding** |
| Inpatient rehabilitation facility or transitional care unit of a nursing home | Patient can tolerate 3 h of rehabilitation therapy/d requiring multiple disciplines (eg, PT, OT, speech therapy) | Medicare Part A pays 100% of charges for days 1–20, patient pays $105/d for days 21–100 with Part A covering the rest, patient pays 100% after day 100 |
| Skilled nursing facility | Patient requires skilled nursing care and cannot tolerate 3 h of therapy/d | Same as above for rehabilitation services associated with hospitalization; long-term stays principally financed out-of-pocket or by Medicaid |
| Home | Physician must certify that patient is able to only occasionally leave the home at great effort | Medicare Part A pays for most nonphysician professional services (eg, nursing, OT, PT); very limited coverage for attendant care (eg, cooking, cleaning) |
| Home/assisted living | Patient able to manage ADLs independently or with informal help | Medicare Part B pays for 80% of most outpatient medical services |
| Hospice (home or facility-based); see also housing alternatives, p 5 | Physician must certify that patient's life expectancy <6 mo (see **Table 68**) | Medicare Part A pays for most professional services and medications related to terminal illness; physician services covered under Part B |

# PREVENTION

## PREVENTIVE TESTS AND PROCEDURES

Table 70. Recommended Primary and Secondary Disease Prevention for Persons Aged 65 and Over

| Preventive Strategy | Frequency |
| --- | --- |
| **USPSTF\* Recommendations for Primary Prevention** | |
| Bone densitometry (women) | at least once after age 65 |
| BP screening | yearly |
| Influenza immunization | yearly |
| Lipid disorder screening | every 5 yr, more often in CAD, diabetes mellitus, PAD, prior stroke |
| Obesity (height and weight) | yearly |
| Pneumonia immunization | once at age 65\*\* |
| Smoking cessation | at every office visit |
| Tetanus immunization | every 10 yr |
| **USPSTF\* Recommendations for Secondary Prevention** | |
| Alcohol abuse screening | unspecified but should be done periodically |
| Depression screening | unspecified but should be done periodically |
| Diabetes mellitus screening | at least once in persons with HTN or hyperlipidemia |
| FOBT and/or sigmoidoscopy or colonoscopy | yearly/every 3–5 yr/every 10 yr |
| Hearing impairment screening | yearly |
| Mammography, clinical breast examination\*\*\* | every 1–2 yr |
| Pap smear† | at least every 3 yr |
| Visual impairment screening | yearly |
| **Other‡ Recommendations for Primary Prevention** | |
| Aspirin to prevent MI | daily |
| Measurement of serum c-reactive protein | at least once in persons with one CAD risk factor |
| Omega-3 fatty acids to prevent MI, stroke | at least 2x/wk (see MI care, p 27) |
| **Other‡ Recommendations for Secondary Prevention** | |
| Skin examination | yearly |
| Breast self-examination | monthly |
| Cognitive impairment screening | yearly |
| Electron-beam computed tomography (EBCT) | at least once in persons with one CAD risk factor |
| PSA and digital rectal examination | yearly |
| TSH in women | yearly |

\* US Preventive Services Task Force. See http://www.ahrq.gov/clinic/uspstfix.htm
\*\* Consider repeating pneumococcal vaccine every 6–7 yr.
\*\*\* Mammograms to age 70 are virtually universally recommended; many organizations, including the USPSTF, recommend that mammography should be continued in women over 70 who have a reasonable life expectancy.
† Pap smear testing can be stopped in most women after age 65. See p 199. Women without a cervix should not have pap smears.
‡ Not endorsed by USPSTF for all older adults, but recommended in selected patients or by other professional organizations.

## ENDOCARDITIS PROPHYLAXIS (AHA GUIDELINES)
### Antibiotic Regimens Recommended (see Table 71)

### Cardiac Conditions Requiring Prophylaxis
*High-Risk Category:*  Prosthetic heart valves, previous endocarditis, surgical systemic pulmonary shunts
*Moderate-Risk Category:*  Acquired valvular dysfunction (eg, rheumatic heart disease), hypertrophic cardiomyopathy, mitral valve prolapse with valvular regurgitation and/or thickened leaflets, most congenital heart malformations

### Procedures Warranting Prophylaxis
*Dental:*  Extractions, periodontal procedures, implants and reimplants, root canals, subgingival placement of antibiotic fibers or strips, initial placement of orthodontic bands but not brackets, intraligamentary local anesthetic injections, teeth cleaning where bleeding is expected
*Respiratory Tract:*  Tonsillectomy and/or adenoidectomy, rigid bronchoscopy, surgery involving respiratory mucosa
*GI Tract:*  Esophageal varices sclerotherapy, esophageal stricture dilation, endoscopic retrograde cholangiography with biliary obstruction, biliary tract surgery, surgery involving intestinal mucosa
*GU Tract:*  Prostatic surgery, cystoscopy, urethral dilation

### Cardiac Conditions Not Requiring Prophylaxis
Previous CABG surgery; mitral valve prolapse without valvular regurgitation; physiologic, functional, or innocent heart murmurs; previous rheumatic fever without valvular dysfunction; cardiac pacemakers; implanted defibrillators; isolated secundum atrial septal defect; surgical repair of atrial or ventricular septal defect

### Procedures Not Warranting Prophylaxis
*Dental:*  Restorative dentistry, local anesthetic injections, intracanal endodontic treatment, rubber dam placement, suture removal, placement of removable prosthodontic or orthodontic appliances, oral impressions, fluoride treatments, oral radiographs, orthodontic appliance adjustment
*Respiratory Tract:*  Endotracheal intubation, flexible bronchoscopy (prophylaxis optional for high-risk patients), ear tube insertion
*GI Tract:*  Transesophageal echocardiography, endoscopy (prophylaxis optional for high-risk patients)
*GU Tract:*  Vaginal hysterectomy (prophylaxis optional for high-risk patients), urethral catheterization of uninfected tissue
*Other:*  Cardiac catheterization, balloon angioplasty

**Table 71. Endocarditis Prophylaxis Regimens**

| Situation | Regimen |
|---|---|
| **Dental, oral, respiratory tract, or esophageal procedures** | |
| Standard general prophylaxis | Amoxicillin 2.0 g po 1 h before procedure |
| Unable to take oral medications | Ampicillin 2.0 g IM or IV ≤30 min before procedure |
| Allergic to penicillin | Clindamycin 600 mg or cephalexin 2.0 g or cefadroxil 2.0 g or azithromycin 500 mg or clarithromycin 500 mg po 1 h before procedure |
| Allergic to penicillin and unable to take oral medications | Clindamycin 600 mg or cefazolin 1.0 g IM or IV ≤30 min before procedure |
| **GU or GI procedures** | |
| High-risk patients | Ampicillin 2.0 g IM or IV + 1 gentamicin 1.5 mg/kg IV or IM (not to exceed 120 mg) ≤30 min before procedure; 6 h later, ampicillin 1.0 g IM or IV or amoxicillin 1.0 g po |
| High-risk patients allergic to ampicillin or amoxicillin | Vancomycin 1.0 g IV over 1–2 h + gentamicin 1.5 mg/kg IV or IM (not to exceed 120 mg); complete injection or infusion ≤30 min before procedure |
| Moderate-risk patients | Amoxicillin 2.0 g po 1 h before procedure or ampicillin 2.0 g IM or IV ≤30 min before procedure |
| Moderate-risk patients allergic to ampicillin or amoxicillin | Vancomycin 1.0 g IV over 1–2 h, complete infusion ≤30 min before procedure |

Note: See **Table 51** for details about antibiotics.
Source: Dajani AS, Taubert KA, Wilson W, et al. Prevention of bacterial endocarditis: Recommendations by the American Heart Association. *JAMA.* 1997;277:1794–1801. Copyright 1997, American Medical Association. All rights reserved. Reprinted with permission.

## PROPHYLAXIS FOR DENTAL PATIENTS WITH TOTAL JOINT REPLACEMENTS (TJR)
**Conditions Requiring:**  Inflammatory arthropathies (eg, rheumatoid arthritis, systemic lupus erythematosus); disease-, drug-, or radiation-induced immunosuppression; type 1 diabetes mellitus; first 2 yr following joint replacement; previous prosthetic joint infection; malnourishment; hemophilia
**Conditions Not Requiring:**  Patients > 2 yr after TJR who do not have one of the above conditions; patients with pins, plates, or screws
**Dental Procedures Warranting:**  see those listed on p 160 for endocarditis
**Suggested Prophylactic Regimens: (all given 1 h before procedure)**
• Not allergic to penicillin: Amoxicillin, cephalexin, or cephradine 2.0 g po
• Not allergic to penicillin and unable to take oral medications: Ampicillin 2.0 g or cefazolin 1.0 g IM or IV
• Allergic to penicillin: Clindamycin 600 mg po
• Allergic to penicillin and unable to take oral medications: Clindamycin 600 mg IV

Source: Modified from American Dental Association and American Academy of Orthopaedic Surgeons. Antibiotic prophylaxis for dental patients with total joint replacements. *JADA,* 1997; 128(7):1004–1007. Copyright © 1997 American Dental Association. All rights reserved. Adapted 2003 with permission.

## EXERCISE PRESCRIPTION
### Before Giving an Exercise Prescription
Screen patient for:
- Musculoskeletal problems: Decreased flexibility, muscular rigidity, weakness, pain, ill-fitting shoes
- Cardiac disease: Consider stress test if patient is beginning a vigorous exercise program and is sedentary with ≥2 cardiac risk factors (male gender, hypertension, smoking, diabetes mellitus, dyslipidemia, obesity, family hx, sedentary life style).

### Individualize the Prescription
Specify short- and long-term goals; include the following components:

***Flexibility:*** Static stretching; daily, >15 sec per muscle group

***Endurance:*** Walking, cycling, swimming at 50%–75% of max HR (220 – age for men; 220 – [0.6 × age] for women); 3–4 ×/wk; goal of 20–30 min duration

***Strength:*** Muscle resistance (weight training); 3 sets (8–15 repetitions) per muscle group 2–3 ×/wk

***Balance:*** Tai Chi, dance, yoga, postural awareness; 1–3 ×/wk

***Patient Information:*** See http://www.niapublications.org/exercisebook/index.asp
See also Assessment and Management of Falls, p 65.

# PROSTATE DISORDERS

## BENIGN PROSTATIC HYPERPLASIA
### Evaluation
Detailed medical hx focusing on the urinary tract physical examination, including a digital rectal examination and a focused neurologic examination; UA; measurement of serum creatinine. Measurement of PSA is optional.

### Management
***Mild Symptoms:*** (eg, AUA score ≤7; see p 217) watchful waiting

***Moderate to Severe Symptoms:*** (eg, AUA score ≥8; see p 217) medical or surgical treatment

***Medical Treatment:*** Combining drugs from different classes may be more effective than single-agent therapy

- $\alpha_1$-**Blockers** (note: sildenafil [*Viagra*], vardenafil [*LEVITRA*], or tadalafil [*Cialis*] can cause hypotension in men receiving $\alpha_1$-blockers):

  **Nonselective:**
  - Terazosin (*Hytrin*) advance as tolerated—days 1–3, 1 mg/d hs; days 4–7, 2 mg; days 8–14, 5 mg; day 15 and beyond, 10 mg [T: 1, 2, 5, 10]
  - Doxazosin (*Cardura*) start 0.5 mg with max of 16 mg/d [T: 1, 2, 4, 8]
  - Prazosin (*Minipress*) start 1 mg/d (first dose hs) or bid with max 20 mg/d [T: 1, 2, 5]

  **Selective:**
  - Tamsulosin (*Flomax*) 0.4 mg half-hour after the same meal each day and increase to 0.8 mg if no response in 2–4 wk [T: 0.4]
  - Alfuzosin ER (*Uroxatral*) 10 mg after the same meal every day [T: 10]

- **5-$\alpha$ Reductase inhibitors:**
  - Finasteride (*Proscar*) 5 mg/d [T: 5]
  - Dutasteride (*Avodart*) 0.5 mg/d [C: 0.5]

***Surgical Management:*** Indicated if recurrent UTI, recurrent or persistent gross hematuria, bladder stones, or renal insufficiency are clearly secondary to BPH or as indicated by symptoms, patient preference, or failure of medical treatment. Options are:
- Transurethral resection of the prostate (TURP).
- Transurethral incision of the prostate (TUIP), which is limited to prostates whose estimated resected tissue weight (if done by TURP) would be 30 g or less.
- Open prostatectomy for large glands.

Source: McConnell JD, Barry MJ, Bruskewitz RC, et al. *Benign Prostatic Hyperplasia: Diagnosis and Treatment.* Clinical Practice Guideline No. 8. Rockville, MD: Agency for Health Care Policy and Research, Public Health Service, US Dept. of Health and Human Services, February 1994. AHCPR Publication No. 94-0582.

## PROSTATE CANCER
**PSA:** See **Table 70**.

### Histology
- Gleason score 2–6 has low 15–20 yr morbidity and mortality; watchful waiting usually appropriate.
- Gleason score ≥7, higher PSA and younger age associated with higher morbidity and mortality; best treatment strategy (surgery, radiation, androgen suppression, etc) is not known.

## Pharmacotherapy

- Use hormonal therapy in ≥ Stage III or T3 (tumor extension beyond prostate capsule); treatment of earlier stage disease is controversial.
- In case of relapse:
  - Withdrawal of antiandrogen may induce remission.
  - Patients often respond when changed to a second antiandrogen.
  - When antiandrogens no longer control disease, adrenal suppression with aminoglutethimide or ketoconazole and hydrocortisone replacement may be effective.

## Therapy for Metastatic Bone Disease

In hormone-therapy cancer and bone metastasis, zoledronic acid reduces the proportion of patients with skeletal-related events or fracture.

Table 72. Common Drugs for Prostate Cancer Therapy

| Class, Agent | Dosage | Metabolism | Adverse Events |
|---|---|---|---|
| **LH-RH agonists** | | | |
| Goserelin acetate implant (*Zoladex*) | 3.6 mg SC q 28 d or 10.8 mg q 3 mo | Rapid urinary and hepatic excretion, no dose adjustment in renal impairment | Hot flushes (60%), breast swelling, libido change, impotence, nausea |
| Leuprolide acetate (*Lupron Depot*) | 7.5 mg IM q mo or 22.5 mg q 3 mo or 30 mg q 4 mo | Unknown; active metabolites for 4–12 wk, dose-dependent | Certain symptoms (obstruction, spinal cord compression, bone pain) may be exacerbated early in treatment; adverse events: hot flushes (60%), edema (12%), pain (7%), nausea, vomiting, impotence, dyspnea, asthenia (all 5%), thrombosis, PE, MI (all 1%); headache as high as 32% |
| Triptorelin (*Trelstar Depot, Trelstar LA*) | Depot: 37.5 mg q 28 d IM LA: 11.25 mg q 84 d | Hepatic metabolism and renal excretion (42% as intact peptide) | Hot flushes, ↑ glucose, ↓ Hb, ↓ RBC, ↑ alk phos, ↑ ALT/AST, skeletal pain, ↑ BUN |
| **Antiandrogens** | | | Class adverse events: |
| Bicalutamide (*Casodex*) | 50 mg po qd [T: 50] | Metabolized in liver, excreted in urine; half-life 10 d at steady state | nausea, hot flushes, breast pain, gynecomastia, hematuria, diarrhea, liver enzyme elevations, galactorrhea |
| Flutamide (*Eulexin*) | 125 mg cap 2 po q 8 h [C: 125] | Renally excreted; half-life 5–6 h | Greatest GI toxicity in the class; severe liver dysfunction reported |
| Nilutamide (*Nilandron*) | 300 mg for 30 d, then 150 mg po qd [T: 50] | 80% protein bound; liver metabolism, renal excretion; half-life 40–60 h | Delayed light adaptation |
| **GnRH antagonist** | | | |
| Abarelix (*Plenaxis*) | 100 mg IM q 28 d | Liver metabolism, 13% renal excretion; half-life 13 d | Hypersensitivity 4%, prolonged QT interval; use limited to initial treatment of advanced cancer |

# PSYCHOTIC DISORDERS

## DIAGNOSIS
### Differential Diagnosis
- Bipolar affective disorder
- Delirium
- Dementia
- Drugs: eg, antiparkinsonian agents, anticholinergics, benzodiazepines or alcohol (including withdrawal), stimulants, corticosteroids, cardiac drugs (eg, digitalis), opioid analgesics
- Late-life delusional (paranoid) disorder
- Major depression
- Physical disorders: hypo- or hyperglycemia, hypo- or hyperthyroidism, sodium or potassium imbalance, Cushing's syndrome, Parkinson's disease, $B_{12}$ deficiency, sleep deprivation, AIDS
- Pain, untreated
- Schizophrenia
- Structural brain lesions: tumor or stroke
- Seizure disorder: eg, temporal lobe

### Risk Factors for Psychotic Symptoms in Elderly Persons
Chronic bed rest, cognitive impairment, female gender, sensory impairment, social isolation

## MANAGEMENT
- Alleviate underlying physical causes.
- Address identifiable psychosocial triggers.
- If psychotic symptoms are severe, frightening, or may affect safety, use antipsychotic.
- Olanzapine, quetiapine, risperidone are first choice because of fewer adverse events (TD extremely high in elderly patients taking typical antipsychotics).

### Table 73. Representative Antipsychotic Medications

| Class, Agent | Dosage* | Formulations | Comments (Metabolism) |
|---|---|---|---|
| **Atypical Antipsychotics** | | | |
| Aripiprazole (*Abilify*) | 10–15 (1) initially; max 30/d | T: 10, 15, 20, 30 | Less geriatrics experience; potential for somnolence; wait 2 wk between dose changes (CYP2D6, 3A4) (L) |
| Clozapine (*Clozaril*) | 25–150 (1) | T: 25, 100 | May be useful for parkinsonism and TD; sedation, orthostasis, anticholinergic effects, agranulocytosis, weight gain; high risk of diabetes mellitus and dyslipidemia (L) |
| ✔Olanzapine (*Zyprexa*) | 2.5–10 (1) | T: 2.5, 5, 7.5, 10, 15, 20; disintegrating tab: 5, 10, 15, 20 | Sedation, anticholinergic effects at high doses, high risk of weight gain, hyperglycemia, risk of diabetes mellitus, risk of cerebrovascular adverse events; dose-related EPS (L) |

✔ = preferred for treating older persons.
* Total mg/d (frequency/d).

(cont.)

#### Table 73. Representative Antipsychotic Medications (cont.)

| Class, Agent | Dosage* | Formulations | Comments (Metabolism) |
|---|---|---|---|
| ✔Quetiapine (*Seroquel*) | 25–800 (1–2) | T: 25, 100, 200, 300 | Sedation, orthostasis, no dose-related EPS; intermediate risk of diabetes mellitus and dyslipidemia; limited geriatric data (L, K) |
| ✔Risperidone (*Risperdal*) | 0.5–1 (1–2) | T: 0.25, 0.5, 1, 2, 3, 4 scored; S: 1 mg/mL | Orthostasis, dose-related EPS; caution in patients at risk of stroke, risk of cerebrovascular adverse events, intermediate risk of diabetes mellitus and dyslipidemia; IM not for acute treatment; do not exceed 6 mg (L, K) |
| Ziprasidone (*Geodon*) | 20–80 (1–2) | IM long-acting: 25, 37.5, and 50 mg/2 mL C: 20, 40, 60, 80 IM: 20 mg/mL | May increase QT$_c$; very limited geriatric data (L) |
| **Low Potency** | | | |
| Thioridazine (eg, *Mellaril*) | 25–200 (1–3) | T: 10, 15, 25, 50, 100, 150, 200; S: 30 mg/mL | Anticholinergic effects, orthostasis, QT$_c$ prolongation, sedation, TD; for acute use only (L, K) |
| **Intermediate Potency** | | | |
| Loxapine (*Loxitane*) | 2.5–20 (1–3) | C: 5, 10, 25, 50; S: 25 mg/mL | Anticholinergic effects, orthostasis, sedation, TD; for acute use only (L, K) |
| **High Potency** | | | |
| Haloperidol (*Haldol*) | 0.5–2 (1–3); depot 100–200 mg IM q 4 wk | T: 0.5, 1, 2, 5, 10, 20; S: conc 2 mg/mL; Inj | EPS, TD; for acute use only (L, K) |

✔ = preferred for treating older persons.
* Total mg/d (frequency/d).

#### Table 74. Management of Adverse Events of Antipsychotic Medications

| Adverse Event | Treatment | Comment |
|---|---|---|
| Drug-induced parkinsonism | Lower dose or switch to atypical antipsychotic | Often dose related |
| Akathisia (motor restlessness) | Switch to atypical antipsychotic, β-blocker (eg, propranolol [*Inderal*] 20–40 mg/d) or low-dose benzodiazepine (eg, lorazepam 0.5 mg bid) | Also seen with atypical antipsychotics; more likely with traditional agents |
| Hypotension | Slow titration; reduce dose; change drug class | More common with low-potency agents |
| Sedation | Reduce dose; give at bedtime; change drug class | More common with low-potency agents |
| TD | Stop drug (if possible); change to atypical antipsychotic | Increased risk in elderly; may be irreversible |

Note: Periodic (q 4 mo) reevaluation of antipsychotic dose and ongoing need is important (see OBRA Regulations, p 219). Older persons are particularly sensitive to adverse events of antipsychotic drugs. They are also at higher risk of developing TD. Periodic use of an adverse-event scale such as the AIMS (p 210) is highly recommended.

## ALLERGIC RHINITIS
### Definition
- The most common atopic disorder.
- Symptoms include rhinorrhea; sneezing; and irritated eyes, nose, and mucous membranes.
- May be seasonal, but in older people is more often perennial.
- Postnasal drip, mainly from chronic rhinitis, is the most common cause of chronic cough.

### Therapy
***Nonpharmacologic:*** Saline and sodium bicarbonate nasal irrigation may be helpful (eg, Sinu*Cleanse*); avoid allergens, eliminate pets and their dander, dehumidify to reduce molds; reduce outdoor exposures during pollen season; reduce house dust mites by encasing pillows and mattresses. Arachnocides reduce mites.

***Pharmacologic:*** Target therapy to symptoms and on whether symptoms are seasonal or perennial; see **Table 75** and **Table 76**.

### Table 75. Choosing Therapy for Allergic Rhinitis or Conjunctivitis

| Agent or Class | Rhinitis | Sneezing | Pruritus | Congestion | Eye Symptoms |
|---|---|---|---|---|---|
| Nasal steroids* | +++ | +++ | ++ | ++ | ++ |
| Ipratropium, nasal* | ++ | | | | 0 |
| Antihistamines**† | ++ | ++ | ++ | + | ++ |
| Pseudoephedrine, nasal‡ | | | | ++++ | 0 |
| Cromolyn, nasal† | + | + | + | + | 0 |
| Leukotriene modifiers | + | 0 | 0 | ++ | ++ |

Note: 0 = drug is not effective; the number of "+'s" grades the drug's effectiveness.

\* Effective in seasonal, perennial, and vasomotor rhinitis.

\*\* Better in seasonal than in perennial rhinitis; nasal, ocular, and oral forms; ocular form effective only for eye symptoms, and nasal form only for nasal symptoms.

† Start before allergy season.

‡ Topical therapy rapid in onset but results in rebound if used for more than a few days; facilitates use of nasal steroids and sleep during severe attacks.

### Table 76. Drug Therapy for Allergic Rhinitis or Conjunctivitis

| Type, Drug | Geriatric Dosage | Formulations | Geriatric Half-Life | Adverse Events |
|---|---|---|---|---|
| **H₁-Receptor Antagonists or Antihistamines** | | | | Class adverse events: |
| ✔Azelastine (*Astelin*) (*Optivar*) | 2 spr bid* <br> 1 gtt OU qid | topical spr 0.1%, 100 spr ophthalmic 0.05% | 22–25 h | bitter taste, nasal burning, sneezing (nasal preparations), eye burning, stinging (ocular preparations) |
| ✔Cetirizine (*Zyrtec*) | 5 mg/d (max) | T: 5, 10; syr 5 mg/5 mL | Prolonged | |
| ✔Desloratadine (*Clarinex*) | 5 mg | T: 5 | 27 h | |

*(cont.)*

**Table 76. Drug Therapy for Allergic Rhinitis or Conjunctivitis (cont.)**

| Type, Drug | Geriatric Dosage | Formulations | Geriatric Half-Life | Adverse Events |
|---|---|---|---|---|
| Emedastine (*Emadine*) | 1 gtt OU qid | 0.05% | | |
| Fexofenadine (✔*Allegra*, *Allegra-D***) | 60 mg po bid; once a day if CrCl <40; D not recommended | T: 30, 60, 180; C: 60 | 14 h | |
| Levocabastine (*Livostin*) | 1 gtt OU qid | 0.05% | | |
| Loratadine (✔*Claritin*, *Claritin-D*,** generic, OTC) | 5–10 mg qd; D not recommended | T: 10; rapid-disintegrating tab 10 mg; syr 1 mg/mL | Metabolites >12 d; wide variation | |
| Chlorpheniramine (eg, *ChlorTrimeton*) | 8–12 mg bid | T: 4, 8, 12; ChT: 2; CR: 8, 12; S: 2 mg/5 mL | 20 h, longer with kidney dysfunction | Sedation, dry mouth, confusion, urinary retention; dries lung secretions |
| Diphenhydramine (eg, *Benadryl*) | 25–50 mg bid | T: 25, 50; S: elixir 12.5 mg/mL | 13.5 h | Same as chlorpheniramine |
| Hydroxyzine (eg, *Atarax*) | 25–30 mg bid | T: 10, 25, 50 | 30 h | Same as chlorpheniramine |
| **Decongestants** | | | | |
| Pseudoephedrine (eg, *Sudafed*, combinations) | 60 mg po q 4–6 h | T: 30, 60; SR: 120; S: elixir 30 mg/5 mL | 2–16 h; varies with urine pH | Arrhythmia, insomnia, anxiety, restlessness, elevated BP, urinary retention in men |
| **Nasal Steroids** | | | | |
| Beclomethasone (eg, *Beconase*, *Vancenase*) | 1 spr bid–qid* | topical spr 16 g (80 spr) | Rapid absorption; hepatic metabolism | Class adverse events: nasal burning, sneezing, bleeding; septal perforation (rare); fungal overgrowth (rare); no significant systemic effects |
| Budesonide (eg, *Rhinocort*) | 2 spr bid or 4 qd* | 7 g (200 spr) | | |
| Dexamethasone (eg, *Dexacort*) | 2 spr bid or tid* | 25 mL (200 spr) | | |
| Flunisolide (eg, *Nasalide*, *Nasarel*) | 2–4 spr bid or tid* | 25 mL (200 spr) | | |
| Fluticasone (eg, *Flonase*) | 2 spr qd* | 16 g (120 spr) | | |
| Mometasone (*Nasonex*) | 2 spr qd* | 17 g (120 spr) | | |
| Triamcinolone (eg, *Nasacort*) | 2–4 spr qd* | 10 g (100 spr) | | |

*(cont.)*

**Table 76. Drug Therapy for Allergic Rhinitis or Conjunctivitis (cont.)**

| Type, Drug | Geriatric Dosage | Formulations | Geriatric Half-Life | Adverse Events |
|---|---|---|---|---|
| **Mast Cell Stabilizers** | | | | |
| Cromolyn (*NasalCrom*) | 1 spr tid–qid;* begin 1–2 wk before exposure to allergen | 2%, 4% | | Nasal irritation, headache, itching of throat |
| Lodoxamide (*Alomide*) | 1–2 gtt OU qid | 0.1% | | Ocular irritation, burning, stinging |
| Nedocromil (*Alocril*) | 1–2 gtt OU bid | 2% | | Headache, ocular irritation, burning, stinging |
| Pemirolast (*Alamast*) | 1–2 gtt OU qid | 0.1% | | Headache, rhinitis, flu-like symptoms, ocular irritation, burning, stinging |
| **Mast Cell Stabilizers and H₁ antagonists** | | | | |
| Ketotifen (*Zaditor*) | 1 gtt OU q 8–12 h | 0.025% | | Conjunctival injection, headache, rhinitis, ocular irritation |
| Oloputadine (*Patanol*) | 1 gtt OU bid | 0.1% | | Cold syndrome, dysgeusia, headache, keratitis, ocular irritation |
| **NSAID** | | | | |
| Ketorolac (*Acular*) | 1 gtt OU qid | 0.5% | | Ocular irritation, burning, stinging |
| **Other** | | | | |
| Ipratropium (*Atrovent NS*) | 2 spr bid–qid* | 0.03, 0.06%† sol | 1.6 h | Epistaxis, nasal irritation, URI, sore throat, nausea. Caution: Do not spray in eyes. |
| Montelukast (*Singulair*) | 10 mg po qd | T: 10 mg; gran 4 mg/packet | | Less effective than nasal steroids |

✔ = preferred for treating older persons.
* Spr per nares.
** *Allegra-D, Claritin-D* are not recommended; both also contain pseudoephedrine. Contraindicated in narrow angle glaucoma, urinary retention, MAOI use within 14 d, severe HTN, or CAD. May cause headache, nausea, insomnia.
† Use 0.06% for treatment of viral upper respiratory infection.

# CHRONIC OBSTRUCTIVE PULMONARY DISEASE
## Definition
A spectrum of chronic respiratory diseases characterized by:
- Airflow limitation
- Cough
- Dyspnea
- Frequent pulmonary infection
- Impaired gas exchange
- Sputum production

## Therapy
***Smoking Cessation:*** Essential at any age. See p 16.

***Rehabilitation:*** Patients at all stages benefit from exercise training, ie, increased exercise tolerance results in decreased dyspnea and fatigue.

***Long-Term Oxygen Therapy:*** For indications, see **Table 81**.

***MDIs:*** Should be used with an AeroChamber (requires separate prescription); educate patients on use. Use a separate AeroChamber for inhaled steroids; wash AeroChamber weekly.

***Stepped Approach:*** Add steps when symptoms inadequately controlled; D/C agent if no improvement. See **Table 77** and **Table 80**.

### Table 77. COPD Therapy

| Stage | Treatment | |
|---|---|---|
| **Mild COPD** | | |
| $FEV_1 \geq 80\%$ | Short-acting $\beta_2$-agonist when needed | |
| **Moderate COPD** | | |
| $50\% \leq FEV_1 < 80\%$ | Regular treatment with one or more bronchodilators* Rehabilitation | Inhaled steroids if significant symptoms and lung function response |
| $30\% \leq FEV_1 < 50\%$ | Regular treatment with one or more bronchodilators* Rehabilitation | Inhaled steroids if significant symptoms and lung function response or if repeated exacerbations |
| **Severe COPD** | | |
| $FEV_1 < 30\%$ or respiratory or right HF | Regular treatment with one or more bronchodilators* | |
| | Inhaled steroids if significant symptoms and lung function response or if repeated exacerbations | |
| | Treatment of complications | |
| | Long-term $O_2$ therapy if respiratory failure | |
| **COPD exacerbation** | | |
| (increased breathlessness, wheezing, cough, sputum) | Increase dose and/or frequency of bronchodilators* | |
| | Consider IV methylxanthine | |
| | Add steroid (eg, methylprednisolone 30–40 mg po qd 10–14 d) | |
| | Add antibiotics if ↑ sputum with ↑ purulence (cover *Streptococcus pneumoniae, Haemophilus influenzae, Moraxella catarrhalis*) | |
| | Check x-ray, ECG, ABG; titrate $O_2$ to 90% sat and recheck ABG | |
| | If there are 2 or more of the following: severe dyspnea, respiratory rate $\geq 25$, $PcO_2$ 45–60, then noninvasive positive pressure ventilation reduces risk of ventilator use and mortality and length of hospital stay | |

*$\beta_2$-agonists, ipratropium, methylxanthines.

Source: Adapted from Global Strategy for the Diagnosis, Management, and Prevention of Chronic Obstructive Pulmonary Disease, Global Initiative for Chronic Obstructive Lung Disease (GOLD). NHLBI/WHO Workshop Report, Executive Summary. National Institutes of Health, National Heart, Lung and Blood Institute. March 2001. NIH Publication No. 2701A (for full report, see http://www.goldcopd.com).

## ASTHMA

### Definition

Chronic inflammatory disorder of the airways; may be triggered by:

- Air pollution
- Allergens
- Chemicals
- Emotional distress
- Exercise
- Tobacco smoke
- Viruses

## Characteristics
Can present at any age, but in old age **cough** is a common presentation, it is less variable and episodic, presents more fixed obstruction, and is more difficult to classify.

*Symptoms:*
- Chest tightness
- Cough
- Reversible and variable PEF
- Shortness of breath
- Wheezing

Symptoms may be confused with HF, COPD; PEF may not be reliable.

## Therapy
### Nonpharmacologic
Avoid triggers; educate patients on disease management, use of MDIs, and peak flow meters (document severity and response to therapy).

### Pharmacologic
Stepped approach:
- Based on severity of symptoms (**Table 78**).
- When symptoms controlled for 3 mo, try stepwise reduction.
- If control not achieved, step up, but first review medication technique, adherence, and avoidance of triggers. (See **Table 79**, **Table 80**.)

MDIs should be used with an AeroChamber (requires separate prescription), and patients should be educated on their use. Use separate AeroChamber for steroids; wash AeroChamber weekly.

#### Table 78. Classification of Asthma Severity

| | Symptoms During Day | Symptoms at Night | PEF or FEV$_1$ | PEF Variability |
|---|---|---|---|---|
| Intermittent | <1/wk; asymptomatic between attacks | <2/mo | ≥80% | <20% |
| Mild, persistent | >2/wk; attacks may affect activity | >2/mo | ≥80% | 20%–30% |
| Moderate, persistent | Daily, attacks affect activity | >1/wk | 60%–80% | >30% |
| Severe, persistent | Continual; limited physical activity | Frequent | ≤60% | >30% |

Source: Adapted from Global Initiative for Asthma, *Global Strategy for Asthma Prevention and Management*. Bethesda, MD: National Heart, Lung, and Blood Institute, April 2002. NIH Publication No. 02-3659. http://www.ginasthma.com

#### Table 79. Asthma Therapy for Adults

| | Daily Medications | Other Options | Geriatric Notes |
|---|---|---|---|
| Step 1 Intermittent | None | Inhaled β$_2$-agonist prn | |
| Step 2 Mild, persistent | Low-dose inhaled steroid | SR-theophylline or cromone or leukotriene inhibitor | Many drug interactions with theophylline; leukotrienes have not been studied in older patients |

*(cont.)*

Table 79. Asthma Therapy for Adults (cont.)

| | Daily Medications | Other Options | Geriatric Notes |
|---|---|---|---|
| Step 3 Moderate, persistent | Low- to medium-dose inhaled steroid plus long-acting inhaled $\beta_2$-agonist | Medium-dose inhaled steroid plus SR-theophylline, or medium-dose inhaled steroid plus either oral $\beta_2$-agonist or leukotriene inhibitor, or high-dose inhaled steroid | Oral $\beta_2$-agonists cause tremors, tachycardia, angina; many older patients have fixed obstruction, and ipratropium is helpful and well tolerated |
| Step 4 Severe, persistent | High-dose inhaled steroid plus long-acting inhaled $\beta_2$-agonist plus one or more of SR-theophylline, leukotriene inhibitor, oral long-acting $\beta_2$-agonist, oral steroid | | |

Sources: Adapted from National Asthma Education and Prevention Program, *NAEPP Working Group Report: Considerations for Diagnosing and Managing Asthma in the Elderly.* Bethesda, MD: National Heart, Lung, and Blood Institute; Feb. 1996. NIH Publication No. 96-3662; and Global Initiative for Asthma, *Global Strategy for Asthma Prevention and Management.* Bethesda, MD: National Heart, Lung, and Blood Institute, April 2002. NIH Publication No. 02-3659. http://www.ginasthma.com

Table 80. Asthma and COPD Medications

| Drug | Dosage | Adverse Events (Metabolism, Excretion) |
|---|---|---|
| **Anticholinergics** | | |
| ✔ Ipratropium (*Atrovent*) | 2–6 puffs qid or 0.5 mg by nebulizer qid | Dry mouth, bitter taste (lung, poorly absorbed; F) |
| Tiotropium | 1 inhalation cap (18 µg) qd | Same as ipratropium (14% K, 86% F) |
| **Short-acting $\beta_2$-Agonists*** | | Class adverse events: tremor, nervousness, headache, palpitations, tachycardia, cough, hypokalemia. Caution: use half-doses in persons with known or suspected coronary disease (L) |
| ✔ Albuterol (*Proventil, Ventolin*) | 2–6 puffs q 4–6 h or 2.5 mg by nebulizer qid; 1.5–3.5 mg bid–qid by nebulizer; ER tablets 4–8 mg po q 12 h | Adverse events more common with oral formulation |
| (*Ventolin Rotacaps*) | 1–2 caps q 4–6 h; dry powder inhaler 200 µg/inhalation | |
| ✔ Bitolterol (*Tornalate*) | 1–3 puffs q 4–6 h | |
| Isoetharine (eg, *Bronkometer, Bronkosol*) | 0.25–0.5 mL of 1% sol; 2 mL NS by nebulizer q 1–4 h; inhaler 1–2 puffs q 4 h | Use limited by short duration of action; not widely used for this reason (lung, L) |
| Levalbuterol (*Xopenex*) | 0.63 mg q 6–8 h | Expensive; no advantage over racemic albuterol (intestine, L) |
| Pirbuterol (*Maxair*) | 2–3 puffs q 4–6 h | Mechanism may be difficult for older patients to trigger (L, K) |

*(cont.)*

## Table 80. Asthma and COPD Medications (cont.)

| Drug | Dosage | Adverse Events (Metabolism, Excretion) |
|------|--------|----------------------------------------|
| **Long-acting β-Agonists**<br>✔ Salmeterol (*Serevent Diskus*) | 1 cap bid; dry powdered inhaler 50 µg/inhalation | Class adverse events: tremor, nervousness, headache, palpitations, tachycardia, cough, hypokalemia; caution: use half-doses in persons with known or suspected coronary disease; not for acute exacerbation (L) |
| ✔ Formoterol (*Foradil*) | 1 puff q 12 h | Onset of action 1–3 min (L, K) |
| **Corticosteroids: Inhaled**<br>✔ Beclomethasone (*Beclovent, Vanceril*) | 2–4 puffs bid–qid [42, 84 µg/puff, max 840 µg/d] | Class adverse events: nausea, vomiting, diarrhea, abdominal pain; oropharyngeal thrush; dosages >1.0 mg/d may cause adrenal suppression, reduce calcium absorption and bone density, and cause bruising (L) |
| ✔ Budesonide (eg, *Pulmicort*) | 1–2 puffs bid–qid [100, 200, 400 µg/puff] | |
| ✔ Dexamethasone (eg, *Dexacort*) | 3 puffs tid–qid [100 µg/puff] | |
| ✔ Flunisolide (eg, *AeroBid*) | 2–4 puffs bid [250 µg/puff] | |
| ✔ Fluticasone (eg, *Flovent*) | 1 puff bid [44, 110, 220 µg/puff] | |
| ✔ Triamcinolone (eg, *Azmacort*) | 2 puffs tid–qid or 4 puffs bid [100 µg/puff] | |
| **Corticosteroids: Oral**<br>Prednisone (eg, *Deltasone, Orasone*) | 20 mg po bid [T: 1, 2.5, 5, 10, 20, 50; elixir 5 mg/5 mL] | Leukocytosis, thrombocytosis, sodium retention, euphoria, depression, hallucination, cognitive dysfunction; other effects with long-term use (L) |
| **Methylxanthines**<br>Long-acting Theophyllines (eg, *Quibron-T/SR*) | 300–400 mg/d [T: 300 bisect, trisect tabs] | Class adverse events: atrial arrhythmias, seizures, increased gastric acid secretion, ulcer, reflux, diuresis; clearance ↓ by 30% after 65 yr; initial dose ≤400 mg/d, titrate using blood levels (L) |
| (eg, *Theo-Dur, Slo-Bid*) | 100–200 mg po bid [T: 100, 200, 300, 450] | |
| (eg, *Uniphyl, Theo-24*) | 400 mg po qd [T: 100, 200, 300, 400] | |
| **Leukotriene Modifiers**<br>Montelukast (*Singulair*) | 10 mg po in AM [T: 10; ChT: 4, 5] | Headache, drowsiness, fatigue, dyspepsia; minimal data in elderly patients; leukotriene-receptor antagonist (L) |

*(cont.)*

### Table 80. Asthma and COPD Medications (cont.)

| Drug | Dosage | Adverse Events (Metabolism, Excretion) |
|---|---|---|
| Zafirlukast (*Accolate*) | 20 mg po bid 1 h before or 2 h after meals [T: 10, 20] | Headache, somnolence, dizziness, nausea, diarrhea, abdominal pain, fever; monitor LFTs; monitor coumarin anticoagulants; leukotriene-receptor antagonist (L, reduced by 50% >65 yr) |
| Zileuton (*Zyflo*) | 600 mg po qid [T: 600] | Dizziness, insomnia, nausea, abdominal pain, abnormal LFTs, myalgia; monitor coumarin anticoagulants; other drug interactions; inhibits synthesis of leukotrienes (L) |
| **Other Medications** | | |
| ✔ Albuterol-Ipratropium (*Combivent*) | 0.09/0.018 mg/puff, 2–3 puffs qid; 3 mg/0.5 mg by nebulizer qid | Same as individual agents (L, K) |
| Cromolyn sodium (eg, *Intal*) | 2–4 puffs or 20-mg caps qid | Because of propellant, use MDI with caution in coronary disease or arrhythmia (L, K) |
| Nedocromil (*Tilade*) | 2 puffs qid | Bitter taste, headache, dizziness, sore throat, cough, chest tightness (K, F) |
| ✔ Salmeterol-Fluticasone combination (*Advair Diskus*) | 1 puff bid (50 µg/100, 250, or 500 µg/inhalation) | |

✔ = preferred for treating older persons.
* Older nonselective $\beta_2$-agonists such as isoproterenol, metoproterenol, epinephrine are not recommended and are more toxic.

### Table 81. Indications for Long-Term Oxygen Therapy*

| PaO$_2$ Level | SaO$_2$ Level | Other |
|---|---|---|
| ≤55 mm Hg | ≤88% | >15 hr/d for benefit[†] |
| 55–59 mm Hg | ≥89% | Signs of tissue hypoxia (ie, cor pulmonale by ECG, HF, hematocrit >55%) |
| ≥60 mm Hg | ≥90% | Desaturation with exercise<br>Desaturation with sleep apnea not corrected by CPAP |

* Titrate O$_2$ saturation to approximately 90%.
† Improves survival, hemodynamics, polycythemia, exercise capacity, lung mechanics, and cognition.
Source: Adapted from Global Strategy for the Diagnosis, Management, and Prevention of Chronic Obstructive Pulmonary Disease, Global Initiative for Chronic Obstructive Lung Disease (GOLD). NHLBI/WHO Workshop Report, Executive Summary. National Institutes of Health, National Heart, Lung and Blood Institute. March 2001. NIH Publication No. 2701A (for full report, see http://www.goldcopd.com).

## COUGH
- Symptom of acute and chronic respiratory and cardiac illnesses.
- Chronic rhinitis is most common cause in older people (see **Table 76**).

### Management
- Identify cause, then treat underlying problem.
- Do not suppress cough in stable COPD.
- For symptomatic relief, see **Table 82**.
- Evaluate for adverse events from other medications, eg, ACE inhibitors.

**Table 82. Antitussives and Expectorants**

| Drug | Dosage | Formulations | Comments (Metabolism) |
|---|---|---|---|
| Benzonatate* (*Tessalon Perles*) | 100 mg po tid (max: 600 mg/d) | C: 100, 200 | Adverse events: CNS stimulation or depression, headache, dizziness, hallucination, constipation (L) |
| Dextromethorphan** (eg, *Robitussin DM*) | 10–30 mL po q 4–8 h | C: 30; S: 10 mg/5 mL | Adverse events: mild drowsiness, fatigue; interacts with fluoxetine, paroxetine; combination may cause serotonin syndrome (L) |
| Guaifenesin** (eg, *Robitussin*) | 5–20 mL po q 4 h | S: 100 mg/5 mL | Adverse events: none at low doses; high doses cause nausea, vomiting, diarrhea, drowsiness, abdominal pain (L) |
| Histussin HC** | 10 mL q 4 h up to 40 mL/d | S: hydrocodone 2.5 mg + phenylephrine 5 mg + chlorpheniramine 2 mg/mL | Adverse events: sedation, constipation, nervousness, tachycardia, hypertension, urinary retention (L) |
| Hydrocodone** (*Hycodan*) | 5 mL po q 4–6 h | S: 5 mg/5 mL | Adverse events include sedation, constipation, confusion (L) |

Note: * = antitussive and expectorant; ** = antitussive.

## PULMONARY EMBOLISM
### Symptoms
Classic triad—dyspnea, chest pain, hemoptysis—occurs in ≤20% of cases.
Consider PE with any of the following:
- Chest pain
- Hemoptysis
- Hypotension
- Hypoxia
- Shortness of breath
- Syncope
- Tachycardia

**Diagnosis**

**Figure 10. Evaluation of Suspected Pulmonary Embolism**

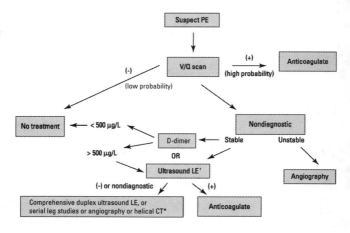

\* Helical CT may not detect peripheral emboli.
† LE lower extremity

**Pharmacologic Therapy**
- Standard therapy for PE remains IV heparin followed by warfarin.
  ○ Heparin: mix infusion 100 U/mL in D5W; cleared through the reticuloendothelial system, half-life of anticoagulation effect 1.5 h
  ○ Warfarin may be started on the same day (see p 18 and **Table 10**)
- Low-molecular-weight heparins (LMWH) appear safe and effective for both DVT and PE (see **Table 12**).
- Acute massive PE (filling defects in 2 or more lobar arteries, or the equivalent, by angiogram) associated with hypotension or severe hypoxia or high pulmonary pressures on echocardiogram should usually be treated with thrombolytic therapy within 48 h of onset (see **Table 12**).

# SEXUAL DYSFUNCTION

## IMPOTENCE (ERECTILE DYSFUNCTION)

### Definition

Inability to achieve erection sufficient for intercourse. Prevalence nearly 70% by age 70.

### Causes

Often multifactorial; >50% of cases arterial, venous, or mixed vascular cause. Also:

- Diabetes mellitus
- Drug adverse events
- Hyperprolactinemia
- Hypogonadism
- Neurologic: eg, disorders of the CNS, spinal cord, or PNS; autonomic neuropathy; temporal lobe epilepsy
- Psychologic: eg, depression, anxiety, bereavement
- Thyroid or adrenal disorders

Decreased bioavailable testosterone is more associated with decreased libido than with erectile dysfunction.

### Evaluation

*History:* Type and duration of problem; relation to surgery, trauma, medication. Problems with orgasm, libido, or penile detumescence are not erectile dysfunction.

*Physical Findings:*

- Neuropathy: orthostatic hypotension, impaired response to Valsalva's maneuver, absent bulbocavernosus or cremasteric reflexes
- Peyronie's disease: penile bands, plaques
- Hypogonadism: diminished male pattern hair, gynecomastia, small (<20–25 mm long) testes

*Assessment:*

- Reduced penile-to-brachial pressure index suggests vascular disease.
- Cavernosometry diagnoses venous leak syndrome; reserved for surgical candidates.
- Test dose of prostaglandin E or papaverine can exclude vascular disease or confirm venous leak syndrome.
- For libido problems check total and bioavailable testosterone, luteinizing hormone, TSH, and prolactin. Most late-life hypogonadism is hypothalamic failure.
- Total testosterone <200 ng/dL is clearly hypogonadal. Levels 200–500 ng/dL are questionable hypogonadism. If symptoms are troublesome, a trial of replacement can be given.
- Because sex hormone binding globulin increases with age, bioavailable testosterone should be a better test in older men. Currently, data are insufficient to set treatment thresholds for bioavailable testosterone for men of different ages.

### Therapy

**Table 83. Management of Male Sexual Dysfunction**

| Cause | Therapy | Comments |
|---|---|---|
| Hypogonadism, poor libido | Testosterone: scrotal transdermal (*Testoderm*) [4, 5, 6] 4–6 mg qd; **or** skin transdermal (*Androderm*) [2.5, 5] 5 mg/d; | |

*(cont.)*

Table 83. **Management of Male Sexual Dysfunction (cont.)**

| Cause | Therapy | Comments |
|---|---|---|
| | **or** testosterone cypionate or enanthate 200 mg IM q 2–4 wk | When given IM, can cause polycythemia, fluid retention, gynecomastia, liver dysfunction, but IM testosterone is inexpensive and generally well tolerated |
| | **or** testosterone gel 1% (*AndroGel* [5 g (50 mg/24 h), 7.5 g (75 mg), 10 g (100 mg)] begin with 5 g pk qam, (*Testim* [5 g (50 mg/24 h)] begin with 5 g pk qam) | Squeeze pk contents into palm of hand and apply, let dry; wash hands immediately. Check serum testosterone after 14 d and adjust dose; do not use in women |
| Neuropathic, vascular, or mixed | Vacuum tumescence devices (*Osbon-Erec Aid, Catalyst Vacuum Device, Pos-T-Vac, Rejoyn*) | Rare: Ecchymosis, reduced ejaculation, coolness of penile tip. Good acceptance in older population; intercourse successful in 70% to 90% of cases |
| | Intracavernosal [5, 10, 20, 40 µg] **or** intraurethral [125, 250, 500, 1000 µg] prostaglandin E (*Alprostadil*) | Risks: hypotension, bruising, bleeding, priapism; erection >4 h requires emergency treatment; intraurethral safer and more acceptable |
| | Penile prosthesis | Complications: infection, mechanical failure, penile fibrosis |
| Organic, psychogenic, or mixed | PDE5 Inhibitors* | All agents: Contraindicated with use of nitrates; caution in vascular disease, least effective in vascular impotence. Metabolism reduced in liver, kidney disease. Adverse events: headache, flushing, dyspepsia, dizziness, rhinitis |
| | Sildenafil (*Viagra*) [25, 50, 100] Start 25 mg 1 h before sexual activity. | Precaution: 50 or 100 mg should not be taken within 4 h of an alpha-blocker; 25 mg may be taken any time. Other adverse events: color tinge in vision, increased sensitivity to light, blurred vision |
| | Vardenafil (*LEVITRA*) [2.5, 5, 10, 20] Start 2.5 mg 1 h before sexual activity. | Contraindicated with use of any alpha-blocker; caution with CYP3A4 inhibitors. |
| | Tadalafil (*Cialis*) [5, 10, 20] Start 5 mg ½–1 h before sexual activity; lasts 24 h. | Contraindicated with use of any alpha-blocker other than tamulosin 0.4 mg; caution with CYP3A4 inhibitors. Other adverse events: back pain, myalgia, pain in limb. |

*There is too little information to predict the extent of interaction of the α-blocker alfuzosin with the PDE5 inhibitors.

## DYSPAREUNIA
### Definition
Pain with intercourse.

### Aggravating Factors
- Gynecologic tumors
- Interstitial cystitis
- Myalgia from overexertion during Kegel's exercises
- Osteoarthritis
- Pelvic fractures
- Retroverted uterus
- Sacral nerve root compression
- Vaginal atrophy from estrogen deprivation
- Vulvar or vaginal infection

### Evaluation

- Ask about sexual problems (eg, changes in libido, partner's function, and health issues).
- Screen for depression.
- Perform pelvic examination for vulvovaginitis, vaginal atrophy, conization (decreased distensibility and narrowing of the vaginal canal), scarring, pelvic inflammatory disease, cystocele, and rectocele.

### Management

- Identify and treat clinical pathology.
- Educate and counsel patients.
- Discuss hormone therapy (see pp 201–203).
- Water-soluble lubricants (eg, *Replens*) are highly effective as monotherapy for those who cannot or will not use hormones, or as a supplement to estrogen.
- For vaginismus (vaginal muscle spasm), trial cessation of intercourse and gradual vaginal dilation may help.
- For diminished libido, short-term use of androgens (which used long-term adversely affect health) may help; refer for counseling or sex therapy.
- Topical estrogens (**Table 84**) treat symptoms and complications of estrogen deficiency such as dyspareunia and recurrent urinary tract infections with minimal systemic absorption.

**Table 84. Topical Estrogens without Systemic Effects**

| Estrogen | Dose |
|---|---|
| Estrogen cream (*Premarin, Ogen, Estrace* [42.5 g]) | Use min dose (0.5 g for *Premarin*, 2 g for *Ogen* and *Estrace*) daily × 2 wk, then 1–3 times/wk thereafter |
| Estradiol vaginal ring (*Estring*) | Insert intravaginally and change q 90 d |
| Estradiol vaginal tablets (*Vagifem*) | Insert 25 μg intravaginally daily × 2 wk, then twice/wk |

## SSRI-INDUCED SEXUAL DYSFUNCTION

- Incidence varies widely, from 1% to 20% of patients making spontaneous reports to 75% when patients are systematically questioned.
- Symptoms include anorgasmia, decreased libido, and ejaculatory dysfunction.
- Tolerance may develop up to 12 wk on treatment.
- Pharmacologic management:
  - For sertraline and citalopram (not other SSRIs), reducing dose or drug holidays (skip or reduce weekend dose) may help.
  - Adjuvant medications reported as effective for this condition in case reports include
    - Bupropion (*Wellbutrin SR, Zyban*) 75–100 mg po qd
    - Mirtazapine (*Remeron*) 15 mg po hs
    - Sildenafil (*Viagra*) 25–100 mg 1 h before intercourse
- Controlled trials of mirtazapine, yohimbine, olanzapine, and bupropion failed to show a benefit different from that of placebo, although most trials were small.

# SKIN ULCERS

## CHRONIC WOUND ASSESSMENT AND TREATMENT
### Wound Assessment
Evaluation of chronic wounds should include the following (see **Table 85** for wound characteristics specific to ulcer type):
- Location
- Wound size and shape: length, width, depth, stage (pressure ulcer), grade (diabetic foot ulcer)
- Wound bed: color, presence of slough, necrotic tissue, granulation tissue, epithelial tissue, undermining or tunneling
- Exudate: purulent versus nonpurulent (serous, serosanguineous)
- Wound edges: distinct, diffuse, rolled under
- Periwound surface: erythema, edema, induration, temperature
- Presence of pain
- Signs of wound infection
  - Increased necrotic tissue
  - Foul odor of exudates
  - Purulent exudates
  - Faint halo of erythema at wound edges
  - Wound breakdown
  - Increasing pain
  - Edema
  - Granulation tissue that bleeds easily
  - Serous exudates with inflammation
  - Nonhealing or enlarging wound
  - Swab culture of limited value in diagnosing infection due to contaminated wound bed

### Wound Treatment
- Remove devitalized tissues and surface contaminants
  - Sharp debridement
  - Autolytic enzymatic preparations (eg, moisture-retaining dressings or hydrogels)
  - Mechanical (eg, wet-to-dry dressings)
  - Chemical (eg, topical enzymes such as *Accuzyme, Santyl*)
  - Cleanse with irrigation or whirlpool using normal saline or lactated Ringer's solution
  - Avoid antiseptics because of cytotoxicity
- Control bacterial burden of wound
  - Monitor for signs of infection
  - Debride all necrotic tissue
  - Limit use of topical antibiotics because of risk of developing resistant organisms
  - Use systemic antibiotics only in presence of spreading cellulitis, sepsis, or osteomyelitis
- Provide moist wound environment and control exudates with dressings (see **Table 86** and **Table 87**)
- Prevent further injury; position to avoid any pressure on the wound
- Support repair process
  - Protein and calories (protein: 1.25–1.5 g/kg/d; calories: 30–35 calories/kg/d)
  - Vitamin and mineral supplements if deficiencies suspected
  - Avoid exposure to cold; vasoconstriction reduces blood flow to wound

Table 85. Wound Characteristics by Ulcer Type

| | Arterial | Diabetic | Pressure | Venous |
|---|---|---|---|---|
| Location | Tips of toes or between toes, on pressure points of foot (eg, heel or lateral foot), or in areas of trauma | Plantar surface of foot, especially over metatarsal heads, toes, and heel | Over bony prominences (eg, trochanter, coccyx, ankle) | Gaiter area, particularly medial malleolus |
| Size and shape | Small craters with well-defined borders | Even wound margins with callus | Variable length, width, depth depending on stage (see staging system, p 186) | Edges may be irregular with depth limited to dermis or shallow subcutaneous tissue |
| Wound bed | Pale or necrotic | Granular tissue unless PAD present | Varies from bright red, shallow crater to deeper crater with slough and necrotic tissue; tunneling and undermining | Ruddy red; yellow slough may be present; undermining or tunneling uncommon |
| Exudate | Minimal amount due to poor blood flow | Variable amount; serous unless infection present | Purulent, becoming serous as healing progresses; foul odor with infection | Copious; serous unless infection present |
| Surrounding skin | Halo of erythema or slight fluctuance indicative of infection | Normal | May be distinct, diffuse, rolled under; erythema, edema, induration if infected | May appear macerated, crusted, or scaling |
| Pain | Cramping or constant deep aching | None, because of neuropathy | Painful, unless sensory function impaired | Variable; may be severe, dull, aching, or bursting in character |

## ARTERIAL ULCERS
### Definition
Any lesion caused by severe tissue ischemia secondary to atherosclerosis.

### Etiologic Factors for Arterial Ulcer Development
- Progressive occlusion
- Minor trauma (eg, footwear)

### Intrinsic Risk Factors
- Peripheral arterial disease (PAD)
- Diabetes mellitus
- Systolic HTN
- Smoking
- Advanced age

## Evaluation
In addition to evaluation under Chronic Wound Assessment (see p 180):
- Determine severity of PAD (see **Table 23**)
  - Venous filling time: Prolonged venous filling (>20 sec) predictive of severe PAD
  - Pedal pulses: Absence of both a dorsalis pedis and a posterior tibialis pulse indicative of PAD
  - Skin temperature: Unilateral coolness and sudden, marked change from proximal to distal
  - Ankle-brachial index (ABI): If ABI value <0.5, wound healing unlikely without revascularization
- Assess wound characteristics (see **Table 85**)
- Assess pain characteristics (see Pain, p 141)

## Prevention and Management
*Protective Skin Care:*
- Inspect feet and legs daily
- Use emollients after bathing to prevent cracking and fissures
- Dry skin between toes to prevent maceration
- Avoid friction and pressure by using lamb's wool or foam between toes
- Use positioning devices to avoid pressure on feet (eg, heel protectors)
*Protection from Mechanical Trauma:*
- Wear proper fitting, protective footwear consistently
- Seek professional foot and nail care
*Protection from Thermal Trauma:*
- Wear warm socks to prevent vasoconstriction
- Avoid exposure of feet and legs to heat-producing devices and hot bathing water

## Local Wound Care
Treatment dictated by adequacy of perfusion and status of wound bed:
- Avoid debridement of necrotic tissue until perfusion status is determined.
- If wound is infected, revascularization procedures, surgical removal of necrotic tissue, and systemic antibiotics are treatments of choice.
- Topical antibiotics should not be relied on to treat infected ischemic wounds and may cause sensitivity reactions.
- If wound is uninfected and dry eschar is present, maintain dry intact eschar as a barrier to bacteria. Application of an antiseptic may decrease bacterial burden on wound surface.
- If wound is uninfected and soft slough and necrotic tissue is present, apply moisture-retaining dressings that allow frequent inspection of wound for signs of infection.
- Assess vascular perfusion and refer for surgical intervention if consistent with overall goals of care.

## DIABETIC FOOT ULCERS
### Definition
Any lesion on the plantar surface of the foot caused by neuropathy.

## Etiologic Factors for Diabetic Ulcer Development
Repetitive stress, unrelieved pressure, and trauma in an insensate foot

### Intrinsic Risk Factors
- Peripheral neuropathy
- Structural foot deformity
- Limited joint mobility
- History of previous ulcers
- History of amputation
- Retinopathy
- Nephropathy
- History of uncontrolled or poorly controlled diabetes
- Advanced age
- Vascular insufficiency
- Poorly fitting footwear

### Evaluation
In addition to evaluation under Chronic Wound Assessment (see p 180):
- Assess the feet in patients with one or more risk factors:
  - Visual inspection for rubor, pallor, callus, dry skin, ingrown toenails, and fissures
  - Vascular assessment for pulses, dorsal vein distention, temperature
  - Sensory assessment for pressure, touch, vibration
  - Motor assessment for joint rigidity, muscle wasting, gait disturbance
- Assess wound characteristics (see **Table 85**)
- Assess for presence of infection:
  - Sudden increase in blood glucose
  - Wound can be probed to the bone—highly sensitive indicator of osteomyelitis
- Determine grade of ulcer (Wagner Classification)
  - Grade 0: Preulcerative lesions; healed ulcers present; bony deformity present
  - Grade 1: Superficial ulcer without subcutaneous tissue involvement
  - Grade 2: Penetration through subcutaneous tissue
  - Grade 3: Ostitis, abscess, or osteomyelitis
  - Grade 4: Gangrene of digit
  - Grade 5: Gangrene of foot requiring disarticulation

### Prevention and Management
- Inspect feet daily
- Use emollients after bathing to prevent cracking and fissures
- Wear proper fitting, protective footwear consistently
- Seek professional foot and nail care
- Avoid exposure to heat-producing devices (eg, heating pads) and hot bathing water

### Local Wound Care
In addition to recommendations under Chronic Wound Treatment (see p 180):
- Debride devitalized tissue and callus: surgical debridement is method of choice for effective, rapid removal of nonviable tissue
- Avoid occlusive dressings due to risk of wound infection
- Offload pressure and stress from foot
  - Avoidance of pressure on foot essential to management of diabetic foot ulcer
  - Use orthotic that redistributes weight on plantar surface of foot when ambulating (eg, total contact cast, *DH Pressure Relief Walker*)

- Topical antibiotics should not be relied on to treat diabetic foot ulcer infections because of development of resistant organisms.

**Pharmacologic Therapy**
- *Regranex*, a recombinant platelet-derived growth factor, applied topically in thin layer to a clean wound bed for 12 h followed by 12 h of saline-moistened gauze dressing
  ○ Must be used in conjunction with offloading of pressure on foot, regular sharp debridement, and maintenance of uninfected status.
  ○ If 30% wound closure has not occurred in 10 wk or complete closure in 20 wk, reevaluate treatment plan and consider surgical intervention (especially if osteomyelitis is present).
  ○ Monitor healing progress; if no signs of healing over 2-wk period, reevaluate factors affecting healing and wound management strategies.

**Surgical Intervention**
- If ulceration is resistant to more conservative therapies or if osteomyelitis is suspected, referral for surgical evaluation is warranted.

**PRESSURE ULCERS**
**Definition**
Any lesion caused by unrelieved pressure resulting in damage of underlying tissue; usually occurs over bony prominence.

**Etiologic Factors for Pressure Ulcer Development**
- Pressure
- Shear
- Friction

**Intrinsic Risk Factors**
- Immobility (eg, chairbound)
- Increased age
- Malnutrition
- Moisture (eg, incontinence)
- Decreased sensory perception

**Table 86. Wound and Pressure Ulcer Products, by Drainage and Stage**

| Product | Drainage | | | Wound Stage | | | |
|---|---|---|---|---|---|---|---|
| | Light | Moderate | Heavy | I | II | III | IV |
| Transparent film | • | | | • | • | | |
| Foam island | • | • | | | • | • | |
| Hydrocolloids | • | • | | | • | • | |
| Petroleum-based nonadherent | • | • | | | • | • | |
| Alginate | | • | • | | | • | • |
| Hydrogel | • | | | | • | • | • |
| Gauze packing (moistened with saline) | | • | • | | | • | • |

Table 87. Common Dressings for Pressure Ulcer Treatment

| Dressing | Indications | Contraindications | Examples |
|---|---|---|---|
| Transparent film | Stage I, II<br>Protection from friction<br>Superficial scrape<br>Autolytic debridement of slough<br>Apply skin prep to intact skin to protect from adhesive | Draining ulcers<br>Suspicion of skin infection or fungus | *Bioclusive*<br>*Tegaderm*<br>*Op-site* |
| Foam island | Stage II, III<br>Low to moderate exudate<br>Can apply as window to secure transparent film | Excessive exudate<br>Dry, crusted wound | *Allevyn*<br>*Lyofoam* |
| Hydrocolloids | Stage II, III<br>Low to moderate drainage<br>Good peri-wound skin integrity<br>Autolytic debridement of slough<br>Left in place 3–5 d<br>Can apply as window to secure transparent film<br>Can apply over alginate to control drainage<br>Must control maceration<br>Apply skin prep to intact skin to protect from adhesive | Poor skin integrity<br>Infected ulcers<br>Wound needs packing | *DuoDERM*<br>*Extra thin film*<br>*DuoDERM*<br>*Tegasorb*<br>*RepliCare*<br>*Comfeel*<br>*Nu-derm* |
| Alginate | Stage III, IV<br>Excessive drainage<br>Apply dressing within wound borders<br>Requires secondary dressing<br>Must use skin prep<br>Must control for maceration | Dry or minimally draining wound<br>Superficial wounds with maceration | *Sorbsan*<br>*Kaltostat*<br>*Algosteril*<br>*AlgiDERM* |
| Hydrogel (amorphous gels) | Stage II, III, IV<br>Needs to be combined with gauze dressing<br>Stays moist longer than saline gauze<br>Changed 1–2 times/d<br>Used as alternative to saline gauze for packing deep wounds with tunnels, undermining<br>Reduces adherence of gauze to wound<br>Must control for maceration | Macerated areas<br>Wounds with excess exudate | *IntraSite gel*<br>*SoloSite gel*<br>*Restore gel* |

(cont.)

**Table 87. Common Dressings for Pressure Ulcer Treatment (cont.)**

| Dressing | Indications | Contraindications | Examples |
|---|---|---|---|
| (gel sheet) | Stage II<br>Needs to be held in place with topper dressing | Macerated areas<br>Wounds with moderate to heavy exudate | *Vigilon*<br>*Restore*<br>*Impregnated Gauze* |
| Gauze packing (moistened with saline) | Stage III, IV<br>Wounds with depth, especially those with tunnels, undermining<br>Must be remoistened often to maintain moist wound environment | | Square 2 × 2s, 4 × 4s<br>*Fluffed Kerlix*<br>*Plain NuGauze* |

Source: Copyright © 2005 by Rita Frantz. Used with permission.

## Evaluation

In addition to evaluation under Chronic Wound Assessment (see p 180)
- Determine intensity of risk status using validated tool, eg, Braden Scale; see Braden BJ, Bergstrom N. Clinical utility of the Braden Scale for predicting pressure sore risk. *Decubitus* 1989;2(3):44–51; for an online version of the scale: http://www.bradenscale.com/bradenscale.htm (for a downloadable PDF file) http://www.ncbi.nlm.nih.gov/books/bv.fcgi?rid=hstat2.section.4947 (in AHRQ pressure ulcer practice guideline).
- Assess wound characteristics (see **Table 85** and below)
- Determine level of tissue injury by using Pressure Ulcer Staging System:
  - **Stage I:** An observable pressure-related alteration of intact skin whose indicators as compared with an adjacent or opposite area on the body may include changes in one or more of the following: skin temperature (warmth or coolness), tissue consistency (firm or boggy feel), and/or sensation (pain, itching). The ulcer appears as a defined area of persistent redness in lightly pigmented skin, whereas in darker skin tones, it may appear with persistent red, blue, or purple hues.
  - **Stage II:** Partial-thickness skin loss involving epidermis and/or dermis; presents as abrasion, blister, or shallow crater.
  - **Stage III:** Full-thickness skin loss involving damage or necrosis of subcutaneous tissue that may extend down to, but not through, underlying fascia; presents as deep crater with or without undermining of adjacent tissue.
  - **Stage IV:** Full-thickness skin loss with extensive destruction, tissue necrosis, or damage to muscle, bone, or supporting structures. May have associated undermining of sinus tracts. Note: eschar-covered ulcers cannot be staged until eschar is removed.

## Prevention and Management

In addition to recommendations under Chronic Wound Treatment (see p 180):
### Protect Wound and Surrounding Skin from Further Trauma
- Avoid positioning directly on the ulcer.
- Employ pressure-reduction strategies:
  - Reposition q 2 h.
  - Use pressure-reducing cushions, mattresses, and heel protectors.

○ Avoid massaging reddened bony prominences.
○ Avoid positioning directly on the trochanter.
• Reduce friction and shear:
○ Maintain head of bed elevation <30 degrees.
○ Use lift sheet to reposition.

### Promote Clean Wound Bed, Prevent Infection
• Debride necrotic tissue, eschar
• Autolytic methods or topical enzymes may be used in conjunction with sharp debridement to facilitate more rapid removal of necrotic tissue.
• Cleanse with each dressing change using normal saline. Irrigate using 8 mm Hg pressure (19-gauge IV catheter and 35-mL syringe) when wound is deep, tunneled, or undermined.

### Maintain Moist Wound Environment (See Table 86 and Table 87)

### Control Exudate (See Table 86 and Table 87)

### Eliminate Dead Space
• Pack dead space (tunnels, undermining) with moistened gauze dressings or strips of calcium alginate

### Diagnose and Treat Infection
• Ensure that necrotic tissue has been debrided completely from wound bed.
• Consider 2-wk trial of topical antibiotic for clean ulcers that are not healing after 2–4 wk optimal care; antibiotic should be effective against gram-negative, gram-positive, and anaerobic organisms.
• Avoid using systemic antibiotics in the absence of advancing cellulitis or systemic infection.

### Support Healing Systemically
• Provide nutritional support (see p 114)
• Provide adequate hydration with oral or parenteral fluids.

### Surgical Repair
• Consider surgical referral for Stage IV pressure ulcers and for severely undermined or tunneled wounds
• Monitor healing progress; in absence of signs of healing over 2-wk period, reevaluate factors affecting healing and wound management strategies

## VENOUS ULCERS
### Definition
Any lesion caused by venous insufficiency precipitated by venous hypertension.

### Etiologic Factors for Venous Ulcer Development
• Venous insufficiency

### Intrinsic Risk Factors
• DVT
• Multiple pregnancies
• Edema
• Ascites

• Congenital anomalies
• Severe trauma to legs
• Tumors
• Sedentary life style or job

**Evaluation**
In addition to evaluation under Chronic Wound Assessment (see p 180):
• Assess status of venous insufficiency
   ○ Lower-extremity edema
   ○ Lipodermatosclerosis (hyperpigmentation and induration around gaiter area)
   ○ Varicosities
   ○ Hemosiderosis
   ○ Venous dermatitis
• Diagnostic studies: Doppler ultrasonography, duplex imaging
• Assess wound characteristics (see **Table 85**)

**Prevention and Management**
*Compression Therapy:*
• Essential component of venous ulcer treatment
• Provides externally applied pressure or static support to lower extremity to facilitate normal venous return
• Therapeutic level of compression is 30–40 mm Hg at the ankle, decreasing toward the knee
• Contraindicated in arterial insufficiency, uncompensated HF, and active thrombus
• Avoid compression therapy when ABI <0.8
• Types of compression therapy:
   ○ Static compression
      ▪ Therapeutic stockings: Use with stable venous insufficiency to prevent ulceration or with an existing ulcer once edema has been controlled.
      ▪ Compression wraps
         □ Combination short- and long-stretch elastic wraps (eg, *Dynaflex, Profore*) provide sustained compression for ambulatory or sedentary patient
         □ Avoid long-stretch elastic wraps (eg, *Ace* bandages, antiembolism hose) that provide subtherapeutic levels of compression
         □ Inelastic devices (paste bandages) and orthotic devices (eg, *Unna's boot, Circ-Aid Thera-Boot*) work by compressing calf during ambulation; most effective for ambulatory patients
   ○ Dynamic compression: Powered devices that propel venous blood upward when applied to lower extremity (eg, intermittent pneumatic pumps, sequential gradient compression devices, A-V impulse device)

**Local Wound Care**
In addition to recommendations under Chronic Wound Treatment (see p 180):
• Use exudate-absorbing dressings (eg, calcium alginate dressings, foam dressings)
• Use skin sealant to protect skin around wound from exudates
• Topical antibiotics should not be relied on to treat venous ulcer infections because of development of resistant organisms.

**Pharmacologic Therapy**
• Pentoxifylline (*Trental*) 400–800 mg tid has been shown to accelerate healing by decreasing blood viscosity and WBC adhesion while increasing fibrinolysis.

**Surgical Intervention**
- If manifestations of chronic venous insufficiency and ulceration are resistant to more conservative therapies or if venous obstruction is present, surgical repair (eg, skin graft) is treatment of choice.
- Monitor healing progress; if no signs of healing over 2-wk period, reevaluate factors affecting healing and wound management strategies.

# SLEEP DISORDERS

## CLASSIFICATION
• Disturbance of the sleep-wake cycle
• Hypersomnolence
• Insomnia (difficulty initiating or maintaining sleep)
• Parasomnias (disorders of arousal, partial arousal, and sleep stage transition)
• Sleep apnea

## SLEEP DISORDERS OTHER THAN SLEEP APNEA
### Risk Factors and Aggravating Factors
***Treatable Associated Medical and Psychiatric Conditions:*** Adjustment disorders, anxiety, bereavement, cough, depression, dyspnea (cardiac or pulmonary), GERD, nocturia, pain, paresthesias, stress

***Medications That Cause or Aggravate Sleep Problems:*** Alcohol, antidepressants, β-blockers, bronchodilators, caffeine, clonidine, cortisone, diuretics, levodopa, methyldopa, nicotine, phenytoin, progesterone, quinidine, reserpine, sedatives, sympathomimetics including decongestants

### Management
Sleep improvements are better sustained over time with behavioral treatment.
***Nonpharmacologic—Measures Recommended to Improve Sleep Hygiene:***
• During the daytime:
  ○ Get out of bed at the same time each morning regardless of how much you slept the night before.
  ○ Exercise daily, but not immediately before bedtime.
  ○ Get adequate exposure to bright light during the day.
  ○ Decrease or eliminate naps, unless necessary part of sleeping schedule.
  ○ Limit or eliminate alcohol, caffeine, and nicotine, especially before bedtime.
• At bedtime:
  ○ Maintain a regular sleeping time, but don't go to bed unless sleepy.
  ○ If hungry, have a light snack before bed (unless there are symptoms of GERD or it is otherwise medically contraindicated), but avoid heavy meals at bedtime.
  ○ Don't read or watch television in bed.
  ○ Relax mentally before going to sleep; don't use bedtime as worry time.
  ○ Relax before bedtime, and maintain a routine period of preparation for bed (eg, washing up and going to the bathroom).
  ○ Control the nighttime environment with comfortable temperature, quietness, darkness.
  ○ Wear comfortable bedclothes.
  ○ If it helps, use soothing noise, for example, a fan or other appliance or a "white noise" machine.
  ○ If unable to fall asleep within 15–20 min, get out of bed and perform soothing activity, such as listening to soft music or reading (but avoid exposure to bright light during these times).
***Pharmacologic—Principles of Prescribing Medications for Sleep Disorders:***
• Use lowest effective dose.
• Use intermittent dosing (2–4 times/wk).

- Prescribe medications for short-term use (no more than 3–4 wk).
- Discontinue medication gradually.
- Be alert for rebound insomnia following discontinuation.

**Table 88. Useful Medications for Sleep Disorders in Elderly Persons**

| Class, Drug | Usual Dose | Formulations | Half-Life | Comments (Metabolism, Excretion) |
|---|---|---|---|---|
| **Antidepressant, sedating** | | | | |
| ✔ Trazodone (*Desyrel*) | 25–150 mg | T: 50, 100, 150, 300 | 12 h | Moderate orthostatic effects; effective for insomnia with or without depression (L) |
| **Benzodiazepine, intermediate-acting** | | | | |
| Estazolam (*ProSom*) | 0.5–1.0 mg | T: 1, 2 | 12–18 h | Rapidly absorbed, effective in initiating sleep; slightly active metabolites that may accumulate (K) |
| Lorazepam (*Ativan*) | 0.25–2 mg | T: 0.5, 1, 2 | 8–12 h | Effective in initiating and maintaining sleep; associated with falls, memory loss, rebound insomnia (K) |
| Temazepam (*Restoril*) | 7.5–15 mg | C: 7.5, 15, 30 | 8–10 h* | Daytime drowsiness may occur with repeated use; effective for sleep maintenance; delayed onset of effect (K) |
| **Nonbenzodiazepine, short-acting** | | | | |
| Zaleplon (*Sonata*) | 5 mg | C: 5, 10 | 1 h | Avoid taking with alcohol or food (L) |
| Zolpidem (*Ambien*) | 5 mg | T: 5, 10 | 1.5–4.5 h** | Confusion and agitation may occur but are rare (L) |
| **CNS depressant, nonbarbiturate and nonbenzodiazepine** | | | | |
| Chloral hydrate (*Aquachloral, Supprettes*) | 500–1000 mg (not to exceed 2 g as single dose or total daily dose) | C: 500; syr 500 mg/5 mL; Sp: 324, 500, 648 | 8 h (active metabolite) | Hypnotic effect lost after 2 wk of continuous use; contraindicated in marked cardiac, hepatic, or renal impairment (K, L) |
| **Hormone** | | | | |
| Melatonin | 0.3–5 mg | various | 1 h | Not regulated by FDA |

✔ = preferred for treating older persons.
\* Can be as long as 30 h in elderly persons.
\*\* 3 h in elderly persons; 10 h in those with hepatic cirrhosis.

## SLEEP APNEA
### Definition
Repeated episodes of apnea (cessation of airflow for ≥10 sec) or hypopnea (transient reduction [≥30% decrease in thoracoabdominal movement or airflow and with at least 4% oxygen desaturation or an arousal] of airflow for ≥10 sec) during sleep with excessive daytime sleepiness or altered cardiopulmonary function.

## Classification
*Obstructive (90% of cases):* Airflow cessation as a result of upper airway closure in spite of adequate respiratory muscle effort
*Central:* Cessation of respiratory effort
*Mixed:* Features of both obstructive and central

## Associated Risk Factors, Clinical Features
Family hx, HTN, increased neck circumference, male gender, obesity, smoking, snoring, upper airway structural abnormalities (eg, soft palate, tonsils)

## Evaluation
• Full night's sleep study (polysomnography) in sleep laboratory indicated for those who habitually snore and either report daytime sleepiness or have observed apnea.
• Results are reported as the apnea-hypopnea index (AHI), which is the number of episodes of apneas and hypopneas per hour of sleep.
• Threshold for CPAP reimbursement by Medicare based on a minimum of 2 h sleep by polysomnography is AHI (1) ≥15 or (2) ≥5 and ≤14 with documented symptoms of excessive daytime sleepiness, impaired cognition, mood disorders, or insomnia, or documented HTN, ischemic heart disease, or hx of stroke.

## Management
*Nonpharmacologic:*
• Use CPAP by nasal mask, nasal prongs, or mask that covers the nose and mouth (considered initial treatment for clinically important sleep apnea).
• Avoid use of alcohol or sedatives.
• Lie in lateral rather than supine position; may be facilitated by soft foam ball in a backpack.
• Lose weight (obese patients).
• Use oral appliances that keep the tongue in an anterior position during sleep or keep the mandible forward.

*Pharmacologic:*
• Modafinil (*Provigil*) 200 mg every morning for excessive daytime sleepiness (CYP3A4 inducer and CYP2C19 inhibitor) [T: 100, 200] L; use in addition to (not in place of) CPAP
• Protriptyline (*Vivactil*) 10–20 mg/d [T: 5, 10] L (men commonly experience urinary hesitancy or frequency and impotence)
• Fluoxetine (*Prozac*) 10–20 mg [T: 10, 20, 40; S: 20 mg/5 mL] L

*Surgical:*
• Tracheostomy (indicated for patients with severe apnea who cannot tolerate positive pressure or when other interventions are ineffective)
• Uvulopalatopharyngoplasty (curative in fewer than 50% of cases)
• Maxillofacial surgery (rare cases)

## OTHER CONDITIONS ASSOCIATED WITH SLEEP DISORDERS
### Nocturnal Leg Cramps
Stretching exercises or use of heating pad 10 min before bedtime may be helpful. Quinine, 200–300 mg po hs [T: 200, 260, 300, 325] may reduce the frequency though not the severity of leg cramps. Cinchonism, hemolysis, thrombocytopenia, and visual disturbances are notable adverse events.

### Restless Legs Syndrome
*Diagnostic Criteria:*
• A compelling urge to move the limbs, usually associated with paresthesias/dysasthesias
• Motor restlessness (eg, floor pacing, tossing and turning in bed, rubbing legs)
• Vague discomfort, usually bilateral, most commonly in calves
• Symptoms exacerbated by rest, especially at night
• Symptoms relieved by movement—jerking, stretching, or shaking of limbs; pacing
*Secondary Causes:*  Iron deficiency, spinal cord and peripheral nerve lesions, uremia, drugs (eg, TCAs, SSRIs, lithium, dopamine antagonists, caffeine)
*Nonpharmacologic Treatment:*
• Sleep hygiene measures (see p 190).
• Avoid alcohol, caffeine, nicotine.
• Rub limbs.
• Use hot or cold baths, whirlpools.
*Pharmacologic Treatment*
• Exclude or treat iron deficiency, peripheral neuropathy.
• If possible, avoid SSRIs, TCAs, lithium, and dopamine antagonists.
Start at low dose, increase as needed:
• First line: dopamine agonists (see **Table 59**) or carbidopa-levodopa (*Sinemet*) 25/100 mg, 1–2 h before bedtime. Patients may develop symptom augmentation that occurs earlier in the day (eg, afternoon instead of evening) and may be more severe. Treatment of augmentation may require reduction of dose or switch to dopamine agonist.
• Second-line agents include carbamazepine and gabapentin (see **Table 60**).
• For refractory cases, benzodiazepines or opioids can be tried.

### Periodic Limb Movement Disorder
*Diagnostic Criteria:*
• Insomnia or excessive sleepiness
• Repetitive, highly stereotyped limb muscle movements (eg, extension of big toes with partial flexion of ankle, knee, and sometimes hip)
• Polysomnographic monitoring showing repetitive episodes of muscle contractions and associated arousals or awakenings
• No evidence of a medical, mental, or other sleep disorder that can account for symptoms
*Treatment:*  Indicated for clinically significant sleep disruption or frequent arousals documented on a sleep study.
• Nonpharmacologic: sleep hygiene measures (see p 190).
• Pharmacologic: See restless legs syndrome, above.

## DEFINITION
Visual acuity 20/40 or worse; severe visual impairment (legal blindness) 20/200 or worse

## EVALUATION
### Acuity Testing
*Near Vision:* Check each eye independently with glasses using handheld Rosenbaum card at 14" or Lighthouse Near Acuity Test at 16".
*Far Vision:* Snellen wall chart at 20'
*Visual Fields:* By confrontation

### Ophthalmoscopic Evaluation
*Tonometry:* Using Tono-pen (portable)

### Causes of Visual Impairment in Decreasing Order of Frequency
*Refractive Error:* Most common cause of impairment
*Cataracts:* Lens opacity on ophthalmoscopic examination. Risk factors: Age, sun exposure, smoking, corticosteroids, diabetes mellitus.
*Age-Related Macular Degeneration (ARMD):* Atrophy of cells in the central macular region of retinal pigmented epithelium; on ophthalmoscopic examination white-yellow patches (drusen) or hemorrhage and scars in advanced stages. Risk factors: Age, smoking, sunlight exposure, family hx, white race.
*Diabetic Retinopathy:* Microaneurysms, dot and blot hemorrhages on ophthalmoscopy with proliferative retinopathy ischemia and vitreous hemorrhage. Risk factors: Chronic hyperglycemia, smoking.
*Glaucoma:* Intraocular pressure >21 mm Hg, optic cupping and nerve head atrophy, and loss of peripheral visual fields. Risk factors: Black race, age, family hx, elevated eye pressures.

## MANAGEMENT
### Prevention
Biennial full eye examinations for persons >65 years of age, annually for diabetic persons

### Nonpharmacologic Interventions
*ARMD:* Photodynamic therapy for some wet forms: monitor for conversion to wet form using Amsler grid daily.
*Cataract:* Reduce UV light exposure. Surgery: AHRQ guidelines (AHCPR Publication No. 93-0542): if acuity 20/50 or worse with symptoms of poor functional acuity; or if 20/40 or better with disabling glare or frequent exposure to low light situations, diplopia, disparity between eyes, or occupational need; or when cataract removal will treat another lens-induced disease (eg, glaucoma); or when cataract coexists with retinal disease requiring unrestricted monitoring (eg, diabetic retinopathy)
*Diabetic Retinopathy:* Laser treatment of proliferative retinopathy or macular edema

*Glaucoma Surgery:* Open angle—laser trabeculoplasty or surgical trabeculectomy; angle closure—laser iridotomy; used primarily when pressures are poorly controlled by topical agents or when visual loss progresses

## Pharmacologic Interventions

*ARMD:* For intermediate or more advanced stages: Zinc oxide 80 mg, cupric oxide 2 mg, β-carotene 15 mg, vitamin C 500 mg, and vitamin E 400 IU taken in divided doses bid reduces risk of progression (eg, *Ocuvite PreserVision* 2 tabs po bid).

*Diabetic Retinopathy:* Glycemic control $HbA_1c$ 7–9%; BP < 130/80; lipid control not well studied (see p 61)

*Glaucoma:* Treat when pressures are >25 mm Hg or with optic nerve damage or visual field loss (see **Table 89**). Instill drops under lower lid, close eye for at least 1 min to reduce systemic absorption; wait 5 min before instilling a second type of drop.

### Table 89. Agents for Treating Glaucoma

| Drug | Strength | Dosage | Comments (Metabolism) |
|---|---|---|---|
| **Adrenergic Agonists (bottles with purple caps)** | | | |
| Apraclonidine (*Iopidine*) | 0.5%, 1% | 1–2 drops tid | Low BP, fatigue, drowsiness, dry mouth, dry nose (unknown) |
| Brimonidine (*Alphagan*) | 0.2% | 1 drop tid | Low BP, fatigue, drowsiness, dry mouth, dry nose (L) |
| (*Alphagan P*) | 0.15% | 1 drop tid | Benzalkonium-chloride free |
| Dipivefrin (*AKPro, Propine*) | 0.1% | 1 drop bid | HTN, headache, tachycardia, arrhythmia (eye, L) |
| Epinephrine (*Epifrin, Glaucon*) | 0.1%–2% | 1 drop qd–bid | HTN, headache, tachycardia, arrhythmia (L) |
| Epinephrine borate (*Epinal*) | 0.25%–0.5% | 1 drop bid | HTN, headache, tachycardia, arrhythmia (L) |
| **β-Blockers (bottles with blue or yellow caps)** | | | Class adverse events: |
| Betaxolol (*Betoptic, Betoptic-S*) | 0.25%, 0.5% | 1–2 drops bid | hypotension, bradycardia, HF, bronchospasm, anxiety, confusion, hallucination, diarrhea, nausea, cramps, lethargy, weakness, masking of hypoglycemia, impotence (L) |
| Carteolol (*Ocupress*) | 1% | 1 drop bid | |
| Levobunolol (*AKBeta, Betagan*) | 0.25%, 0.5% | 1 drop bid | |
| Metipranolol (*OptiPranolol*) | 0.3% | 1 drop bid | |
| Timolol drops (*Betimol, Timoptic*) | 0.25%, 0.5% | 1 drop bid | |
| **Miotics, Direct-Acting (bottles with green caps)** | | | |
| Pilocarpine gel (*Pilopine HS*) | 4% | 1/2" qhs | Systemic cholinergic effects (tissues, K) |
| (*Ocusert*) | 20, 40 µg/h | Weekly | |

*(cont.)*

| Table 89. Agents for Treating Glaucoma (cont.) | | | |
|---|---|---|---|
| **Drug** | **Strength** | **Dosage** | **Comments (Metabolism)** |
| Pilocarpine (*Adsorbocarpine, Akarpine, Isopto Carpine, Pilagan, Pilocar, Piloptic, Pilostat*) | 0.25%–10% | 1 drop qid | Systemic cholinergic effects are rare (K) |
| **Miotics, Cholinesterase Inhibitors (bottles with green caps)** | | | Class adverse events: |
| Demecarium (*Humorsol*) | 0.125%, 0.25% | 1–2 drops bid | cholinomimetic effects (sweating, tremor, headache, salivation), confusion, high or low BP, bradycardia, bronchoconstriction, urinary frequency, cramps, diarrhea, nausea, deterioration of mental status in persons with AD |
| Echothiophate (*Phospholine*) | 0.03%–0.25% | 1 drop bid | |
| Isoflurophate (*Floropryl*) | 0.025% oint | 0.25" strip 8–72 h | |
| Physostigmine (*Eserine, Fisostin, Isopto Eserine*) | 0.25% oint | 1" tid | (L) |
| **Carbonic Anhydrase Inhibitors (bottles with orange caps)** | | | |
| ***Topical*** | | | Caution in kidney failure (K) |
| ✔Brinzolamide (*Azopt*) | 1% | 1 drop tid | |
| ✔Dorzolamide (*Trusopt*) | 2% | 1 drop tid | |
| ***Oral*** | | | Class adverse events: |
| Acetazolamide (eg, *Diamox*) | 125–500 mg, 500 mg SR | 250–500 mg bid–qid, 500 SR bid | fatigue, weight loss, paresthesias, depression, COPD exacerbation, cramps, diarrhea, kidney failure, blood dyscrasias, hypokalemia, acidosis; not recommended in kidney failure (K) |
| Dichlorphenamide (*Daranide*) | 50 mg | 25–50 mg qd–tid | |
| Methazolamide (eg, *Neptazane*) | 25–50 mg | 50–100 mg bid–tid | (L,K) |
| **Prostaglandin Analogues** | | | Class adverse events: |
| | | | change in eye color and periorbital tissues, hyperemia, itching; expensive (K, L) |
| Bimatoprost (*Lumigan*) | 0.03% | 1 drop hs | (L,K,F) |
| Latanoprost (*Xalatan*) | 0.005% | 1 drop hs | (L) |
| Travoprost (*Travatan*) | 0.004% | 1 drop hs | (L) |
| Unoprostone (*Rescula*) | 0.15% | 1 drop hs | (L) |

(cont.)

| Table 89. Agents for Treating Glaucoma (cont.) | | | |
|---|---|---|---|
| Drug | Strength | Dosage | Comments (Metabolism) |
| **Other Topical** | | | |
| Dorzolamide/timolol (*Cosopt*) | 0.2%, 0.05% | 1 drop bid | Unusual taste, ocular itching, burning (K, L) |

✔ = preferred for treating older persons.
Note:  Patients may not know names of drugs but instead refer to them by the color of the bottle cap. The usual color scheme is referenced above.

## Low-Vision Services
• These services address the full range of functional vision impairment from blindness to partial sight. Refer patients with uncompensated visual loss that reduces function.
• The service will recommend optical aids:
  ◦ Magnifiers with lights
  ◦ Wearable telescopes for distance vision
  ◦ Closed-circuit television to enlarge text
  ◦ A variety of high-technology devices are available and under development (see products at *www.lighthouse.org*).
  ◦ Optical aids (like the above) may improve mood as opposed to traditional aids such as talking books, Braille watches, etc, which do not.
• Strategies include magnification, improved illumination, increased contrast, and auditory and tactile feedback.
• Environmental modifications that improve function include color contrast, floor lamps to reduce glare, and motion sensors to turn on lights.
• Many states have "Services for the Visually Impaired" through the state health department.

## Dry Eye Syndrome
***Symptoms:*** Itchy or sandy (foreign body sensation)
***Etiology:*** Many; consider autoimmune (Sjögren's syndrome), drug-induced, refer to ophthalmology for diagnostic assistance.
***Therapy:***
• Artificial tear formulations (eg, *HypoTears*)
• Viscoelastic tear formulations containing either chondroitin sulfate or hyaluronic acid are not better than artificial tears.
• Cyclosporine ophthalmic emulsion 0.05% (*Restasis*) 1 gtt OU q 12 h. Indicated when tear production is suppressed by inflammation. Does not increase tears in persons using topical anti-inflammatories or punctal plugs. Adverse events: burning, hyperemia, discharge, pain, blurring.

## Acute Conjunctivitis
***Symptoms:*** Red eye, foreign body sensation, discharge, photophobia
***Signs:*** Conjunctival hyperemia and discharge. Visual acuity, pupillary light reflexes, and visual fields are normal. If eye functions are abnormal, refer to ophthalmology for urgent diagnosis.
***Differential diagnosis:*** Acute iritis, acute glaucoma, episcleritis, or scleritis.
***Etiology:*** Viral, bacterial, chlamydial, chemical, foreign body

*Viral versus bacterial:* **Viral**—profuse tearing, minimal exudation, preauricular adenopathy common, monocytes in stained scrapings and exudates;
**bacterial**—moderate tearing, profuse exudation, preauricular adenopathy uncommon, bacteria and polymorphonuclear cells in stained scrapings and exudates;
**both**—minimal itching, generalized hyperemia, occasional sore throat and fever.
*Treatment:* Majority are viral; treat symptoms with artificial tears and cool compresses. If purulent discharge, suspect bacterial; start broad-spectrum topical antibiotics (see **Table 51**). If severe, obtain culture and Gram's stain, then start treatment. If signs and symptoms fail to improve in 24–48 h, refer to ophthalmologist. If vision decreased or severe pain, refer to ophthalmologist immediately.
*Other:* Frequent hand washing and use of separate towels to avoid spread.

| Table 90. Treatment for Acute Bacterial Conjunctivitis* | | |
|---|---|---|
| Agent | Formulations** | Comments |
| Ciprofloxacin (*Ciloxan Ophthalmic*) | 0.3% sol, 0.3% oint | Very broad spectrum, well tolerated, a 1st choice in severe cases, expensive |
| Erythromycin ophthalmic (*AK-Mycin, Ilotycin*) | 5 mg/g oint | Good if staphylococcal blepharitis is present |
| Gatifloxacin (*Tequin*) | 0.3% sol | Very broad spectrum, well tolerated, a 1st choice in severe cases, expensive |
| Moxifloxacin (*Avelox*) | 0.5% sol | Very broad spectrum, well tolerated, a 1st choice in severe cases, expensive |
| Norfloxacin (*Chibroxin*) | 0.3% sol | Very broad spectrum, well tolerated, a 1st choice in severe cases, expensive |
| Ofloxacin (*Floxin, Ocuflox Ophthalmic*) | 0.3% sol, 0.3% oint | Very broad spectrum, well tolerated, a 1st choice in severe cases, expensive |
| Sulfacetamide sodium (*Sodium Sulamyd*) | 10%, 30% drops, 10% oint | Same coverage as trimethoprim and polymyxin |
| Tobramycin (*AKTob, Tobrex*) | 3 mg/g oint, 3 mg/mL sol | Well tolerated, but more corneal toxic |
| Trimethoprim and polymyxin (*Polytrim*) | 1 mg/mL, 10,000 IU/mL sol | Well tolerated but some gaps in coverage |

* Do not use steroid or steroid-antibiotic preparations in initial treatment.

** In mild cases solution is applied qid and gel or ointments bid for 5–7 d. In more severe cases solution is applied q 2–3 h, ointment qid; as the eye improves, solution is applied qid and ointment, bid.

## Systemic Medications with Ocular Adverse Events (symptoms, signs)
- Amiodarone: halos, blurred vision, corneal changes, optic neuropathy
- Anticholinergics: blurry near vision, angle-closure glaucoma (rare)
- Cisplatin: decreased central and color vision, optic disk edema, neuritis, corneal blindness
- Corticosteroids: cataracts, glaucoma
- Digoxin: yellowish orange vision; snowy, flickering vision
- Ethambutol or INH: loss of color vision, visual acuity, visual field
- Hydroxychloroquine or chloroquine: loss of color vision, visual acuity, visual field
- Niacin: decreased visual field, maculopathy
- Sildenafil: color tinge in vision (often blue haze), increased sensitivity to light, blurred vision (may be PDE5 inhibitor class effect)

## PREVENTION (See also **Table 70**)
- Annual breast and pelvic and perineal examination
- Annual mammography if life expectancy >4 yr
- Discuss HRT risks/benefits with patients on treatment
- One negative Pap smear after 65 yr if low risk (ie, single established sexual partner, good prior screening, no hx of abnormal Pap smear)
- Osteoporosis evaluation (see p 138)

## COMMON DISORDERS
### Breast Cancer
*Prevention:* Also see **Table 70**. Tamoxifen 20 mg po qd reduces breast cancer risk by 49% in women at high risk. For risk assessment see prevention section of http://www.cancer.gov/cancerinfo/pdq/prevention/breast/healthprofessional

*Monitoring:*
- History, physical
- LFTs, calcium every 4–6 mo for 5 yr, then yearly
- Annual mammography, pelvic, and FOBT

*Oral Hormone Adjuvant Therapy:* Postmenopausal women with estrogen receptor (ER) or progesterone receptor (PR) positive tumors at high risk for recurrence (tumors greater than 1 cm, or positive nodes) should be treated with oral adjuvant therapy for 5 yr, even when treated with chemotherapy. See **Table 91**.

*Adjuvant Chemotherapy:* Reduces recurrence risk for receptor-negative tumors. There is an additional 5% to 10% reduction in recurrence in ER- or PR-positive tumors treated with both tamoxifen and chemotherapy. Tamoxifen is first-line therapy except in women with thromboembolic or cerebrovascular disease, in which case anastrazole is the preferred agent. Also use anastrazole if intolerant to tamoxifen.

*Therapy for Metastatic Bone Disease:* Pamidronate or zoledronic acid reduces morbidity and delays time to onset of bone symptoms. Consult oncology.

| Table 91. Oral Agents for Breast Cancer Treatment | | | | |
|---|---|---|---|---|
| Class, Agent | Dosage | Formulations | Monitoring | Comments |
| **Anti-estrogen Drugs** | | | | |
| Fulvestrant (*Faslodex*) | 250 mg IM 1/mo in 1 or 2 injections | Inj | Blood chemistry, lipids | Has potent CYP3A4 inhibitors; GI reactions, anesthesia, pain (back, pelvic, headache), hot flushes |
| Tamoxifen* (*Nolvadex*) | 20 mg po qd | T: 10, 20 | Annual eye exam; endometrial cancer screening | Drug interactions: erythromycin, calcium channel blockers; ↑ risk of thrombosis |
| Toremifene (*Fareston*) | 60 mg po qd | T: 60 | CBC, Ca, LFTs, BUN, Cr | Drug interactions with CYP3A4–6 inhibitors and inducers (see **Table 7**); ↑ warfarin effect |

*(cont.)*

Table 91. Oral Agents for Breast Cancer Treatment (cont.)

| Class, Agent | Dosage | Formulations | Monitoring | Comments |
|---|---|---|---|---|
| **Aromatase Inhibitors**[†] | | | | |
| Anastrazole (*Arimidex*) | 1 mg po qd | T: 1 | Periodic CBC, lipids, serum chemistry profile | Preferred aromatase inhibitor as alternative to tamoxifen for adjuvant; first-line for metastatic disease or tamoxifen failure |
| Exemestane (*Aromasin*) | 25 mg po qd | T: 25 | Periodic WBC with differential, lipids, serum chemistry profile | First-line adjuvant therapy for hormone-responsive metastatic disease or tamoxifen failure |
| Letrozole (*Femara*) | 2.5 mg po qd | T: 2.5 | Periodic CBC, LFTs, TSH | First-line adjuvant therapy for hormone-responsive metastatic disease or tamoxifen failure |

\* Reduce dose if CrCl <10 mL/min.
† All have randomized trial data showing superiority to tamoxifen alone.

## Vulvar Diseases
### Non-neoplastic:
• Lichen sclerosus—Common on vulva of middle-aged and older women; causes 1/3 of benign vulvar lesions, extends to perirectal areas (classic hourglass appearance); lesions are white to pink macules or papules, may coalesce; symptoms are none or itching, soreness, or dyspareunia. Must biopsy for diagnosis: Associated with squamous cell cancer in 4% to 5%. R$_x$: Clobetasol propionate 0.05% qd–bid for 8–12 wk; then taper gradually to zero. Long-term follow-up advised.
• Squamous hyperplasia—Raised white keratinized lesions difficult to distinguish from VIN; must biopsy to exclude malignancy. R$_x$: Betamethasone dipropionate 0.05% for 6–8 wk, then 1% hydrocortisone if symptoms persist; long-term follow-up advised.
### Neoplastic:
• VIN—Most often seen in postmenopausal women; asymptomatic or may cause pruritus; appear as hypo- or hyperpigmented keratinized lesions; often multifocal; inspection ± colposcopy with biopsy of most worrisome lesions; lesions graded on degree of atypia. R$_x$: surgical or other ablative therapy.
• Vulvar malignancy—Half of cases occur in women aged >70 yr; 80% are squamous cell, with melanoma, sarcoma, basal cell, and adenocarcinoma <20%; biopsy any suspicious lesion. R$_x$: radical surgery is preferred treatment.

## Postmenopausal Bleeding
Bleeding after 1 yr of amenorrhea:
• Exclude malignancy, identify source, treat symptoms.
• Examine genitalia, perineum, rectum.
• If endometrial source, use endometrial biopsy or vaginal probe ultrasound to assess endometrial thickness (<5 mm virtually excludes malignancy).
• D&C when endometrium not otherwise adequately assessed.
• Women on combination continuous estrogen and progesterone who bleed after 12 mo need evaluation.

- Those on cyclic replacement with bleeding at unexpected times (ie, bleeding other than during the second week of progesterone therapy) need evaluation.
- Women on unopposed estrogen who bleed at any time need evaluation.

## Hot Flushes
- Vasomotor symptoms respond to estrogen (see **Table 93**) in dose-response fashion; start low dose, titrate to effect.
- If estrogen cannot be taken, try one of the less effective alternatives:
  ○ Megestrol (*Megace*): [T: 20, 40] 20 mg qd–bid
  ○ Venlafaxine (*Effexor*) 75–150 mg/d
  ○ Fluoxetine (*Prozac*) 20 mg/d
  ○ Paroxetine (*Paxil CR*) 12.5–25 mg/d
  ○ Gabapentin (*Neurontin*) usually 300–600 tid [C: 100, 300, 400; T: 600, 800; S: 250/5 mL]
  ○ Clonidine (*Catapres, Duraclon*): [T: 0.1, 0.2, 0.3] 0.1–0.3 mg/d; use lowest effective dose, watch for orthostatic ↓ BP and rebound ↑ BP if used intermittently

## Vaginal Prolapse
- Child-bearing and other causes of increased intra-abdominal pressure weaken connective tissue and muscles supporting the genital organs, leading to prolapse.
- Symptoms include: Pelvic pressure, back pain, fecal or urinary incontinence, difficulty evacuating the rectum. Symptoms may be present even with mild prolapse.
- The degree of prolapse and organs involved dictate therapy; no therapy if asymptomatic.
- Estrogen and Kegel's exercises may help in mild cases.
- Pessary or surgery indicated with greater symptoms. Surgery needed for 4th-degree symptomatic prolapse.
- Precise anatomic defect(s) dictates the surgical approach.
- A common (ACOG) classification for degrees of prolapse:
  ○ First degree—extension to mid-vagina
  ○ Second degree—approaching hymenal ring
  ○ Third degree—at hymenal ring
  ○ Fourth degree—beyond hymenal ring

## Atrophic Vaginitis
Atrophic vaginitis can be treated with topical estrogens (see **Table 84**).

## HORMONE THERAPY
### Estrogen Therapy
- Current understanding of risks for women >65 yr old on estrogen replacement are given in **Table 92**.
- If the patient has a uterus, estrogen can be combined with progesterone to reduce risk of endometrial cancer.
- Some women prefer unopposed estrogen and annual endometrial biopsy.
- Common regimens are given in **Table 93**.
- Older women can get hot flushes if estrogen is discontinued suddenly. Tapering (eg, qod for 1–2 mo and then q 3 d for a few months) is better tolerated.

Table 92. Hormone Therapy Risks and Benefits After Age 65

| Outcome | Estrogen | Estrogen/Progesterone |
|---|---|---|
| MI | none | ↑* |
| Thromboembolic | ↑ DVT | ↑ DVT,PE |
| Stroke | ↑ | ↑ |
| Breast cancer | possibly ↓ | ↑** |
| Hip fracture | ↓ | ↓ |
| Colon cancer | none | ↓ |
| Endometrial cancer | ↑ | no change or ↓ |
| Gallbladder disease | ↑ | ↑ |
| Urogenital disease† | ↓ | ↓ |
| Dementia | unknown | ↑ |
| Ovarian cancer | ↑ | unknown |

* No increase in CHD mortality
** No clear increase in breast cancer mortality in Women's Health Initiative (WHI)
† Dyspareunia, UTI, vaginal dryness, and possibly incontinence

**Contraindications:**
- Undiagnosed vaginal bleeding
- Thromboembolic disease
- Breast cancer
- Endometrial cancer greater than Stage 1
- Possibly gallbladder disease
- CHD

Table 93. Common Regimens for Systemic Hormone Therapy*

| Preparation | Starting Dosage (mg/d) | Cyclic Dosing | Continuous Dosing | Formulations |
|---|---|---|---|---|
| **Oral** | | | | |
| Conjugated equine estrogen (*Premarin*)** | 0.3–0.625 | — | Daily | T: 0.3, 0.625, 0.9, 1.25, 2.5 |
| Conjugated synthetic estrogen (*Cenestin*) | 0.625 | — | Daily | T: 0.625, 0.9, 1.25 |
| Esterified estrogen (eg, *Estratab, Menest*)** | 0.3–0.625 | — | Daily | T: 0.3, 0.625, 1.25, 2.5 |
| Estropipate (*Ogen, Ortho-Est*)** | 0.625 | — | Daily | T: 0.625, 1.25, 2.5 |
| Micronized 17-β estradiol (*Estrace*)** | 0.5–1 | — | Daily | T: 0.5, 1, 2 |
| **Oral Combinations** | | | | |
| Conjugated estrogen *and* medroxyprogesterone (*Prempro*) | 0.625, 0.45 1.5, 2.5, 5 | — | Daily | Fixed dose 0.625/2.5 or 0.625/5 or 0.45/1.5 |
| Conjugated estrogen *and* medroxyprogesterone (*Premphase*) | 0.625 5 | Days 1–28 Days 15–28 | — | Fixed dose 0.625 days 1–14, 0.625/5 days 15–28 |

*(cont.)*

| Preparation | Starting Dosage (mg/d) | Cyclic Dosing | Continuous Dosing | Formulations |
|---|---|---|---|---|
| Estradiol *and* norethindrone (*FEMHRT 1/5*) | 1 5 | — | Daily | Fixed dose 1.0/5 |
| **Transdermal** | | | | |
| Transdermal estrogen | | | | |
| (*Alora*) | 0.05–0.75 | — | Biweekly | 0.05 0.075, 0.1 |
| (*Bio-E-Gel*) | 0.75 | — | Apply 1 packet topically daily | Gel (0.06%), 1.25 g/packet |
| (*Estrasorb*) | 0.05 | — | Apply 2 packets topically daily | Emulsion, 1.74 g/packet |
| (*Estraderm*)** | 0.05–0.75 | — | Biweekly | 0.05, 0.1 |
| (*Vivelle*)** | 0.0375–0.05 | — | Biweekly | 0.025, 0.0375, 0.05, 0.075, 0.1 |
| (*Climara*)** | 0.025–0.05 | — | Weekly | 0.025, 0.05, 0.075, 0.1 |
| (*FemPatch*) | 0.025–0.05 | — | Weekly | 0.025 |
| (*EstroGel*) | 0.75 | — | Daily | Metered-dose pump: 1.25 g/pump (0.75 mg estradiol) |
| Estradiol *and* norethindrone (*CombiPatch*) | 0.05/0.14 | Biweekly for 3 wk, 1 wk off | — | 0.05/0.14, 0.05/0.25 |
| **Other** | | | | |
| Femring | 0.05 | — | Intravaginal ring, change q 90 d | 0.05, 0.10 |
| Medroxyprogesterone (*Cycrin, Provera*) | 2.5–10 | 5–10 mg, days 1–14 | 2.5–5 mg daily | T: 2.5, 5, 10 |

Table 93. **Common Regimens for Systemic Hormone Therapy\* (cont.)**

\* See also **Table 84** for topical estrogens without systemic effects.
\*\* FDA approved for long-term use to prevent osteoporosis.

## MINI-COG ASSESSMENT INSTRUMENT FOR DEMENTIA

The Mini-Cog assessment instrument combines an uncued 3-item recall test with a clock-drawing test (CDT). The Mini-Cog can be administered in about 3 min, requires no special equipment, and is relatively uninfluenced by level of education or language variations.

### Administration

The test is administered as follows:

1. Instruct the patient to listen carefully to and remember 3 unrelated words and then to repeat the words.
2. Instruct the patient to draw the face of a clock, either on a blank sheet of paper, or on a sheet with the clock circle already drawn on the page. After the patient puts the numbers on the clock face, ask him or her to draw the hands of the clock to read a specific time, such as 11:20. These instructions can be repeated, but no additional instructions should be given. Give the patient as much time as needed to complete the task. The CDT serves as the recall distractor.
3. Ask the patient to repeat the 3 previously presented words.

### Scoring

Give 1 point for each recalled word after the CDT distractor. Score 1–3.
  ○ A score of 0 indicates positive screen for dementia.
  ○ A score of 1 or 2 with an abnormal CDT indicates positive screen for dementia.
  ○ A score of 1 or 2 with a normal CDT indicates negative screen for dementia.
  ○ A score of 3 indicates negative screen for dementia.
The CDT is considered normal if all numbers are present in the correct sequence and position, and the hands readably display the requested time.

Source: Adapted in part from Borson S, Scanlan J, Brush M, Vitaliano P, Dokmak A. The mini-cog: a cognitive "vital signs" measure for dementia screening in multi-lingual elderly. *Int J Geriatr Psychiatry* 2000; 15(11):1021–1027.

Mini-Cog™ Copyright 2000 and 2004 by Soo Borsen and James Scanlon. All rights reserved. Described here under license from the University of Washington, solely for use as a clinical aid. Any other use is strictly prohibited. To obtain information on the Mini-Cog™ contact Soo Borsen at soob@u.washington.edu.

## PHYSICAL SELF-MAINTENANCE SCALE (ACTIVITIES OF DAILY LIVING, OR ADLs)

In each category, circle the item that most closely describes the person's highest level of functioning and record the score assigned to that level (either 1 or 0) in the blank at the beginning of the category.

**A. Toilet** _____
1. Care for self at toilet completely; no incontinence ..................................................1
2. Needs to be reminded, or needs help in cleaning self, or has rare (weekly at most) accidents...........................................................................................................0
3. Soiling or wetting while asleep more than once a week.............................................0
4. Soiling or wetting while awake more than once a week.............................................0
5. No control of bowels or bladder ..........................................................................0

**B. Feeding** _____

1. Eats without assistance. . . . . . . . . . . . . . . . . . . . . . . . . . . . . . . . . . . . . . . . . . . . . . . . . . . . . .1
2. Eats with minor assistance at meal times and/or with special preparation of food, or help in cleaning up after meals . . . . . . . . . . . . . . . . . . . . . . . . . . . . . . . . . . . . . . . . . . . . . . . . .0
3. Feeds self with moderate assistance and is untidy . . . . . . . . . . . . . . . . . . . . . . . . . . . . . . .0
4. Requires extensive assistance for all meals . . . . . . . . . . . . . . . . . . . . . . . . . . . . . . . . . . .0
5. Does not feed self at all and resists efforts of others to feed him or her . . . . . . . . . . . . . . . .0

**C. Dressing** _____

1. Dresses, undresses, and selects clothes from own wardrobe . . . . . . . . . . . . . . . . . . . . . . .1
2. Dresses and undresses self, with minor assistance . . . . . . . . . . . . . . . . . . . . . . . . . . . . . .0
3. Needs moderate assistance in dressing and selection of clothes. . . . . . . . . . . . . . . . . . . . .0
4. Needs major assistance in dressing, but cooperates with efforts of others to help . . . . . . . . .0
5. Completely unable to dress self and resists efforts of others to help . . . . . . . . . . . . . . . . . .0

**D. Grooming (neatness, hair, nails, hands, face, clothing)** _____

1. Always neatly dressed, well-groomed, without assistance . . . . . . . . . . . . . . . . . . . . . . . . .1
2. Grooms self adequately with occasional minor assistance, eg, with shaving. . . . . . . . . . . . .0
3. Needs moderate and regular assistance or supervision with grooming . . . . . . . . . . . . . . . . .0
4. Needs total grooming care, but can remain well-groomed after help from others . . . . . . . . . .0
5. Actively negates all efforts of others to maintain grooming . . . . . . . . . . . . . . . . . . . . . . . . .0

**E. Physical Ambulation** _____

1. Goes about grounds or city . . . . . . . . . . . . . . . . . . . . . . . . . . . . . . . . . . . . . . . . . . . . . . . .1
2. Ambulates within residence on or about one block distant. . . . . . . . . . . . . . . . . . . . . . . . . .0
3. Ambulates with assistance of (check one)
   a ( ) another person, b ( ) railing, c ( ) cane, d ( ) walker, e ( ) wheelchair . . . . . . . . . . . . .0
   1.___Gets in and out without help. 2.___Needs help getting in and out
4. Sits unsupported in chair or wheelchair, but cannot propel self without help. . . . . . . . . . . . .0
5. Bedridden more than half the time . . . . . . . . . . . . . . . . . . . . . . . . . . . . . . . . . . . . . . . . . .0

**F. Bathing** _____

1. Bathes self (tub, shower, sponge bath) without help. . . . . . . . . . . . . . . . . . . . . . . . . . . . . .1
2. Bathes self with help getting in and out of tub. . . . . . . . . . . . . . . . . . . . . . . . . . . . . . . . . . .0
3. Washes face and hands only, but cannot bathe rest of body . . . . . . . . . . . . . . . . . . . . . . . .0
4. Does not wash self, but is cooperative with those who bathe him or her. . . . . . . . . . . . . . . .0
5. Does not try to wash self and resists efforts to keep him or her clean. . . . . . . . . . . . . . . . . .0

For scoring interpretation and source, see note following the next instrument.

# INSTRUMENTAL ACTIVITIES OF DAILY LIVING SCALE (IADLs)

In each category, circle the item that most closely describes the person's highest level of functioning and record the score assigned to that level (either 1 or 0) in the blank at the beginning of the category.

**A. Ability to Use Telephone** _____

1. Operates telephone on own initiative; looks up and dials numbers. . . . . . . . . . . . . . . . . . . . .1
2. Dials a few well-known numbers. . . . . . . . . . . . . . . . . . . . . . . . . . . . . . . . . . . . . . . . . . . . .1
3. Answers telephone, but does not dial. . . . . . . . . . . . . . . . . . . . . . . . . . . . . . . . . . . . . . . . .1
4. Does not use telephone at all. . . . . . . . . . . . . . . . . . . . . . . . . . . . . . . . . . . . . . . . . . . . . . .0

**B. Shopping** _____

1. Takes care of all shopping needs independently. . . . . . . . . . . . . . . . . . . . . . . . . . . . . . . . .1
2. Shops independently for small purchases. . . . . . . . . . . . . . . . . . . . . . . . . . . . . . . . . . . . . .0
3. Needs to be accompanied on any shopping trip. . . . . . . . . . . . . . . . . . . . . . . . . . . . . . . . . .0
4. Completely unable to shop. . . . . . . . . . . . . . . . . . . . . . . . . . . . . . . . . . . . . . . . . . . . . . . . .0

**C. Food Preparation**                                                         ___
   1. Plans, prepares, and serves adequate meals independently. . . . . . . . . . . . . . . . . . . . . . . . . . . .1
   2. Prepares adequate meals if supplied with ingredients. . . . . . . . . . . . . . . . . . . . . . . . . . . . . . .0
   3. Heats and serves prepared meals or prepares meals, but does not maintain
      adequate diet. . . . . . . . . . . . . . . . . . . . . . . . . . . . . . . . . . . . . . . . . . . . . . . . . . . . . . . . . . . . . . . .0
   4. Needs to have meals prepared and served. . . . . . . . . . . . . . . . . . . . . . . . . . . . . . . . . . . . . . .0

**D. Housekeeping**                                                             ___
   1. Maintains house alone or with occasional assistance (eg, heavy-work
      domestic help). . . . . . . . . . . . . . . . . . . . . . . . . . . . . . . . . . . . . . . . . . . . . . . . . . . . . . . . . . . . . .1
   2. Performs light daily tasks such as dishwashing, bedmaking. . . . . . . . . . . . . . . . . . . . . . . .1
   3. Performs light daily tasks, but cannot maintain acceptable level of cleanliness. . . . . . . . . . .1
   4. Needs help with all home maintenance tasks. . . . . . . . . . . . . . . . . . . . . . . . . . . . . . . . . . . . .1
   5. Does not participate in any housekeeping tasks. . . . . . . . . . . . . . . . . . . . . . . . . . . . . . . . . .0

**E. Laundry**                                                                  ___
   1. Does personal laundry completely. . . . . . . . . . . . . . . . . . . . . . . . . . . . . . . . . . . . . . . . . . . . .1
   2. Launders small items; rinses socks, stockings, etc. . . . . . . . . . . . . . . . . . . . . . . . . . . . . . .1
   3. All laundry must be done by others. . . . . . . . . . . . . . . . . . . . . . . . . . . . . . . . . . . . . . . . . . . .0

**F. Mode of Transportation**                                                   ___
   1. Travels independently on public transportation or drives own car. . . . . . . . . . . . . . . . . . . .1
   2. Arranges own travel via taxi, but does not otherwise use public transportation. . . . . . . . . .1
   3. Travels on public transportation when assisted or accompanied by another. . . . . . . . . . . . .1
   4. Travel limited to taxi or automobile with assistance of another. . . . . . . . . . . . . . . . . . . . . .0
   5. Does not travel at all. . . . . . . . . . . . . . . . . . . . . . . . . . . . . . . . . . . . . . . . . . . . . . . . . . . . . . . .0

**G. Responsibility for Own Medications**                                       ___
   1. Is responsible for taking medication in correct dosages at correct time. . . . . . . . . . . . . . .1
   2. Takes responsibility if medication is prepared in advance in separate dosages. . . . . . . . . .0
   3. Is not capable of dispensing own medication. . . . . . . . . . . . . . . . . . . . . . . . . . . . . . . . . . . .0

**H. Ability to Handle Finances**                                               ___
   1. Manages financial matters independently (budgets, writes checks, pays rent
      and bills, goes to bank); collects and keeps track of income. . . . . . . . . . . . . . . . . . . . . . .1
   2. Manages day-to-day purchases, but needs help with banking, major
      purchases, etc. . . . . . . . . . . . . . . . . . . . . . . . . . . . . . . . . . . . . . . . . . . . . . . . . . . . . . . . . . . . .1
   3. Incapable of handling money. . . . . . . . . . . . . . . . . . . . . . . . . . . . . . . . . . . . . . . . . . . . . . . . . .0

Scoring Interpretation: For ADLs, the total score ranges from 0 to 6, and for IADLs, from 0 to 8. In some categories, only the highest level of function receives a 1; in others, two or more levels have scores of 1 because each describes competence that represents some minimal level of function. These screens are useful for indicating specifically how a person is performing at the present time. When they are also used over time, they serve as documentation of a person's functional improvement or deterioration.

Source: Lawton MP, Brody EM. Assessment of older people: self-maintaining and instrumental activities of daily living. *Gerontologist* 1969, 9:179–186. Copyright by the Gerontological Society of America. Reproduced by permission of the publisher.

## GERIATRIC DEPRESSION SCALE (GDS, SHORT FORM)

Choose the best answer for how you felt over the past week.

   1. Are you basically satisfied with your life?                     yes/**no**
   2. Have you dropped many of your activities and interests?         **yes**/no
   3. Do you feel that your life is empty?                            **yes**/no
   4. Do you often get bored?                                         **yes**/no

5. Are you in good spirits most of the time?     yes/**no**
6. Are you afraid that something bad is going to happen to you?     **yes**/no
7. Do you feel happy most of the time?     yes/**no**
8. Do you often feel helpless?     **yes**/no
9. Do you prefer to stay at home, rather than going out and doing new things?     **yes**/no
10. Do you feel you have more problems with memory than most?     **yes**/no
11. Do you think it is wonderful to be alive now?     yes/**no**
12. Do you feel pretty worthless the way you are now?     **yes**/no
13. Do you feel full of energy?     yes/**no**
14. Do you feel that your situation is hopeless?     **yes**/no
15. Do you think that most people are better off than you are?     **yes**/no

Score 1 point for each bolded answer. Cut-off: normal (0–5), above 5 suggests depression.

Source: Courtesy of Jerome A. Yesavage, MD. For 30 translations of the GDS, see
http://www.stanford.edu/~yesavage/GDS.html
For additional information on administration and scoring, refer to the following references:
Sheikh JI, Yesavage JA. Geriatric Depression Scale: recent evidence and development of a shorter version. *Clin Gerontol.* 1986;5:165–172.
Feher EP, Larrabee GJ, Crook TH 3rd. Factors attenuating the validity of the Geriatric Depression Scale in a dementia population. *J Am Geriatr Soc.* 1992;40:906–909.
Yesavage JA, Brink TL, Rose TL et al. Development and validation of a geriatric depression rating scale: a preliminary report. *J Psychiatr Res.* 1983;17:27.

## BRIEF HEARING LOSS SCREENER

    **Points**

1. Age:_____     _____
   *If age >70 years = 1 point*
2. Sex: Male_____ Female_____     _____
   *If male = 1 point*
3. Highest grade attended:     _____
   12th grade or less_____
   higher than 12th grade_____
   *If ≤12th grade = 1 point*
4. Have you ever had deafness or trouble hearing with one or both ears?     __0__
   Yes_____, continue to Question #5.
   No_____, go to Question #6.
   *No points assigned to this question.*
5. Did you ever see a doctor about it?     _____
   Yes_____ No_____
   *If "Yes" = 2 points*
6. Without a hearing aid, can you usually hear and understand what a person says     _____
   without seeing his/her face if that person whispers to you from across the room?
   Yes_____ No_____
   *If "No" = 1 point*
7. Without a hearing aid, can you usually hear and understand what a person says     _____
   without seeing his/her face if that person talks to you in a normal voice from
   across the room?
   Yes_____ No_____
   *If "No" = 2 points*

**TOTAL**     _____

*3 or more points is a positive score indicating the need for further evaluation.*

**Test Characteristics of This Screener With Established Hearing Loss Criteria**

| | Sensitivity | Specificity | Pos Predictive Value | Neg Predictive Value |
|---|---|---|---|---|
| Ventry-Weinstein criteria | 80% | 80% | 45% | 95% |
| High-frequency pure-tone average | 59% | 88% | 76% | 77% |

Source: Reuben DB, Walsh K, Moore AA, et al. Hearing loss in community-dwelling older persons: national prevalence data and identification using simple questions. *J Am Geriatr Soc.* 1998;46:1011. Reprinted with permission.

## PERFORMANCE-ORIENTED MOBILITY ASSESSMENT (POMA)

### Balance

*Chair:* Instructions: Place a hard armless chair against a wall. The following maneuvers are tested.

1. Sitting down
   - 0 = unable without help or collapses (plops) into chair *or* lands off center of chair
   - 1 = able and does not meet criteria for 0 or 2
   - 2 = sits in a smooth, safe motion *and* ends with buttocks against back of chair and thighs centered on chair
2. Sitting balance
   - 0 = unable to maintain position (marked slide forward or leans forward or to side)
   - 1 = leans in chair slightly or slight increased distance from buttocks to back of chair
   - 2 = steady, safe, upright
3. Arising
   - 0 = unable without help or loses balance or requires >three attempts
   - 1 = able but requires three attempts
   - 2 = able in ≤two attempts
4. Immediate standing balance (first 5 seconds)
   - 0 = unsteady, marked staggering, moves feet, marked trunk sway or grabs object for support
   - 1 = steady but uses walker or cane or mild staggering but catches self without grabbing object
   - 2 = steady without walker or cane or other support

### Stand

5a. Side-by-side standing balance
   - 0= unable *or* unsteady *or* holds ≤3 seconds
   - 1= able *but* uses cane, walker, or other support *or* holds for 4–9 seconds
   - 2= narrow stance without support for 10 seconds
5b. Timing __ __.__ seconds
6. Pull test (person at maximum position attained in #5, examiner stands behind and exerts mild pull back at waist)
   - 0 = begins to fall
   - 1 = takes more than two steps back
   - 2 = fewer than two steps backward and steady
7a. Able to stand on right leg unsupported
   - 0 = unable *or* holds onto any objects *or* able for <3 seconds
   - 1 = able for 3 or 4 seconds
   - 2 = able for 5 seconds
7b. Timing __ __.__ seconds

8a. Able to stand on left leg unsupported
   0 = unable *or* holds onto any object *or* able for <3 seconds
   1 = able for 3 or 4 seconds
   2 = able for 5 seconds
8b. Timing __ __.__ seconds
9a. Semitandem stand
   0 = unable to stand with one foot half in front of other with feet touching *or* begins to fall *or* holds for ≤3 seconds
   1 = able for 4 to 9 seconds
   2 = able to semitandem stand for 10 seconds
9b. Timing __ __.__ seconds
10a. Tandem stand
   0 = unable to stand with one foot in front of other *or* begins to fall *or* holds for ≤3 seconds
   1 = able for 4 to 9 seconds
   2 = able to tandem stand for 10 seconds
10b. Timing __ __.__ seconds
11. Bending over (to pick up a pen off floor)
   0 = unable *or* is unsteady
   1 = able, but requires more than one attempt to get up
   2 = able and is steady
12. Toe stand
   0 = unable
   1 = able but <3 seconds
   2 = able for 3 seconds
13. Heel stand
   0 = unable
   1 = able but <3 seconds
   2 = able for 3 seconds

*Gait:* Instructions: Person stands with examiner, walks down 10-ft walkway (measured). Ask the person to walk down walkway, turn, and walk back. The person should use customary walking aid.

*Bare Floor* (flat, even surface)
1. Type of surface: 1 = linoleum or tile; 2 = wood; 3 = cement or concrete; 4 = other_____ [not included in scoring]
2. Initiation of gait (immediately after told to "go")
   0 = any hesitancy or multiple attempts to start
   1 = no hesitancy
3. Path (estimated in relation to tape measure). Observe excursion of foot closest to tape measure over middle 8 feet of course.
   0 = marked deviation
   1 = mild or moderate deviation *or* uses walking aid
   2 = straight without walking aid
4. Missed step (trip or loss of balance)
   0 = yes, and would have fallen *or* more than two missed steps
   1 = yes, but appropriate attempt to recover *and* no more than two missed steps
   2 = none
5. Turning (while walking)
   0 = almost falls
   1 = mild staggering, but catches self, uses walker or cane
   2 = steady, without walking aid

6.   Step over obstacles (to be assessed in a separate walk with two shoes placed on course 4 feet apart)

   0 = begins to fall at any obstacle or unable or walks around any obstacle or >two missed steps

   1 = able to step over all obstacles, but some staggering and catches self or one to two missed steps

   2 = able and steady at stepping over all four obstacles with no missed steps

Source: Courtesy of Mary E. Tinetti, MD. Adapted with permission.

## ABNORMAL INVOLUNTARY MOVEMENT SCALE (AIMS)

### Examination Procedure

Either before or after completing the examination procedure, observe the patient unobtrusively, at rest (eg, in waiting room). The chair to be used in this examination should be a hard, firm one without arms.

 1. Ask patient to remove shoes and socks.
 2. Ask patient whether there is anything in his/her mouth (ie, gum, candy, etc) and if there is, to remove it.
 3. Ask patient about the **current** condition of his/her teeth. Ask patient if he/she wears dentures. Do teeth or dentures bother patient **now**?
 4. Ask patient whether he/she notices any movements in mouth, face, hands, or feet. If yes, ask to describe and to what extent they **currently** bother patient or interfere with his/her activities.
 5. Have patient sit in chair with hands on knees, legs slightly apart, and feet flat on floor. (Look at entire body for movements while in this position.)
 6. Ask patient to sit with hands hanging unsupported. If male, between legs, if female wearing a dress, hanging over knees. (Observe hands and other body areas.)
 7. Ask patient to open mouth. (Observe tongue at rest within mouth.) Do this twice.
 8. Ask patient to protrude tongue. (Observe abnormalities of tongue movement.) Do this twice.
 9. Ask patient to tap thumb with each finger as rapidly as possible for 10–15 seconds; separately with right hand, then with left hand. (Observe facial and leg movements.)
10. Flex and extend patient's left and right arms (one at a time). (Note any rigidity.)
11. Ask patient to stand up. (Observe in profile. Observe all body areas again, hips included.)
12. Ask patient to extend both arms outstretched in front with palms down. (Observe trunk, legs, and mouth.)
13. Have patient walk a few paces, turn, and walk back to chair. (Observe hands and gait.) Do this twice.

***Instructions:*** Complete examination procedure before making ratings. Rate highest severity observed.

Code:
   1 None
   2 Minimal, may be extreme normal
   3 Mild
   4 Moderate
   5 Severe

## Facial and Oral Movements

1. Muscles of facial expression (eg, movements of forehead, eyebrows, periorbital area, cheeks; including frowning, blinking, smiling, grimacing)

   1        2        3        4        5

2. Lips and perioral area (eg, puckering, pouting, smacking)

   1        2        3        4        5

3. Jaw (eg, biting, clenching, chewing, mouth opening, lateral movement)

   1        2        3        4        5

4. Tongue (rate only increase in movement both in and out of mouth, NOT inability to sustain movement)

   1        2        3        4        5

## Extremity Movements

5. Upper (arms, wrists, hands, fingers). Include choreic movements (ie, rapid, objectively purposeless, irregular, spontaneous), athetoid movements (ie, slow, irregular, complex, serpentine). Do NOT include tremor (ie, repetitive, regular, rhythmic).

   1        2        3        4        5

6. Lower (legs, knees, ankles, toes). (Eg, lateral knee movement, foot tapping, heel dropping, foot squirming, inversion and eversion of foot)

   1        2        3        4        5

## Trunk Movements

7. Neck, shoulders, hips (eg, rocking, twisting, squirming, pelvic gyrations)

   1        2        3        4        5

## Global Judgments

8. Severity of abnormal movements
   1. None, normal
   2. Minimal
   3. Mild
   4. Moderate
   5. Severe
9. Incapacitation due to abnormal movements
   1. None, normal
   2. Minimal
   3. Mild
   4. Moderate
   5. Severe
10. Patient's awareness of abnormal movements (rate only patient's report)
    1. No awareness
    2. Aware, no distress
    3. Aware, mild distress
    4. Aware, moderate distress
    5. Aware, severe distress

## Dental Status

11. Current problems with teeth and/or dentures
    1  No
    2  Yes
12. Does patient usually wear dentures?
    1  No
    2  Yes

Source: Adapted from Department of Health and Human Services, Public Health Service, Alcohol, Drug Abuse and Mental Health Administration, National Institute of Mental Health. *Treatment Strategies in Schizophrenia Study*. ADM-117. Revised 1985.

## PAIN SCALES FOR ASSESSING PAIN INTENSITY
Use copies of pain scales that are large enough for older patients to see comfortably (14-point font or larger).

### Faces Pain Scale
Place an X under the face that best represents the severity or intensity of your pain right now.

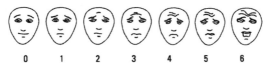

Source: Reprinted from *Pain*, 41(2), Bien D, Reeve R, Champion G, et al. The Faces Pain Scale for the self-assessment of the severity of pain experienced by children: development and initial validation, and preliminary investigation for ratio scale properties. 139–150, Copyright 1990, with permission from the International Association for the Study of Pain.

### 0–10 Numeric Rating Scales
**Verbal:** On a scale of 0–10, with 0 being no pain and 10 being the most intense pain imaginable, what would you rate the severity or intensity of your pain right now? _____

Source: Keela Herr, 2005.

**Visual:** Circle the number that best represents the severity or intensity of your pain right now.

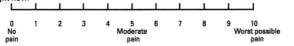

Source: Carr DB, Jacox AK, Chapman CR, et al. *Acute Pain Management: Operative Medical Procedures and Trauma*. Clinical Practice Guideline No. 1. Rockville, MD: AHCPR, Public Health Service, US Dept of Health and Human Services; February 1992. AHCPR Publication No. 92-0032.

## Verbal Descriptor Scale

Place an X beside the words that best describe the severity or intensity of your pain right now. Mark one set of words.

—— Most Intense Pain Imaginable
—— Very Severe Pain
—— Severe Pain
—— Moderate Pain
—— Mild Pain
—— Slight Pain
—— No Pain

Source: Keela Herr, 2005.

## Reference

AGS Panel on Persistent Pain in Older Persons. The management of persistent pain in older persons. *J Am Geriatr Soc.* 2002;50(6, Suppl):S205–S224.

## Brief Pain Inventory (Short Form)

### Brief Pain Inventory (Short Form)

Date: ___/___/___                                    Time: _____

Name: _____  _____  _____
            Last                          First                    Middle Initial

1. Throughout our lives, most of us have had pain from time to time (such as minor headaches, sprains, and toothaches). Have you had pain other than these every-day kinds of pain today?

   1. Yes                                                    2. No

2. On the diagram, shade in the areas where you feel pain. Put an X on the area that hurts the most.

Front          Back
Right  Left    Left  Right

3. Please rate your pain by circling the one number that best describes your pain at its **worst** in the last 24 hours.

   0      1      2      3      4      5      6      7      8      9      10
   No                                                                   Pain as bad as
   Pain                                                                 you can imagine

4. Please rate your pain by circling the one number that best describes your pain at its **least** in the last 24 hours.

   0      1      2      3      4      5      6      7      8      9      10
   No                                                                   Pain as bad as
   Pain                                                                 you can imagine

5. Please rate your pain by circling the one number that best describes your pain on the **average**.

   0      1      2      3      4      5      6      7      8      9      10
   No                                                                   Pain as bad as
   Pain                                                                 you can imagine

6. Please rate your pain by circling the one number that tells how much pain you have **right now**.

   0      1      2      3      4      5      6      7      8      9      10
   No                                                                   Pain as bad as
   Pain                                                                 you can imagine

Page 1 of 2

STUDY ID #: _____ DO NOT WRITE ABOVE THIS LINE   HOSPITAL #: _____

Date: ___/___/___                                                    Time: _____
Name: _____
           Last                    First              Middle Initial

**7.  What treatments or medications are you receiving for your pain?**

_____
_____

**8.  In the last 24 hours, how much relief have pain treatments or medications provided? Please circle the one percentage that most shows how much relief you have received.**

| 0% | 10% | 20% | 30% | 40% | 50% | 60% | 70% | 80% | 90% | 100% |
|----|-----|-----|-----|-----|-----|-----|-----|-----|-----|------|
| No Relief | | | | | | | | | | Complete Relief |

**9.  Circle the one number that describes how, during the past 24 hours, pain has interfered with your:**

**A.  General Activity**

| 0 | 1 | 2 | 3 | 4 | 5 | 6 | 7 | 8 | 9 | 10 |
|---|---|---|---|---|---|---|---|---|---|----|
| Does not Interfere | | | | | | | | | | Completely Interferes |

**B.  Mood**

| 0 | 1 | 2 | 3 | 4 | 5 | 6 | 7 | 8 | 9 | 10 |
|---|---|---|---|---|---|---|---|---|---|----|
| Does not Interfere | | | | | | | | | | Completely Interferes |

**C.  Walking Ability**

| 0 | 1 | 2 | 3 | 4 | 5 | 6 | 7 | 8 | 9 | 10 |
|---|---|---|---|---|---|---|---|---|---|----|
| Does not Interfere | | | | | | | | | | Completely Interferes |

**D.  Normal Work (includes both work outside the home and housework)**

| 0 | 1 | 2 | 3 | 4 | 5 | 6 | 7 | 8 | 9 | 10 |
|---|---|---|---|---|---|---|---|---|---|----|
| Does not Interfere | | | | | | | | | | Completely Interferes |

**E.  Relations with other people**

| 0 | 1 | 2 | 3 | 4 | 5 | 6 | 7 | 8 | 9 | 10 |
|---|---|---|---|---|---|---|---|---|---|----|
| Does not Interfere | | | | | | | | | | Completely Interferes |

**F.  Sleep**

| 0 | 1 | 2 | 3 | 4 | 5 | 6 | 7 | 8 | 9 | 10 |
|---|---|---|---|---|---|---|---|---|---|----|
| Does not Interfere | | | | | | | | | | Completely Interferes |

**G.  Enjoyment of life**

| 0 | 1 | 2 | 3 | 4 | 5 | 6 | 7 | 8 | 9 | 10 |
|---|---|---|---|---|---|---|---|---|---|----|
| Does not Interfere | | | | | | | | | | Completely Interferes |

Page 2 of 2

Worst pain, or the arithmetic mean of the 4 severity items (items 3, 4, 5, and 6), can be used as measures of pain severity. The arithmetic mean of the 7 interference item (items 9A-G) can be used as a measure of pain interference. Scores on the BPI pain severity items are defined as mild (1–4), moderate (5–6), and severe (7–10). The tool can be used to follow the course of pain and response to interventions.

## KARNOFSKY SCALE

This 10-point scale is a quick and easy way to indicate how a patient is feeling on a given day, without going through several multiple-choice questions or symptom surveys.

| Score | Description |
|-------|-------------|
| 100 | Able to work; normal, no complaints, no evidence of disease |
| 90 | Able to work; able to carry on normal activity, minor symptoms |
| 80 | Able to work; normal activity with effort, some symptoms |
| 70 | Unable to work or carry on normal activity, cares for self independently |
| 60 | Mildly disabled, dependent; requires occasional assistance, cares for most needs |
| 50 | Moderately disabled, dependent; requires considerable assistance and frequent care |
| 40 | Severely disabled, dependent; requires special care and assistance |
| 30 | Severely disabled; hospitalized, death not imminent |
| 20 | Very sick; active supportive treatment needed |
| 10 | Moribund; fatal processes rapidly progressing |

Source: Karnofsky DA, Burchenal JH. The clinical evaluation of chemotherapeutic agents in cancer. In: MacLeon CM, ed. *Evaluation of Chemotherapeutic Agents.* Columbia University Press; 1949:196.

## PALLIATIVE PERFORMANCE SCALE, VERSION 2 (PPSv2)

| % | Ambulation | Activity and Evidence of Disease | Self-care | Intake | Conscious Level |
|---|-----------|----------------------------------|-----------|--------|-----------------|
| 100 | Full | Normal activity and work, no evidence of disease | Full | Normal | Full |
| 90 | Full | Normal activity and work, some evidence of disease | Full | Normal | Full |
| 80 | Full | Normal activity with effort, some evidence of disease | Full | Normal or reduced | Full |
| 70 | Reduced | Unable normal job/work, significant disease | Full | Normal or reduced | Full |
| 60 | Reduced | Unable hobby/housework, significant disease | Occasional assistance necessary | Normal or reduced | Full or confusion |
| 50 | Mainly sit/lie | Unable to do any work, extensive disease | Considerable assistance required | Normal or reduced | Full or confusion |
| 40 | Mainly in bed | Unable to do most activity, extensive disease | Mainly assistance | Normal or reduced | Full or drowsy, ± confusion |
| 30 | Totally bed bound | Unable to do any activity, extensive disease | Total care | Normal or reduced | Full or drowsy, ± confusion |
| 20 | As above | As above | Total care | Minimal to sips | Full or drowsy, ± confusion |
| 10 | As above | As above | Total care | Mouth care only | Drowsy or coma ± confusion |
| 0 | Death | — | — | — | — |

The Palliative Performance Scale, version 2 (PPSv2), copyright 2001, Victoria Hospice Society. Reprinted with permission. Instructions for use of PPSv2 can be found at: http://www.victoriahospice.org/ed_tools.html
The PPSv2 replaces the first PPS published in Anderson F et al., Palliative performance scale (PPS): A new tool. *J Pall Care* 1996;(9)4:26-32.

## REISBERG FUNCTIONAL ASSESSMENT STAGING (FAST) SCALE

This 16-item scale is designed to parallel the progressive activity limitations associated with AD. Stage 7 identifies the threshold of activity limitation that would support a prognosis of ≤ 6 mo.

| FAST Scale Item | Activity Limitation Associated with AD |
|---|---|
| Stage 1 | No difficulty, either subjectively or objectively |
| Stage 2 | Complains of forgetting location of objects; subjective work difficulties |
| Stage 3 | Decreased job functioning evident to coworkers; difficulty in traveling to new locations |
| Stage 4 | Decreased ability to perform complex tasks (eg, planning dinner for guests; handling finances) |
| Stage 5 | Requires assistance in choosing proper clothing |
| Stage 6 | Decreased ability to dress, bathe, and toilet independently |
| Substage 6a | Difficulty putting clothing on properly |
| Substage 6b | Unable to bathe properly; may develop fear of bathing |
| Substage 6c | Inability to handle mechanics of toileting (ie, forgets to flush, does not wipe properly) |
| Substage 6d | Urinary incontinence |
| Substage 6e | Fecal incontinence |
| Stage 7 | Loss of speech, locomotion, and consciousness |
| Substage 7a | Ability to speak limited (1–5 words a day) |
| Substage 7b | All intelligible vocabulary lost |
| Substage 7c | Nonambulatory |
| Substage 7d | Unable to smile |
| Substage 7e | Unable to hold head up |

Source: Reisberg, B. Functional assessment staging (FAST), *Psychopharmacol Bull.* 1988;24(4):653–659. Copyright Media Works Media LLC. Reprinted with permission.

## AUA SYMPTOM INDEX FOR BPH

| Questions to be answered (circle one number on each line) | Not at all | Less than 1 time in 5 | Less than half the time | About half the time | More than half the time | Almost always |
|---|---|---|---|---|---|---|
| 1. Over the past month or so, how often have you had a sensation of not emptying your bladder completely after you finished urinating? | 0 | 1 | 2 | 3 | 4 | 5 |
| 2. Over the past month or so, how often have you had to urinate again less than two hours after you finished urinating? | 0 | 1 | 2 | 3 | 4 | 5 |

*(cont.)*

| Questions to be answered (circle one number on each line) | Not at all | Less than 1 time in 5 | Less than half the time | About half the time | More than half the time | Almost always |
|---|---|---|---|---|---|---|
| 3. Over the past month or so, how often have you found you stopped and started again several times when you urinated? | 0 | 1 | 2 | 3 | 4 | 5 |
| 4. Over the past month or so, how often have you found it difficult to postpone urination? | 0 | 1 | 2 | 3 | 4 | 5 |
| 5. Over the past month or so, how often have you had a weak urinary stream? | 0 | 1 | 2 | 3 | 4 | 5 |
| 6. Over the past month or so, how often have you had to push or strain to begin urination? | 0 | 1 | 2 | 3 | 4 | 5 |
| 7. Over the last month, how many times did you most typically get up to urinate from the time you went to bed at night until the time you got up in the morning? | none | 1 time | 2 times | 3 times | 4 times | 5 or more times |

AUA Symptom Score = sum of questions 1–7 =_____. For interpretation, see p 163.

Source: Barry MJ, Fowler FJ Jr, O'Leary MP et al. The American Urological Association symptom index for benign prostatic hyperplasia. *J Urol.* 1992;148(5):1549–1557. Reprinted with permission.

## MEDICATION APPROPRIATENESS ASSESSMENT

To assess the appropriateness of a drug, the following questions should be considered in view of the patient's medical problems and current medications. For combination drugs, the questions should be considered for each drug. See also p 9.
• Is there an indication for the drug?
• Is the medication effective for the condition?
• Is the dosage correct?
• Are the directions correct?
• Are the directions practical?
• Are there clinically significant drug-drug interactions?
• Are there clinically significant drug-disease/condition interactions?
• Is there unnecessary duplication with other drug(s)?
• Is the duration of therapy acceptable?
• Is this drug the least expensive alternative compared with others of equal utility?

Source: Adapted from Hanlon JT, Schmader KE, Samsa GP, et al. A method for assessing drug therapy appropriateness. *J Clin Epidemiol* 1992; 45(10):1045–51, copyright (1992) with permission from Elsevier.

# OBRA REGULATIONS

US Health Care Financing Administration (in 2001 renamed Centers for Medicare and Medicaid Services, or CMS) regulations regarding the use of certain medications in nursing homes are contained in the Omnibus Budget Reconciliation Act (OBRA) of 1987.

## ANTIDEPRESSANT MEDICATIONS

### Table 94. Recommended Maximum Doses of Antidepressants

| Drug | Usual Max Daily Dose (mg) for Age ≥65 | Usual Max Daily Dose (mg) |
|---|---|---|
| Amitriptyline (*Elavil*) | 150 | 300 |
| Amoxapine (*Asendin*) | 200 | 400 |
| Desipramine (*Norpramin*) | 150 | 300 |
| Doxepin (*Adapin, Sinequan*) | 150 | 300 |
| Imipramine (*Tofranil*) | 150 | 300 |
| Maprotiline (*Ludiomil*) | 150 | 300 |
| Nortriptyline (*Aventyl, Pamelor*) | 75 | 150 |
| Protriptyline (*Vivactil*) | 30 | 60 |
| Trazodone (*Desyrel*) | 300 | 600 |
| Trimipramine (*Surmontil*) | 150 | 300 |

## ANTIPSYCHOTIC MEDICATIONS

Indications for appropriate use of antipsychotic medications are outlined in OBRA. In addition to psychotic disorders, these indications include specific nonpsychotic behavior associated with organic mental syndromes:
- Agitated psychotic symptoms (biting, kicking, scratching, assertive and belligerent behavior, sexual aggressiveness) that present a danger to themselves or others or interfere with family's and/or staff's ability to provide care (activities of daily living, or ADLs)
- Psychotic symptoms (hallucinations, delusions, paranoia)
- Continual (24-h) crying out and screaming

Behavior less responsive to antipsychotic therapy includes:
- Repetitive, bothersome behavior (ie, pacing, wandering, repeated statements or words, calling out, fidgeting)
- Poor self-care
- Unsociability
- Indifference to surroundings
- Uncooperative behavior
- Restlessness
- Impaired memory
- Anxiety
- Depression
- Insomnia

If antipsychotic therapy is to be used for one or more of these symptoms only, then the use of antipsychotic agents is inappropriate. Because of their anticholinergic properties, antipsychotic agents may worsen these symptoms, especially symptoms of sedation and lethargy, as well as enhance "confusion."

Selection of an antipsychotic agent should be based on the adverse-event profile since all antipsychotic agents are equally effective at equivalent doses. Coadministration of two or more antipsychotics does not have any pharmacologic basis or clinical advantage. Coadministration of two or more antipsychotic agents does not improve clinical response and increases the potential for adverse events.

Once behavior control is obtained, assess patient to determine if precipitating event (stress from drugs, fluid or electrolyte changes, infection, changes in environment) has been resolved or patient has accommodated to the environment or situation. Determine whether the antipsychotic can be decreased in dose or tapered off completely by monitoring selected target symptoms for which the antipsychotic therapy was initiated. OBRA 1987 requires attempts at dose reduction within a 6-month period unless documented as to why this cannot be done. Identifying target symptoms is essential for adequate monitoring. Because of adverse events, intermittent use (not prn) is preferable (ie, only when patient has behavior warranting use of these agents). For the recommended doses of antipsychotics, see **Table 95**.

**Table 95. Recommended Maximum Doses of Antipsychotics**

| Drug | Usual Max Daily Dose (mg) for Age ≥65 | Usual Max Daily Dose (mg) | Daily Oral Dose (mg) for Residents with Organic Mental Syndromes |
|---|---|---|---|
| Acetophenazine (*Tindal*) | 150 | 300 | 20 |
| Chlorpromazine (*Thorazine*) | 800 | 1600 | 75 |
| Chlorprothixene (*Taractan*) | 800 | 1600 | 75 |
| Clozapine (*Clozaril*) | 25 | 450 | 50 |
| Fluphenazine (*Prolixin*) | 20 | 40 | 4 |
| Haloperidol (*Haldol*) | 50 | 100 | 4 |
| Loxapine (*Loxitane*) | 125 | 250 | 10 |
| Mesoridazine (*Serentil*) | 250 | 500 | 25 |
| Molindone (*Moban*) | 112 | 225 | 10 |
| Olanzapine (*Zyprexa*) | — | 20 | 10 |
| Quetiapine (*Seroquel*) | — | 800 | 200 |
| Perphenazine (*Trilafon*) | 32 | 64 | 8 |
| Promazine (*Sparine*) | 50 | 500 | 150 |
| Risperidone (*Risperdal*) | 1 | 16 | 2 |
| Thioridazine (*Mellaril*) | 400 | 800 | 75 |
| Thiothixene (*Navane*) | 30 | 60 | 7 |
| Trifluoperazine (*Stelazine*) | 40 | 80 | 8 |
| Trifluopromazine (*Vesprin*) | 100 | 20 | — |

## ANXIOLYTIC MEDICATIONS

The use of anxiolytics is acceptable as long as other disease processes that could explain anxious behavior have been excluded. Daily use, at any dose, is for <4 consecutive months, unless an attempt at dose reduction is unsuccessful. Proper indications include:

- Generalized anxiety disorder
- Organic mental syndrome (including dementia associated with agitation)
- Panic disorders
- Anxiety associated with other psychiatric disorder (eg, depression, adjustment disorder)

**Table 96. Recommended Maximum Doses of Anxiolytics\***

| Drug | Usual Daily Dose (mg) for Age ≥65 | Usual Daily Dose (mg) for Age <65 |
|---|---|---|
| Alprazolam (*Xanax*) | 2 | 4 |
| Clorazepate (*Tranxene*) | 30 | 60 |
| Chlordiazepoxide (*Librium*) | 40 | 100 |
| Diazepam (*Valium*) | 20 | 60 |
| Halazepam (*Paxipam*) | 80 | 160 |
| Lorazepam (*Ativan*) | 3 | 6 |
| Meprobamate (*Miltown*) | 600 | 1600 |
| Oxazepam (*Serax*) | 60 | 90 |
| Prazepam (*Centrax*) | 30 | 60 |

\* CMS-OBRA guidelines strongly urge clinicians not to use barbiturates, glutethimide, and ethchlorvynol because of their adverse events, pharmacokinetics, and addiction potential in the elderly person. Also, CMS discourages use of long-acting benzodiazepines in treating the elderly person.

## HYPNOTIC MEDICATIONS

Hypnotics are allowed for 10 consecutive days of use. If three unsuccessful attempts at dose reduction occur, then it is clinically contraindicated to reduce.

**Table 97. Recommended Maximum Doses of Hypnotics\***

| Drug | Usual Max Single Dose (mg) for Age ≥65 | Usual Max Single Dose (mg) |
|---|---|---|
| Alprazolam (*Xanax*) | 0.25 | 1.5 |
| Amobarbital (*Amytal*) | 150 | 300 |
| Butabarbital (*Butisol*) | 100 | 200 |
| Chloral hydrate (*Noctec*) | 750 | 1500 |
| Chloral hydrate (*various*) | 500 | 1000 |
| Diphenhydramine (*Benadryl*) | 25 | 50 |
| Ethchlorvynol (*Placidyl*) | 500 | 1000 |
| Flurazepam (*Dalmane*) | 15 | 30 |
| Glutethimide (*Doriden*) | 500 | 1000 |
| Halazepam (*Paxipam*) | 20 | 40 |
| Hydroxyzine (*Atarax*) | 50 | 100 |
| Lorazepam (*Ativan*) | 1 | 2 |
| Methyprylon (*Noludar*) | 200 | 400 |
| Oxazepam (*Serax*) | 15 | 30 |
| Phenobarbital (*Nembutal*) | 100 | 200 |
| Secobarbital (*Seconal*) | 100 | 200 |

*(cont.)*

**Table 97. Recommended Maximum Doses of Hypnotics\* (cont.)**

| Drug | Usual Max Single Dose (mg) for Age ≥65 | Usual Max Single Dose (mg) |
|------|----------------------------------------|----------------------------|
| Temazepam (*Restoril*) | 15 | 30 |
| Triazolam (*Halcion*) | 0.125 | 0.5 |

\* CMS-OBRA guidelines strongly urge clinicians not to use barbiturates, glutethimide, and ethchlorvynol because of their adverse effects, pharmacokinetics, and addiction potential in the elderly person. Also, CMS discourages use of long-acting benzodiazepines in treating the elderly person.

# CMS CRITERIA: INAPPROPRIATE DRUG USE IN NURSING HOMES

On July 1, 1999, HCFA (the US Health Care Financing Administration, renamed in 2001 the Centers for Medicare and Medicaid Services, or CMS) modified its regulations regarding medication use by nursing home residents who are 65 years of age or older. As part of their review, surveyors will determine if the resident is taking any medications considered to have a high potential ("high severity") for severe adverse drug reactions (ADRs) or medications with a high potential for less severe ("low severity") ADRs. Residents receiving any medications will be monitored for ADRs. If an ADR is identified, the rationale for the medication use must be justified and considered appropriate. If it is not, a deficiency will be cited.

Persons wishing additional information are advised to contact the American Society of Consultant Pharmacists.

The medications specified in **Table 98** are considered "high severity" by CMS and should be considered potentially inappropriate for use in treating elderly persons.

### Table 98. Drugs Considered "High Severity" by CMS

| Class or Drug | Comments |
| --- | --- |
| Amitriptyline (*Elavil*) | May be used for neurogenic pain if an evaluation of risk vs. benefit of the drug is documented, including consideration of alternative therapies |
| Chlorpropamide (*Diabinese*) | |
| Digoxin, in dosages >0.125 mg/d | Unless an atrial arrhythmia is being treated; high severity is considered if started within the past month |
| Disopyramide (*Norpace*) | |
| GI antispasmodics (belladonna alkaloids, clidinium, dicyclomine, hyoscyamine, propantheline) | Use for short periods (not over 7 d) on an intermittent basis (not more frequently than q 3 mo) does not require review by the surveyor |
| Meperidine, oral | If started within past month |
| Methyldopa | If started within past month |
| Pentazocine | |
| Ticlopidine | Review by the surveyor is not necessary in individuals who receive it because they have had a previous stroke or have evidence of stroke precursors (ie, TIAs) and cannot tolerate aspirin |

The drug-diagnosis combinations specified in **Table 99** are considered "high severity" by CMS and should be considered potentially inappropriate for use in treating elderly persons.

### Table 99. Diagnosis-Drug Combinations Considered "High Severity" by CMS

| Class or Drug | Diagnosis | Comments |
| --- | --- | --- |
| Sedatives, hypnotics | COPD | Short-acting benzodiazepines are acceptable |
| NSAIDs | Active or recurrent gastritis, peptic ulcer disease, GERD | COX-2 inhibitors are not included on the list of NSAIDs |

*(cont.)*

**Table 99. Diagnosis-Drug Combinations Considered "High Severity" by CMS (cont.)**

| Class or Drug | Diagnosis | Comments |
|---|---|---|
| Metoclopramide | Seizures or epilepsy | |
| ASA, NSAIDs, dipyridamole, ticlopidine | Anticoagulation | |
| Anticholinergic drugs | BPH | |
| TCAs | Arrhythmias | If started within past month |

The medications listed in **Table 100** are considered "low severity" by CMS and should be considered as potentially inappropriate in treating elderly patients.

**Table 100. Drugs Considered "Low Severity" by CMS**

| Class or Drug | Comments |
|---|---|
| Antihistamines | That is, with anticholinergic properties |
| Cyclandelate | |
| Digoxin, in dosages >0.125 mg/d | Unless an atrial arrhythmia is being treated; high severity is considered if started within the past month |
| Diphenhydramine | Review by a surveyor is not necessary if used for a short time (not over 7 d) on an intermittent basis (not more frequently than q 3 mo) for allergies |
| Dipyridamole | |
| Ergot mesylates (eg, *Hydergine*) | |
| Indomethacin | Short-term use (eg, 1 wk) is considered acceptable for treatment of gouty arthritis |
| Meperidine, oral | If therapy longer than 1 mo |
| Muscle relaxants (eg, carisoprodol, chlorzoxazone, cyclobonzaprine, dantrolene, metaxalone, methocarbarnol, orphenadrine) | Use for short periods (not over 7 d) on an intermittent basis (not more frequently than q 3 mo) does not require review |

The drug-diagnosis combinations specified in **Table 101** are considered "low severity" by the CMS and should be considered potentially inappropriate in all elderly patients.

**Table 101. Diagnosis-Drug Combinations Considered "Low Severity" by CMS**

| Class or Drug | Diagnosis | Comments |
|---|---|---|
| Corticosteroids | Diabetes mellitus | If started within past month |
| Potassium supplements or ASA (>325 mg/d) | Active or recurrent gastritis, peptic ulcer disease, or GERD | Use of potassium supplements to treat low potassium levels until they return to the normal range is permissible if prescriber determines that use of fresh fruits and vegetables or other dietary supplementation is not adequate or possible |

*(cont.)*

Table 101. Diagnosis-Drug Combinations Considered "Low Severity" by CMS (cont.)

| Class or Drug | Diagnosis | Comments |
|---|---|---|
| Antipsychotics | Seizures or epilepsy | Treatment of acute psychosis for 72 h or less is permissible |
| Narcotic drugs, including propoxyphene | BPH | Review by the surveyor is not necessary if use is for short duration (7 d or less) on an intermittent basis (once q 3 mo) for symptoms of an acute, self-limiting condition |
| Bladder relaxants (flavoxate, oxybutynin, bethanechol) | BPH | Review by the surveyor is not necessary if use is for short duration (7 d or less) on an intermittent basis (once q 3 mo) for symptoms of an acute, self-limiting condition |
| Anticholinergic antihistamines, GI antispasmodics, anticholinergic antidepressants, and narcotic drugs (including propoxyphene) | Constipation | Constipation can be worsened. Review by the surveyor is not necessary if use is for short duration (7 d or less) on an intermittent basis (once q 3 mo) for symptoms of an acute self-limiting condition |
| Antiparkinson medications | Constipation | Constipation can be worsened |
| Decongestants, theophylline, methylphenidate, SSRI antidepressants and desipramine, MAOIs, $\beta$-agonists | Insomnia | Insomnia can be worsened |

# IMPORTANT TELEPHONE NUMBERS AND WEB SITES

**General Information on Aging**

| | | |
|---|---|---|
| AGS Foundation for Health in Aging | www.healthinaging.org | 800-563-4916 |
| Administration on Aging | www.aoa.gov | 202-619-0724 |
| American Association of Retired Persons | www.aarp.org | 888-OUR-AARP (888-687-2277) |
| American Geriatrics Society | www.americangeriatrics.org | 800-247-4779 |
| American Medical Directors Association | www.amda.com | 800-876-2632 |
| American Society of Consultant Pharmacists | www.ascp.com | 800-355-2727 |
| Assisted Living Federation of America | www.alfa.org | 703-691-8100 |
| Children of Aging Parents | www.caps4caregivers.org | 800-227-7294 |
| CDC National Prevention Information Network | www.cdcnpin.org | 800-458-5231 |
| Family Caregiver Alliance | www.caregiver.org | 800-445-8106 |
| Medicare Hotline | www.medicare.gov | 800-MEDICARE (800-633-4227) |
| National Adult Day Services Association | www.nadsa.org | 800-558-5301 |
| National Council on the Aging | www.ncoa.org | 202-479-1200 |
| National Institute on Aging | www.nia.nih.gov | 800-222-2225 |

**Elder Mistreatment**

| | | |
|---|---|---|
| National Center on Elder Abuse | www.elderabusecenter.org | 202-898-2586 |

**End-of-Life**

| | | |
|---|---|---|
| Last Acts Partnership | www.lastactspartnership.org | 800-989-WILL (800-989-9455) |
| National Hospice and Palliative Care Organization | www.nhpco.org | 800-658-8898 for hospice referral |

**Smoking Cessation**

| | | |
|---|---|---|
| American Cancer Society | www.cancer.org (search on "quit smoking") | 800-ACS-2345 (800-227-2345) |
| American Lung Association | www.lungusa.org | 800-LUNG-USA (800-586-4872) |
| CDC National Center for Chronic Disease Prevention and Health Promotion | www.cdc.gov/tobacco/how2quit.htm | 800-311-3435 |
| National Cancer Institute | www.smokefree.gov | 877-44U-QUIT (877-448-7848) TTY: 800-332-8615 |

**Specific Health Problems**

| | | |
|---|---|---|
| Alzheimer's Association | www.alz.org | 800-272-3900 |
| American Cancer Society | www.cancer.org | 800-ACS-2345 (800-227-2345) |
| Alzheimer's Disease Education and Referral Center | www.alzheimers.org | 800-438-4380 |
| American Academy of Ophthalmology | www.aao.org | 800-222-3937 |

| | | |
|---|---|---|
| American Association for Geriatric Psychiatry | www.aagponline.org | 301-654-7850 |
| American College of Obstetricians and Gynecologists | www.acog.com | 800-673-8444 |
| American Diabetes Association | www.diabetes.org | 800-DIABETES (800-342-2383) |
| American Foundation for the Blind | www.afb.org | 800-AFB-LINE (800-232-5463) |
| American Heart Association | www.americanheart.org | 800-AHA-USA1 (800-242-8721) |
| American Lung Association | www.lungusa.org | 800-LUNG-USA (800-586-4872) |
| American Obesity Association | www.obesity.org | 202-776-7711 |
| American Pain Society | www.ampainsoc.org | 847-375-4715 |
| American Parkinson Disease Association | www.apdaparkinson.com | 800-223-2732 |
| American Urological Association | www.auanet.org | 410-727-1100 |
| Arthritis Foundation | www.arthritis.org | 800-283-7800 |
| Better Hearing Institute | www.betterhearing.org | 800-EARWELL (800-327-9355) |
| Lighthouse International | www.lighthouse.org | 800-829-0500 |
| Meals On Wheels Association of America | www.mowaa.org | 703-548-5558 |
| National Association for Continence | www.nafc.org | 800-BLADDER (800-252-3337) |
| National Diabetes Information Clearinghouse | www.diabetes.niddk.nih.gov | 800-860-8747 |
| National Digestive Disease Information Clearinghouse | www.digestive.niddk.nih.gov | 800-891-5389 |
| National Eye Institute | www.nei.nih.gov | 301-496-5248 |
| National Heart, Lung and Blood Institute | www.nhlbi.nih.gov | 301-592-8573 |
| National Institute of Arthritis and Musculoskeletal and Skin Diseases | www.niams.nih.gov | 877-22-NIAMS (877-226-4267) |
| National Institute of Mental Health | www.nimh.nih.gov | 866-615-NIMH (866-615-6464) |
| National Institute of Neurological Disorders and Stroke | www.ninds.nih.gov | 800-352-9424 |
| National Institute on Deafness and Other Communication Disorders | www.nidcd.nih.gov | 800-241-1044 TTY: 800-241-1055 |
| National Kidney and Urologic Diseases Information Clearinghouse | www.kidney.niddk.nih.gov | 800-891-5390 |
| National Osteoporosis Foundation | www.nof.org | 800-223-9994 |
| National Parkinson Foundation | www.parkinson.org | 800-327-4545 |
| Self Help for Hard of Hearing People | www.hearingloss.org | 301-657-2248 TTY: 301-657-2249 |
| Sexuality Information and Education Council of the US | www.siecus.org | 212-819-9770 |
| The Simon Foundation for Continence | www.simonfoundation.org | 800-23-SIMON (800-237-4666) |

Page references followed by *t* and *f* indicate tables and figures, respectively.
Trade names are in *italics*.

**A**

Abandonment, 7*t*
Abarelix *(Plenaxis),* 164*t*
Abbreviations, iii–vii
Abciximab *(ReoPro),* 25*t*
Abdominal massage, 90
Abdominal radiograph, 89
Abdominal surgery, 20*t*
*Abelcet* (amphotericin B lipid complex), 104*t*
ABI (ankle-brachial index), 182
*Abilify* (aripiprazole)
    for agitation, 47*t*
    for psychosis, 165*t*
Abnormal Involuntary Movement Scale (AIMS), 210–212
*Absorbine Jr. Antifungal* (tolnaftate), 56*t*
Abuse
    alcohol, 15–16, 143, 159*t*
    elder, 7–8, 7*t*–8*t*, 226
    tobacco, 17*t*
Acarbose *(Precose),* 62*t*
*Accolate* (zafirlukast), 174*t*
*Accupril. See also* Quinapril
    for HTN, 36*t*
*Accuzyme,* 180
*Ace* bandages, 188
ACE (angiotensin-converting enzyme) inhibitors
    for acute MI, 26
    antihypertensive combinations, 37*t*
    for chronic angina, 27
    for chronic kidney failure, 108
    and coexisting conditions, 36*t*
    for diabetes mellitus, 62
    for diastolic dysfunction, 29
    drug interactions, 11
    for heart failure, 28
    for HTN, 32, 35*t*–36*t*
    target doses in HF, 29*t*
Acebutolol *(Sectral),* 34*t*
*Aceon. See also* Perindopril
    for HTN, 36*t*
Acetaminophen. *See* APAP

Acetazolamide *(Diamox),* 196*t*
Acetophenazine *(Tindal),* 220*t*
Acetylsalicylic acid. *See* ASA
*Achromycin. See also* Tetracycline
    for peptic ulcer disease, 72
ACIP (Advisory Committee on Immunization Practices) guidelines, 95
*AcipHex* (rabeprazole), 70*t*
*Aclovate* (alclometasone dipropionate), 57*t*
Acoustic neuroma, 80
Acquired immune deficiency syndrome (AIDS), 165
ACTH stimulation test, 59
*Actiq. See also* Fentanyl
    for pain, 147*t*
Activities of daily living (ADLs)
    in falls prevention, 68
    instrumental, 205–206
    pain management, 144
    Physical Self-Maintenance Scale, 204–205
*Actonel. See also* Risedronate
    for osteoporosis, 139
*Actos. See also* Pioglitazone
    for diabetes mellitus, 63*t*
*Actron* (ketoprofen), 125*t*
*Actron 200* (ketoprofen SR), 125*t*
Acuity testing, 194
*Acular. See also* Ketorolac
    for allergic rhinitis or conjunctivitis, 169*t*
Acute bacterial conjunctivitis, 197–198
    treatment for, 198*t*
Acute coronary syndrome
    anticoagulant therapy, 20*t*
    antithrombotic therapy, 25*t*
    management, 24–25
    subacute pharmacologic management, 26
Acute kidney failure, 107
    determinants for hospice eligibility, 152*t*

Acute tubular necrosis, 107
Acyclovir *(Zovirax),* 95t
AD (Alzheimer's disease). *See also*
    Dementia
    diagnosis, 44
    progression, 44
    resources, 226
    risk and protective factors, 45
*Adalat CC. See also* Nifedipine
    for HTN, 35t
*Adapin. See also* Doxepin
    recommended max dose, 219t
Addiction, 143
Adenocarcinoma, 200
Adenosine stress test, 24
Adhesive capsulitis, 118
ADLs (activities of daily living)
    in falls prevention, 68
    instrumental, 205–206
    pain management, 144
    Physical Self-Maintenance Scale,
        204–205
Adrenal insufficiency, 59
    corticosteroids for, 59t
Adrenergic agonists, 195t
$\alpha_2$-Adrenergic agonists, 34t
$\beta$-Adrenergic agonists
    for asthma and COPD, 173t
    CMS criteria for inappropriate use,
        225t
    for pneumonia, 92
$\beta_2$-Adrenergic agonists
    for asthma, 171t, 172t
    for asthma and COPD, 172t, 173t
    for COPD, 170t
Adrenergic inhibitors, 33t–35t
$\alpha$-Adrenergic inhibitors. *See* $\alpha$-blockers
$\beta$-Adrenergic inhibitors. *See* $\beta$-blockers
Adrenocorticotropic hormone, 127
*Adsorbocarpine* (pilocarpine), 196t
*Advair Diskus* (salmeterol-fluticasone),
    174t
Advance directives
    end-of-life decisions, 152
    preoperative care, 157
*Advicor* (lovastatin with niacin), 31t
*Advil. See also* Ibuprofen
    for arthritis, 125t

Advisory Committee on Immunization
        Practices (ACIP) guidelines, 95
Aerobic exercise. *See* Exercise
*AeroBid. See also* Flunisolide
    for asthma and COPD, 173t
AeroChambers
    for asthma, 171
    for COPD, 170
AF (atrial fibrillation), 38
    anticoagulation for, 18t
    antihypertensive therapy and, 36t
Age-related macular degeneration
        (ARMD)
    causes, 194
    nonpharmacologic interventions, 194
    pharmacologic interventions, 195
*Aggrastat* (tirofiban), 25t
*Aggrenox* (ASA and dipyridamole), 131
Aggression
    agitation treatment guidelines, 47t–48t
    in dementia, 45
Agitation
    in dementia, 45
    treatment guidelines, 47t–48t
AIDS (acquired immune deficiency
        syndrome), 165
AIMS (Abnormal Involuntary Movement
        Scale), 210–212
*Akarpine* (pilocarpine), 196t
Akathisia, 166t
*AKBeta* (levobunolol), 195t
*AK-Mycin* (erythromycin ophthalmic),
    198t
*AKPro* (dipivefrin), 195t
*AKTob. See also* Tobramycin
    for acute bacterial conjunctivitis, 198t
*Alamast* (pemirolast), 169t
Albumin
    in malnutrition, 114
    relation to phenytoin, 135t
Albuterol *(Proventil, Ventolin, Ventolin
        Rotacaps)*
    for asthma and COPD, 172t
    for hyperkalemia, 113
Albuterol-ipratropium *(Combivent),* 174t
Alclometasone dipropionate *(Aclovate),*
    57t

**INDEX (CONT.)**

Alcohol
  and aging, 15
  drug interactions, 16
  guidelines for moderate drinking, 16
  and osteoporosis, 138
  and sleep problems, 190
  warfarin interactions, 18
Alcohol abuse, 15–16
  risk factors for addiction, 143
  screening, 159t
*Aldactazide* (spironolactone with HCTZ),
    37t
*Aldactone* (spironolactone)
  for HF, 29
  for HTN, 33t
*Aldomet. See also* Methyldopa
  for HTN, 34t
*Aldoril* (methyldopa with HCTZ), 37t
Aldosterone antagonists
  for HF, 29
  for HTN, 36t
Alendronate *(Fosamax)*
  bone outcomes, 140t
  effects on other outcomes, level of
    evidence, and risks of, 140t
  for osteoporosis, 139
*Aleve* (naproxen), 125t
Alfuzosin, 178t
Alfuzosin ER *(UroXatral)*, 163
*AlgiDERM. See also* Alginate
  for pressure ulcers, 185t
Alginate *(Algosteril, AlgiDERM, Kaltostat,
    Sorbsan)*
  for pressure ulcers, 185t
  wound and pressure ulcer products,
    184t
*Algosteril. See also* Alginate
  for pressure ulcers, 185t
*Allegra* (fexofenadine), 168t
*Allegra-D* (fexofenadine), 168t, 169t
Allergic rhinitis, 167
  choosing therapy for, 167t
  drug therapy for, 167t–169t
*Allevyn. See also* Foam island
  for pressure ulcers, 185t

Allopurinol *(Zyloprim, Lopurin)*
  for chronic gout, 127t
  warfarin interactions, 18
*Alocril. See also* Nedocromil
  for allergic rhinitis or conjunctivitis,
    169t
*Alomide* (lodoxamide), 169t
*Alora* (transdermal estrogen), 203t
$\alpha$-blockers ($\alpha$-adrenergic inhibitors)
  and coexisting conditions, 36t
  combined $\alpha$- and $\beta$-blockers, 34t–35t,
    36t
  drug interactions, 178t
  herbal medicine interactions, 14t
$\alpha_1$-blockers ($\alpha_1$-adrenergic inhibitors)
  for BPH, 163
  for HTN, 33t
*Alphagan* (brimonidine), 195t
*Alphagan P* (brimonidine), 195t
Alprazolam *(Xanax)*
  drug and metabolic interactions, 12t
  recommended max dose (anxiolytic),
    221t
  recommended max dose (hypnotic),
    221t
Alprostadil (prostaglandin E), 178t
*Altace. See also* Ramipril
  for HTN, 36t
Altered mental status, 42–43
Alternative medications, 13t–14t
*Altocor. See also* Lovastatin
  for dyslipidemia, 30t
Aluminum
  and constipation, 73
  food interactions, 10
Alveolar-arterial oxygen gradient, 1
Alzheimer's Association
  caregiver issues, 48
  resources, 226
Alzheimer's disease (AD). *See also*
    Dementia
  diagnosis, 44
  progression, 44
  resources, 226
  risk and protective factors, 45

Amantadine *(Symmetrel)*
    for influenza, 96*t*
    for Parkinson's disease, 133*t*
*Amaryl* (glimepiride), 62*t*
*Ambien. See also* Zolpidem
    for sleep disorders, 191*t*
*AmBisome* (amphotericin B liposomal), 105*t*
Amcinonide *(Cyclocort)*, 57*t*
American Urological Association (AUA), 217–218
Amikacin *(Amikin)*, 101*t*
*Amikin* (amikacin), 101*t*
Amiloride *(Midamor)*, 33*t*
Amiloride hydrochloride with HCTZ *(Moduretic)*, 37*t*
Aminoglutethimide, 164
Aminoglycosides
    for community-acquired pneumonia, 92*t*, 93*t*
    for hospital-acquired pneumonia, 93
    for infectious diseases, 101*t*
    for nursing-home–acquired pneumonia, 93
    for urosepsis, 94
Aminosalicylic acid, 11
Amiodarone
    for AF, 38
    digoxin interactions, 11
    drug and metabolic interactions, 11*t*–12*t*
    ocular adverse events, 198
    warfarin interactions, 18
Amitriptyline *(Elavil)*
    antidepressants to avoid, 51
    CMS regulations, 223*t*
    drug and metabolic interactions, 11*t*
    recommended max dose, 219*t*
Amlodipine *(Norvasc)*, 35*t*
Amlodipine besylate with benazepril hydrochloride *(Lotrel)*, 37*t*
Amobarbital *(Amytal)*, 221*t*
Amoxapine *(Asendin)*
    antidepressants to avoid, 51
    recommended max dose, 219*t*
Amoxicillin *(Amoxil)*
    with clarithromycin and lansoprazole *(Prevpac)*, 71*t*

for community-acquired pneumonia, 92*t*
for cystitis, 94
for endocarditis prophylaxis, 161, 161*t*
for *H pylori*-induced ulcerations, 71*t*
for infectious diseases, 98*t*
for peptic ulcer disease, 72
Amoxicillin-clavulanate *(Augmentin)*
    for community-acquired pneumonia, 92*t*, 93*t*
    for cystitis, 94
    for folliculitis, 55*t*
    for infectious diseases, 99*t*
*Amoxil. See also* Amoxicillin
    for infectious diseases, 98*t*
    for peptic ulcer disease, 72
*Amphotec* (amphotericin B colloidal dispersion), 105*t*
Amphotericin B *(Fungizone)*
    colloidal dispersion *(Amphotec)*, 105*t*
    for dermatologic conditions, 56*t*
    for infectious diseases, 104*t*
    lipid complex *(Abelcet)*, 104*t*
    liposomal *(AmBisome)*, 105*t*
Ampicillin
    for cellulitis, 55*t*
    for cystitis, 94
    for endocarditis prophylaxis, 161, 161*t*
    for infectious diseases, 98*t*
Ampicillin-sulbactam *(Unasyn)*
    for community-acquired pneumonia, 92*t*
    for infectious diseases, 99*t*
Amsler grid, 194
*Amytal* (amobarbital), 221*t*
Analgesics. *See also* APAP; ASA
    for arthritis, 124*t*–126*t*
    for claudication pain, 39
    dosage, 145
    drug and metabolic interactions, 12*t*
    initial dosing for PCA, 144*t*
    management of adverse events, 145–146
    for osteoarthritis, 122, 123*f*
    for pain management, 144–146, 146*t*–147*t*
    patient-controlled, 143–144, 144*t*
    selection of agents, 144–145

INDEX (CONT.)

*Anaprox* (naproxen sodium), 126*t*
*Anaspaz. See also* Hyoscyamine
  for UI, 87*t*
Anastrazole *(Arimidex),* 199, 200*t*
*Ancef. See also* Cefazolin
  for infectious diseases, 100*t*
*Ancobon* (flucytosine), 105*t*
*Androderm* (testosterone), 177*t*
*AndroGel* (testosterone gel), 178*t*
Androgens
  for diminished libido, 179
  warfarin interactions, 18
Anemia, 81–84
  associated with deficiency, 84*t*
  and chronic kidney failure, 108
  hypoproliferative, 82*f,* 83*f*
  of unknown cause, 84
Angina
  antihypertensive therapy and, 36*t*
  chronic, 27
  unstable, 24–25, 26
Angioedema, 55*t*
Angiography
  magnetic resonance, 131
  pulmonary, 176*f*
Angioplasty, percutaneous
  for PAD, 39
  for Q-wave MI, 25
Angiotensin II receptor blockers. *See*
  ARBs
Angiotensin-converting enzyme
  inhibitors. *See* ACE inhibitors
Anistreplase, 25
Ankle-brachial index (ABI), 182
Anorectal physiology tests, 89
*Ansaid* (flurbiprofen), 125*t*
*Anspor* (cephradine), 100*t*
Antacids
  and constipation, 73
  digoxin interactions, 11
  for GERD, 70
  for stress-ulcer prevention, 72
Anthralin, 54*t*
Anthropometrics, 114
Antiandrogens, 164, 164*t*

Antiarrhythmics
  fall risks, 67
  for heart failure, 29
Antibiotic-associated diarrhea, 76–77
Antibiotics, 98*t*–106*t*
  for acute conjunctivitis, 198
  for arterial ulcer infection, 182
  for community-acquired pneumonia,
    92*t*–93*t*
  for COPD, 170*t*
  endocarditis prophylaxis regimens,
    161*t*
  for folliculitis, 55*t*
  food interactions, 10
  for *H pylori,* 71
  for halitosis at end of life, 154
  for infectious diseases, 98*t*–106*t*
  for peptic ulcer disease, 72
  preoperative, 156
  for pressure ulcer infection, 187
  for skin ulcer infection, 180
  and tinnitus, 80
  for UTIs, 94
  warfarin interactions, 18
  for wound infection, 187
Anticholinergics
  for asthma and COPD, 172*t*
  CMS criteria for inappropriate use,
    224*t,* 225*t*
  and dementia, 46
  ocular adverse events, 198
  for Parkinson's disease, 133*t*
Anticoagulation, 18–20. *See also* Heparin;
  Warfarin
  in absence of active bleeding or
    severe bleeding risk, 18*t*
  acute, 19–20
  for acute coronary syndrome, 25*t*
  for acute MI, 24
  for acute stroke, 131
  for AF, 38
  for cardioembolic stroke, 131
  CMS criteria for inappropriate use,
    224*t*
  for DVT/PE prophylaxis and treatment,
    19*t*–20*t*

for heart failure, 29
herbal medicine interactions, 13t
for PE, 176f
preoperative, 157
for stroke prevention, 131
Anticonvulsants
fall risks, 67
herbal medicine interactions, 13t
and osteoporosis, 138
for pain relief, 148t
Antidepressants. See also MAOIs; SSRIs;
    TCAs
for anxiety disorders, 22
choosing, 49–50
CMS criteria for inappropriate use,
    225t
contraindicated in older adults, 51
for depression, 50t–51t
fall risks, 67
food interactions, 11
herbal medicine interactions, 13t
for pain relief, 148t
recommended max doses, 219t
for sleep disorders, 191t
Antidiarrheals
for fecal incontinence, 90
prescribing information, 76t
Antidiuretic hormone, 109
Antiemetics, 75t
Antiepileptic therapy
prescribing information, 134t–135t
for seizures, 134
Anti-estrogen drugs, 199t
Antifungals
for dermatologic conditions, 54t
for infectious diseases, 104t–106t
oral, 56t
prescribing information, 56t
topical, 56t
Antihistamines
for allergic rhinitis or conjunctivitis,
    167t–168t
CMS criteria for inappropriate use,
    224t, 225t
for dermatologic conditions, 55t
fall risks, 67
food interactions, 11

Antihypertensives
and coexisting conditions, 36t–37t
combinations, 37t
for emergencies and urgencies, 32–33
fall risks, 67
for HTN management, 32
oral agents, 33t–36t
Anti-inflammatory drugs, nonsteroidal.
    See NSAIDs
Antineoplastics, 11
Antiparkinsonian agents, 225t
Antiplatelet therapy
for acute coronary syndrome, 25t
herbal medicine interactions, 13t
for PAD, 39, 39t
for stroke prevention, 131
Antipseudomonal agents
for community-acquired pneumonia,
    92t
for hospital-acquired pneumonia, 93
for infectious diseases, 99t, 100t
for nursing-home–acquired
    pneumonia, 93
Antipsychotics
adverse events, 166t
for anxiety disorders, 22
atypical, 48t, 68t
CMS criteria for inappropriate use,
    225t
for delirium, 43
fall risks, 68t
food interactions, 11
OBRA regulations, 219–220
prescribing information, 165t–166t
for psychotic disorders, 165
recommended max doses, 220t
Antiseptics, 182
Antispasmodics, 223t, 225t
Antistaphylococcal penicillins
for infectious diseases, 99t
for skin and soft-tissue infections, 55t
Antithrombotic therapy, 25t
Antithymocyte globulin, 84
Antithyroids, 18
Antitussives, 175t
Antivert. See also Meclizine
for nausea and vomiting, 75t

## INDEX (CONT.)

Antiviral therapy
for herpes zoster, 95, 95*t*
for influenza, 95–96, 96*t*
*Anturane* (sulfinpyrazone), 127*t*
Anxiety, 21–23
benzodiazepines for, 23*t*
at end of life, 155
treatment guidelines, 48*t*
Anxiolytics
for dyspnea, 154
OBRA regulations, 220–221
recommended max doses, 221*t*
Aortic stenosis, 38–39
anticoagulation for DVT/PE
prophylaxis and treatment, 19*t*
Aortic valve replacement surgery
anticoagulation for, 18*t*
for aortic stenosis, 39
APAP (acetaminophen) *(Tylenol)*
for acute lumbar strain (low back pain
syndrome), 119
for acute pain and short-term
management, 143
for arthritis, 124*t*
for back pain, 120
for chronic disk degeneration, 119
with codeine, 146*t*
drug interactions, 11*t*
extended release *(Tylenol ER)*, 124*t*
with hydrocodone *(Lorcet, Lortab,
Vicodin)*, 145, 146*t*
management of adverse events, 145
metabolic interactions, 11*t*
with opioid, 123*f*
for osteoarthritis, 119, 123*f*
with oxycodone *(Percocet, Tylox)*, 146*t*
for pain, 146*t*
for shoulder pain, 118
with tramadol *(Ultracet)*, 145, 147*t*
Aphasia, 135*t*–136*t*
Apnea-hypopnea index, 192
Appetite, decreased. *See also*
Malnutrition
drug interactions, 10
Appetite stimulants, 115
Apraclonidine *(Lopidine)*, 195*t*

*Apresoline* (hydralazine), 35*t*
*Aquachloral. See also* Chloral hydrate
for sleep disorders, 191*t*
*Aquaphor*, 55*t*
Arachnocides, 167
*Aranesp* (darbepoetin alfa), 84*t*
ARBs (angiotensin II receptor blockers)
antihypertensive combinations, 37*t*
for chronic kidney failure, 108
and coexisting conditions, 36*t*
for diabetes mellitus type 2, 62
for heart failure, 29
for HTN, 36*t*
target doses in HF, 29*t*
Argatroban, 20*t*
*Aricept. See also* Donepezil
for cognitive dysfunction in AD, 47
for cognitive enhancement, 47*t*
*Arimidex. See also* Anastrazole
for breast cancer, 200*t*
Aripiprazole *(Abilify)*
for agitation, 47*t*
for psychosis, 165*t*
*Aristocort. See also* Triamcinolone
for adrenal insufficiency, 59*t*
for dermatologic conditions, 57*t*
*Arixtra* (fondaparinux), 20*t*
ARMD (age-related macular
degeneration)
causes, 194
nonpharmacologic interventions, 194
pharmacologic interventions, 195
*Aromasin* (exemestane), 200*t*
Aromatase inhibitors, 200*t*
*Artane* (trihexyphenidyl), 133*t*
Arterial blood gases, 1
Arterial disease, peripheral (PAD), 39–40
classes of disease, 39*t*
evaluation of, 182
Arterial oxygen
alveolar-arterial oxygen gradient, 1
partial pressure of (Pa$O_2$), 1
Arterial ulcers, 181–182
wound characteristics, 181*t*
Arteriovenous fistula access referral, 109
Arteritis, giant cell (temporal), 128

Arthritis. *See also* Osteoarthritis
acute arthritis, 128
acute gouty arthritis, 126
APAP and NSAIDs for, 124t–126t
chronic, 127
crystal-induced, 127
and falls, 68
pain relief, 148t
pseudogout, 127
resources, 227
*Arthropan* (choline salicylate), 124t
Arthroscopy, 118
*Arthrotec* (diclofenac with misoprostol), 125t
Artificial tears
for acute conjunctivitis, 198
for dry eye syndrome, 197
ASA (acetylsalicylic acid or aspirin)
for acute coronary syndrome, 25t
for acute MI, 24
for acute stroke, 131
for AF, 38
for anticoagulation, 18t
for arthritis, 124t
for chronic angina, 27
CMS criteria for inappropriate use, 224t
for diabetes mellitus, 62
with dipyridamole *(Aggrenox),* 131
for dizziness, 129t
enteric-coated, 124t
extended release *(Ext Release Bayer 8 Hour, ZORprin),* 124t
with hydrocodone *(Lortab ASA),* 146t
for MI prevention, 159t
with oxycodone *(Percodan),* 146t
for PAD, 39
for stroke prevention, 131
and tinnitus, 80
for vertigo, 130t
warfarin interactions, 18
*Asendin* (amoxapine)
antidepressants to avoid, 51
recommended max dose, 219t
*Aspercreme* (trolamine salicylate), 149t
Aspirin. *See* ASA

Assessment, 4
ADLs, 204–205
balance, 208–210
BPH, 217–218
cardiac risk, 156, 156f
cognitive status, 45, 47, 157, 204
coronary risk, 156f
depression, 206–207
dimensions of, 4t
functional, 67, 143, 204–205, 205–206, 217
gait, 67, 209
hearing, 207–208
of impotence, 177
instrumental ADLs, 205–206
instruments, 204–218
involuntary movement, abnormal, 210–212
Karnofsky Scale, 216
medication appropriateness, 218
mobility, 67, 208–210
nutritional, 114, 157
pain, 142f, 213–215
Palliative Performance Scale (PPS), 216
Performance-Oriented Mobility Assessment (POMA), 208–210
preoperative, 156–157, 157
psychosocial, 143
pulmonary, 176f
pulmonary risk, 156–157
for risk of addiction with opioid use, 143
wound, 180
Assisted living facilities
housing alternatives, 5
sites of post-hospital care, 158t
Assisted suicide, 153
Assistive devices
functional assessment, 67
for hearing, 79
for osteoarthritis, 122
for preventing falls, 68t
Assistive listening devices, 79
*Astelin* (azelastine), 167t
Asthma, 170–174
classification of, 171t
medications for, 172t–174t
therapy for, 171t–172t

**INDEX (CONT.)**

*Astramorph PF. See also* Morphine
    for pain, 146*t*
*Atacand. See also* Candesartan
    for HTN, 36*t*
*Atacand-HCT* (candesartan with HCTZ),
    37*t*
*Atarax. See also* Hydroxyzine
    for allergic rhinitis or conjunctivitis,
        168*t*
    recommended max dose, 221*t*
Atenolol *(Tenormin)*
    for acute MI, 24–25
    for AF, 38
    with chlorthalidone *(Tenoretic),* 37*t*
    for HTN, 34*t*
    perioperative, 157
    for tremors, 129*t*
*Ativan. See also* Lorazepam
    for anxiety, 23*t*
    for delirium, 43
    recommended max dose (anxiolytic),
        221*t*
    recommended max dose (hypnotic),
        221*t*
    for sleep disorders, 191*t*
Atorvastatin *(Lipitor)*
    drug and metabolic interactions, 12*t*
    for dyslipidemia, 30*t*
Atrial fibrillation (AF), 38
    anticoagulation for, 18*t*
    antihypertensive therapy and, 36*t*
Atrial tachycardia, 36*t*
Atropine
    with diphenoxylate *(Lomotil),* 76*t*
    for excessive secretions, 155
*Atrovent. See also* Ipratropium
    for asthma and COPD, 172*t*
*Atrovent NS. See also* Ipratropium
    for allergic rhinitis or conjunctivitis,
        169*t*
Attapulgite *(Kaopectate),* 76*t*
AUA Symptom Index for BPH, 217–218
Audiometry
    evaluation of hearing impairment, 78
    evaluation of tinnitus, 80

*Augmentin. See also* Amoxicillin-
    clavulanate
    for infectious diseases, 99*t*
Autolytic pressure ulcer debridement,
    187
Autolytic skin ulcer debridement, 180
A-V impulse device, 188
*Avalide* (irbesartan with HCTZ), 37*t*
*Avandamet* (rosiglitazone and
    metformin), 63*t*
*Avandia* (rosiglitazone), 63*t*
*Avapro. See also* Irbesartan
    for HTN, 36*t*
*Avelox. See also* Moxifloxacin
    for acute bacterial conjunctivitis, 198*t*
    for infectious diseases, 102*t*
*Aventyl. See also* Nortriptyline
    for depression, 51*t*
    for painful neuropathy, 136
    recommended max dose, 219*t*
*Avinza* (morphine), 147*t*
*Avodart* (dutasteride), 163
*Axid* (nizatidine), 71*t*
*Azactam. See also* Aztreonam
    for infectious diseases, 99*t*
Azelaic acid *(Azelex, Finacea, Finevin),*
    54*t*
Azelastine *(Astelin, Optivar),* 167*t*
*Azelex* (azelaic acid), 54*t*
Azithromycin *(Zithromax)*
    for community-acquired pneumonia,
        92*t*–93*t*
    for endocarditis prophylaxis, 161*t*
    for infectious diseases, 102*t*
*Azmacort. See also* Triamcinolone
    for asthma and COPD, 173*t*
*Azopt* (brinzolamide), 196*t*
Azotemia, prerenal, 107
Aztreonam *(Azactam)*
    for community-acquired pneumonia,
        93*t*
    for infectious diseases, 99*t*
    for urosepsis, 94

B

Back pain, 119–120
*Backache* (magnesium salicylate), 124t
Baclofen *(Lioresal)*, 149t
Bacterial conjunctivitis, acute, 197–198
    treatment for, 198t
Bacteriuria
    catheter care, 88
    definition, 93–94
*Bactocill* (oxacillin), 99t
*Bactrim* (co-trimoxazole), 103t
*Bactroban* (mupirocin), 55t
Balance assessment, 208–210
Balance exercises
    exercise prescription, 162
    for prevention of falls, 67, 68t
Balance impairment, 68t
Barbiturates
    recommended max doses (anxiolytic),
        221t
    recommended max doses (hypnotic),
        222t
    warfarin interactions, 18
Basal cell carcinoma, 200
Basic energy (caloric) requirements, 115
Beclomethasone *(Beclovent, Beconase,
        Vancenase, Vanceril)*
    for allergic rhinitis or conjunctivitis,
        168t
    for asthma and COPD, 173t
*Beclovent*. See also Beclomethasone
    for asthma and COPD, 173t
*Beconase*. See also Beclomethasone
    for allergic rhinitis or conjunctivitis,
        168t
Behavioral therapy
    for anxiety, 22
    for dementia, 46
    for dizziness, 129t
    for drop attacks, 130t
    for falls, 67
    for sleep disorders, 190
    for smoking cessation, 17
    for UI, 86–87
Belladonna alkaloids, 223t

*Benadryl*. See also Diphenhydramine
    for allergic rhinitis or conjunctivitis,
        168t
    recommended max dose, 221t
Benazepril *(Lotensin)*
    with amlodipine besylate *(Lotrel)*, 37t
    with HCTZ *(Lotensin HTC)*, 37t
    for HTN, 35t
    target dose in HF, 29t
Bendroflumethiazide with nadolol
        *(Corzide)*, 37t
*Benecol*, 30
*Benemid* (probenecid), 127t
*Ben-Gay* (methylsalicylate and menthol)
    for osteoarthritis, 123f
    for pain relief, 149t
*Benicar*. See also Olmesartan
    for HTN, 36t
Benign paroxysmal positional vertigo,
        130t
Benign prostatic hyperplasia (BPH), 163
    antihypertensive therapy and, 36t
    AUA symptom index, 217–218
    CMS criteria for inappropriate drug
        use, 224t, 225t
Benzodiazepines
    for akathisia, 166t
    for anxiety, 23, 23t
    for delirium, 43
    fall risks, 67, 68t
    for pain at end of life, 153
    recommended max doses (anxiolytic),
        221t
    recommended max doses (hypnotic),
        222t
    for restless legs syndrome, 193
    for sleep disorders, 191t
Benzonatate *(Tessalon Perles)*, 175t
Benztropine *(Cogentin)*
    and dementia, 46
    for Parkinson's disease, 133t
β-blockers (β-adrenergic inhibitors)
    for acute MI, 24–25
    for akathisia, 166t
    antihypertensive combinations, 37t
    for anxiety disorders, 22
    for chronic angina, 27
    and coexisting conditions, 36t

## INDEX (CONT.)

β-blockers (*continued*)
  combined α- and β-blockers, 34*t*–35*t*,
    36*t*
  for diastolic dysfunction, 29
  for glaucoma, 195*t*
  for HF, 28
  for HTN, 32, 34*t*
  for hyperthyroidism, 60
  perioperative use, 157
  for subacute MI, 26
  for tremors, 129*t*
β-carotene, 195
*Betagan* (levobunolol), 195*t*
β-lactams
  for hospital-acquired pneumonia, 93
  for infectious diseases, 98*t*–101*t*
  for nursing-home–acquired
    pneumonia, 93
Betamethasone *(Celestone)*, 59*t*
Betamethasone dipropionate *(Diprolene,
  Diprolene AF, Diprosone)*
  for dermatologic conditions, 57*t*, 58*t*
  for vulvar squamous hyperplasia, 200
Betamethasone valerate *(Valisone)*, 57*t*
Betaxolol *(Betoptic, Betoptic-S, Kerlone)*
  for glaucoma, 195*t*
  for HTN, 34*t*
Bethanechol *(Urecholine)*
  CMS criteria for inappropriate use,
    225*t*
  for GERD, 71*t*
*Betimol* (timolol drops), 195*t*
*Betoptic. See also* Betaxolol
  for glaucoma, 195*t*
*Betoptic-S. See also* Betaxolol
  for glaucoma, 195*t*
*Bextra* (valdecoxib), 126*t*
*Biaxin. See also* Clarithromycin
  for infectious diseases, 102*t*
  for peptic ulcer disease, 72
*Biaxin XL. See also* Clarithromycin
  for infectious diseases, 102*t*
Bicalutamide *(Casodex)*, 164*t*
Bicipital tendinitis, 118
Biguanides, 62*t*
Bimatoprost *(Lumigan)*, 196*t*

*Bioclusive. See also* Transparent film
  for pressure ulcers, 185*t*
*Bio-E-Gel* (transdermal estrogen), 203*t*
Biofeedback
  for osteoarthritis, 122
  for pain management, 144
Bioprosthetic heart valves, 18*t*
Bipolar disorders, 52
  bipolar affective disorder, 165
  long-term treatment of, 52*t*–53*t*
Bisacodyl *(Dulcolax)*
  for constipation, 73, 73*t*
  for fecal incontinence, 90
Bismuth subsaliclyate *(Pepto-Bismol)*
  for diarrhea, 76*t*
  for *H pylori*-induced ulcerations, 72*t*
  for peptic ulcer disease, 72
Bisoprolol *(Zebeta)*
  for HF, 28
  for HTN, 34*t*
  perioperative, 157
Bisoprolol fumarate with HCTZ *(Ziac)*, 37*t*
Bisphosphonates
  for metastatic bone pain, 153
  for osteoporosis, 139
Bitolterol *(Tornalate)*, 172*t*
Bladder outlet obstruction
  classification of, 85
  evaluation of, 86
Bladder relaxants, 225*t*
Bladder stress test, 86
Bladder-sphincter dyssynergia, 85
Blepharitis, 198*t*
Blindness. *See* Visual impairment
*Blocadren. See also* Timolol
  for HTN, 34*t*
Blood gases, arterial, 1
Blood glucose monitoring, 61
Blood pressure
  high, 31–33
  home monitoring, 32
  low, 59*t*, 69*t*, 129*t*, 166*t*
  management in chronic kidney failure,
    108
  management in PAD, 39

management in stroke, 131
screening, 159t
Blood urea nitrogen (BUN)/creatinine ratio, 109
BMD (bone mineral density)
  definition of osteoporosis, 138
  drugs for osteoporosis and, 140t
BMI (body mass index)
  formula, 1
  in HTN, 32
  post MI, 27
BNP (brain natriuretic peptide), 28
Board-and-cares, 5
Body mass index (BMI)
  formula, 1
  in HTN, 32
  post MI, 27
Body weight
  ideal, 1
  lean, 1
Bone densitometry, 159t
Bone disease, metastatic
  in breast cancer, 199
  pain relief, 153
  in prostate cancer, 164
Bone marrow biopsy, 83f
Bone mineral density (BMD)
  definition of osteoporosis, 138
  drugs for osteoporosis and, 140t
Bone pain, metastatic, 153
Boost Basic, 115t
Boost Plus, 115t
Boost with Fiber, 116t
Bowel obstruction, 154–155
Bowel training, 90
BPH (benign prostatic hyperplasia), 163
  antihypertensive therapy and, 36t
  AUA symptom index, 217–218
  CMS criteria for inappropriate drug use, 224t, 225t
Braden Scale, 186
Bradykinesia, 132
Brain natriuretic peptide (BNP), 28
Brain tumor, 165
Bran, 73
Breast cancer, 199
  drugs for osteoporosis and, 140t
  oral agents for, 199t–200t

Breast examination
  for prevention, 199
  recommendations, 159t
Brief Hearing Loss Screener, 207–208
Brief Pain Inventory
  assessment instrument, 214–215
  in pain, 143
Brimonidine (Alphagan, Alphagan P), 195t
Brinzolamide (Azopt), 196t
Broca's aphasia, 135t
Bromocriptine (Parlodel), 133t
Bronchodilators
  for asthma and COPD, 172t–174t
  for COPD, 170t
  for dyspnea, 154
  preoperative, 156
Bronchospasm, 36t
Bronkometer (isoetharine), 172t
Bronkosol (isoetharine), 172t
Budesonide (Pulmicort, Rhinocort)
  for allergic rhinitis or conjunctivitis, 168t
  for asthma and COPD, 173t
Bumetanide (Bumex)
  for HTN, 33t
  for hyperkalemia, 112, 113
  for UI, 87
Bumex. See also Bumetanide
  for HTN, 33t
BUN/creatinine ratio, 109
Bupropion (Wellbutrin, Wellbutrin SR, Zyban)
  for depression, 50, 50t
  drug and metabolic interactions, 12t
  for smoking cessation, 16
  for SSRI-induced sexual dysfunction, 179
  for tobacco abuse, 17t
Bursitis
  subacromial, 118
  trochanteric, 120
BuSpar. See also Buspirone
  for agitation, 48t
  for anxiety, 23
Buspirone (BuSpar)
  for agitation, 48t
  for anxiety, 23
  drug and metabolic interactions, 12t

## INDEX (CONT.)

Butabarbital *(Butisol)*, 221*t*
*Butisol* (butabarbital), 221*t*
Bypass surgery
coronary artery, 25*t*, 26
peripheral artery, 39

C
CABG (coronary artery bypass grafting)
for acute coronary syndrome, 25*t*
for acute MI, 26
CAD (coronary artery disease), 24–26
diagnostic tests, 24
drugs for osteoporosis and, 140*t*
ICD placement for, 41
Cadaveric kidney transplant, 109
Caffeine
for fecal incontinence, 90
for postural hypotension, 69*t*
and sleep problems, 190
CAGE questionnaire, 15
Caged ball or caged disk valve, 18*t*
*Calan SR* (verapamil SR), 35*t*
*Calcimar. See also* Calcitonin
for osteoporosis, 139
Calcipotriene, 54*t*
Calcitonin *(Calcimar, Cibacalcin, Miacalcin, Osteocalcin, Salmonine)*
bone outcomes, 140*t*
effects on other outcomes, level of evidence, and risks of, 140*t*
for osteoporosis, 139
for vertebral compression fracture, 120
Calcitriol *(Rocaltrol)*
for hypocalcemia, 108
for vitamin D insufficiency, 108
Calcium
antacids with, 73
for chronic kidney failure, 108
drug interactions, 10
for HTN, 32
for osteoporosis, 138
for prevention of falls, 67
Calcium alginate dressings
for pressure ulcers, 187
for venous ulcers, 188

Calcium antagonists
for acute MI, 26
antihypertensive combinations, 37*t*
for chronic angina, 27
and coexisting conditions, 36*t*
for diastolic dysfunction, 29
drug and metabolic interactions, 12*t*
for HTN, 35*t*
for hyperthyroidism, 60
for systolic dysfunction, 29
Calcium carbonate, 108
Calcium channel blockers. *See* Calcium antagonists
Calcium citrate, 108
Calcium gluconate, 113
Calcium pyrophosphate, 127
*Calmoseptine*, 55*t*
Caloric requirements
calculating, 115
for wound repair, 180
CAM (Confusion Assessment Method), 42
*Campho-Phenique* (camphor and phenol), 149*t*
Camphor and phenol *(Campho-Phenique)*, 149*t*
Camphor-menthol-phenol *(Sarna)*, 148*t*
Cancer
breast, 140*t*, 199, 199*t*–200*t*
colorectal, 140*t*
determinants for hospice eligibility, 151*t*
metastatic bone disease, 153, 164, 199
prostate cancer, 163–164, 164*t*
resources, 226
screening (secondary prevention), 159*t*
vulvar, 200
*Cancidas* (caspofungin), 105*t*
Candesartan *(Atacand)*
with HCTZ *(Atacand-HCT)*, 37*t*
for HTN, 36*t*
target dose in HF, 29*t*
Candidiasis
antibiotics for, 105*t*
at end of life, 154
topical antifungals for, 56*t*

treatment, 54t
CAPD (central auditory processing disorders), 78
*Capoten.* See also Captopril
for HTN, 35t
*Capozide* (captopril with HCTZ), 37t
Capsaicin *(Capsin, Capzasin, No Pain-HP, R-Gel, Zostrix)*
for osteoarthritis, 122, 123f
for pain, 149t
for painful neuropathy, 136
*Capsin.* See also Capsaicin
for pain, 149t
Capsulitis, adhesive, 118
Captopril *(Capoten)*
food interactions, 10
with HCTZ *(Capozide)*, 37t
for HTN, 35t
target dose in HF, 29t
*Capzasin.* See also Capsaicin
for pain, 149t
*Carafate.* See also Sucralfate
for GERD, 71t
Carbamazepine *(Tegretol, Tegretol XR)*
for agitation, 48t
for bipolar disorders, 52t
drug and metabolic interactions, 11t–12t
for epilepsy, 134t
for painful neuropathy, 136
for restless legs syndrome, 193
warfarin interactions, 18
Carbamide peroxide *(Cerumenex, Debrox)*, 79
Carbapenem, 99t
Carbenicillin indanyl sodium *(Geocillin)*, 99t
*Carbex* (selegiline), 133t
Carbidopa-levodopa *(Sinemet, Sinemet CR)*
for Parkinson's disease, 133t
for restless legs syndrome, 193
Carbonic anhydrase inhibitors, 196t
*Cardene* (nicardipine), 35t
*Cardene SR* (nicardipine), 35t
Cardiac catheterization, 24
Cardiac diagnostic tests, 24
Cardiac enzymes, 24

Cardiac risk assessment, preoperative, 156
reducing cardiac risk in noncardiac surgery, 156f
Cardiac risk factors
evaluation and assessment, 31
exercise prescription for, 162
Cardiac syncope
classification of, 40t
evaluation of, 40
Cardiac troponins, 24
Cardioembolic stroke, 131
Cardiomyopathy
anticoagulation for, 18t
ICD placement for, 41
Cardiovascular diseases, 24–41
and chronic kidney failure, 108
determinants for hospice eligibility, 151t
endocarditis prophylaxis, 160
exercise prescription, 162
resources, 227
and risks with surgery, 156
Cardioversion, 38
*Cardizem CD* (diltiazem), 35t
*Cardizem SR* (diltiazem), 35t
*Cardura* (doxazosin)
for BPH, 163
for HTN, 33t
Caregiving. See also Elder mistreatment
caregiver issues, 48
resources, 226
risk factors for inadequate or abusive caregiving, 7
*Carfin.* See also Warfarin
prescribing information, 18
Carisoprodol
CMS regulations, 224t
for pain management, 146
*Carnation Instant Breakfast,* 115
Carotid endarterectomy, 132t
Carotid stenosis, 132t
Carpal tunnel syndrome, 121
Carteolol *(Cartrol, Ocupress)*
for glaucoma, 195t
for HTN, 34t
*Cartrol.* See also Carteolol
for HTN, 34t

**INDEX (CONT.)**

Carvedilol *(Coreg)*
  for HF, 28
  for HTN, 35t
*Casodex* (bicalutamide), 164t
Caspofungin *(Cancidas)*, 105t
*Cataflam* (diclofenac), 124t
*Catalyst Vacuum Device*, 178t
*Catapres. See also* Clonidine
  for hot flushes, 201
  for HTN, 34t
*Catapres-TTS. See also* Clonidine
  for HTN, 34t
Cataracts
  causes, 194
  nonpharmacologic interventions, 194
  preoperative care, 157
Catechol *O*-methyltransferase (COMT)
  inhibitors, 133t
Catheters, 88
Cavernosometry, 177
CBT (cognitive-behavior therapy), 22
*Ceclor* (cefaclor), 100t
*Cedax* (ceftibuten), 101t
Cefaclor *(Ceclor)*, 100t
Cefadroxil *(Duricef)*
  for endocarditis prophylaxis, 161t
  for infectious diseases, 100t
*Cefadyl* (cephapirin), 100t
Cefamandole *(Mandol)*, 100t
Cefazolin *(Ancef, Kefzol)*
  for endocarditis prophylaxis, 161, 161t
  for infectious diseases, 100t
Cefdinir *(Omnicef)*, 101t
Cefditoren *(Spectracef)*, 101t
Cefepime *(Maxipime)*, 101t
Cefixime *(Suprax)*, 101t
*Cefizox* (ceftizoxime), 101t
Cefmetazole *(Zefazone)*, 100t
*Cefobid* (cefoperazone), 101t
Cefoperazone *(Cefobid)*, 101t
*Cefotan* (cefotetan), 100t
Cefotaxime *(Claforan)*
  for community-acquired pneumonia,
    92t
  for infectious diseases, 101t
Cefotetan *(Cefotan)*, 100t

Cefoxitin *(Mefoxin)*, 100t
Cefpodoxime *(Vantin)*
  for community-acquired pneumonia,
    92t
  for infectious diseases, 101t
Cefprozil *(Cefzil)*
  for community-acquired pneumonia,
    92t
  for infectious diseases, 100t
Ceftazidime *(Ceptaz, Fortaz)*, 101t
Ceftibuten *(Cedax)*, 101t
*Ceftin. See also* Cefuroxime axetil
  for infectious diseases, 100t
Ceftizoxime *(Cefizox)*, 101t
Ceftriaxone *(Rocephin)*
  for community-acquired pneumonia,
    92t
  for infectious diseases, 101t
Cefuroxime axetil *(Ceftin)*
  for community-acquired pneumonia,
    92t
  for infectious diseases, 100t
*Cefzil. See also* Cefprozil
  for infectious diseases, 100t
Celecoxib *(Celebrex)*
  for arthritis, 126t
  drug and metabolic interactions,
    11t–12t
*Celestone* (betamethasone), 59t
*Celexa. See also* Citalopram
  for agitation, 47t
  for depression, 50t
Cellulitis, 55t, 180
*Cenestin. See also* Estrogen
  for systemic hormone therapy, 202t
Centers for Medicare and Medicaid
    Services (CMS)
  criteria for inappropriate drug use,
    223–225
  diagnosis-drug combinations
    considered "high severity", 223t–224t
  diagnosis-drug combinations
    considered "low severity", 224t–225t
  drugs considered "high severity", 223t
  drugs considered "low severity", 224t

OBRA regulations, 219–222
Central auditory processing disorders (CAPD), 78
Central nervous system (CNS) depressants, 191t
*Centrax* (prazepam), 221t
Cephalexin *(Keflex)*
  for cystitis, 94
  for endocarditis prophylaxis, 161, 161t
  for infectious diseases, 100t
Cephalosporins
  for hospital-acquired pneumonia, 93
  for infectious diseases, 100t, 101t
  for nursing-home–acquired pneumonia, 93
  for skin and soft-tissue infections, 55t
  for urosepsis, 94
Cephalothin *(Keflin)*, 100t
Cephapirin *(Cefadyl)*, 100t
Cephradine *(Anspor)*, 100t, 161
*Cephulac* (lactulose), 74t
*Ceptaz* (ceftazidime), 101t
Cerebellar tremor, 129t
Cerebral disease, ischemic, 129t
Cerumen removal, 79
*Cerumenex* (carbamide peroxide), 79
Cervical spondylosis, 129t
Cetirizine *(Zyrtec)*, 167t
Chemical dependency, 144
Chemical skin ulcer debridement, 180
Chemotherapy
  for breast cancer, 199
  and tinnitus, 80
Chest pain, acute, 24
Chest percussion, 92
*Chibroxin. See also* Norfloxacin
  for acute bacterial conjunctivitis, 198t
*Chlamydia pneumoniae*
  community-acquired pneumonia, 91
  nursing-home–acquired pneumonia, 91
Chloral hydrate *(Aquachloral, Noctec, Supprettes)*
  recommended max dose, 221t
  for sleep disorders, 191t
Chloramphenicol *(Chloromycetin)*, 103t
Chlordiazepoxide *(Librium)*
  for anxiety, 23

recommended max dose, 221t
*Chloromycetin* (chloramphenicol), 103t
Chloroquine, 198
Chlorothiazide *(Diuril)*, 33t
Chlorothiazide with reserpine *(Diupres)*, 37t
Chlorpheniramine *(Chlor-Trimeton)*
  for allergic rhinitis or conjunctivitis, 168t
  drug and metabolic interactions, 12t
  with hydrocodone and phenylephrine *(Histussin HC)*, 175t
Chlorpromazine *(Thorazine)*
  for delirium, 43
  recommended max dose, 220t
Chlorpropamide *(Diabinese)*, 223t
Chlorprothixene *(Taractan)*, 220t
Chlorthalidone *(Hygroton)*
  with atenolol *(Tenoretic)*, 37t
  for HTN, 33t
*Chlor-Trimeton. See also* Chlorpheniramine
  for allergic rhinitis or conjunctivitis, 168t
Chlorzoxazone
  CMS regulations, 224t
  for pain management, 146
*ChoiceDM* beverage, 116t
*ChoiceDM TF*, 116t
Cholesterol, serum
  in malnutrition, 115
  in stroke prevention, 131
Cholesterol screening. *See* Dyslipidemia
Cholesterol-lowering diet, 30
Cholesterol-lowering drugs, 30t–31t
Cholesterol-lowering margarines, 30
Cholestyramine
  digoxin interactions, 11
  warfarin interactions, 18
Cholestyramine resin *(Questran)*, 77
Choline magnesium salicylate *(Tricosal, Trilisate)*, 124t
Choline salicylate *(Arthropan)*, 124t
Cholinergic urticaria, 55t
Cholinesterase inhibitors
  for cognitive dysfunction in AD, 46
  cognitive enhancers, 47t
  for glaucoma, 196t

## INDEX (CONT.)

Chondrocalcinosis, 128
Chondroitin
  common herbal and alternative
    medications, 13*t*
  for osteoarthritis, 122
Chronic disease anemia, 81
Chronic kidney failure, 108–109
  determinants for hospice eligibility,
    152*t*
Chronic obstructive pulmonary disease
  (COPD), 169–170
  CMS criteria for inappropriate drug
    use, 223*t*
  medications for, 172*t*–174*t*
  preoperative risk assessment, 156
  resources, 226, 227
  therapy for, 170*t*
Chronic wounds, 180
  wound characteristics, 181*t*
*Cialis* (tadalafil)
  for BPH, 163
  for male sexual dysfunction, 178*t*
*Cibacalcin. See also* Calcitonin
  for osteoporosis, 139
Ciclopirox *(Loprox, Penlac)*, 56*t*
Cigarette smoke-drug interactions, 11*t*
Cilastatin-imipenem *(Primaxin)*, 99*t*
Cilostazol *(Pletal)*, 39
*Ciloxan Ophthalmic. See also*
    Ciprofloxacin
  for acute bacterial conjunctivitis, 198*t*
Cimetidine *(Tagamet)*
  drug and metabolic interactions,
    11*t*–12*t*
  for GERD, 70*t*
  warfarin interactions, 18
*Cinobac* (cinoxacin), 102*t*
Cinoxacin *(Cinobac)*, 102*t*
*Cipro. See also* Ciprofloxacin
  for infectious diseases, 102*t*
Ciprofloxacin *(Ciloxan Ophthalmic, Cipro)*
  for acute bacterial conjunctivitis, 198*t*
  for community-acquired pneumonia,
    92*t*
  drug interactions, 11
  for infectious diseases, 102*t*

*Circ-Aid Thera-Boot*, 188
Cisplatin, 198
Citalopram *(Celexa)*
  for agitation, 47*t*
  for depression, 50*t*
  SSRI-induced sexual dysfunction, 179
*CitriSource*, 116*t*
*Citrobacter*, 94
*Citroma* (magnesium citrate), 74*t*
*Citrucel. See also* Methylcellulose
  for constipation, 74*t*
*Claforan. See also* Cefotaxime
  for infectious diseases, 101*t*
*Clarinex* (desloratadine), 167*t*
Clarithromycin *(Biaxin, Biaxin XL)*
  for community-acquired pneumonia,
    92*t*–93*t*
  drug and metabolic interactions, 12*t*
  for endocarditis prophylaxis, 161*t*
  food interactions, 10
  for *H pylori*-induced ulcerations, 71*t*,
    72*t*
  for infectious disease, 102*t*
  with lansoprazole and amoxicillin
    *(Prevpac)*, 71*t*
  for peptic ulcer disease, 72
  for rosacea, 54*t*
*Claritin* (loratadine), 168*t*
*Claritin-D* (loratadine), 168*t*, 169*t*
Claudication
  in PAD, 39*t*
  treatment of, 39
Clavicle, rotator tendon impingement on,
  118
Clavulanate-amoxicillin *(Augmentin)*
  for folliculitis, 55*t*
  for infectious diseases, 99*t*
*Clenia* (sodium sulfacetamide), 54*t*
*Cleocin. See also* Clindamycin
  for infectious diseases, 103*t*
Clidinium, 223*t*
*Climara* (transdermal estrogen), 203*t*
Clindamycin *(Cleocin)*
  for community-acquired pneumonia,
    92*t*
  for endocarditis prophylaxis, 161, 161*t*

for folliculitis, 55t
for hospital-acquired pneumonia, 93
for infectious diseases, 103t
for nursing-home–acquired
pneumonia, 93
*Clinoril* (sulindac), 126t
Clobetasol propionate *(Temovate)*
for dermatologic conditions, 58t
for lichen sclerosus, 200
Clocortolone pivalate *(Cloderm)*, 57t
*Cloderm* (clocortolone pivalate), 57t
Clofibrate, 18
Clomipramine, 12t
Clonidine *(Catapres, Catapres-TTS,
Duraclon)*
food interactions, 11
for hot flushes, 201
for HTN, 34t
Clopidogrel *(Plavix)*
for acute coronary syndrome, 25t
for acute MI, 24
for PAD, 39
for stroke prevention, 131
Clorazepate *(Tranxene)*, 221t
*Clostridium difficile*
antibiotics for, 104t
diagnosis of, 76
pseudomembranous colitis, 76
Clotrimazole *(Cruex, Lotrimin, Mycelex)*
for candidiasis, 154
for dermatologic conditions, 56t
Clozapine *(Clozaril)*
and dementia, 46
drug and metabolic interactions,
11t–12t
for psychosis, 165t
recommended max dose, 220t
*Clozaril. See also* Clozapine
for psychosis, 165t
recommended max dose, 220t
CMS. *See* Centers for Medicare and
Medicaid Services
CNS depressants, 191t
Cochlear implants, 79
Codeine
with APAP, 146t
drug and metabolic interactions, 12t
for pain, 146t

*Cogentin. See also* Benztropine
for Parkinson's disease, 133t
Cognitive enhancers, 47t
Cognitive impairment
in Alzheimer's disease, 46
in delirium, 42
and falls, 68, 69t
and pain assessment, 141, 142f
progression, 44
screening, 159t
UI and, 86
Cognitive status assessment
in cognitive dysfunction in AD, 47
in dementia, 45
Mini-Cog Assessment Instrument for
Dementia, 204
preoperative, 157
Cognitive-behavior therapy (CBT), 22
*Colace. See also* Docusate
for constipation, 73t
to remove ear war, 79
*ColBenemid* (probenecid with
colchicine), 127t
Colchicine
for acute gouty flare, 126–127
for chronic gout, 127t
for hyperuricemia following acute
flare, 127
with probenecid *(ColBenemid, Col-
Probenecid, Proben-C)*, 127t
for pseudogout, 128
Colesevelam *(WelChol)*, 31t
Colestipol, 11
Colitis, antibiotic-associated
pseudomembranous, 76–77
Colonoscopy
in fecal incontinence, 89
recommendations, 159t
Colorectal cancer, 140t
Colposcopy, 200
Colposuspension, retropubic, 88
*Col-Probenecid* (probenecid with
colchicine), 127t
Coma, myxedema, 60
*CombiPatch* (estradiol and
norethindrone), 203t
*Combivent* (albuterol-ipratropium), 174t

**INDEX (CONT.)**

*Comfeel. See also* Hydrocolloids
  for pressure ulcers, 185*t*
Communication with hearing-impaired
      persons, 79
Community-acquired cystitis, 94
Community-acquired pneumonia
    empiric antibiotic therapy, 92*t*–93*t*
    expected organisms, 91
*Compazine* (prochlorperazine), 75*t*
Compression fractures, vertebral, 120
Compression therapy, 188
COMT inhibitors, 133*t*
*Comtan* (entacapone), 133*t*
Conduction aphasia, 136*t*
Conductive hearing loss
    aggravating factors, 78
    classification, 78
Confusion Assessment Method (CAM),
      42
Congestion, nasal, 167*t*
Congestive heart failure. *See* Heart
      failure
Conjunctival hyperemia, 197
Conjunctivitis, 197–198
    choosing therapy for, 167*t*
    drug therapy for, 167*t*–169*t*
    treatment for, 198*t*
Constipation, 73
    CMS criteria for inappropriate drug
      use, 225*t*
    at end of life, 154
    and fecal incontinence, 90
    medications for, 73*t*–74*t*
Continuing care retirement communities,
      5
Continuous positive airway pressure
      (CPAP), 192
COPD. *See* Chronic obstructive
      pulmonary disease
*Cordran* (flurandrenolide), 57*t*
*Coreg* (carvedilol)
    for HF, 28
    for HTN, 35*t*
*Corgard* (nadolol), 34*t*
Coronary angioplasty, percutaneous, 25

Coronary artery bypass grafting (CABG)
    for acute coronary syndrome, 25*t*
    for acute MI, 26
Coronary artery disease (CAD), 24–26
    diagnostic tests, 24
    drugs for osteoporosis and, 140*t*
    ICD placement for, 41
Coronary risk assessment, preoperative,
      156*t*
*Cortef. See also* Hydrocortisone
    for adrenal insufficiency, 59*t*
Corticosteroids. *See also* Glucocorticoids
    for acute bacterial conjunctivitis, 198*t*
    for acute disk herniation, 119
    for adrenal insufficiency, 59, 59*t*
    for allergic rhinitis or conjunctivitis,
      167*t*, 168*t*
    for asthma, 171*t*, 172*t*, 173*t*
    for back pain, 120
    for bicipital tendinitis, 118
    for carpal tunnel syndrome, 121
    for chronic disk degeneration, 119
    CMS criteria for inappropriate use,
      224*t*
    for COPD, 170*t*, 173*t*
    for frozen shoulder (adhesive
      capsulitis), 118
    for herpes zoster, 95
    for malnutrition, dehydration at end of
      life, 155
    for neurodermatitis, 54*t*
    ocular adverse events, 198
    for osteoarthritis, 119, 122, 123*f*
    and osteoporosis, 138
    for pain relief, 148*t*
    preoperative, 156
    for psoriasis, 54*t*
    for scabies, 54*t*
    topical, 56*t*–58*t*
    for trochanteric bursitis, 120
    warfarin interactions, 18
Cortisone *(Cortone)*
    for adrenal insufficiency, 59*t*
    and sleep problems, 190
*Cortone. See also* Cortisone
    for adrenal insufficiency, 59*t*

*Cortrosyn* (cosyntropin), 127
*Corzide* (nadolol with
    bendroflumethiazide), 37*t*
*Cosopt* (dorzolamide/timolol), 197*t*
Cosyntropin *(Cortrosyn)*, 127
Co-trimoxazole *(Bactrim)*, 103*t*
Cough, 175
    antitussives and expectorants, 175*t*
    with asthma, 171
*Coumadin. See also* Warfarin
    prescribing information, 18
Counterirritants, 148*t*–149*t*
COX-2 inhibitors
    for acute pain and short-term
        management, 143
    for arthritis, 126*t*
    for osteoarthritis, 122, 123*f*
    for pain management, 145
*Cozaar. See also* Losartan
    for HTN, 36*t*
CPAP (continuous positive airway
    pressure), 192
Cr (creatinine), 109
Cramps, leg, 193
*Crescendo* TIA, 131
*Crestor* (rosuvastatin), 30*t*
Cromolyn *(NasalCrom)*
    for allergic rhinitis or conjunctivitis,
        167*t*, 169*t*
    for asthma, 171*t*
Cromolyn sodium *(Intal)*, 174*t*
Cross-cultural geriatrics, 8
Crotamiton *(Eurax)*, 54*t*
*Cruex. See also* Clotrimazole
    prescribing information, 56*t*
Crystal-induced arthritis, 127
*Cubicin* (daptomycin), 103*t*
Cultural identity, 8
Cupric oxide, 195
Cushing's syndrome, 165
*Cutivate* (fluticasone propionate), 57*t*
Cyclandelate, 224*t*

Cyclobenzaprine
    CMS regulations, 224*t*
    for pain management, 146
*Cyclocort* (amcinonide), 57*t*
Cyclosporine
    drug and metabolic interactions, 12*t*
    ophthalmic emulsion *(Restasis)*, 197
    for pancytopenia, 84
    for psoriasis, 54*t*
*Cycrin. See also* Medroxyprogesterone
    for systemic hormone therapy, 203*t*
*Cymbalta. See also* Duloxetine
    for depression, 50*t*
    for pain, 148*t*
    for painful neuropathy, 136
CYP substrates, inducers, and inhibitors,
    11*t*–12*t*
Cystitis
    classification, 85
    empiric antibiotic management, 94
*Cystospaz. See also* Hyoscyamine
    for UI, 87*t*
Cytochrome P-450. *See* CYP substrates,
    inducers, and inhibitors
*Cytotec* (misoprostol), 122

D
Dalfopristin/quinupristin *(Synercid)*, 104*t*
*Dalmane. See also* Flurazepam
    recommended max dose, 221*t*
Dalteparin *(Fragmin)*
    for acute coronary syndrome, 25*t*
    for DVT/PE, 20*t*
Danaparoid *(Organan)*, 20*t*
Dance, 162
Dantrolene, 224*t*
Daptomycin *(Cubicin)*, 103*t*
*Daranide* (dichlorphenamide), 196*t*
Darbepoetin alfa *(Aranesp)*, 84*t*
Darifenacin *(Enablex)*, 87*t*
*Daypro* (oxaprozin), 126*t*
D&C (dilation and curettage), 200
D/C cardioversion, 38
D-dimer, 176*f*
Deafness. *See* Hearing impairment
Debridement
    for diabetic foot ulcers, 183

**INDEX (CONT.)**

Debridement (*continued*)
  for pressure ulcers, 187
  for skin ulcers, 180
*Debrox* (carbamide peroxide), 79
*Decaderm* (dexamethasone phosphate),
  56*t*
*Decadron. See also* Dexamethasone
  for adrenal insufficiency, 59*t*
  for inflammation due to malignant
    obstruction, 155
Decision making, informed, 5, 6*f*
*Declomycin* (demeclocycline), 112
Decongestants
  for allergic rhinitis or conjunctivitis,
    168*t*
  CMS criteria for inappropriate use,
    225*t*
Deep heat, 122
Deep-vein thrombosis (DVT)
  anticoagulation for prophylaxis and
    treatment, 19*t*–20*t*
  drugs for osteoporosis and, 140*t*
  prophylaxis, 157
  treatment, 176
Dehydration, 109. *See also* Hydration
  and delirium, 43
  at end of life, 155
Delirium, 42–43
  differential diagnosis, 165
*Deliver,* 116*t*
*Delta-Cortef* (prednisolone), 59*t*
*Deltasone. See also* Prednisone
  for adrenal insufficiency, 59*t*
  for asthma and COPD, 173*t*
Delusional (paranoid) disorder, late-life,
  165
Delusions, 45
*Demadex. See also* Torsemide
  for HTN, 33*t*
Demecarium (*Humorsol*), 196*t*
Demeclocycline (*Declomycin*), 112
Dementia, 44–48
  and delirium, 42
  dementia syndrome, 44
  determinants for hospice eligibility,
    151*t*

  differential diagnosis, 165
  Mini-Cog Assessment Instrument for
    Dementia, 204
  and osteoporosis, 138
  pharmacologic management of, 43
  preoperative risk, 157
Dental procedures, endocarditis
    prophylaxis for
  for patients with total joint
    replacements, 161
  procedures warranting prophylaxis,
    160
  regimens, 161*t*
Dental status, 212
*Depacon. See also* Valproic acid
  for bipolar disorders, 52*t*
  for epilepsy, 135*t*
*Depade* (naltrexone), 16
*Depakene. See also* Valproic acid
  for bipolar disorders, 52*t*
  for epilepsy, 135*t*
*Depakote* (divalproex sodium). *See also*
    Valproic acid
  for agitation, 48*t*
  for bipolar disorders, 52*t*
  for epilepsy, 135*t*
*Depo-Medrol. See also*
    Methylprednisolone
  for adrenal insufficiency, 59*t*
*Deponit. See also* Nitroglycerin
  dosage and formulations, 27*t*
*Depo-Provera. See also*
    Medroxyprogesterone
  for agitation, 48*t*
Depression, 49–53
  agitation treatment guidelines, 47*t*
  in Alzheimer's disease, 45
  antihypertensive therapy and, 36*t*
  differential diagnosis, 165
  at end of life, 155
  and falls, 68, 69*t*
  Geriatric Depression Scale (GDS),
    206–207
  screening, 159*t*
  and tinnitus, 80

Dermatitis, seborrheic
  topical antifungals for, 56*t*
  treatment, 54*t*
Dermatologic conditions, 54–58
  conditions common in elderly persons, 54*t*–55*t*
  resources, 227
Dermatomes, 3*f*
*Dermatop* (prednicarbate), 57*t*
Dermatophytoses, 56*t*
Desipramine *(Norpramin)*
  CMS criteria for inappropriate use, 225*t*
  for depression, 49–50, 51*t*
  drug and metabolic interactions, 12*t*
  for pain relief, 148*t*
  for painful neuropathy, 136
  recommended max dose, 219*t*
Desloratadine *(Clarinex)*, 167*t*
Desonide *(DesOwen, Tridesilon)*, 57*t*
*DesOwen* (desonide), 57*t*
Desoximetasone *(Topicort)*, 57*t*
*Desyrel. See also* Trazodone
  for agitation, 48*t*
  for depression, 51*t*
  recommended max dose, 219*t*
  for sleep disorders, 191*t*
*Detrol* (tolterodine)
  for depression, 50
  for UI, 87*t*
*Detrol LA. See also* Tolterodine
  for UI, 87*t*
Detrusor contractility, impaired
  classification of, 85
  management of, 87
Detrusor hyperactivity with impaired contractility (DHIC)
  classification of, 85
  evaluation of, 86
  management of, 87
Detrusor instability, 86
*Dexacort. See also* Dexamethasone
  for allergic rhinitis or conjunctivitis, 168*t*
  for asthma and COPD, 173*t*
Dexamethasone *(Decadron, Dexacort, Dexone, Hexadrol)*
  for adrenal insufficiency, 59*t*

  for allergic rhinitis or conjunctivitis, 168*t*
  for asthma and COPD, 173*t*
  for inflammation due to malignant obstruction, 155
  for malnutrition, dehydration, 155
Dexamethasone phosphate *(Decaderm)*, 56*t*
*Dexedrine* (dextroamphetamine), 153
*Dexone. See also* Dexamethasone
  for adrenal insufficiency, 59*t*
Dextroamphetamine *(Dexedrine)*, 153
Dextromethorphan *(Robitussin DM)*
  for cough, 175*t*
  drug and metabolic interactions, 12*t*
Dextrose solution
  for hyperkalemia, 112, 113
  for parenteral nutrition, 117*t*
*DH Pressure Relief Walker*, 183
DHIC (detrusor hyperactivity with impaired contractility)
  classification of, 85
  evaluation of, 86
  management of, 87
*Diaβeta* (glyburide), 62*t*
Diabetes control
  in chronic kidney failure, 108
  post MI, 27
Diabetes insipidus, 110
Diabetes mellitus, 61–64
  antihypertensive therapy and, 36*t*
  CMS criteria for inappropriate drug use, 224*t*
  eye examinations, 194
  insulin preparations, 63*t*
  lactose-free oral and enteral formulations, 116*t*
  oral agents for, 62*t*–63*t*
  and PAD, 39
  resources, 227
  screening, 159*t*
Diabetic neuropathy, 136
Diabetic peripheral neuropathy, 149*t*
Diabetic retinopathy
  causes, 194
  nonpharmacologic interventions, 194
  pharmacologic interventions, 195

**INDEX** (CONT.)

Diabetic ulcers, 182–184
  wound characteristics, 181*t*
*Diabinese* (chlorpropamide), 223*t*
Dialysis
  for acute kidney failure, 107
  for chronic kidney failure, 109
  hemodialysis, 109
  for hyperkalemia, 113
  peritoneal dialysis, 109
*Diamox* (acetazolamide), 196*t*
Diarrhea, 75–76
  antibiotic-associated, 76–77
  antidiarrheals, 76*t*
  at end of life, 155
  with enteral feedings, 117
  and hyponatremia, 111
Diastolic dysfunction
  evaluation and assessment, 27
  pharmacologic management, 29
Diazepam *(Valium)*
  for anxiety, 23
  drug and metabolic interactions, 12*t*
  recommended max dose, 221*t*
Dichlorphenamide *(Daranide)*, 196*t*
Diclofenac *(Cataflam, Voltaren, Voltaren-XR)*
  for arthritis, 124*t*
  with misoprostol *(Arthrotec)*, 125*t*
Dicloxacillin *(Dycill, Pathocil)*, 99*t*
Dicyclomine, 223*t*
Diflorasone diacetate *(Florone, Maxiflor, Psorcon)*, 58*t*
*Diflucan. See also* Fluconazole
  for dermatologic conditions, 56*t*
  for infectious diseases, 105*t*
  for onychomycosis, 54*t*
Diflunisal *(Dolobid)*, 125*t*
Digital rectal examination, 159*t*
Digital stimulation, 90
Digoxin *(Lanoxin, Lanoxicaps)*
  for AF, 38
  CMS regulations, 223*t*, 224*t*
  drug interactions, 11
  for HF, 28–29
  ocular adverse events, 198

Dihydropyridines
  and coexisting conditions, 36*t*, 37*t*
  drug and metabolic interactions, 12*t*
  for HTN, 35*t*
*Dilacor XR* (diltiazem), 35*t*
*Dilantin. See also* Phenytoin
  for epilepsy, 135*t*
Dilation and curettage (D&C), 200
*Dilatrate SR* (isosorbide dinitrate), 26*t*
*Dilaudid. See also* Hydromorphone
  for pain, 146*t*
Diltiazem
  for AF, 38
  digoxin interactions, 11
  drug and metabolic interactions, 11*t*–12*t*
  enteral nutrition interactions, 117
Diltiazem SR *(Cardizem CD, Cardizem SR, Dilacor XR, Tiazac)*, 35*t*
Dimenhydrinate *(Dramamine)*, 75*t*
*Diovan. See also* Valsartan
  for HTN, 36*t*
*Diovan-HCT* (valsartan with HCTZ), 37*t*
Diphenhydramine *(Benadryl)*
  for allergic rhinitis or conjunctivitis, 168*t*
  CMS regulations, 224*t*
  and dementia, 46
  for painful mucositis, 154
  recommended max dose, 221*t*
Diphenoxylate with atropine *(Lomotil)*, 76*t*
Dipivefrin *(AKPro, Propine)*, 195*t*
*Diprolene. See also* Betamethasone dipropionate
  for dermatologic conditions, 58*t*
*Diprolene AF. See also* Betamethasone dipropionate
  for dermatologic conditions, 57*t*
*Diprosone. See also* Betamethasone dipropionate
  for dermatologic conditions, 57*t*
Dipyridamole *(Persantine)*
  with ASA *(Aggrenox)*, 131
  CMS criteria for inappropriate use, 224*t*
  stress test, 24
  for stroke prevention, 131

Direct current (D/C) cardioversion, 38
Direct thrombin inhibitors, 20t
*Disalcid* (salsalate), 124t
Discharge planning, 157
Disk degeneration, chronic, 119
Disk herniation, acute, 119
Disopyramide *(Norpace)*
    for AF, 38
    CMS regulations, 223t
*Ditropan. See also* Oxybutynin
    for UI, 87t
*Ditropan XL. See also* Oxybutynin
    for UI, 87t
*Diupres* (reserpine with chlorothiazide),
    37t
Diuretics
    antihypertensive combinations, 37t
    and coexisting conditions, 36t, 37t
    for dyspnea, 154
    fall risks, 69t
    food interactions, 11
    for HF, 28, 29
    for HTN, 32, 33t
    for hyperkalemia, 112, 113
    and hyponatremia, 111
    potassium-sparing, 11
    and sleep problems, 190
    for vertigo, 130t
*Diuril* (chlorothiazide), 33t
Divalproex *(Depakote, Epival)*
    for agitation or aggression, 48t
    for sexual aggression, impulse-control
        symptoms in men, 48t
Dizziness, 129t–130t
DNR (do-not-resuscitate) orders, 152
*Doan's* (magnesium salicylate), 124t
Dobutamine stress test, 24
Docusate *(Colace)*
    for constipation, 73t
    for fecal incontinence, 90
    to remove ear wax, 79
*Dolobid* (diflunisal), 125t
Donepezil *(Aricept)*
    for cognitive dysfunction in AD, 47
    for cognitive enhancement, 47t
    drug and metabolic interactions, 12t
Do-not-resuscitate (DNR) orders, 152

Dopamine, 133t
Dopamine agonists
    for Parkinson's disease, 133t
    for restless legs syndrome, 193
Dopamine antagonists, 193
Dopamine reuptake inhibitors, 133t
Doppler studies, carotid, 131
*Doriden. See also* Glutethimide
    recommended max dose, 221t
Dorzolamide *(Trusopt)*, 196t
Dorzolamide/timolol *(Cosopt)*, 197t
Doxazosin *(Cardura)*
    for BPH, 163
    for HTN, 33t
Doxepin *(Adapin, Sinequan, Zonalon)*
    antidepressants to avoid, 51
    for hives, 55t
    recommended max dose, 219t
Doxycycline *(Vibramycin)*
    for community-acquired pneumonia,
        92t
    for infectious diseases, 103t
    for rosacea, 54t
*Dramamine* (dimenhydrinate), 75t
Dressings
    for arterial ulcers, 182
    for diabetic foot ulcers, 184
    for pressure ulcers, 185t–186t, 187
    for skin ulcers, 180
    for venous ulcers, 188
    wound and pressure ulcer products,
        184t
DRIP mnemonic, 85
Dronabinol, 115
"Drop arm" sign, 118
Drop attacks, 130t
Drug abuse, 143
Drug interactions
    alcohol interactions, 16
    CYP drug and metabolic interactions,
        11t–12t
    drug-drug interactions, 11
Drug metabolism, 10
Drug prescribing. *See* Pharmacotherapy
Dry eye syndrome, 197
*Dulcolax* (bisacodyl), 73t
Duloxetine *(Cymbalta)*
    for depression, 50, 50t

**INDEX (CONT.)**

Duloxetine *(Cymbalta)* *(continued)*
  for pain, 148*t*
  for painful neuropathy, 136
*DuoDERM. See also* Hydrocolloids
  for pressure ulcers, 185*t*
Durable power of attorney for health
  care, 152
*Duraclon. See also* Clonidine
  for hot flushes, 201
*Duragesic. See also* Fentanyl,
    transdermal
  for pain, 147*t*
*Duramorph. See also* Morphine
  for pain, 146*t*
*Duricef. See also* Cefadroxil
  for infectious diseases, 100*t*
Dutasteride *(Avodart)*, 163
DVT (deep-vein thrombosis)
  anticoagulation for prophylaxis and
    treatment, 19*t*–20*t*
  drugs for osteoporosis and, 140*t*
  prophylaxis, 157
  treatment, 176
*Dyazide* (triamterene with HCTZ), 37*t*
*Dycill* (dicloxacillin), 99*t*
*Dynabac* (dirithromycin), 102*t*
*DynaCirc* (isradipine), 35*t*
*DynaCirc CR* (isradipine), 35*t*
*Dynaflex*, 188
*Dyrenium* (triamterene), 33*t*
Dysgeusia, 10
Dyskinesias, 132
Dyslipidemia, 30
  in acute MI, 26
  antihypertensive therapy and, 36*t*
  in diabetes, 61–62
  drug regimens for, 30*t*–31*t*
  post MI, 27
  screening, 159*t*
  treatment indications, 30
Dyspareunia, 178–179
Dysphagia, 154
Dyspnea
  with COPD, 170
  at end of life, 154
Dyssynergia, 85

E
Ear wax removal, 79
Echinacea, 13*t*
Echocardiography
  in acute stroke, 131
  in AF, 38
  in aortic stenosis, 38
  in CAD, 24
*EC-Naprosyn* (naproxen), 125*t*
Econazole nitrate *(Spectazole)*, 56*t*
*Effexor. See also* Venlafaxine
  for depression, 51*t*
  for hot flushes, 201
*Effexor XR. See also* Venlafaxine
  for depression, 51*t*
Elastic wraps, 188
*Elavil. See also* Amitriptyline
  antidepressants to avoid, 51
  CMS regulations, 223*t*
  recommended max dose, 219*t*
*Eldepryl* (selegiline), 133*t*
Elder mistreatment, 7–8
  resources, 226
  signs that raise suspicion of, 7*t*–8*t*
Electrical stimulation, 86
Electrocardiography, 112
Electroconvulsive therapy
  for depression, 52
  for psychotic depression, 50
Electron-beam computed tomography
    (EBCT), 159*t*
*Elimite* (permethrin), 54*t*
*Elocon* (mometasone furoate), 58*t*
*Eltroxin. See also* Levothyroxine
  for hypothyroidism, 60
*Emadine* (emedastine), 168*t*
Embolism, pulmonary (PE), 175–176
  anticoagulation for, 19*t*–20*t*
  anticoagulation in absence of active
    bleeding or severe bleeding risk,
    18*t*
  drugs for osteoporosis and, 140*t*
  evaluation of suspected PE, 176*f*
Emedastine *(Emadine)*, 168*t*
*Enablex* (darifenacin), 87*t*

Enalapril *(Vasotec)*
    for HTN, 35*t*
    target dose in HF, 29*t*
Enalapril maleate with felodipine
        *(Lexxel)*, 37*t*
Enalapril maleate with HCTZ *(Vaseretic)*,
        37*t*
Endocarditis prophylaxis
    AHA Guidelines, 160–161
    perioperative, 157
    regimens, 161*t*
Endocrine disorders, 59–64
End-of-life care, 150–155
    resources, 226
End-of-life decisions, 150–153
Enemas
    for chronic constipation, 73
    for fecal incontinence, 90
    for hyperkalemia, 112, 113
*Enemeez,* 90
Energy requirements, 115
Energy supplements, 115
*Enlive,* 116*t*
Enoxacin *(Penetrex),* 102*t*
Enoxaparin *(Lovenox)*
    for acute coronary syndrome, 25*t*
    for DVT/PE prophylaxis and treatment,
        19*t*
*Ensure,* 116*t*
*Ensure Fiber with FOS,* 116*t*
*Ensure Plus,* 116*t*
Entacapone *(Comtan),* 133*t*
Enteral nutrition
    drug interactions, 116–117
    lactose-free products, 115*t*–116*t*
    for malnutrition, 115
    for stress-ulcer prevention, 72
*Enterobacter*
    in noncatheterized patients, 94
    in nursing-home–catheterized
        patients, 94
*Enterococcus faecium,* vancomycin-
        resistant, 104*t*
Environmental modification
    for delirium, 43
    in end-of-life care, 153
    for prevention of falls, 67, 68*t*
    for visual impairment, 197

*Epifrin. See also* Epinephrine
    for glaucoma, 195*t*
Epilepsy
    antiepileptic therapy, 134, 134*t*–135*t*
    CMS criteria for inappropriate drug
        use, 224*t,* 225*t*
*Epinal* (epinephrine borate), 195*t*
Epinephrine *(Epifrin, EpiPen, Glaucon)*
    for angioedema, 55*t*
    for asthma and COPD, 174*t*
    for glaucoma, 195*t*
Epinephrine borate *(Epinal),* 195*t*
*EpiPen. See also* Epinephrine
    for angioedema, 55*t*
*Epival. See also* Divalproex
    for agitation, 48*t*
Eplerenone *(Inspra)*
    for HF, 30
    for HTN, 33*t*
Epley's maneuver, 130*t*
Epoetin alfa *(Epogen),* 84*t*
*Epogen* (epoetin alfa), 84*t*
Eprosartan *(Teveten)*
    for HTN, 36*t*
    target dose in HF, 29*t*
Eptifibatide *(Integrilin),* 25*t*
*Epulor,* 116*t*
Erectile dysfunction, 177–178
Ergocalciferol (vitamin D$_2$), 108
Ergot mesylates *(Hydergine),* 224*t*
Ertapenem *(Invanz)*
    for community-acquired pneumonia,
        92*t*
    for infectious diseases, 99*t*
Erysipelas, 55*t*
Erythrocyte sedimentation rate (ESR), 1
Erythromycin
    for community-acquired pneumonia,
        92*t*–93*t*
    digoxin interactions, 11
    drug and metabolic interactions, 12*t*
    prescribing information, 102*t*–103*t*
    for skin and soft-tissue infections, 55*t*
    and tinnitus, 80
Erythromycin ophthalmic *(AK-Mycin,
        Ilotycin),* 198*t*
Erythropoietin, 84*t*
Erythropoietin-darbopoetin, 108

**INDEX** (CONT.)

*Escherichia coli,* 94
Escitalopram *(Lexapro)*
    for anxiety disorders, 22
    for depression, 50*t*
*Eserine* (physostigmine), 196*t*
*Esidrix* (HCTZ), 33*t*
*Eskalith. See also* Lithium
    for bipolar disorders, 52*t*
*Eskalith CR. See also* Lithium
    for bipolar disorders, 52*t*
Esmolol, 11
Esomeprazole *(Nexium),* 70*t*
Esophageal procedures, endocarditis
    prophylaxis regimens, 161*t*
Esophagitis, 140*t*
ESR (erythrocyte sedimentation rate), 1
Essential tremor
    antihypertensive therapy and, 36*t*
    classification of, 129*t*
Estazolam *(ProSom),* 191*t*
*Estrace. See also* Estradiol
    for dyspareunia, 179*t*
    for systemic hormone therapy, 202*t*
*Estraderm* (transdermal estrogen), 203*t*
Estradiol *(Estrace)*
    drug and metabolic interactions,
        11*t*–12*t*
    with norethindrone *(CombiPatch),* 203*t*
    with norethindrone *(FEMHRT 1/5),* 203*t*
    for systemic hormone therapy, 202*t*
    vaginal ring *(Estring),* 179*t*
    vaginal tablets *(Vagifem),* 179*t*
*Estrasorb* (transdermal estrogen), 203*t*
*Estratab* (estrogen), 202*t*
*Estring* (estradiol vaginal ring), 179*t*
*EstroGel* (transdermal estrogen), 203*t*
Estrogen
    equine *(Premarin),* 48*t,* 179*t,* 202*t*
    esterified *(Estratab, Menest),* 202*t*
    with medroxyprogesterone *(Prempro,
        Premphase),* 202*t*
    with progesterone, 140*t,* 200–201, 202*t*
    synthetic *(Cenestin),* 202*t*
    transdermal *(Alora),* 203*t*
    warfarin interactions, 18

Estrogen therapy, 201–202
    and AD, 47
    for agitation, 48*t*
    for atrophic vaginitis, 201
    bone outcomes, 140*t*
    for dyspareunia, 179, 179*t*
    effects on other outcomes, level of
        evidence, and risks of, 140*t*
    for hot flushes, 201
    for osteoporosis, 139
    in postmenopausal bleeding, 201
    for recurrent urinary tract infections,
        179
    regimens, 202*t*–203*t*
    risks and benefits, 202*t*
    topical, 179, 179*t,* 201
    for UI, 87
    for vaginal prolapse, 201
Estropipate *(Ogen, Ortho-Est)*
    for dyspareunia, 179*t*
    for systemic hormone therapy, 202*t*
Ethambutol
    for active tuberculosis, 98, 98*t*
    ocular adverse events, 198
Ethchlorvynol *(Placidyl)*
    recommended max dose (anxiolytic),
        221*t*
    recommended max dose (hypnotic),
        221*t,* 222*t*
Ethnic groups, 8
Etodolac *(Lodine)*
    for arthritis, 125*t*
    extended release *(Lodine XL),* 125*t*
Etretinate, 54*t*
*Eucerin,* 55*t*
*Eulexin* (flutamide), 164*t*
*Eurax* (crotamiton), 54*t*
Euthanasia, 153
*Evista. See also* Raloxifene
    for osteoporosis, 139
*Exelon* (rivastigmine), 47*t*
Exemestane *(Aromasin),* 200*t*
Exercise(s)
    for back pain, 120
    for balance, 67
    for chronic angina, 27

Exercise(s) (*continued*)
  for COPD, 170
  for fecal incontinence, 90
  for HF, 28
  for HTN, 32
  for nocturnal leg cramps, 193
  for osteoarthritis, 122
  for osteoporosis, 138
  for PAD, 39
  for pain management, 144
  for Parkinson's disease, 132
  pelvic muscle (Kegel's), 86, 201
  prescription, 162
  for preventing falls, 68*t*
  rectal sphincter, 90
  for shoulder pain, 118
  for sleep hygiene, 190
  for vaginal prolapse, 201
  for vertigo, 130*t*
Expectorants, 175*t*
Exploitation, 7*t*
*Ext Release Bayer 8 Hour* (aspirin), 124*t*
Extremity movements, 211
Eye examinations, 194
Eye symptoms, 167*t*
Ezetimibe *(Zetia)*, 31*t*
Ezetimibe/simvastatin combination
      *(Vytorin)*, 31*t*

F
Faces Pain Scale, 212
Facial movements, abnormal, 211
Facial weakness, 135*t*
*Factive. See also* Gemifloxacin
  for infectious diseases, 102*t*
Factor Xa inhibitors, 20*t*
Failure to thrive, 151*t*
Falls, 65–69
  assessment and management, 66*f*
  risk factors and interventions, 68*t*–69*t*
Famciclovir *(Famvir)*, 95*t*
Family Caregiver Alliance, 48
Famotidine *(Pepcid)*, 71*t*
*Famvir* (famciclovir), 95*t*
Far vision testing, 194
*Fareston* (toremifene), 199*t*
*Faslodex* (fulvestrant), 199*t*
FAST scale, 217

Fasting glucose, impaired, 61
Fatigue
  with COPD, 170
  at end of life, 153
Fecal incontinence (FI), 88–90
Fecal occult blood test (FOBT), 159*t*
Feeding, tube, 116–117
*Feldene. See also* Piroxicam
  for arthritis, 126*t*
Felodipine *(Plendil)*
  with enalapril maleate *(Lexxel)*, 37*t*
  for HTN, 35*t*
*Femara* (letrozole), 199*t*
*FEMHRT 1/5* (estradiol and
      norethindrone), 203*t*
*FemPatch* (transdermal estrogen), 203*t*
Femring, 203*t*
FENa (fractional excretion of sodium)
  in acute kidney failure, 107
  in dehydration, 109
Fenofibrate *(Tricor)*, 31*t*
Fenoprofen *(Nalfon)*, 125*t*
Fentanyl *(Actiq)*
  for dyspnea, 154
  for pain, 147*t*
  transdermal *(Duragesic)*, 145, 147*t*
Ferrous polysaccharide, 84*t*
Ferrous sulfate
  for anemia associated with deficiency,
      84*t*
  for hyperproliferative anemia with
      normal or low MCV, 83*f*
FEun (fractional excretion of urea), 107
Feverfew, 13*t*
Fexofenadine *(Allegra, Allegra-D)*, 168*t*,
      169*t*
FI (fecal incontinence), 88–90
Fibrillation, atrial (AF), 38
  anticoagulation for, 18*t*
  antihypertensive therapy and, 36*t*
Fibrillation, ventricular (VF), 41
*Finacea* (azelaic acid), 54*t*
Finasteride *(Proscar)*, 14*t*, 163
*Finevin* (azelaic acid), 54*t*
Fish oil, 27
*Fisostin* (physostigmine), 196*t*

**INDEX (CONT.)**

*Flagyl. See also* Metronidazole
  for antibiotic-associated diarrhea, 77
  for infectious diseases, 104*t*
  for peptic ulcer disease, 72
Flavoxate, 225*t*
Flecainide, 11
*Fleet* (sodium phosphate/biphosphate
    emollient enema), 74*t*
*Flomax* (tamsulosin), 163
*Flonase. See also* Fluticasone
  for allergic rhinitis or conjunctivitis,
    168*t*
*Florinef* (fludrocortisone)
  for adrenal insufficiency, 59*t*
  for hyperkalemia, 113
  for postural hypotension, 69*t*
*Florone* (diflorasone diacetate), 58*t*
*Floropryl* (isoflurophate), 196*t*
*Flovent. See also* Fluticasone
  for asthma and COPD, 173*t*
*Floxin. See also* Ofloxacine
  for acute bacterial conjunctivitis, 198*t*
Fluconazole *(Diflucan)*
  for candidiasis, 154
  for dermatologic conditions, 56*t*
  drug and metabolic interactions,
    11*t*–12*t*
  for infectious diseases, 105*t*
  for onychomycosis, 54*t*
Flucytosine *(Ancobon)*, 105*t*
Fludrocortisone *(Florinef)*
  for adrenal insufficiency, 59*t*
  for hyperkalemia, 113
  for postural hypotension, 69*t*
*Fluffed Kerlix. See also* Gauze packing
  for pressure ulcers, 186*t*
Fluid replacement
  in acute kidney failure, 107
  in chronic constipation, 73
  in dehydration, 109
  in hypernatremia, 110
Fluid requirements, 115
*Flumadine* (rimantadine), 96*t*
Flunisolide *(AeroBid, Nasalide, Nasarel)*
  for allergic rhinitis or conjunctivitis,
    168*t*

  for asthma and COPD, 173*t*
Fluocinolone acetonide *(Synalar)*, 57*t*
Fluocinonide
  high potency *(Lidex-E)*, 57*t*
  higher potency *(Lidex)*, 58*t*
Fluoroquinolones. *See also* Quinolones
  for community-acquired pneumonia,
    92*t*–93*t*
  for cystitis or UTI, 94
  drug and metabolic interactions, 11*t*
  for hospital-acquired pneumonia, 93
  for nursing-home–acquired
    pneumonia, 93
  for urosepsis, 94
Fluoxetine *(Prozac)*
  for anxiety disorders, 22
  for depression, 50*t*
  dextromethorphan interactions, 175*t*
  drug and metabolic interactions, 12*t*
  enteral nutrition interactions, 117
  for hot flushes, 201
  for sleep apnea, 192
Fluphenazine *(Prolixin)*, 220*t*
Flurandrenolide *(Cordran)*, 57*t*
Flurazepam *(Dalmane)*
  for anxiety, 23
  recommended max dose, 221*t*
Flurbiprofen *(Ansaid)*, 125*t*
Flutamide *(Eulexin)*, 164*t*
Fluticasone *(Flonase, Flovent)*
  for allergic rhinitis or conjunctivitis,
    168*t*
  for asthma and COPD, 173*t*
  salmeterol-fluticasone *(Advair
    Diskus)*, 174*t*
Fluticasone propionate *(Cutivate)*, 57*t*
Fluvastatin *(Lescol)*
  drug and metabolic interactions, 11*t*
  for dyslipidemia, 30*t*
Fluvoxamine *(Luvox)*
  for anxiety disorders, 22
  for depression, 50*t*

drug and metabolic interactions, 11*t*–12*t*
Foam island *(Allevyn, Lyofoam)*
  for pressure ulcers, 185*t*
  for venous ulcers, 188
  wound and pressure ulcer products, 184*t*
FOBT (fecal occult blood test), 159*t*
Folate
  for anemia associated with deficiency, 84*t*
  for giant cell arteritis, 128
Folate deficiency, anemia of, 81
Folic acid
  for homocystinemia, 27
  for hypoproliferative anemia, 82*f*
Folliculitis, 55*t*
Fondaparinux *(Arixtra),* 20*t*
Food-drug interactions, 10
Foot ulcers, diabetic, 182–184
*Foradil* (formoterol), 173*t*
Formoterol *(Foradil),* 173*t*
Formulas, 1–3, 1*t*
*Fortaz* (ceftazidime), 101*t*
*Forteo.* See also Teriparatide
  for osteoporosis, 139
*Fosamax.* See also Alendronate
  for osteoporosis, 139
Fosinopril *(Monopril)*
  with HCTZ *(Monopril H),* 37*t*
  for HTN, 36*t*
  target dose in HF, 29*t*
Fractional excretion of sodium (FENa)
  in acute kidney failure, 107
  in dehydration, 109
Fractional excretion of urea (FEun), 107
Fractures
  drugs for osteoporosis and, 140*t*
  hip, 121
  osteoporotic, 138
  vertebral compression, 120
*Fragmin* (dalteparin)
  for acute coronary syndrome, 25*t*
  for DVT/PE, 20*t*
Frontotemporal dementia, 45
Frozen shoulder, 118
Fulvestrant *(Faslodex),* 199*t*
*Fulvicin P/G* (griseofulvin), 105*t*

Functional assessment
  ADLs, 204–205
  in falls, 67
  instrumental ADLs, 205–206
  in pain, 143
  Reisberg Functional Assessment Staging (FAST) scale, 217
Fungal infections
  community-acquired, 91
  hospital-acquired, 91
*Fungizone* (amphotericin B)
  for dermatologic conditions, 56*t*
  for infectious diseases, 104*t*
Furosemide *(Lasix)*
  for acute kidney failure, 107
  for HTN, 33*t*
  for hyperkalemia, 113
  and tinnitus, 80

**G**
Gabapentin *(Neurontin)*
  for epilepsy, 134*t*
  for hot flushes, 201
  for painful neuropathy, 136
  for restless legs syndrome, 193
  for tremor, 129*t*
*Gabitril Filmtabs* (tiagabine), 135*t*
GAD. *See* Generalized anxiety disorder
Gait, and falls, 68*f*
Gait assessment
  functional, 67
  Performance-Oriented Mobility Assessment (POMA), 209
Galantamine *(Reminyl),* 47*t*
*Garamycin.* See also Gentamicin
  for infectious diseases, 101*t*
Garlic, 13*t*
Gastritis
  CMS criteria for inappropriate drug use, 223*t*, 224*t*
  resources, 227
Gastroesophageal reflux disease (GERD), 70
  CMS criteria for inappropriate drug use, 223*t*, 224*t*
  pharmacologic management of, 70*t*–71*t*
Gastrointestinal (GI) antispasmodics, 225*t*

**INDEX** (CONT.)

Gastrointestinal (GI) diseases, 70–77
Gastrointestinal (GI) procedures,
    endocarditis prophylaxis for
    procedures warranting, 160
    regimens, 161*t*
Gastrostomy, percutaneous venting, 154
Gastrostomy tube feedings, 117
Gatifloxacin *(Tequin)*
    for acute bacterial conjunctivitis, 198*t*
    for community-acquired pneumonia,
        92*t*–93*t*
    for infectious diseases, 102*t*
Gauze packing *(Fluffed Kerlix, Plain
        NuGauze)*
    for diabetic foot ulcers, 184
    for pressure ulcers, 186*t*, 187
    wound and pressure ulcer products,
        184*t*
GDS (Geriatric Depression Scale),
    206–207
Gemfibrozil *(Lopid)*, 31*t*
Gemifloxacin *(Factive)*
    for community-acquired pneumonia,
        92*t*–93*t*
    for infectious diseases, 102*t*
Generalized anxiety disorder (GAD)
    antidepressants approved for, 22
    benzodiazepine management of, 23
    buspirone management of, 23
    DSM-IV criteria, 21
    nonpharmacologic management of, 22
Genitourinary (GU) procedures,
    endocarditis prophylaxis for
    procedures warranting, 160
    regimens, 161*t*
Gentamicin *(Garamycin)*
    for endocarditis prophylaxis, 161*t*
    for infectious diseases, 101*t*
*Geocillin* (carbenicillin indanyl sodium),
    99*t*
*Geodon. See also* Ziprasidone
    for delirium, 43
    for psychosis, 166*t*

GERD (gastroesophageal reflux disease),
    70
    CMS criteria for inappropriate drug
        use, 223*t*, 224*t*
    pharmacologic management of,
        70*t*–71*t*
Geriatric Depression Scale (GDS),
    206–207
GI (gastrointestinal) antispasmodics, 225*t*
GI (gastrointestinal) diseases, 70–77
GI (gastrointestinal) procedures,
    endocarditis prophylaxis for
    procedures warranting, 160
    regimens, 161*t*
Giant cell (temporal) arteritis, 128
Ginger, 13*t*
*Ginkgo biloba*, 13*t*, 47
Ginseng, 13*t*
Glaucoma
    agents for treating, 195*t*–197*t*
    causes of, 194
    nonpharmacologic interventions, 195
    pharmacologic interventions, 195
*Glaucon. See also* Epinephrine
    for glaucoma, 195*t*
Glimepiride *(Amaryl)*, 62*t*
Glipizide *(Glucotrol, Glucotrol XL)*
    for diabetes mellitus, 62*t*
    drug and metabolic interactions, 11*t*
    with metformin *(METAGLIP)*, 63*t*
Global aphasia, 136*t*
Global judgments, 211
*Glucerna*, 116*t*
*Glucerna* shake, 116*t*
Glucocorticoids. *See also* Corticosteroids
    for angioedema, 55*t*
    drug and metabolic interactions, 12*t*
    for hives, 55*t*
*Glucophage. See also* Metformin
    for diabetes mellitus, 62*t*
*Glucophage XR. See also* Metformin
    for diabetes mellitus, 62*t*
Glucosamine
    common herbal and alternative
        medications, 13*t*
    for osteoarthritis, 122, 123*f*

Glucose, fasting, impaired, 61
Glucose tolerance, impaired, 61
α-Glucosidase inhibitors, 61, 62t
*Glucotrol. See also* Glipizide
  for diabetes mellitus, 62t
*Glucotrol XL. See also* Glipizide
  for diabetes mellitus, 62t
*Glucovance* (glyburide and metformin),
  63t
Glutethimide *(Doriden)*
  recommended max dose (anxiolytic),
    221t
  recommended max dose (hypnotic),
    221t, 222t
Glyburide *(Diaβeta, Micronase)*
  for diabetes mellitus, 62t
  with metformin *(Glucovance),* 63t
  micronized *(Glynase),* 62t
Glycemic control
  for diabetic retinopathy, 195
  for PAD, 39
Glycerine suppository, 90
Glycoprotein IIb/IIIa inhibitors
  for acute coronary syndrome, 25t
  for acute MI, 24
Glycopyrrolate, 155
*Glynase* (glyburide), 62t
*Glyset* (miglitol), 62t
GnRH agonists, 164t
Gonadotropin-releasing hormone (GnRH)
  agonists, 164t
Goserelin acetate implant *(Zoladex),* 164t
Gout, 126–127
  medications for, 127t
  pseudogout, 127–128
Gouty arthritis, acute, 126
Gouty flare, acute, 126–127
Grapefruit juice, 12t
*Grifulvin V* (griseofulvin), 105t
Griseofulvin *(Fulvicin P/G, Grifulvin V)*
  drug and metabolic interactions, 12t
  for infectious diseases, 105t
Group B streptococcus, 91
GU (genitourinary) procedures,
  endocarditis prophylaxis for
  procedures warranting, 160
  regimens, 161t
Guaifenesin *(Robitussin),* 175t

Guanabenz *(Wytensin),* 34t
Guanadrel *(Hylorel),* 34t
Guanethidine *(Ismelin),* 34t
Guanfacine *(Tenex),* 34t

H
*H pylori* infection
  FDA-approved treatments, 71t–72t
  peptic ulcer disease, 71–72
$H_1$ receptor antagonists
  for allergic rhinitis or conjunctivitis,
    167t–168t, 169t
  for angioedema, 55t
  for cholinergic reactions, 55t
  for hives, 55t
$H_2$ receptor antagonists
  for GERD, 70t–71t
  for *H pylori*-induced ulcerations, 72t
  for hives, 55t
  for stress-ulcer prevention, 72
*Habitrol* (transdermal nicotine patch), 17t
*Haemophilus influenzae*
  in community-acquired pneumonia, 91
  COPD therapy, 170t
  in nursing-home–acquired pneumonia,
    91
Halazepam *(Paxipam)*
  recommended max dose (anxiolytic),
    221t
  recommended max dose (hypnotic),
    221t
Halcinonide *(Halog),* 58t
*Halcion. See also* Triazolam
  recommended max dose, 222t
*Haldol. See also* Haloperidol
  for agitation, 47t
  for delirium, 43
  for nausea and vomiting, 155
  for psychosis, 166t
  recommended max dose, 220t
Halitosis, 154
Hallucinations, 45
Halobetasol propionate *(Ultravate),* 58t
*Halog* (halcinonide), 58t
Haloperidol *(Haldol)*
  for agitation, 47t
  for delirium, 43
  drug and metabolic interactions, 12t

**INDEX (CONT.)**

Haloperidol (*continued*)
  for nausea and vomiting, 155
  for psychosis, 166*t*
  recommended max dose, 220*t*
Harris-Benedict energy requirement
    equations, 115
Hazardous drinking, 15
HCFA (Health Care Financing
    Administration). *See* Centers for
    Medicare and Medicaid Services
    (CMS)
HCTZ (hydrochlorothiazide) *(Esidrix,*
    *HydroDIURIL, Oretic)*
  antihypertensive combinations, 37*t*
  for HTN, 33*t*
HDL (high-density lipoprotein)
  in acute MI, 26
  in diabetes, 61–62
Headache, 149*t*
Health Care Financing Administration
    (HCFA). *See* Centers for Medicare
    and Medicaid Services (CMS)
Health care proxy, 152
*Health Shake,* 115
Hearing aids, 79
Hearing impairment, 78–80
  Brief Hearing Loss Screener, 207–208
  effects and rehabilitation, 79*t*
  resources, 227
  screening, 159*t*
Heart disease. *See also* Cardiovascular
    diseases
  anticoagulation in absence of active
    bleeding or severe bleeding risk,
    18*t*
  determinants for hospice eligibility,
    151*t*
  end-stage, 151*t*
  ICD placement for, 41
  resources, 227
  valvular, 18*t*
Heart failure (HF), 27–29
  anticoagulation for, 18*t*
  antihypertensive therapy and, 36*t*
  drugs useful in treating, 33*t*–36*t*
  ICD placement for, 41

  staging, 28*t*
  target doses of ACE inhibitors and
    ARBs, 29*t*
Heat therapy
  for osteoarthritis, 122
  for pain management, 144
Heel protectors
  for arterial ulcers, 182
  for pressure ulcers, 186
*Helicobacter pylori* infection
  FDA-approved treatments, 71*t*–72*t*
  peptic ulcer disease, 71–72
*Helidac. See also* Tetracycline
  for *H pylori*-induced ulcerations, 72*t*
Hematologic disorders, 81–84
Hemiparesis, 135*t*
Hemiplegia, 135*t*
Hemodialysis, 109
Hemorrhagic stroke, 131
Heparin *(Hep-Lock). See also*
    Anticoagulation
  for acute coronary syndrome, 25*t*
  for acute stroke, 131
  cessation before surgery, 19
  for DVT, 19*t,* 176
  LMWH, 19*t*–20*t*
  and osteoporosis, 138
  for PE, 19*t,* 176
Heparin-induced thrombocytopenia, 20*t*
Heparinoids, 19*t*
Hepatitis B vaccines, 109
*Hep-Lock. See also* Heparin
  for acute coronary syndrome, 25*t*
  for DVT/PE prophylaxis and treatment,
    19*t*
Herbal medications, 13*t*–14*t*
Herpes zoster ("shingles"), 94–95
  antiviral treatments, 95*t*
  post-herpetic neuralgia, 95
*Hexadrol. See also* Dexamethasone
  for adrenal insufficiency, 59*t*
HF. *See* Heart failure
High-density lipoprotein (HDL)
  in acute MI, 26
  in diabetes, 61–62
High-fiber diet, 61

Hip fracture, 121
  drugs for osteoporosis and, 140t
Hip fracture surgery
  anticoagulation for DVT/PE
    prophylaxis and treatment, 19t, 20t
  hip fracture treatment, 121
Hip pain, 120–121
Hip protectors, 67, 68t
Hip replacement
  anticoagulation for DVT/PE
    prophylaxis and treatment, 19t, 20t
  for hip fracture, 121
  for osteoarthritis, 120
Hip surgery, 18t
*Histussin HC* (hydrocodone +
    phenylephrine + chlorpheniramine),
    175t
Hives, 55t
HMG-CoA, 31t
HMG-CoA reductase inhibitors, 30t–31t
Home BP monitoring, 32
Home evaluation, 67
Homocystinemia, 27
Hormone therapy, 201–203
  bone outcomes, 140t
  for breast cancer, 199
  for dyspareunia, 179
  effects on other outcomes, level of
    evidence, and risks, 140t
  estrogen therapy, 201–202
  GnRH agonists, 164t
  LH-RH agonists, 164t
  for malnutrition, dehydration, 155
  for osteoporosis, 139
  for prostate cancer, 164
  regimens, 202t–203t
  risks and benefits, 202t
  for sleep disorders, 191t
  for UI, 87
Hospice, 150–151
  determinants for hospice, 151t–152t
  resources, 226
  sites of post-hospital care, 158t
Hospital-acquired pneumonia, 91
Hot flushes, 201
  drugs for osteoporosis and, 140t
  hormone therapy for, 201
Housing alternatives, 5

HTN (hypertension), 31–33
  combination drugs for, 37t
  post MI, 27
*Humalog* (insulin lispro), 63t
*Humorsol* (demecarium), 196t
*Humulin. See also* Insulin
  preparations, 63t
*Hyalgan* (sodium hyaluronan), 122
Hyaluronan, 122
Hyaluronic acid, 123f
*Hycodan* (hydrocodone), 175t
*Hydergine* (ergot mesylate), 224t
Hydralazine *(Apresoline)*
  for HF, 29
  for HTN, 35t
Hydration. *See also* Dehydration
  for bowel obstruction, 154
  for pressure ulcers, 187
Hydrochlorothiazide. *See* HCTZ
Hydrocodone *(Hycodan)*
  with APAP *(Lorcet, Lortab, Vicodin)*,
    145, 146t
  with ASA *(Lortab ASA)*, 146t
  for cough, 175t
  with ibuprofen *(Vicoprofen)*, 146t
  with phenylephrine and
    chlorpheniramine *(Histussin HC)*,
    175t
Hydrocolloids *(Comfeel, DuoDERM, extra*
    *thin film DuoDERM, Nu-derm,*
    *RepliCare, Tegasorb)*
  for pressure ulcers, 185t
  wound and pressure ulcer products,
    184t
Hydrocortisone *(Cortef, Hydrocortone)*
  for adrenal insufficiency, 59, 59t
  for intertrigo, 54t
  for prostate cancer, 164
  for seborrheic dermatitis, 54t
  for squamous hyperplasia, 200
  for xerosis, 55t
Hydrocortisone acetate *(Hytone)*, 56t
Hydrocortisone butyrate *(Locoid)*, 57t
Hydrocortisone valerate *(Westcort)*, 57t
*Hydrocortone. See also* Hydrocortisone
  for adrenal insufficiency, 59t
*HydroDIURIL* (HCTZ), 33t

## INDEX (CONT.)

Hydrogel
    amorphous gels *(IntraSite gel, Restore gel, SoloSite gel)*, 185t
    gel sheets *(Restore Impregnated Gauze, Vigilon)*, 186t
    for skin ulcers, 180
    wound and pressure ulcer products, 184t
Hydromorphone *(Dilaudid, Hydrostat)*
    extended release *(Palladone)*, 147t
    initial dosing for PCA, 144t
    for pain, 146t
*Hydropres* (reserpine with HCTZ), 37t
*Hydrostat. See also* Hydromorphone
    for pain, 146t
Hydroxychloroquine
    digoxin interactions, 11
    ocular adverse events, 198
Hydroxyzine *(Atarax)*
    for allergic rhinitis or conjunctivitis, 168t
    and dementia, 46
    recommended max dose, 221t
*Hygroton* (chlorthalidone), 33t
Hylan G-F 20 *(Synvisc)*, 122
*Hylorel* (guanadrel), 34t
Hyoscyamine *(Anaspaz, Cystospaz, Levsin, Levsin/SL)*
    CMS regulations, 223t
    for spasm, pain, and vomiting, 155
    for UI, 87t
Hyperemia, conjunctival, 197
Hyperglycemia
    differential diagnosis, 165
    and hyponatremia, 111
Hyperkalemia, 112–113
    and chronic kidney failure, 108
Hyperlipidemia. *See* Dyslipidemia
Hypernatremia, 110
Hyperparathyroidism, secondary, 108
Hyperphosphatemia, 108
Hypersomnolence, 190
Hypertension (HTN), 31–33
    combination drugs for, 37t
    post MI, 27

Hypertensive emergencies and urgencies, 32–33
Hyperthyroidism, 60
    antihypertensive therapy and, 36t
    differential diagnosis, 165
Hypertonic sodium gain, 110
Hyperuricemia, 127
Hypnosis, 144
Hypnotics
    CMS criteria for inappropriate use, 223t
    fall risks, 67, 68t
    OBRA regulations, 221
    recommended max doses, 221t–222t
    for sleep disorders, 191t
Hypoalbuminemia
    and antiepileptic therapy, 135t
    definition of, 114
Hypoaldosteronism, hyporeninemic, 109
Hypocalcemia, 108
Hypocholesterolemia, 114
Hypodermoclysis, 154
Hypoglycemia, 165
Hypogonadism
    management of, 177t–178t
    physical findings, 177
Hyponatremia, 111
Hypoproliferative anemia
    with elevated MCV, 82f
    with normal or low MCV, 83f
Hyporeninemic hypoaldosteronism, 109
*HypoTears*, 197
Hypotension
    drug-induced, 166t
    orthostatic (postural), 59t, 69t, 129t, 166t
Hypothyroidism, 60
    differential diagnosis, 165
Hypotonic hyponatremia, 111
Hypotonic sodium loss, 110
*Hytone* (hydrocortisone acetate), 56t
*Hytrin* (terazosin)
    for BPH, 163
    for HTN, 33t
*Hyzaar* (losartan potassium with HCTZ), 37t

I

IADLs (Instrumental Activities of Daily Living) Scale, 205–206
Ibuprofen *(Advil, Motrin, Nuprin)*
  for arthritis, 125*t*
  digoxin interactions, 11
  drug and metabolic interactions, 11*t*
  with hydrocodone *(Vicoprofen)*, 146*t*
ICDs (implantable cardioverter defibrillators)
  placement, 41
  post MI, 27
*Icy Hot* (methylsalicylate and menthol)
  for osteoarthritis, 123*f*
  for pain relief, 149*t*
Ideal body weight, 1
Idiopathic venous thrombosis, 18*t*
*Ilotycin* (erythromycin ophthalmic), 198*t*
*Imdur* (isosorbide mononitrate), 26*t*
Imipenem-cilastatin *(Primaxin)*, 99*t*
Imipramine *(Tofranil)*
  antidepressants to avoid, 51
  drug and metabolic interactions, 11*t*–12*t*
  recommended max dose, 219*t*
  for UI, 87*t*
Immunization
  influenza, 95, 159*t*
  pneumonia, 159*t*
  tetanus, 159*t*
*Imodium A-D* (loperamide)
  for diarrhea, 76*t*
  for diarrhea and excessive secretions, 155
Impetigo, 55*t*
Implantable cardioverter defibrillators (ICDs)
  placement, 41
  post MI, 27
Impotence, 177–178
Impulse-control symptoms in men, 48*t*
Incontinence, fecal (FI), 88–90
Incontinence, urinary (UI), 85–88
  antihypertensive therapy and, 36*t*
  classification of, 85
  drugs to treat, 87*t*–88*t*
  estrogen for, 87
  mixed, 85, 87*t*

  overflow, 85
  resources, 227
  stress, 85, 86, 88*t*
  urge, 36*t*, 50, 85, 87*t*
Indapamide *(Lozol)*, 33*t*
*Inderal. See also* Propranolol
  for akathisia, 166*t*
  for HTN, 34*t*
*Inderal LA. See also* Propranolol
  for HTN, 34*t*
*Inderide* (propranolol with HCTZ), 37*t*
*Inderide LA* (propranolol with HCTZ), 37*t*
*Indochron. See also* Indomethacin
  for arthritis, 125*t*
*Indochron SR. See also* Indomethacin
  for arthritis, 125*t*
*Indocin. See also* Indomethacin
  for arthritis, 125*t*
Indomethacin *(Indochron, Indochron SR, Indocin, Indocin SR)*
  for arthritis, 125*t*
  CMS regulations, 224*t*
  digoxin interactions, 11
  for pain management, 146
Infections
  antibiotics for, 98*t*–106*t*
  arterial ulcers, 182
  fungal, 91
  *H pylori*, 71–72
  herpes zoster ("shingles"), 94–95, 95*t*
  influenza, 95–96, 96*t*, 159*t*
  pneumonia, 91–93
  pressure ulcers, 187
  prevention of, 187
  skin and soft-tissue, 55*t*
  skin ulcers, 180
  tuberculosis, 97–99, 97*t*, 98*t*
  urinary tract, 93–94, 179
  wound, 182
Infectious diseases, 91–106
  antibiotics for, 98*t*–106*t*
Influenza, 95–96
  antiviral treatment, 96*t*
  immunization, 159*t*
Informed decision making, 5, 6*f*
*Infumorph. See also* Morphine
  for pain, 146*t*

**INDEX** (CONT.)

INH (isoniazid)
    for active tuberculosis, 98, 98*t*
    drug and metabolic interactions, 12*t*
    for latent tuberculosis, 97*t*
    ocular adverse events, 198
Inhalers
    metered-dose (MDIs), 170, 171
    for nicotine replacement therapy, 17*t*
Injection therapy, 144
*Innohep* (tinzaparin), 20*t*
*InnoPran XL. See also* Propranolol
    for HTN, 34*t*
Insomnia
    classification, 190
    CMS criteria for inappropriate drug
      use, 225*t*
    management, 191
*Inspra* (eplerenone)
    for HF, 30
    for HTN, 33*t*
Instrumental Activities of Daily Living
    (IADLs) Scale, 205–206
Insulin *(Humulin, Novolin)*
    for diabetes mellitus, 61
    for hyperkalemia, 113
    long-acting *(Ultralente)*, 63*t*
    preparations, 63*t*
    zinc *(Lente)*, 63*t*
Insulin aspart *(NovoLog)*, 63*t*
Insulin glargine *(Lantus)*, 63*t*
Insulin lispro *(Humalog)*, 63*t*
*Intal* (cromolyn sodium), 174*t*
*Integrilin* (eptifibatide), 25*t*
Intermittent pneumatic pumps, 188
Intertrigo, 54*t*
Intestinal obstruction, 154–155
Intra-articular injections
    for acute gouty flare, 126
    for osteoarthritis, 122
*IntraSite gel*, 185*t*
Intubation, nasogastric, 154
*Invanz. See also* Ertapenem
    for infectious diseases, 99*t*
Iodine, radioactive, 60

Ipratropium *(Atrovent, Atrovent NS)*
    albuterol-ipratropium *(Combivent)*,
      174*t*
    for allergic rhinitis or conjunctivitis,
      167*t*, 169*t*
    for asthma and COPD, 172*t*
    for COPD, 170*t*
Irbesartan *(Avapro)*
    drug and metabolic interactions, 11*t*
    with HCTZ *(Avalide)*, 37*t*
    for HTN, 36*t*
    target dose in HF, 29*t*
Iridotomy, laser, 195
Iron deficiency anemia, 81
Iron dextran, 84*t*
Iron therapy
    for anemia associated with deficiency,
      84*t*
    for hyperproliferative anemia with
      normal or low MCV, 83*f*
Iron-drug interactions, 10
Ischemic cerebral disease, 129*t*
*Ismelin* (guanethidine), 34*t*
*ISMO* (isosorbide mononitrate), 26*t*
*Isocal*, 116*t*
Isocarboxazid *(Marplan)*, 51*t*
Isoetharine *(Bronkometer, Bronkosol)*,
    172*t*
Isoflurophate *(Floropryl)*, 196*t*
Isoniazid (INH)
    for active tuberculosis, 98, 98*t*
    drug and metabolic interactions,
      11*t*–12*t*
    for latent tuberculosis, 97*t*
    ocular adverse events, 198
Isoproterenol, 174*t*
*Isoptin SR* (verapamil), 35*t*
*Isopto Carpine* (pilocarpine), 196*t*
*Isopto Eserine* (physostigmine), 196*t*
*Isordil* (isosorbide dinitrate), 26*t*, 27*t*
*Isordil Tembids* (isosorbide dinitrate), 26*t*
Isosorbide dinitrate *(Isordil, Sorbitrate)*,
    26*t*, 27*t*
Isosorbide dinitrate SR *(Isordil Tembids,
    Dilatrate SR)*, 26*t*

Isosorbide mononitrate *(ISMO, Monoket),* 26*t*
Isosorbide mononitrate SR *(Imdur),* 26*t*
Isradipine *(DynaCirc, DynaCirc CR),* 35*t*
Itraconazole *(Sporanox)*
  for dermatologic conditions, 56*t*
  drug and metabolic interactions, 11*t*–12*t*
  for infectious diseases, 105*t*
  for onychomycosis, 54*t*
Ivermectin *(Stromectol),* 54*t*

J
Jejunostomy tube feedings, 117
*Jevity,* 116*t*
Jobst stockings, 69*t*
Joint replacement, total
  anticoagulation for, 20*t*
  endocarditis prophylaxis, 161
  for hip fracture, 121
  for osteoarthritis, 122

K
*Kabikinase.* See also Streptokinase
  for DVT/PE, 20*t*
*Kadian* (morphine), 147*t*
*Kaltostat.* See also Alginate
  for pressure ulcers, 185*t*
Kaolin-pectin, 11
*Kaopectate* (attapulgite), 76*t*
Karnofsky Scale, 216
Kava kava, 13*t*
*Kayexalate* (sodium polystyrene sulfonate), 112, 113
*Keflex.* See also Cephalexin
  for infectious diseases, 100*t*
*Keflin* (cephalothin), 100*t*
*Kefzol.* See also Cefazolin
  for infectious diseases, 100*t*
Kegel's exercises
  for detrusor instability, 86
  for stress incontinence, 86
  for vaginal prolapse, 201
*Kenacort.* See also Triamcinolone
  for adrenal insufficiency, 59*t*
*Kenalog.* See also Triamcinolone
  for adrenal insufficiency, 59*t*
  for dermatologic conditions, 57*t*

*Keppra* (levetiracetam), 134*t*
*Kerlone.* See also Betaxolol
  for HTN, 34*t*
*Ketalar* (ketamine), 153
Ketamine *(Ketalar),* 153
*Ketek.* See also Telithromycin
  for infectious diseases, 102*t*
Ketoconazole *(Nizoral, Nizoral A-D)*
  for dermatologic conditions, 56*t*
  drug and metabolic interactions, 11*t*–12*t*
  for infectious diseases, 105*t*
  for prostate cancer, 164
  for seborrheic dermatitis, 54*t*
Ketolides, 102*t*
Ketoprofen *(Actron, Orudis)*
  for arthritis, 125*t*
  sustained release *(Actron 200, Oruvail),* 125*t*
Ketorolac *(Acular, Toradol)*
  for allergic rhinitis or conjunctivitis, 169*t*
  for arthritis, 125*t*
Ketotifen *(Zaditor),* 169*t*
Kidney disorders, 107–113
  acute kidney failure, 107, 152*t*
  chronic kidney failure, 108–109, 152*t*
  resources, 227
Kidney transplantation, 109
*Klebsiella,* 94
Knee replacement, 19*t,* 20*t*
Knee surgery, 18*t*
*K-well* (lindane), 54*t*
Kyphoplasty, 120, 139

L
Labetalol *(Normodyne, Trandate),* 35*t*
Laboratory tests, preoperative, 157
Labyrinthitis, 130*t*
β-Lactam/β-lactamase inhibitors
  for hospital-acquired pneumonia, 93
  for infectious diseases, 98*t*–102*t*
  for nursing-home–acquired pneumonia, 93
Lactose-free oral and enteral products, 115*t*–116*t*
Lactulose *(Cephulac),* 74*t*

## INDEX (CONT.)

*Lamictal* (lamotrigine)
  for bipolar disorders, 53*t*
  for epilepsy, 134*t*
  for painful neuropathy, 136
*Lamisil* (terbinafine)
  for fungal infections, 56*t*
  for infectious diseases, 106*t*
  for onychomycosis, 54*t*
*Lamisil AT. See also* Terbinafine
  prescribing information, 56*t*
Lamotrigine *(Lamictal)*
  for bipolar disorders, 53*t*
  for epilepsy, 134*t*
  for painful neuropathy, 136
*Lanoxicaps. See also* Digoxin
  for HF, 28–29
*Lanoxin. See also* Digoxin
  for HF, 28–29
Lansoprazole *(Prevacid)*
  with clarithromycin and amoxicillin
    *(Prevpac),* 71*t*
  enteral nutrition interactions, 117
  for GERD, 70*t*
  for *H pylori*-induced ulcerations, 71*t*
*Lantus* (insulin glargine), 63*t*
Laser iridotomy, 195
Laser trabeculoplasty, 195
*Lasix. See also* Furosemide
  for HTN, 33*t*
Latanoprost *(Xalatan),* 196*t*
Late-life delusional (paranoid) disorder,
  165
Laxatives
  for chronic constipation, 73
  for constipation, 74*t*
  for constipation at end of life, 154
  for fecal incontinence, 90
  for pain management, 145
  tube feeding, 117
LDL (low-density lipoprotein)
  in acute MI, 26
  in diabetes, 61
  nonpharmacologic management, 30
  in stroke prevention, 131
Lean body weight, 1
Left ventricular dysfunction, 18*t*

Leg cramps, nocturnal, 193
Legal blindness, 194
*Legionella*
  in community-acquired pneumonia, 91
  hospital- or nursing-home–acquired,
    empiric antibiotic therapy for, 93
  testing for, 91
*Lente* (insulin, zinc), 63*t*
Lepirudin *(Refludan),* 20*t*
*Lescol. See also* Fluvastatin
  for dyslipidemia, 30*t*
Letrozole *(Femara),* 199*t*
Leukotriene inhibitors, 171*t,* 172*t*
Leukotriene modifiers
  for allergic rhinitis or conjunctivitis,
    167*t*
  for asthma and COPD, 173*t*–174*t*
Leuprolide acetate *(Lupron Depot),* 164*t*
Levalbuterol *(Xopenex),* 172*t*
*Levaquin. See also* Levofloxacin
  for infectious diseases, 102*t*
*Levatol* (penbutolol), 34*t*
Levetiracetam *(Keppra),* 134*t*
*LEVITRA* (vardenafil)
  for BPH, 163
  for male sexual dysfunction, 178*t*
Levobunolol *(AKBeta, Betagan),* 195*t*
Levocabastine *(Livostin),* 168*t*
Levodopa
  for periodic limb movement disorder,
    193
  and sleep problems, 190
Levodopa-carbidopa *(Sinemet)*
  for Parkinson's disease, 133*t*
  for restless legs syndrome, 193
  sustained-release *(Sinemet CR),* 133*t*
Levofloxacin *(Levaquin)*
  for community-acquired pneumonia,
    92*t*–93*t*
  for infectious diseases, 102*t*
Levorphanol, 145
*Levo-T. See also* Levothyroxine
  for hypothyroidism, 60
*Levothroid. See also* Levothyroxine
  for hypothyroidism, 60

Levothyroxine *(Eltroxin, Levo-T, Levothroid, Levoxyl, Synthroid)*
food interactions, 10
for hypothyroidism, 60
*Levoxyl. See also* Levothyroxine
for hypothyroidism, 60
*Levsin. See also* Hyoscyamine
for UI, 87t
*Levsin/SL. See also* Hyoscyamine
for spasm, pain, and vomiting, 155
Lewy body dementia. *See also* Dementia
clinical features, 45
pharmacologic treatment, 46
*Lexapro* (escitalopram), 50t
*Lexxel* (felodipine with enalapril maleate), 37t
LH-RH agonists, 164t
Libido problems
assessment of, 177
management of, 177t–178t, 179
*Librium. See also* Chlordiazepoxide
recommended max dose, 221t
Lichen sclerosus, 200
*Lidex* (fluocinonide), 58t
*Lidex-E* (fluocinonide), 57t
Lidocaine *(Lidoderm)*
for osteoarthritis, 122
for pain, 149t
for painful mucositis, 154
for painful neuropathy, 136
*Lidoderm. See also* Lidocaine
for pain, 149t
for painful neuropathy, 136
Lighthouse Near Acuity Test, 194
Limb salvage, 39, 39t
Lindane *(K-well, Scabene)*, 54t
Linezolid *(Zyvox)*, 104t
α-Linolenic acid, 27
*Lioresal* (baclofen), 149t
Liothyronine with thyroxine *(Thyrolar)*, 60
Lipid disorders
in diabetes, 61
screening, 159t
Lipid emulsions, 117t
Lipidemia. *See* Dyslipidemia
Lipid-lowering therapy
for acute MI, 26
for dyslipidemia, 30

in PAD, 39
*Lipitor. See also* Atorvastatin
for dyslipidemia, 30t
Liquid conversions, 1t
*Liquid Pred. See also* Prednisone
for adrenal insufficiency, 59t
Lisinopril *(Prinivil, Zestril)*
with HCTZ *(Prinzide, Zestoretic)*, 37t
for HTN, 36t
target dose in HF, 29t
Lithium *(Eskalith, Eskalith CR, Lithobid)*
for bipolar disorders, 52t
and constipation, 73
and osteoporosis, 138
for restless legs syndrome, 193
*Lithobid. See also* Lithium
for bipolar disorders, 52t
Living wills, 152
*Livostin* (levocabastine), 168t
*Locoid* (hydrocortisone butyrate), 57t
*Lodine* (etodolac), 125t
*Lodine XL* (etodolac), 125t
*Lodoxamide (Alomide)*, 169t
Lomefloxacin *(Maxaquin)*, 102t
*Lomotil* (diphenoxylate with atropine), 76t
*Loniten* (minoxidil), 35t
Loop diuretics
and coexisting conditions, 36t, 37t
for HTN, 33t
for hyperkalemia, 112, 113
and tinnitus, 80
for UI, 87
Loperamide *(Imodium A-D)*
for diarrhea, 76t
for diarrhea and excessive secretions, 155
for fecal incontinence, 90
*Lopid* (gemfibrozil), 31t
*Lopidine* (apraclonidine), 195t
*Lopressor* (metoprolol)
for acute MI, 25
for HTN, 34t
*Lopressor HCT* (metoprolol with HCTZ), 37t
*Loprox* (ciclopirox), 56t
*Lopurin. See also* Allopurinol
for chronic gout, 127t
*Lorabid* (loracarbef), 100t

**INDEX (CONT.)**

Loracarbef *(Lorabid),* 100*t*
Loratadine *(Claritin, Claritin-D),* 168*t*
Lorazepam *(Ativan)*
  for akathisia, 166*t*
  for anxiety, 23*t*
  for delirium, 43
  for dyspnea, 154
  recommended max dose (anxiolytic), 221*t*
  recommended max dose (hypnotic), 221*t*
  for sleep disorders, 191*t*
*Lorcet. See also* Hydrocodone with APAP
  for pain, 146*t*
*Lortab. See also* Hydrocodone with APAP
  for pain, 146*t*
*Lortab ASA* (hydrocodone and ASA), 146*t*
Losartan *(Cozaar)*
  drug and metabolic interactions, 11*t*
  for HTN, 36*t*
  target dose in HF, 29*t*
Losartan potassium with HCTZ *(Hyzaar),* 37*t*
*Lotensin. See also* Benazepril
  for HTN, 35*t*
*Lotensin HTC* (benazepril hydrochloride with HCTZ), 37*t*
*Lotrel* (amlodipine besylate with benazepril hydrochloride), 37*t*
Lovastatin *(Mevacor, Altocor)*
  drug and metabolic interactions, 12*t*
  for dyslipidemia, 30*t*
  with niacin *(Advicor),* 31*t*
*Lovenox* (enoxaparin)
  for acute coronary syndrome, 25*t*
  for DVT/PE prophylaxis and treatment, 19*t*
Low back pain syndrome, 119
Low-density lipoprotein (LDL)
  in acute MI, 26
  in diabetes, 61
  nonpharmacologic management, 30
  in stroke prevention, 131
Low-fat diet
  for HTN, 32
  for PAD, 39

Low-vision services, 197
Loxapine *(Loxitane)*
  for psychosis, 166*t*
  recommended max dose, 220*t*
*Loxitane* (loxapine)
  for psychosis, 166*t*
  recommended max dose, 220*t*
*Lozol* (indapamide), 33*t*
Lubricants, water-soluble *(Replens),* 179
*Ludiomil* (maprotiline)
  antidepressants to avoid, 51
  recommended max dose, 219*t*
Lumbar spinal stenosis, 119–120
Lumbar spine, unstable, 119
Lumbar strain, acute, 119
Lumbosacral nerve root compression, 2*t*
*Lumigan* (bimatoprost), 196*t*
*Luminal. See also* Phenobarbital
  for epilepsy, 135*t*
*Lupron Depot* (leuprolide acetate), 164*t*
Luteinizing hormone-releasing hormone (LH-RH) agonists, 164*t*
*Luvox. See also* Fluvoxamine
  for depression, 50*t*
*Lyofoam. See also* Foam island
  for pressure ulcers, 185*t*

**M**
*Maalox* (magnesium-aluminum hydroxide), 154
*Macrodantin* (nitrofurantoin), 104*t*
Macrolides
  for community-acquired pneumonia, 92*t*–93*t*
  for infectious diseases, 102*t*
  for pneumonia, 93
Macular degeneration, age-related (ARMD)
  causes of, 194
  nonpharmacologic interventions for, 194
  pharmacologic interventions for, 195
Macular edema, 194
Magnesium
  drug interactions, 10
  for HTN, 32

Magnesium citrate *(Citroma)*, 74t
Magnesium hydroxide *(Milk of Magnesia)*, 74t
Magnesium salicylate *(Backache, Doan's, Mobigesic)*, 124t
Magnesium-aluminum hydroxide *(Maalox)*, 154
Magnetic resonance angiography, 131
Malnutrition, 114–117
    at end of life, 155
Mammography
    for prevention, 199
    recommendations, 159t
*Mandol* (cefamandole), 100t
Mania
    acute, 52
    late-onset, 52
MAO B inhibitors, 133t
MAOIs (monoamine oxidase inhibitors)
    CMS criteria for inappropriate use, 225t
    for depression, 51t
    fall risks, 67
    herbal medicine interactions, 13t
Maprotiline *(Ludiomil)*
    antidepressants to avoid, 51
    recommended max dose, 219t
*Marplan* (isocarboxazid), 51t
Mast cell stabilizers, 169t
*Mavik. See also* Trandolapril
    for HTN, 36t
*Maxair* (pirbuterol), 172t
*Maxaquin* (lomefloxacin), 102t
*Maxiflor* (diflorasone diacetate), 58t
Maxillofacial surgery, 192
*Maxipime* (cefepime), 101t
*Maxzide* (triamterene with HCTZ), 37t
MDIs (metered-dose inhalers)
    for asthma, 171
    for COPD, 170
Mechanical aortic heart valve, 18t
Mechanical mitral heart valve, 18t
Mechanical skin ulcer debridement, 180
Mechanical ventilation, 92
Meclizine *(Antivert)*
    for nausea and vomiting, 75t
    for vertigo, 130t
Meclofenamate sodium, 125t

Medication Appropriateness Index, 218
*Medrol. See also* Methylprednisolone
    for adrenal insufficiency, 59t
Medroxyprogesterone *(Cycrin, Depo-Provera, Provera)*
    for agitation, 48t
    with estrogen *(Prempro, Premphase)*, 202t
    for systemic hormone therapy, 203t
Mefenamic acid *(Ponstel)*, 125t
*Mefoxin* (cefoxitin), 100t
*Megace* (megestrol), 201
Megestrol *(Megace)*, 201
Megestrol acetate
    for malnutrition, 115
    for malnutrition, dehydration, 155
Meglitinides, 62t
Melanoma, vulvar, 200
Melatonin, 191t
*Mellaril. See also* Thioridazine
    for delirium, 43
    for psychosis, 166t
    recommended max dose, 220t
Meloxicam *(Mobic)*, 125t
Memantine *(Namenda)*
    for cognitive dysfunction in AD, 47
    for cognitive enhancement, 47t
Memory. *See* Cognitive impairment; Dementia
*Menest* (estrogen), 202t
Ménière's disease
    audiometry, 80
    management of, 130t
Menopause. *See also* Hormone therapy
    dyspareunia, 178–179
    early, and osteoporosis, 138
    hot flushes, 140t, 201
Men's health
    benign prostatic hyperplasia (BPH), 36t, 163, 217–218, 224t, 225t
    erectile dysfunction, 177–178
    impulse-control symptoms, 48t
    prostate cancer, 163–164, 164t
    prostate disorders, 163–164
    prostate-specific antigen (PSA), 159t
    sexual dysfunction, 177t–178t
Mental status, altered, 42–43

**INDEX** (CONT.)

Menthol
camphor-menthol-phenol *(Sarna)*, 148*t*
with methylsalicylate *(Ben-Gay, Icy Hot)*, 149*t*
Meperidine
CMS regulations, 223*t*, 224*t*
for pain management, 146
Meprobamate *(Miltown)*, 221*t*
Meropenem *(Merrem IV)*, 99*t*
*Merrem IV* (meropenem), 99*t*
Mesoridazine *(Serentil)*, 220*t*
*METAGLIP* (glipizide and metformin), 63*t*
*Metamucil. See also* Psyllium
for constipation, 74*t*
*Metaprel. See also* Metaproterenol
for glaucoma, 196*t*
Metaproterenol *(Metaprel)*
for asthma and COPD, 174*t*
for glaucoma, 196*t*
Metastatic bone disease
in breast cancer, 199
pain relief, 153
in prostate cancer, 164
Metaxalone
CMS regulations, 224*t*
for pain management, 146
Metered-dose inhalers (MDIs)
for asthma, 171
for COPD, 170
Metformin *(Glucophage, Glucophage XR)*
for diabetes mellitus, 61, 62*t*
with glipizide *(METAGLIP)*, 63*t*
with glyburide *(Glucovance)*, 63*t*
with rosiglitazone *(Avandamet)*, 63*t*
Methadone
morphine dose equivalents and conversion to, 148*t*
for pain management, 145
prescribing and monitoring, 147–148
Methazolamide *(Neptazane)*, 196*t*
Methicillin-resistant *S aureus*, 93
Methimazole *(Tapazole)*, 60
Methocarbamol
CMS regulations, 224*t*
for pain management, 146

Methotrexate
for giant cell arteritis, 128
for psoriasis, 54*t*
Methylcellulose *(Citrucel)*
for constipation, 74*t*
tube feeding, 117
Methyldopa *(Aldomet)*
CMS regulations, 223*t*
with HCTZ *(Aldoril)*, 37*t*
for HTN, 34*t*
Methylphenidate *(Ritalin)*
CMS criteria for inappropriate use, 225*t*
for depression, 50, 50*t*
for weakness, fatigue, 153
Methylprednisolone *(Medrol, Solu-Medrol, Depo-Medrol)*
for adrenal insufficiency, 59*t*
for carpal tunnel syndrome, 121
for COPD, 170*t*
for malnutrition, dehydration, 155
for vertigo, 130*t*
Methylprednisolone acetate, 122
Methylsalicylate, 123*f*
Methylsalicylate and menthol *(Ben-Gay, Icy Hot)*, 149*t*
Methylxanthines
for asthma and COPD, 173*t*
for COPD, 170*t*
Methyprylon *(Noludar)*, 221*t*
*Meticorten. See also* Prednisone
for adrenal insufficiency, 59*t*
Metipranolol *(OptiPranolol)*, 195*t*
Metoclopramide *(Reglan)*
CMS criteria for inappropriate use, 224*t*
digoxin interactions, 11
for GERD, 71*t*
for high gastric residual volume problems, 117
for nausea and vomiting, 75*t*
Metolazone *(Mykrox, Zaroxolyn)*
for HTN, 33*t*
for hyperkalemia, 112, 113
Metoprolol *(Lopressor)*
for acute MI, 25

for AF, 38
drug and metabolic interactions, 12*t*
with HCTZ *(Lopressor HCT)*, 37*t*
for HTN, 34*t*
Metoprolol XL *(Toprol XL)*
for HF, 28
for HTN, 34*t*
*MetroCream. See also* Metronidazole
for rosacea, 54*t*
*MetroGel. See also* Metronidazole
for infectious diseases, 104*t*
for rosacea, 54*t*
Metronidazole *(Flagyl, MetroCream, MetroGel, Noritate)*
for antibiotic-associated diarrhea, 77
for *H pylori*-induced ulcerations, 72*t*
for infectious diseases, 104*t*
for peptic ulcer disease, 72
for rosacea, 54*t*
*Mevacor. See also* Lovastatin
for dyslipidemia, 30*t*
MI (myocardial infarction), 24–26
anticoagulation in absence of active bleeding or severe bleeding risk, 18*t*
antihypertensive therapy and, 36*t*
*Miacalcin. See also* Calcitonin
for osteoporosis treatment, 139
*Micardis. See also* Telmisartan
for HTN, 36*t*
*Micardis-HCT* (telmisartan with HCTZ), 37*t*
*Micatin. See also* Miconazole
prescribing information, 56*t*
Miconazole *(Micatin, Monistat-Derm, Monistat IV)*
for dermatologic conditions, 56*t*
for infectious diseases, 106*t*
Microalbuminuria, 64
Microenemas, 90
*Micronase* (glyburide), 62*t*
*Midamor* (amiloride), 33*t*
Midodrine *(ProAmatine)*, 69*t*
Miglitol *(Glyset)*, 62*t*
*Milk of Magnesia* (magnesium hydroxide), 74*t*
*Miltown* (meprobamate), 221*t*
Mineral supplements, 180

Mini-Cog Assessment Instrument for Dementia
assessment instrument, 204
in cognitive dysfunction in AD, 47
in dementia, 45
preoperative, 157
Mini-Mental State Examination (MMSE)
in cognitive dysfunction in AD, 47
in dementia, 45
preoperative, 157
progression, 44
*Minipress* (prazosin)
for BPH, 163
for HTN, 33*t*
*Minitran. See also* Nitroglycerin
dosage and formulations, 27*t*
*Minocin. See also* Minocycline
for infectious diseases, 103*t*
Minocycline *(Minocin)*
for infectious diseases, 103*t*
for rosacea, 54*t*
Minoxidil *(Loniten)*, 35*t*
Miotics, 195*t*–196*t*
*MiraLax* (PEG), 74*t*
*Mirapex* (pramipexole), 133*t*
Mirtazapine *(Remeron)*
for depression, 49, 50*t*
for SSRI-induced sexual dysfunction, 179
for weight loss, 115
Misoprostol *(Cytotec)*
with diclofenac *(Arthrotec)*, 125*t*
for osteoarthritis, 122, 123*f*
Mitral valve replacement surgery, 18*t*
MMSE (Mini-Mental State Examination)
in cognitive dysfunction in AD, 47
in dementia, 45
preoperative, 157
progression, 44
*Moban* (molindone), 220*t*
*Mobic* (meloxicam), 125*t*
*Mobigesic* (magnesium salicylate), 124*t*
Mobility assessment
in falls, 67
Performance-Oriented Mobility Assessment (POMA), 208–210
Modafinil *(Provigil)*
for excessive daytime sleepiness, 192

**INDEX (CONT.)**

Modafinil (*continued*)
  for weakness, fatigue, 153
*Moduretic* (amiloride hydrochloride with
  HCTZ), 37t
Moexipril (*Univasc*)
  with HCTZ (*Uniretic*), 37t
  for HTN, 36t
  target dose in HF, 29t
Moisture-retaining dressings
  for arterial ulcers, 182
  for skin ulcers, 180
Molindone (*Moban*), 220t
*Momentum* (magnesium salicylate), 124t
Mometasone (*Nasonex*), 168t
Mometasone furoate (*Elocon*), 58t
*Monistat IV. See also* Miconazole
  for infectious diseases, 106t
*Monistat-Derm. See also* Miconazole
  prescribing information, 56t
Monoamine oxidase B inhibitors, 133t
Monoamine oxidase inhibitors (MAOIs)
  CMS criteria for inappropriate use,
    225t
  for depression, 51t
  fall risks, 67
  herbal medicine interactions, 13t
Monobactam, 99t
*Mono-Gesic* (salsalate), 124t
*Monoket* (isosorbide mononitrate), 26t
*Monopril. See also* Fosinopril
  for HTN, 36t
*Monopril H* (fosinopril with HCTZ), 37t
Montelukast (*Singulair*)
  for allergic rhinitis or conjunctivitis,
    169t
  for asthma and COPD, 173t
Mood disorder, 145
*Moraxella catarrhalis*
  in community-acquired pneumonia, 91
  COPD therapy, 170t
Morphine (*Astramorph PF, Duramorph,
  Infumorph, MSIR, MS/L, MS/S,
  OMS Concentrate, RMS, Roxanol*)
  dose equivalents and conversion to
    methadone, 148t
  for dyspnea, 154

  extended release (*Avinza, Kadian, MS
    Contin, Oramorph SR*), 147t
  initial dosing for PCA, 144t
  for pain, 146t
Morphine sulfate, 25
Motor function, 2t
Motor restlessness (akathisia), 166t
*Motrin. See also* Ibuprofen
  for arthritis, 125t
Moxifloxacin (*Avelox*)
  for acute bacterial conjunctivitis, 198t
  for community-acquired pneumonia,
    92t–93t
  for infectious diseases, 102t
*MS Contin* (morphine), 147t
*MSIR. See also* Morphine
  for pain, 146t
*MS/L. See also* Morphine
  for pain, 146t
*MS/S. See also* Morphine
  for pain, 146t
Mucosal protective agents, 71t
Mucositis, painful, 154
Mupirocin (*Bactroban*), 55t
Muscle relaxants, 224t
Musculoskeletal disorders, 118–128
  exercise prescription, 161
  resources, 227
*Mycelex. See also* Clotrimazole
  prescribing information, 56t
*Mycobacterium pneumoniae,* 93
*Mycobacterium tuberculosis*
  in community-acquired pneumonia, 91
  testing for, 91
  treatment of, 98
Mycoses, superficial
  antibiotics for, 106t
  topical antifungals for, 56t
*Mycostatin* (nystatin), 56t
*Mykrox. See also* Metolazone
  for HTN, 36t
Myocardial infarction (MI), 24–26
  anticoagulation in absence of active
    bleeding or severe bleeding risk,
    18t
  antihypertensive therapy and, 36t

*Mysoline* (primidone), 129*t*
Myxedema coma, 60

N

Nabumetone *(Relafen)*, 125*t*
Nadolol *(Corgard)*
    with bendroflumethiazide *(Corzide)*, 37*t*
    for HTN, 34*t*
Nafcillin, 99*t*
Naftifine *(Naftin)*, 56*t*
*Naftin* (naftifine), 56*t*
Nalbuphine, 146
*Nalfon* (fenoprofen), 125*t*
Naltrexone *(Depade, REVIA, Trexan)*, 16
*Namenda* (memantine)
    for cognitive dysfunction in AD, 47
    for cognitive enhancement, 47*t*
*Naprelan* (naproxen), 125*t*
*Naprosyn* (naproxen), 125*t*
Naproxen *(Aleve, Naprosyn)*
    for arthritis, 125*t*
    delayed release *(EC-Naprosyn)*, 125*t*
    extended release *(Naprelan)*, 125*t*
Naproxen sodium *(Anaprox)*, 126*t*
Narcotics. See Opioids
*Nardil* (phenelzine), 51*t*
*Nasacort. See also* Triamcinolone
    for allergic rhinitis or conjunctivitis, 168*t*
Nasal steroids, 167*t*, 168*t*
*NasalCrom. See also* Cromolyn
    for allergic rhinitis or conjunctivitis, 169*t*
*Nasalide. See also* Flunisolide
    for allergic rhinitis or conjunctivitis, 168*t*
*Nasarel. See also* Flunisolide
    for allergic rhinitis or conjunctivitis, 168*t*
Nasogastric intubation, 154
*Nasonex* (mometasone), 168*t*
Nateglinide *(Starlix)*, 62*t*
Nausea and vomiting, 74–75
    antiemetics, 75*t*
    at end of life, 155
*Navane* (thiothixene), 220*t*
Near vision testing, 194

*Nebcin. See also* Tobramycin
    for infectious diseases, 101*t*
Nedocromil *(Alocril, Tilade)*
    for allergic rhinitis or conjunctivitis, 169*t*
    for asthma and COPD, 174*t*
Nefazodone *(Serzone)*
    for depression, 51*t*
    drug and metabolic interactions, 12*t*
Neglect, elder
    risk factors for, 7
    signs that raise suspicion of, 7*t*
*Nembutal. See also* Phenobarbital
    recommended max dose, 221*t*
*Neptazane* (methazolamide), 196*t*
Nerve roots, 2*t*
Neuralgia, post-herpetic, 95
Neuroaxial analgesia, 144
Neurodermatitis, 54*t*
Neuroimaging, 46
Neuroleptics. See Antipsychotics
Neurologic disorders, 129–137
Neuromodulation, 144
*Neurontin. See also* Gabapentin
    for epilepsy, 134*t*
    for hot flushes, 201
    for painful neuropathy, 136
Neuropathy
    with impotence, 177
    painful, 136, 145
    peripheral, 136, 137*f*, 149*t*
    with UI, 86
New York Heart Association (NYHA)
    heart failure staging, 28*t*
*Nexium* (esomeprazole), 70*t*
Niacin
    for dyslipidemia, 31*t*
    with lovastatin *(Advicor)*, 31*t*
    ocular adverse events, 198
Nicardipine *(Cardene)*
    for HTN, 35*t*
    sustained release *(Cardene SR)*, 35*t*
*NicoDerm* (nicotine patch), 17*t*
*Nicorette* (polacrilex gum), 17*t*
Nicotine replacement therapy
    for smoking cessation, 16
    for tobacco abuse, 17*t*
*Nicotrol* (nicotine patch), 17*t*

## INDEX (CONT.)

*Nicotrol inhaler* (nicotine replacement), 17*t*
*Nicotrol NS* (nicotine replacement), 17*t*
Nifedipine
  digoxin interactions, 11
  sustained release (*Adalat CC, Procardia XL*), 35*t*
*Nilandron* (nilutamide), 164*t*
*Nilstat* (nystatin), 56*t*
Nilutamide (*Nilandron*), 164*t*
*Nipride* (sodium nitroprusside), 32
Nisoldipine (*Sular*), 35*t*
Nitrates
  for acute MI, 26
  for chronic angina, 27
  dosages and formulations, 26*t*–27*t*
  drug interactions, 11
*Nitrek. See also* Nitroglycerin
  dosage and formulations, 27*t*
*Nitro-Bid. See also* Nitroglycerin
  dosage and formulations, 26*t*, 27*t*
*Nitrodisc. See also* Nitroglycerin
  dosage and formulations, 27*t*
*Nitro-Dur. See also* Nitroglycerin
  dosage and formulations, 27*t*
Nitrofurantoin (*Macrodantin*), 104*t*
Nitroglycerin (*Deponit, Minitran, Nitrek, Nitro-Bid, Nitrodisc, Nitro-Dur, Nitrol, Nitrolingual, Nitrostat, Transderm-Nitro*)
  for acute angina, 27
  for acute MI, 25, 26
  dosage and formulations, 26*t*, 27*t*
  for heart failure, 29
*Nitrol. See also* Nitroglycerin
  dosage and formulations, 27*t*
*Nitrolingual. See also* Nitroglycerin
  dosage and formulations, 27*t*
*Nitrostat. See also* Nitroglycerin
  dosage and formulations, 27*t*
Nizatidine (*Axid*), 71*t*
*Nizoral. See also* Ketoconazole
  for dermatologic conditions, 56*t*
  for infectious diseases, 105*t*
*Nizoral A-D. See also* Ketoconazole
  for dermatologic conditions, 56*t*

NMDA antagonists, 47*t*
*No Pain-HP. See also* Capsaicin
  for pain, 149*t*
*Noctec. See also* Chloral hydrate
  recommended max dose, 221*t*
Nocturnal leg cramps, 193
*Noludar* (methyprylon), 221*t*
*Nolvadex. See also* Tamoxifen
  for breast cancer, 199*t*
Noncardioembolic stroke, 131
Nonsteroidal anti-inflammatory drugs. *See* NSAIDs
Norethindrone with estradiol (*CombiPatch*), 203*t*
Norethindrone with estradiol (*FEMHRT 1/5*), 203*t*
Norfloxacin (*Noroxin, Chibroxin*)
  for acute bacterial conjunctivitis, 198*t*
  for infectious diseases, 103*t*
*Noritate. See also* Metronidazole
  for rosacea, 54*t*
*Normodyne* (labetalol), 35*t*
*Noroxin. See also* Norfloxacin
  for infectious diseases, 103*t*
*Norpace* (disopyramide), 223*t*
*Norpramin. See also* Desipramine
  for depression, 51*t*
  for painful neuropathy, 136
  recommended max dose, 219*t*
Nortriptyline (*Aventyl, Pamelor*)
  for depression, 49–50, 51*t*
  drug and metabolic interactions, 11*t*
  for pain relief, 148*t*
  for painful neuropathy, 136
  recommended max dose, 219*t*
  for tobacco abuse, 17*t*
*Norvasc* (amlodipine), 35*t*
*Novolin. See also* Insulin preparations, 63*t*
*NovoLog* (insulin aspart), 63*t*
NSAIDs (nonsteroidal anti-inflammatory drugs)
  for acute gouty flare, 126
  for acute lumbar strain (low back pain syndrome), 119, 120

for acute pain and short-term management, 143
for allergic rhinitis or conjunctivitis, 169t
for arthritis, 124t–126t
for back pain, 120
for chronic disk degeneration, 119
CMS criteria for inappropriate use, 223t, 224t
dosage, 145
herbal medicine interactions, 13t
management of adverse events, 146
nonselective, 122, 123f
for osteoarthritis, 119, 122, 123f
for pain management, 143, 145
for polymyalgia rheumatica, 128
for shoulder pain, 118
and tinnitus, 80
warfarin interactions, 18
*Nu Basics,* 116t
*Nu Basics Plus,* 116t
*Nu-derm. See also* Hydrocolloids
for pressure ulcers, 185t
*Numorphan* (oxymorphone), 147t
*Nuprin. See also* Ibuprofen
for arthritis, 125t
Nursing-home patients
catheter care, 88
CMS criteria for inappropriate drug use, 223–225
community-acquired pneumonia, 93t
fecal incontinence treatment, 90
housing alternatives, 5
influenza prophylaxis and treatment, 95–96
malnutrition, 114
OBRA regulations, 219–222
scheduled visit checklist, 5
sites of post-hospital care, 158t
Nursing-home–acquired cystitis, 94
Nursing-home–acquired pneumonia
empiric antibiotic therapy, 93
expected organisms, 91
*Nutren 1. 0,* 116t
*Nutren 1. 0 with fiber,* 116t
*Nutren 2. 0,* 116t

Nutriceuticals, 122
Nutrient-drug interactions, 10
Nutrition
at end of life, 155
enteral, 72, 115, 115t–116t, 116
oral, 115, 115t–116t
parenteral, 117, 117t
Nutritional assessment
with malnutrition, 114
preoperative, 157
Nutritional supplements, 115
Nutritional support
for diabetes mellitus, 61
at end of life, 155
lactose-free products, 115t–116t
for malnutrition, 115
for pressure ulcers, 187
for skin ulcers, 180
NYHA (New York Heart Association) heart failure staging, 28t
Nystatin *(Mycostatin, Nilstat, Nystex),* 56t
*Nystex* (nystatin), 56t

O
Oatmeal baths
for scabies, 54t
for xerosis, 55t
Obesity
management of HTN, 32
post MI, 27
resources, 227
screening, 159t
OBRA (Omnibus Budget Reconciliation Act) regulations, 219–222
Obsessive-compulsive disorder (OCD)
antidepressants approved for, 22
benzodiazepine management of, 23
nonpharmacologic management of, 22
Obstruction, bowel, 154–155
Obstructive pulmonary disease, chronic (COPD), 169–170
CMS criteria for inappropriate drug use, 223t
medications for, 172t–174t
preoperative risk assessment, 156
resources, 226, 227
therapy for, 170t
Obstructive sleep apnea, 192

**INDEX (CONT.)**

Occupational therapy (OT)
   for falls prevention, 67
   for osteoarthritis, 122
   for pain management, 144
OCD (obsessive-compulsive disorder)
   antidepressants approved for, 22
   benzodiazepine management of, 23
   nonpharmacologic management of, 22
Octreotide *(Sandostatin)*, 155
*Ocuflox Ophthalmic. See also* Ofloxacin
   for acute bacterial conjunctivitis, 198t
*Ocupress. See also* Carteolol
   for glaucoma, 195t
*Ocusert* (pilocarpine gel), 195t
*Ocuvite*, 195
Ofloxacin *(Floxin, Ocuflox Ophthalmic,*
     *Roxin)*
   for acute bacterial conjunctivitis, 198t
   for infectious diseases, 103t
*Ogen* (estropipate)
   for dyspareunia, 179t
   for systemic hormone therapy, 202t
Olanzapine *(Zyprexa, Zydis)*
   for acute mania, 52
   for agitation, 47t, 48t
   for delirium, 43
   for depression, 50
   drug and metabolic interactions, 11t
   for preventing falls, 68t
   for psychosis, 165t
   for psychotic disorders, 165
   recommended max dose, 220t
   for SSRI-induced sexual dysfunction,
     179
Olmesartan *(Benicar)*
   for HTN, 36t
   target dose in HF, 29t
Olopatadine *(Patanol)*, 169t
Omega-3 fatty acids
   for MI, stroke prevention, 159t
   post MI, 27
Omeprazole *(Prilosec)*
   drug and metabolic interactions,
     11t–12t
   enteral nutrition interactions, 117
   for GERD, 70t

   for *H pylori*-induced ulcerations, 71t
   warfarin interactions, 18
Omnibus Budget Reconciliation Act
   (OBRA) regulations, 219–222
*Omnicef* (cefdinir), 101t
*OMS Concentrate. See also* Morphine
   for pain, 146t
Ondansetron *(Zofran)*, 155
Onychomycosis
   topical antifungals for, 56t
   treatment, 54t
Opioids
   with acetaminophen, 123f
   for acute pain and short-term
     management, 143
   assessment for risk of addiction with,
     143
   CMS criteria for inappropriate use,
     225t
   dosage, 145
   for dyspnea, 154
   management of adverse events, 145
   for osteoarthritis, 122
   for pain, 145, 146t–147t
   for pain at end of life, 153
   for painful neuropathy, 136
   for restless legs syndrome, 193
*Op-site. See also* Transparent film
   for pressure ulcers, 185t
Optical aids, 197
*OptiPranolol* (metipranolol), 195t
*Optivar* (azelastine), 167t
Oral movements, abnormal, 211
Oral nutrition
   lactose-free products, 115t–116t
   for malnutrition, 115
Oral procedures, endocarditis
   prophylaxis for
   for dental patients with total joint
     replacements, 161
   procedures warranting, 160
   regimens, 161t
Oral statements, 152
*Oramorph SR* (morphine), 147t
*Orasone. See also* Prednisone
   for adrenal insufficiency, 59t

for asthma and COPD, 173t
*Oretic* (HCTZ), 33t
*Organan* (danaparoid), 20t
Orphenadrine, 224t
*Ortho-Est. See also* Estropipate
  for systemic hormone therapy, 202t
Orthostatic hypotension
  corticosteroids for, 59t
  dizziness in, 129t
  drug-induced, 166t
  preventing falls with, 69t
Orthostatic syncope
  classification of, 40t
  evaluation of, 40
  management of, 40
Orthotics
  for diabetic foot ulcers, 183
  for trochanteric bursitis, 120
  for venous ulcers, 188
*Orudis* (ketoprofen), 125t
*Oruvail* (ketoprofen), 125t
*Osbon-Erec Aid* (vacuum tumescence
  device), 178t
Oseltamivir *(Tamiflu)*, 96t
Osmolality
  calculated, 1
  in hyponatremia, 110
*Osmolite,* 116t
Osteoarthritis, 122
  APAP and NSAIDs for, 124t–126t
  in back, 119
  and falls, 69t
  in hip, 120
  pain relief, 148t
  pharmacologic management, 123f
  resources, 227
*Osteocalcin. See also* Calcitonin
  for osteoporosis, 139
Osteomyelitis
  surgical intervention, 184
  wound treatment, 180
Osteoporosis, 138–140
  antihypertensive therapy and, 36t
  bone outcomes of drugs for, 140t
  effects on other outcomes, level of
    evidence, and risks of drugs for,
    140t
  resources, 227

OT (occupational therapy)
  for falls prevention, 67
  for osteoarthritis, 122
  for pain management, 144
Overflow incontinence. *See also* Urinary
  incontinence
  classification, 85
Oxacillin *(Bactocill),* 99t
Oxaprozin *(Daypro),* 126t
Oxazepam *(Serax)*
  for anxiety, 23t
  recommended max dose (anxiolytic),
    221t
  recommended max dose (hypnotic),
    221t
Oxcarbazepine *(Trileptal)*
  drug and metabolic interactions, 12t
  for epilepsy, 134t
*Oxy IR* (oxycodone), 146t
Oxybutynin *(Ditropan, Ditropan XL,
  Oxytrol)*
  CMS criteria for inappropriate use,
    225t
  and dementia, 46
  for UI, 87t
Oxycodone *(Oxy IR, Roxicodone)*
  with APAP *(Percocet, Tylox),* 146t
  with ASA *(Percodan),* 146t
  extended release *(OxyContin),* 147t
  for pain, 146t
*OxyContin* (oxycodone), 147t
Oxygen
  alveolar-arterial oxygen gradient, 1
  partial pressure of, arterial (PaO$_2$), 1
Oxygen therapy
  for acute MI, 24
  COPD therapy, 170
  for dyspnea, 154
  long-term, 170t, 174t
  for pneumonia, 92
Oxymorphone *(Numorphan),* 147t
*Oxytrol. See also* Oxybutynin
  for UI, 87t

P
PAD (peripheral arterial disease), 39–40
  classes of disease, 39t

**INDEX (CONT.)**

PAD (*continued*)
  evaluation of, 182
Pain, 141–149
  acute, 141, 143–144
  adjuvant drugs for, 148*t*–149*t*
  arthritic, 122, 123*f*, 124*t*–126*t*
  assessment, 142*f*, 212–215
  back, 119–120
  bowel obstruction, 155
  carpal tunnel syndrome, 121
  chronic, 141, 144
  differential diagnosis, 165
  at end of life, 153
  hip, 120–121
  in intercourse, 178
  metastatic bone, 153
  neuropathic, 145
  nonrheumatic, 121
  opioids for, 146*t*–147*t*
  resources, 227
  shoulder, 118
Pain crisis, 153
Pain scales, 212–215
Painful neuropathy, 136
*Palladone* (hydromorphone), 147*t*
Palliative care, 150–155
  resources, 226
Palliative Performance Scale (PPS), 216
Pallidotomy, 132
*Pamelor. See also* Nortriptyline
  for depression, 51*t*
  for painful neuropathy, 136
  recommended max dose, 219*t*
Pamidronate, 199
Pancytopenia, 84
Panic attack, 21–22
Panic disorder
  antidepressants approved for, 22
  benzodiazepine management of, 23
  differential diagnosis, 22
  nonpharmacologic management of, 22
Pantoprazole *(Protonix)*, 70*t*
PaO₂ (partial pressure of oxygen,
    arterial), 1
Pap smear
  for prevention, 199

  recommendations, 159*t*
Paranoid (delusional) disorder, late-life,
    165
Parasomnias, 190
Parenteral nutrition
  for malnutrition, 117
  solutions, 117*t*
Parkinsonism
  classification of, 129*t*
  drug-induced, 166*t*
Parkinson's disease, 132
  classification of, 129*t*
  differential diagnosis, 165
  drugs for, 133*t*
  and falls, 69*t*
  resources, 227
*Parlodel* (bromocriptine), 133*t*
*Parnate* (tranylcypromine), 51*t*
Paroxetine *(Paxil, Paxil CR)*
  for anxiety disorders, 22
  for depression, 50*t*
  dextromethorphan interactions, 175*t*
  drug and metabolic interactions, 12*t*
  for hot flushes, 201
Partial pressure of oxygen, arterial
    (PaO₂), 1
*Patanol* (olopatadine), 169*t*
*Pathocil* (dicloxacillin), 99*t*
Patient-controlled analgesia (PCA)
  for acute pain and short-term
    management, 143–144
  initial dosing, 144*t*
*Paxil. See also* Paroxetine
  for depression, 50*t*
*Paxil CR. See also* Paroxetine
  for depression, 50*t*
  for hot flushes, 201
*Paxipam* (halazepam)
  recommended max dose (anxiolytic),
    221*t*
  recommended max dose (hypnotic),
    221*t*
PCA (patient-controlled analgesia)
  for acute pain and short-term
    management, 143–144
  initial dosing, 144*t*

PDE5 inhibitors, 178t
PE (pulmonary embolism), 175–176
    anticoagulation for, 19t–20t
    anticoagulation in absence of active
        bleeding or severe bleeding risk,
        18t
    drugs for osteoporosis and, 140t
    evaluation of suspected PE, 176f
Pedal pulse, 182
Pediapred (prednisolone), 59t
PEG (MiraLax), 74t
Pelvic muscle (Kegel's) exercises
    for detrusor instability, 86
    for stress incontinence, 86
    for vaginal prolapse, 201
Pemirolast (Alamast), 169t
Penbutolol (Levatol), 34t
Penetrex (enoxacin), 102t
Penicillin G
    for hospital-acquired pneumonia, 93
    for infectious diseases, 98t
    for nursing-home–acquired
        pneumonia, 93
Penicillin VK, 99t
Penicillinase-resistant penicillins,
    99t–100t
Penicillins
    for infectious diseases, 98t–99t, 100t
    for skin and soft-tissue infections, 55t
Penile prosthesis, 178t
Penile-to-brachial pressure index, 177
Penlac (ciclopirox), 56t
Pentazocine
    CMS regulations, 223t
    for pain management, 146
Pentoxifylline (Trental)
    for PAD, 39
    for venous ulcers, 188
Pepcid (famotidine), 71t
Peptic ulcer disease, 71–72
    CMS criteria for inappropriate drug
        use, 223t, 224t
Pepto-Bismol (bismuth subsalicylate)
    for diarrhea, 76t
    for H pylori–induced ulcerations, 72t
    for peptic ulcer disease, 72
Percocet (oxycodone with APAP), 146t
Percodan (oxycodone with ASA), 146t

Percutaneous angioplasty, for PAD, 39
Percutaneous transluminal coronary
    angioplasty (PTCA), 25
Percutaneous venting gastrostomy, 154
Perennial rhinitis, 167
Performance-oriented mobility
    assessment (POMA), 208–210
Pergolide (Permax), 133t
Perindopril (Aceon)
    for HTN, 36t
    target dose in HF, 29t
Periodic limb movement disorder, 193
Perioperative management, 157
Peripheral arterial disease (PAD), 39–40
    classes of disease, 39t
    evaluation of, 182
Peripheral neuropathy, 136
    diagnosis of, 137f
    pain relief, 149t
Peripheral parenteral nutrition, 117
Peritoneal dialysis, 109
Permax (pergolide), 133t
Permethrin (Elimite), 54t
Perphenazine (Trilafon), 220t
Persantine. See also Dipyridamole
    for stroke prevention, 131
Personality disorder, 145
Pessaries
    for UI, 86
    for vaginal prolapse, 201
Pet therapy, 46
Petroleum-based nonadherent dressing
    (Adaptic, Vaseline gauze,
    Xerofoam), 184t
Peyronie's disease, 177
Pharmacodynamics, 10t
Pharmacokinetics, 10t
Pharmacotherapy
    appropriate, 9–14, 218
    CMS criteria for use in nursing homes,
        223–225
    criteria for drugs of choice for older
        adults, 9–10
    drug-drug interactions, 11
    enteral nutrition interactions, 116–117
    fall risks, 67, 68t
    food interactions, 10
    metabolic interactions, 11t–12t

INDEX (CONT.)

Pharmacotherapy (*continued*)
    nutrient interactions, 10
    systemic medications with ocular
      adverse events, 198
Phenelzine (*Nardil*), 51*t*
Phenobarbital (*Luminal, Nembutal*)
    drug and metabolic interactions,
      11–12*t*
    for epilepsy, 135*t*
    recommended max dose, 221*t*
Phenol
    camphor and phenol (*Campho-
      Phenique*), 149*t*
    camphor-menthol-phenol (*Sarna*), 148*t*
Phenothiazines, 67
Phenylephrine + chlorpheniramine +
    hydrocodone (*Histussin HC*), 175*t*
Phenytoin (*Dilantin*)
    drug interactions, 11*t*–12*t*
    enteral nutrition interactions, 116
    for epilepsy, 135*t*
    food or nutrient interactions, 10
    metabolic interactions, 11*t*–12*t*
    monitoring, 135*t*
    warfarin interactions, 18
Phobia, social, 22
Phospholine (echothiophate), 196*t*
Photocoagulation, 194
Physical abuse, 7*t*
Physical restraints, 43
Physical self-maintenance scale,
    204–205
Physical therapy (PT)
    for balance and strength training, 129*t*
    for bicipital tendinitis, 118
    for dizziness, 129*t*
    for frozen shoulder (adhesive
      capsulitis), 118
    for osteoarthritis, 122
    for pain management, 144
    preoperative, 156
    for preventing falls, 68*t*
    for rotator cuff tears, 118
    for rotator cuff tendinitis, subacromial
      bursitis, or rotator tendon
      impingement on clavicle, 118
    for UI, 86
Physiologic tremor, 129*t*
Physostigmine (*Eserine, Fisostin, Isopto
    Eserine*), 196*t*
Pilagan (pilocarpine), 196*t*
Pilocar (pilocarpine), 196*t*
Pilocarpine (*Adsorbocarpine, Akarpine,
    Isopto Carpine, Pilagan, Pilocar,
    Piloptic, Pilostat*), 196*t*
Pilocarpine gel (*Ocusert, Pilopine HS*),
    195*t*
Pilopine HS (pilocarpine gel), 195*t*
Piloptic (pilocarpine), 196*t*
Pilostat (pilocarpine), 196*t*
Pindolol (*Visken*), 34*t*
Pioglitazone (*Actos*)
    for diabetes mellitus, 63*t*
    drug and metabolic interactions, 12*t*
Piperacillin (*Pipracil*), 99*t*
Piperacillin–tazobactam (*Zosyn*), 100*t*
Pipracil (piperacillin), 99*t*
Pirbuterol (*Maxair*), 172*t*
Piroxicam (*Feldene*), 126*t*
    drug and metabolic interactions, 11*t*
Placidyl. See also Ethchlorvynol
    recommended max dose, 221*t*
Plain NuGauze. See also Gauze packing
    for pressure ulcers, 186*t*
Plavix (clopidogrel)
    for acute coronary syndrome, 25*t*
    for acute MI, 24
    for PAD, 39
    for stroke prevention, 131
Plenaxis (abarelix), 164*t*
Plendil (felodipine), 35*t*
Pletal (cilostazol), 39
Pneumococcal vaccine, 159*t*
Pneumonia, 91–93
    empiric antibiotic therapy, 92*t*–93*t*
Pneumonia immunization, 159*t*
Pneumovax, 109
Polacrilex gum (*Nicorette*), 17*t*
Polydipsia, 111
Polyethylene glycol (PEG) (*MiraLax*), 74*t*
Polymyalgia rheumatica, 128

Polymyxin with trimethoprim *(Polytrim)*, 198*t*
Polythiazide *(Renese)*, 33*t*
*Polytrim* (trimethoprim and polymyxin), 198*t*
POMA (performance-oriented mobility assessment), 208–210
*Ponstel* (mefenamic acid), 125*t*
Positive pressure ventilation, 170*t*
Post-herpetic neuralgia, 95
Postmenopausal bleeding, 200–201
Post-traumatic stress disorder, 22
Postural awareness, 162
Postural hypotension
  corticosteroids for, 59*t*
  dizziness in, 129*t*
  drug-induced, 166*t*
  preventing falls with, 69*t*
Postural impingement of vertebral artery, 130*t*
*Pos-T-Vac* (vacuum tumescence device), 178*t*
Potassium
  for HTN, 32
  for volume depletion (dehydration), 109
Potassium imbalance, 165
Potassium supplements
  CMS criteria for inappropriate use, 224*t*
  drug interactions, 11
  for HTN, 32
Potassium-sparing drugs, 33*t*
PPS (Palliative Performance Scale), 216
Pramipexole *(Mirapex)*, 133*t*
*Prandin* (repaglinide), 62*t*
*Pravachol* (Pravachol), 30*t*
Pravastatin *(Pravachol)*, 30*t*
Prazepam *(Centrax)*, 221*t*
Prazosin *(Minipress)*
  for BPH, 163
  for HTN, 33*t*
Prealbumin, 114
*Precose* (acarbose), 62*t*
Pre-diabetes, 61
Prednicarbate *(Dermatop)*, 57*t*
Prednisolone *(Delta-Cortef, Prelone Syrup, Pediapred)*, 59*t*

Prednisone *(Deltasone, Liquid Pred, Meticorten, Orasone)*
  for acute gouty flare, 127
  for adrenal insufficiency, 59*t*
  for asthma and COPD, 173*t*
  for carpal tunnel syndrome, 121
  for giant cell arteritis, 128
  for hives, 55*t*
  for malnutrition, dehydration, 155
  for polymyalgia rheumatica, 128
*Prelone Syrup* (prednisolone), 59*t*
*Premarin* (equine estrogen)
  for agitation, 48*t*
  for dyspareunia, 179*t*
  for systemic hormone therapy, 202*t*
*Premphase* (estrogen and medroxyprogesterone), 202*t*
*Prempro* (estrogen and medroxyprogesterone), 202*t*
Preoperative care, 156–157
  reducing cardiac risk in noncardiac surgery, 156*f*
Prerenal azotemia, 107
Presbycusis
  audiometry, 80
  classification of, 78
Prescribing, appropriate, 218
*PreserVision*, 195
Pressure stockings
  for preventing falls, 69*t*
  for UI, 87
  for venous ulcers, 188
Pressure ulcers, 184–187
  dressings for, 185*t*–186*t*
  wound and pressure ulcer products, 184*t*
  wound characteristics, 181*t*
*Prevacid. See also* Lansoprazole
  for GERD, 70*t*
Prevention, 159–162
  DVT, 157
  endocarditis, 157, 160–161, 161*t*
  falls, 67, 68*t*–69*t*
  gynecologic, 199
  influenza, 95
  recommendations, 159*t*
  stress ulcer, 72

**INDEX (CONT.)**

*Prevpac* (lansoprazole + clarithromycin + amoxicillin), 71*t*
*Prilosec. See also* Omeprazole
for GERD, 70*t*
*Primaxin* (imipenem-cilastatin), 99*t*
Primidone *(Mysoline)*, 129*t*
*Prinivil. See also* Lisinopril
for HTN, 36*t*
*Prinzide* (lisinopril with HCTZ), 37*t*
*ProAmatine* (midodrine), 69*t*
*Pro-Banthine. See also* Propantheline
for UI, 87*t*
*Proben-C* (probenecid with colchicine), 127*t*
Probenecid *(Benemid)*
for chronic gout, 127*t*
with colchicine *(ColBenemid, Col-Probenecid)*, 127*t*
*Procardia XL. See also* Nifedipine
for HTN, 35*t*
Prochlorperazine *(Compazine)*, 75*t*
*Profore*, 188
Progesterone with estrogen
effects on other outcomes, level of evidence, and risks of, 140*t*
for hormone therapy, 201
in postmenopausal bleeding, 200–201
risks and benefits, 202*t*
Prokinetic agents, 71*t*
*Prolixin* (fluphenazine), 220*t*
Promazine *(Sparine)*, 220*t*
Propafenone, 38
Propantheline *(Pro-Banthine)*
CMS regulations, 223*t*
for UI, 87*t*
*Propine* (dipivefrin), 195*t*
Propoxyphene
CMS criteria for inappropriate use, 225*t*
drug and metabolic interactions, 11*t*–12*t*
for pain management, 146
warfarin interactions, 18
Propranolol *(Inderal)*
for akathisia, 166*t*
with HCTZ *(Inderide, Inderide LA)*, 37*t*

Propranolol, long-acting *(Inderal LA, InnoPran XL)*
for HTN, 34*t*
for tremor, 129*t*
Propylthiouracil, 60
*Proscar* (finasteride), 163
*Proshield*, 55*t*
*ProSom* (estazolam), 191*t*
Prostaglandin analogues, 196*t*
Prostaglandin E *(Alprostadil)*, 178*t*
Prostate cancer, 163–164
drugs for, 164*t*
Prostate disorders, 163–164
Prostatectomy, 163
Prostate-specific antigen (PSA), 159*t*
Prostatic hyperplasia, benign (BPH), 163
antihypertensive therapy and, 36*t*
AUA symptom index, 217–218
CMS criteria for inappropriate drug use, 224*t*, 225*t*
*ProStep* (transdermal nicotine patch), 17*t*
Prosthesis, penile, 178*t*
Prosthetic heart valves, 18*t*
Protein requirements, 180
Protein restriction, 108
Protein supplements, 115
Proteinuria, 108
*Proteus*, 94
*Protonix* (pantoprazole), 70*t*
Proton-pump inhibitors
for GERD, 70*t*
for *H pylori*-induced ulcerations, 72*t*
for osteoarthritis, 122, 123*f*
for stress-ulcer prevention, 72
Protriptyline *(Vivactil)*
antidepressants to avoid, 51
recommended max dose, 219*t*
for sleep apnea, 192
*Proventil* (albuterol), 172*t*
*Provera. See also* Medroxyprogesterone
for systemic hormone therapy, 203*t*
*Providencia*, 94
*Provigil* (modafinil)
for excessive daytime sleepiness, 192

for weakness, fatigue, 153
*Prozac. See also* Fluoxetine
  for depression, 50*t*
  for hot flushes, 201
  for sleep apnea, 192
Pruritus, 167*t*
PSA (prostate-specific antigen), 159*t*
Pseudoephedrine *(Sudafed, Sudafed XR)*
  for allergic rhinitis or conjunctivitis,
    167*t*, 168*t*
  for UI, 88*t*
Pseudogout, 127–128
Pseudohyponatremia, 111
Pseudomembranous colitis, antibiotic-
    associated, 76–77
*Pseudomonas aeruginosa*
  empiric antibiotic therapy, 92*t*–93*t*
  UTI or urosepsis, 94
Psoralen plus ultraviolet light (PUVA), 54*t*
*Psorcon* (diflorasone diacetate), 58*t*
Psoriasis, 54*t*
Psychiatric resources, 227
Psychological abuse, 8*t*
Psychosis, acute
  agitation treatment guidelines, 47*t*
  CMS criteria for inappropriate drug
    use, 225*t*
Psychosocial assessment, 143
Psychostimulants, 153
Psychotic disorders, 165–166
  agitation treatment guidelines, 47*t*–48*t*
  psychotic depression, 50
  representative antipsychotic
    medications, 165*t*–166*t*
Psyllium *(Metamucil)*
  for constipation, 74*t*
  digoxin interactions, 11
  for pain management, 145
  tube feeding, 117
PT. *See* Physical therapy
PTCA (percutaneous transluminal
    coronary angioplasty), 25
*Pulmicort. See also* Budesonide
  for asthma and COPD, 173*t*
Pulmonary angiography, 176*f*
Pulmonary assessment, 176*f*
Pulmonary disease, chronic obstructive
    (COPD), 169–170

CMS criteria for inappropriate drug
    use, 223*t*
medications for, 172*t*–174*t*
preoperative risk assessment, 156
resources, 226, 227
therapy for, 170*t*
Pulmonary disease, end-stage, 151*t*
Pulmonary embolism (PE), 175–176
  anticoagulation for, 19*t*–20*t*
  anticoagulation in absence of active
    bleeding or severe bleeding risk,
    18*t*
  drugs for osteoporosis and, 140*t*
  evaluation of suspected PE, 176*f*
Pulmonary risk assessment,
    preoperative, 156–157
PUVA (psoralen plus ultraviolet light), 54*t*
Pyrazinamide
  for active tuberculosis, 98, 98*t*
  for latent tuberculosis, 97*t*

**Q**
Quality of life, 150
*Questran* (cholestyramine resin), 77
Quetiapine *(Seroquel)*
  for acute mania, 52
  for agitation, 47*t*
  drug and metabolic interactions, 12*t*
  for preventing falls, 68*t*
  for psychosis, 165, 166*t*
  for psychotic depression, 50
  for psychotic disorders, 50, 165, 166*t*
  recommended max dose, 220*t*
*Quibron-T/SR. See also* Theophylline-SR
  for asthma and COPD, 173*t*
Quinapril *(Accupril)*
  for HTN, 36*t*
  target dose in HF, 29*t*
Quinidine
  digoxin interactions, 11
  drug and metabolic interactions, 12*t*
Quinine
  digoxin interactions, 11
  and tinnitus, 80
Quinolones. *See also* Fluoroquinolones
  drug-food or -nutrient interactions, 10
  for infectious diseases, 102*t*–103*t*
Quinupristin/dalfopristin *(Synercid)*, 104*t*

## INDEX (CONT.)

Q-wave MI
    management, 25
    thrombolytic therapy, 25–26

## R

Rabeprazole *(AcipHex)*, 70*t*
Radioactive iodine ablation, 60
Radionuclide ventriculography, 28
Radionuclides, 153
Raloxifene *(Evista)*
    bone outcomes, 140*t*
    effects on other outcomes, level of
        evidence, and risks of, 140*t*
    for osteoporosis, 139
Ramipril *(Altace)*
    for HTN, 36*t*
    target dose in HF, 29*t*
Range-of-motion programs, 144
Ranitidine *(Zantac)*, 71*t*
Ranitidine bismuth citrate (RBC)
    for *H pylori*-induced ulcerations, 72*t*
    for peptic ulcer disease, 72
RBC (ranitidine bismuth citrate)
    for *H pylori*-induced ulcerations, 72*t*
    for peptic ulcer disease, 72
Rectal sphincter exercises, 90
5-α Reductase inhibitors, 163
*Refludan* (lepirudin), 20*t*
Reflux, gastroesophageal (GERD), 70
    CMS criteria for inappropriate drug
        use in, 223*t*, 224*t*
    pharmacologic management of,
        70*t*–71*t*
*Reglan. See also* Metoclopramide
    for GERD, 71*t*
    for high gastric residual volume
        problems, 117
    for nausea and vomiting, 75*t*
*Regranex*, 184
Rehabilitation
    in acute stroke, 131
    for COPD, 170
    of hearing loss, 79*t*
    for moderate COPD, 170*t*
    in pain management, 144
    perioperative, 157

sites of post-hospital care, 158*t*
Rehydration
    for acute kidney failure, 107
    for pneumonia, 92
    for volume depletion (dehydration),
        109
Reisberg Functional Assessment Staging
    (FAST) scale, 217
*Rejoyn* (vacuum tumescence device),
    178*t*
*Relafen* (nabumetone), 125*t*
*Relenza* (zanamivir), 96*t*
*Remeron. See also* Mirtazapine
    for depression, 50*t*
    for SSRI-induced sexual dysfunction,
        179
*Reminyl* (galantamine), 47*t*
*Renagel* (sevelamer), 108
Renal artery stenosis, 32
Renal dialysis, 107
Renal insufficiency
    anemia of, 81
    antiepileptic therapy and, 135*t*
    antihypertensive therapy and, 36*t*
Renal replacement therapy, 109
*Renese* (polythiazide), 33*t*
*ReoPro* (abciximab), 25*t*
Repaglinide *(Prandin)*, 62*t*
*Replens* (water-soluble lubricant), 179
*RepliCare. See also* Hydrocolloids
    for pressure ulcers, 185*t*
*Requip* (ropinirole), 133*t*
*Rescula* (unoprostone), 196*t*
Reserpine *(Serpasil)*
    with chlorothiazide *(Diupres)*, 37*t*
    with HCTZ *(Hydropres)*, 37*t*
    for HTN, 34*t*
Residential care facilities, 5
Resistance training, 68*t*
*Resource*, 116*t*
*Resource Benecalorie*, 116*t*
Respiratory diseases, 167–176
Respiratory tract procedures,
        endocarditis prophylaxis for
    procedures warranting, 160
    regimens, 161*t*

Respiratory viruses, 91
*Restasis* (cyclosporine ophthalmic emulsion), 197
Restless legs syndrome, 193
*Restore gel,* 185*t*
*Restore Impregnated Gauze,* 186*t*
*Restoril* (temazepam)
  recommended max dose, 222*t*
  for sleep disorders, 191*t*
Retinopathy, diabetic
  causes of, 194
  nonpharmacologic interventions for, 194
  pharmacologic interventions for, 195
Retirement communities, continuing care, 5
Retropubic colposuspension, 88
Revascularization, 182
*REVIA* (naltrexone), 16
*R-Gel. See also* Capsaicin
  for pain, 149*t*
Rhinitis, 167
  choosing therapy for, 167*t*
  drug therapy for, 167*t*–169*t*
  drugs for osteoporosis and, 140*t*
*Rhinocort. See also* Budesonide
  for allergic rhinitis or conjunctivitis, 168*t*
Rifabutin, 12*t*
Rifampin
  for active tuberculosis, 98, 98*t*
  drug and metabolic interactions, 11*t*–12*t*
  for latent tuberculosis, 97*t*
  warfarin interactions, 18
Rimantadine *(Flumadine),* 96*t*
Risedronate *(Actonel)*
  bone outcomes, 140*t*
  effects on other outcomes, level of evidence, and risks of, 140*t*
  for osteoporosis, 139
*Risperdal. See also* Risperidone
  for agitation, 47*t*
  for psychosis, 166*t*
  recommended max dose, 220*t*
*Risperdal Consta* (risperidone IM), 43
Risperidone *(Risperdal)*
  for acute mania, 52

  for agitation, 47*t*
  for depression, 50
  drug and metabolic interactions, 12*t*
  for preventing falls, 68*t*
  for psychosis, 165, 166*t*
  for psychotic depression, 50
  for psychotic disorders, 50, 165, 166*t*
  recommended max dose, 220*t*
Risperidone IM *(Risperdal Consta),* 43
*Ritalin. See also* Methylphenidate
  for depression, 50*t*
  for weakness, fatigue, 153
Rivastigmine *(Exelon),* 47*t*
*RMS. See also* Morphine
  for pain, 146*t*
*Robitussin* (guaifenesin), 175*t*
*Robitussin DM. See also* Dextromethorphan
  for cough, 175*t*
*Rocaltrol. See also* Calcitriol
  for hypocalcemia, 108
*Rocephin. See also* Ceftriaxone
  for infectious diseases, 101*t*
Ropinirole *(Requip),* 133*t*
Rosacea, 54*t*
Rosenbaum card testing for near vision, 194
Rosiglitazone *(Avandia)*
  for diabetes mellitus, 63*t*
  with metformin *(Avandamet),* 63*t*
*Rosula* (sodium sulfacetamide), 54*t*
Rosuvastatin *(Crestor),* 30*t*
Rotator cuff tears, 118
Rotator cuff tendinitis, 118
Rotator tendon impingement on clavicle, 118
*Roxanol. See also* Morphine
  for pain, 146*t*
*Roxicodone* (oxycodone), 146*t*
*Roxin. See also* Ofloxacin
  for infectious diseases, 103*t*

**S**
*Salflex* (salsalate), 124*t*
Salicylates, nonacetylated, 124*t*
Salicylic acid, 54*t*
Saline and sodium bicarbonate (Sinu*Cleanse*), 167

## INDEX (CONT.)

Salmeterol *(Serevent Diskus),* 173*t*

Salmeterol-fluticasone *(Advair Diskus),* 174*t*

*Salmonine. See also* Calcitonin
for osteoporosis, 139

Salsalate *(Disalcid, Mono-Gesic, Salflex),* 124*t*

Salt restriction
for HF, 28
for vertigo, 130*t*

SAMe (S-adenosylmethionine), 13*t*

*Sanctura* (trospium), 87*t*

*Sandostatin* (octreotide), 155

*Santyl,* 180

Sarcoma, vulvar, 200

*Sarna* (camphor-menthol-phenol), 148*t*

Saw palmetto, 14*t*

SBP (systolic blood pressure)
management. *See also* Blood
pressure
for stroke prevention, 131

*Scabene* (lindane), 54*t*

Scabies, 54*t*

Schizophrenia, 165

Sciatica
acute disk herniation, 119
acute lumbar strain (low back pain
syndrome), 119
osteoarthritis and chronic disk
degeneration, 119

Scopolamine
for excessive secretions, 155
for spasm, pain, and vomiting, 155

Seborrheic dermatitis
topical antifungals for, 56*t*
treatment, 54*t*

Secobarbital *(Seconal),* 221*t*

*Seconal* (secobarbital), 221*t*

Secretions, excessive, 155
diarrhea and, 155

*Sectral* (acebutolol), 34*t*

Sedation
drug-induced, 166*t*
end-of-life care, 153

Sedatives
CMS criteria for inappropriate use, 223*t*
fall risks, 67, 68*t*
for sleep disorders, 191*t*

Seizures, 134
CMS criteria for inappropriate drug
use, 224*t*, 225*t*
differential diagnosis, 165

Selective serotonin-reuptake inhibitors.
*See* SSRIs

Selegiline *(Carbex, Eldepryl),* 133*t*

Self-examination, breast, 159*t*

Self-maintenance physical scale (ADLs), 204–205

Self-monitoring, blood glucose, 61

Senior citizen housing, 5

Senna *(Senokot),* 73, 74*t*

*Senokot* (senna), 74*t*

Sensorineural hearing loss
aggravating factors, 78
classification of, 78

Sensory impairments
and delirium, 43
and dizziness, 129*t*

Sepsis, 180

*Serax* (oxazepam)
for anxiety, 23*t*
recommended max dose (anxiolytic), 221*t*
recommended max dose (hypnotic), 221*t*

*Serentil* (mesoridazine), 220*t*

*Serevent Diskus* (salmeterol), 173*t*

*Seroquel. See also* Quetiapine
for agitation, 47*t*
for psychosis, 166*t*
recommended max dose, 220*t*

Serotonin 1A partial agonists, 23

*Serpasil* (reserpine), 34*t*

Sertraline *(Zoloft)*
for anxiety disorders, 22
for depression, 50*t*
SSRI-induced sexual dysfunction, 179

*Serzone. See also* Nefazodone
for depression, 51*t*

Sevelamer *(Renagel),* 108
Sexual aggression, 48*t*
Sexual dysfunction, 177–179
  male, 177*t*–178*t*
  resources, 227
  SSRI-induced, 179
Sharp ulcer debridement
  for diabetic foot ulcers, 184
  for pressure ulcers, 187
  for skin ulcers, 180
Shingles (herpes zoster), 94–95
  antiviral treatments, 95*t*
  post-herpetic neuralgia, 95
Shoulder pain, 118
SIADH (syndrome of inappropriate
  secretion of antidiuretic hormone),
  111–112
Sigmoidoscopy, 159*t*
Sildenafil *(Viagra)*
  for BPH, 163
  drug and metabolic interactions, 12*t*
  for male sexual dysfunction, 178*t*
  ocular adverse events, 198
  for SSRI-induced sexual dysfunction,
  179
Simvastatin *(Zocor)*
  drug and metabolic interactions, 12*t*
  for dyslipidemia, 30*t*
*Sinemet* (levodopa-carbidopa)
  for Parkinson's disease, 133*t*
  for restless legs syndrome, 193
*Sinemet CR* (levodopa-carbidopa), 133*t*
*Sinequan. See also* Doxepin
  antidepressants to avoid, 51
  recommended max dose, 219*t*
*Singulair. See also* Montelukast
  for allergic rhinitis or conjunctivitis,
  169*t*
  for asthma and COPD, 173*t*
Sinu*Cleanse* (saline and sodium
  bicarbonate), 167
Skilled nursing facility, 158*t*
Skin care
  and fecal incontinence, 90
  protective, 182
Skin examination
  recommendations, 159*t*
  resources, 227

Skin graft, 189
Skin infections, 55*t*
Skin losses, 111
Skin maceration, 55*t*
Skin ulcers, 180–189
  wound characteristics, 181*t*
Sleep apnea, 191–192
Sleep deprivation, 165
Sleep disorders, 190–193
  CMS criteria for inappropriate drug
  use, 225*t*
  medications for, 191*t*
Sleep hygiene measures
  for delirium, 43
  for periodic limb movement disorder,
  193
  for sleep disorders other than sleep
  apnea, 190
*Slo-Bid. See also* Theophylline-SR
  for asthma and COPD, 173*t*
Smoking
  drug and metabolic interactions, 11*t*
  and osteoporosis, 138
Smoking cessation, 16–17
  for chronic kidney failure, 108
  for COPD, 169
  for diabetes mellitus, 61
  for GERD, 70
  for HTN, 32
  for PAD, 39
  post MI, 27
  preoperative, 156
  resources, 226
*Smooth and Cool,* 55*t*
Sneezing, 167*t*
Snellen wall chart, 194
Social phobia, 22
Sodium, fractional excretion of (FENa)
  in acute kidney failure, 107
  in dehydration, 109
Sodium bicarbonate
  for allergic rhinitis, 167
  for chronic kidney failure, 108
  for hyperkalemia, 113
Sodium bicarbonate and saline
  (Sinu*Cleanse*), 167
Sodium disorders, 110, 111
Sodium hyaluronan *(Hyalgan),* 122

## INDEX (CONT.)

Sodium nitroprusside *(Nipride)*, 32
Sodium phosphate/biphosphate emollient enema *(Fleet)*, 74t
Sodium polystyrene sulfonate (SPS, *Kayexalate*), 112, 113
Sodium salicylate *(Uracel)*, 124t
*Sodium Sulamyd* (sulfacetamide sodium), 198t
Sodium sulfacetamide *(Clenia, Rosula)*, 54t
*Sofarin. See also* Warfarin
    prescribing information, 18
Soft-tissue infections, 55t
*SoloSite gel*, 185t
*Solu-Medrol. See also* Methylprednisolone
    for adrenal insufficiency, 59t
Somatization, 144
*Sonata* (zaleplon), 191t
Sorbitol
    for chronic constipation, 73
    for constipation, 74t
*Sorbitrate* (isosorbide dinitrate), 26t, 27t
*Sorbsan. See also* Alginate
    for pressure ulcers, 185t
Sotalol, 38
Soybean formulas, 116
Sparfloxacin *(Zagam)*, 103t
*Sparine* (promazine), 220t
Spasm, pain, and vomiting, 155
Spasms, muscular, 149t
*Spectazole* (econazole nitrate), 56t
*Spectracef* (cefditoren), 101t
Spironolactone *(Aldactone)*
    digoxin interactions, 11
    with HCTZ *(Aldactazide)*, 37t
    for HF, 29
    for HTN, 33t
Splinting
    for carpal tunnel syndrome, 121
    for osteoarthritis, 122
    for pain management, 144
*Sporanox. See also* Itraconazole
    for dermatologic conditions, 56t
    for infectious diseases, 105t
    for onychomycosis, 54t

Squamous cell carcinoma, vulvar, 200
Squamous hyperplasia, 200
SSRIs (selective serotonin-reuptake inhibitors)
    for agitation, 47t
    CMS criteria for inappropriate use, 225t
    for depression, 49, 50t
    fall risks, 67
    for pain relief, 148t
    for painful neuropathy, 136
    and restless legs syndrome, 193
    and sexual dysfunction, 179
    with tolterodine, 50
    warfarin interactions, 18
St. John's wort
    antidepressants to avoid, 51
    common herbal and alternative medications, 14t
    digoxin interactions, 11
    drug and metabolic interactions, 12t
    herbal medication interactions, 13t
Staphylococcal blepharitis, 198t
*Staphylococcus aureus*
    methicillin-resistant, 93
    in nursing-home–acquired pneumonia, 91
*Starlix* (nateglinide), 62t
Statin therapy, 61
*Stelazine* (trifluoperazine), 220t
Steroids. *See* Corticosteroids; Glucocorticoids
Stockings, pressure
    for preventing falls, 69t
    for UI, 87
    for venous ulcers, 188
Strength training
    for dizziness, 129t
    exercise prescription, 162
    for preventing falls, 67, 68t
*Streptase. See also* Streptokinase
    for DVT/PE, 20t
*Streptococcus pneumoniae*
    in community-acquired pneumonia, 91
    COPD therapy, 170t
    empiric antibiotic therapy for, 93

in nursing-home–acquired pneumonia, 91

Streptokinase (Kabikinase, Streptase)
  for DVT/PE, 20t
  for Q-wave MI, 25

Streptomycin
  for active tuberculosis, 98, 98t
  for infectious diseases, 101t

Stress, post-traumatic, 22

Stress incontinence. See also Urinary incontinence
  classification, 85
  drugs to treat, 88t
  management, 86

Stress testing
  bladder, 86
  cardiac, 24

Stress ulcers, 72–73

Stretching exercises
  for nocturnal leg cramps, 193
  prescription, 162

Stroke
  acute, 130–131
  differential diagnosis, 165
  drugs for osteoporosis and, 140t
  prevention, 131
  resources, 227

Stromectol (ivermectin), 54t

Subacromial bursitis, 118

Sucralfate (Carafate)
  drug interactions, 11
  for GERD, 71t
  for stress-ulcer prevention, 72
  warfarin interactions, 18

Sudafed. See also Pseudoephedrine
  for allergic rhinitis or conjunctivitis, 168t
  for UI, 88t

Sudafed XR. See also Pseudoephedrine
  for allergic rhinitis or conjunctivitis, 168t
  for UI, 88t

Sular (nisoldipine), 35t

Sulfacetamide sodium (Sodium Sulamyd), 198t

Sulfasalazine
  digoxin interactions, 11
  for psoriasis, 54t

Sulfinpyrazone (Anturane), 127t

Sulfonamides, 11

Sulfonylureas, 61, 62t

Sulindac (Clinoril), 126t

Sumycin. See also Tetracycline
  for peptic ulcer disease, 72

Supprettes. See also Chloral hydrate
  for sleep disorders, 191t

Suprax (cefixime), 101t

Surgery
  abdominal, 20t
  for acute disk herniation, 119
  for acute MI, 26
  anticoagulation cessation prior to, 19
  anticoagulation for DVT/PE prophylaxis and treatment, 19t, 20t
  anticoagulation in absence of active bleeding or severe bleeding risk, 18t
  for aortic stenosis, 39
  for arterial ulcers, 182
  for back pain, 120
  for bowel obstruction, 154
  for BPH, 163
  cardiac risk assessment for, 156f
  for carpal tunnel syndrome, 121
  for cataract, 157, 194
  for diabetic foot ulcers, 184
  DVT prophylaxis, 157
  endocarditis prophylaxis, 160
  for fecal incontinence, 90
  for frozen shoulder (adhesive capsulitis), 118
  for GERD, 70
  for glaucoma, 195
  for hip fracture, 19t, 20t, 121
  ICD placement, 41
  maxillofacial, 192
  for osteoarthritis, 122
  for PAD, 39
  for Parkinson's disease, 132
  perioperative management, 157
  preoperative care, 156–157, 156f
  for pressure ulcers, 187
  pulmonary risk assessment for, 156–157
  for rotator cuff tears, 118
  sites of post-hospital care, 158t

**INDEX (CONT.)**

Surgery (*continued*)
  for sleep apnea, 192
  for UI, 88
  for unstable lumbar spine, 119
  for vaginal prolapse, 201
  for venous ulcers, 189
  for vulvar malignancy, 200
*Surmontil* (trimipramine)
  antidepressants to avoid, 51
  recommended max dose, 219*t*
*Symmetrel* (amantadine)
  for influenza, 96*t*
  for Parkinson's disease, 133*t*
*Synacthen Depot* (tetracosactin), 59
*Synalar* (fluocinolone acetonide), 57*t*
Syncope, 40
  classification of, 40*t*
  ICD placement for, 41
Syndrome of inappropriate secretion of
    antidiuretic hormone (SIADH),
    111–112
*Synercid* (quinupristin/dalfopristin), 104*t*
*Synthroid. See also* Levothyroxine
  for hypothyroidism, 60
*Synvisc* (hylan G-F 20), 122
Systolic blood pressure (SBP)
  management. *See also* Blood
    pressure
  for stroke prevention, 131
Systolic dysfunction
  evaluation and assessment, 27
  pharmacologic management, 28–29

**T**
T scores, 138
T$_3$ (liothyronine)
  for depression, 50
  with thyroxine (*Thyrolar*), 60
T$_4$ (thyroxine)
  enteral nutrition interactions, 116
  for hypothyroidism, 60
  with liothyronine (*Thyrolar*), 60
  and osteoporosis, 138
Tachycardia, atrial, 36*t*
Tacrolimus, 12*t*
Tadalafil (*Cialis*)
  for BPH, 163
  for male sexual dysfunction, 178*t*
*Tagamet. See also* Cimetidine
  for GERD, 70*t*
Tai Chi
  exercise prescription, 162
  for preventing falls, 67, 68*t*
*Take Control*, 30
*Tamiflu* (oseltamivir), 96*t*
Tamoxifen (*Nolvadex*)
  for breast cancer, 199, 199*t*
  drug and metabolic interactions,
    11*t*–12*t*
  warfarin interactions, 18
Tamsulosin (*Flomax*), 163
Tamulosin, 178*t*
*Tapazole* (methimazole), 60
*Taractan* (chlorprothixene), 220*t*
Tardive dyskinesia (TD), 166*t*
*Tarka* (verapamil hydrochloride with
    trandolapril), 37*t*
*Tasmar* (tolcapone), 133*t*
TCAs (tricyclic antidepressants)
  CMS criteria for inappropriate use,
    224*t*
  and dementia, 46
  for depression, 51*t*
  fall risks, 67
  for pain relief, 149*t*
  for painful neuropathy, 136
  for restless legs syndrome, 193
TD (tardive dyskinesia), 166*t*
TDD (telephone device for the deaf), 79
*Tegaderm. See also* Transparent film
  for pressure ulcers, 185*t*
*Tegasorb. See also* Hydrocolloids
  for pressure ulcers, 185*t*
*Tegretol. See also* Carbamazepine
  for agitation, 48*t*
  for bipolar disorders, 52*t*
  for epilepsy, 134*t*
  for painful neuropathy, 136
*Tegretol XR. See also* Carbamazepine
  for bipolar disorders, 52*t*
  for epilepsy, 134*t*
  for painful neuropathy, 136

Telephone device for the deaf (TDD), 79
Telithromycin *(Ketek)*
    drug and metabolic interactions, 12*t*
    for infectious diseases, 102*t*
Telmisartan *(Micardis)*
    with HCTZ *(Micardis-HCT)*, 37*t*
    for HTN, 36*t*
    target dose in HF, 29*t*
Temazepam *(Restoril)*
    recommended max dose, 222*t*
    for sleep disorders, 191*t*
*Temovate.* See also Clobetasol
    propionate
    for dermatologic conditions, 58*t*
Temperature conversions, 1*t*
Temporal (giant cell) arteritis, 128
Tendinitis
    bicipital, 118
    rotator cuff, 118
*Tenex* (guanfacine), 34*t*
*Tenoretic* (atenolol with chlorthalidone),
    37*t*
*Tenormin.* See also Atenolol
    for acute MI, 24–25
    for HTN, 34*t*
*Tequin.* See also Gatifloxacin
    for acute bacterial conjunctivitis, 198*t*
    for infectious diseases, 102*t*
Terazosin *(Hytrin)*
    for BPH, 163
    for HTN, 33*t*
Terbinafine *(Lamisil, Lamisil AT)*
    for fungal infections, 56*t*
    for infectious diseases, 106*t*
    for onychomycosis, 54*t*
Teriparatide *(Forteo)*
    bone outcomes, 140*t*
    for osteoporosis, 139
*Tessalon Perles* (benzonatate), 175*t*
*Testim* (testosterone gel), 178*t*
*Testoderm* (testosterone), 177*t*
Testosterone
    scrotal transdermal *(Testoderm)*, 177*t*
    skin transdermal *(Androderm)*, 177*t*
Testosterone cypionate or enanthate,
    178*t*
Testosterone gel *(AndroGel, Testim)*, 178*t*
Tests, preventive, 159*t*

Tetanus immunization, 159*t*
Tetracosactin *(Synacthen Depot)*, 59
Tetracycline *(Achromycin, Helidac,
    Sumycin)*
    for cellulitis, 55*t*
    digoxin interactions, 11
    for *H pylori*-induced ulcerations, 72*t*
    for infectious diseases, 103*t*
    for peptic ulcer disease, 72
    for pneumonia, 93
    for rosacea, 54*t*
*Teveten.* See also Eprosartan
    for HTN, 36*t*
Thalamotomy, 132
*Theo-24.* See also Theophylline-SR
    for asthma and COPD, 173*t*
*Theo-Dur.* See also Theophylline-SR
    for asthma and COPD, 173*t*
Theophylline, 225*t*
Theophylline-SR *(Quibron-T/SR, Slo-Bid,
    Theo-24, Theo-Dur, Uniphyl)*
    for asthma, 171*t*, 172*t*, 173*t*
    for COPD, 173*t*
Thiamine, 43
Thiazide diuretics
    and coexisting conditions, 36*t*, 37*t*
    for HTN, 32, 33*t*
    for hyperkalemia, 112, 113
Thiazolidinediones
    for diabetes mellitus, 61, 63*t*
Thioridazine *(Mellaril)*
    for delirium, 43
    and dementia, 46
    for psychosis, 166*t*
    recommended max dose, 220*t*
Thiothixene *(Navane)*, 220*t*
Third-spacing, 111
Thirst, impaired, 110
*Thorazine* (chlorpromazine)
    for delirium, 43
    recommended max dose, 220*t*
Thrombin inhibitors, 20*t*
Thrombocytopenia, heparin-induced, 20*t*
Thrombolytic therapy
    for acute stroke, 131
    for anticoagulation, 20*t*
    for PE, 176
    for Q-wave MI, 25–26

## INDEX (CONT.)

Thrombosis
    deep-vein (DVT), 19t–20t, 140t, 157, 176
    idiopathic venous, 18t
Thyroid hormone, 18
Thyroid-stimulating hormone (TSH), 159t
*Thyrolar* (thyroxine and liothyronine), 60
Thyrotoxicosis, 60
Thyroxine (T$_4$)
    enteral nutrition interactions, 116
    for hypothyroidism, 60
    with liothyronine *(Thyrolar)*, 60
    and osteoporosis, 138
TIA (transient ischemic attack)
    crescendo, 131
    and dizziness, 130t
    management of, 131
*Tiazac* (diltiazem), 35t
*Ticar* (ticarcillin), 99t
Ticarcillin *(Ticar)*, 99t
Ticarcillin–clavulanate *(Timentin)*, 100t
*Ticlid. See also* Ticlopidine
    for stroke prevention, 131
Ticlopidine *(Ticlid)*
    CMS criteria for inappropriate use, 224t
    CMS regulations, 223t
    drug and metabolic interactions, 11t
    for stroke prevention, 131
*Tilade. See also* Nedocromil
    for asthma and COPD, 174t
Tilt-table testing, 40
*Timentin* (ticarcillin–clavulanate), 100t
*Timolide* (timolol maleate with HCTZ), 37t
Timolol *(Blocadren)*
    drug and metabolic interactions, 12t
    for HTN, 34t
Timolol drops *(Betimol, Timoptic)*, 195t
Timolol maleate with HCTZ *(Timolide)*, 37t
Timolol/dorzolamide *(Cosopt)*, 197t
*Timoptic* (timolol drops), 195t
*Tinactin* (tolnaftate), 56t
*Tindal* (acetophenazine), 220t
Tinnitus, 79–80
Tinzaparin *(Innohep)*, 20t
Tiotropium, 172t

Tirofiban *(Aggrastat)*, 25t
TMP/SMZ (trimethoprim/sulfamethoxazole), 103t
TMP/SMZ (trimethoprim/sulfamethoxazole) DS, 94
Tobacco abuse. *See also* Smoking
    pharmacotherapy for, 17t
Tobramycin *(AKTob, Nebcin, Tobrex)*
    for acute bacterial conjunctivitis, 198t
    for infectious diseases, 101t
*Tobrex. See also* Tobramycin
    for acute bacterial conjunctivitis, 198t
*Tofranil. See also* Imipramine
    antidepressants to avoid, 51
    recommended max dose, 219t
    for UI, 87t
Toilet training, 90
Tolbutamide, 11
Tolcapone *(Tasmar)*, 133t
*Tolectin* (tolmetin), 126t
Tolmetin *(Tolectin)*, 126t
Tolnaftate *(Absorbine Jr. Antifungal, Tinactin)*, 56t
Tolterodine *(Detrol, Detrol LA)*
    for depression, 50
    for UI, 87t
Tonometry, 194
Tono-Pen, 194
*Topamax* (topiramate), 135t
*Topicort* (desoximetasone), 57t
Topiramate *(Topamax)*, 135t
*Toprol XL* (metoprolol XL)
    for HF, 28
    for HTN, 34t
*Toradol. See also* Ketorolac
    for arthritis, 125t
Toremifene *(Fareston)*, 199t
*Tornalate* (bitolterol), 172t
Torsemide *(Demadex)*
    for HTN, 33t
    for hyperkalemia, 112, 113
Total body water, 110

Total joint replacement
anticoagulation for DVT/PE
prophylaxis and treatment, 19*t*, 20*t*
endocarditis prophylaxis, 161
for hip fracture, 121
for osteoarthritis, 122
Total parenteral nutrition, 117
Trabeculectomy, 195
Tracheostomy, 192
Tramadol *(Ultram)*
with APAP *(Ultracet),* 145, 147*t*
drug and metabolic interactions, 12*t*
for osteoarthritis, 122, 123*f*
for pain, 147*t*
for painful neuropathy, 136
*Trandate* (labetalol), 35*t*
Trandolapril *(Mavik)*
for HTN, 36*t*
target dose in HF, 29*t*
with verapamil hydrochloride *(Tarka),*
37*t*
Transcutaneous electrical nerve
stimulation
for osteoarthritis, 122
for pain management, 144
for painful neuropathy, 136
Transdermal estrogen *(Alora, Bio-E-Gel,
Estrasorb, Estraderm, Vivelle,
Climara, FemPatch, EstroGel),* 203*t*
Transdermal fentanyl *(Duragesic)*
for pain, 145, 147*t*
Transdermal hormone therapy, 203*t*
Transdermal lidocaine patches
*(Lidoderm)*
for pain, 149*t*
for painful neuropathy, 136
Transdermal nicotine patches *(Habitrol,
NicoDerm, Nicotrol, ProStep),* 17*t*
Transdermal scopolamine
for excessive secretions, 155
for spasm, pain, and vomiting, 155
Transdermal testosterone *(Androderm,
Testoderm),* 177*t*
*Transderm-Nitro.* See also Nitroglycerin
dosage and formulations, 27*t*
Transesophageal echocardiography
in acute stroke, 131
in AF, 38

Transferrin, 114
Transient ischemic attack (TIA)
crescendo, 131
and dizziness, 130*t*
management of, 131
Transparent film *(Bioclusive, Tegaderm,
Op-site)*
for pressure ulcers, 185*t*
wound and pressure ulcer products,
184*t*
Transplantation, kidney, 109
Transthoracic echocardiography, 131
Transurethral incision of the prostate
(TUIP), 163
Transurethral resection of the prostate
(TURP), 163
*Tranxene* (clorazepate), 221*t*
Tranylcypromine *(Parnate),* 51*t*
*Travatan* (travoprost), 196*t*
Travoprost *(Travatan),* 196*t*
Trazodone *(Desyrel)*
for agitation, 48*t*
for depression, 51*t*
drug and metabolic interactions, 12*t*
recommended max dose, 219*t*
for sleep disorders, 191*t*
*Trelstar Depot* (triptorelin), 164*t*
*Trelstar LA* (triptorelin), 164*t*
Tremors
antihypertensive therapy and, 36*t*
cerebellar, 129*t*
classification of, 129*t*
essential tremor, 36*t,* 129*t*
nonpharmacologic management, 132
physiologic, 129*t*
*Trental* (pentoxifylline)
for PAD, 39
for venous ulcers, 188
*Trexan* (naltrexone), 16
Triamcinolone acetonide *(Aristocort,
Azmacort, Kenacort, Kenalog,
Nasacort)*
for adrenal insufficiency, 59*t*
for allergic rhinitis or conjunctivitis,
168*t*
for asthma and COPD, 173*t*
for dermatologic conditions, 57*t*
for intertrigo, 54*t*

**INDEX** (CONT.)

Triamcinolone acetonide (*continued*)
 for osteoarthritis, 122
 for seborrheic dermatitis, 54*t*
Triamcinolone hexacetonide, 122
Triamterene (*Dyrenium*)
 with HCTZ (*Dyazide, Maxzide*), 37*t*
 for HTN, 33*t*
Triazolam (*Halcion*)
 drug and metabolic interactions, 12*t*
 recommended max dose, 222*t*
Tricor (fenofibrate), 31*t*
Tricosal (choline magnesium salicylate), 124*t*
Tricyclic antidepressants. *See* TCAs
Tridesilon (desonide), 57*t*
Trifluoperazine (*Stelazine*), 220*t*
Trifluopromazine (*Vesprin*), 220*t*
Trihexy (trihexyphenidyl), 133*t*
Trihexyphenidyl (*Artane, Trihexy*), 133*t*
Trilafon (perphenazine), 220*t*
Trileptal. *See also* Oxcarbazepine
 for epilepsy, 134*t*
Trilisate (choline magnesium salicylate), 124*t*
Trimethoprim and polymyxin (*Polytrim*), 198*t*
Trimethoprim/sulfamethoxazole
 (TMP/SMZ), 103*t*
Trimethoprim/sulfamethoxazole DS, 94
Trimipramine (*Surmontil*)
 antidepressants to avoid, 51
 recommended max dose, 219*t*
Triptorelin (*Trelstar Depot, Trelstar LA*), 164*t*
Trochanteric bursitis, 120
Trolamine salicylate (*Aspercreme*), 149*t*
Troponins, cardiac, 24
Trospium (*Sanctura*), 87*t*
Trovafloxacin (*Trovan*), 103*t*
Trovan (trovafloxacin), 103*t*
Trunk movements, 211
Trusopt (dorzolamide), 196*t*
TSH (thyroid-stimulating hormone), 159*t*
Tube feeding
 drug interactions, 10
 tips for successful tube feeding, 117

Tuberculosis, infectious, 97–99
 identification of high-risk patients, 97*t*
 treatment of active infection, 98*t*
 treatment of latent infection, 97*t*
Tubular necrosis, 107
TUIP (transurethral incision of the
 prostate), 163
TURP (transurethral resection of the
 prostate), 163
TwoCal HN, 116*t*
Tylenol. *See also* APAP
 for arthritis, 124*t*
Tylenol ER (APAP extended release), 124*t*
Tylox (oxycodone with APAP), 146*t*

**U**

UI. *See* Urinary incontinence
Ulcers
 arterial, 181–182, 181*t*
 diabetic, 181*t*, 182–184
 *H pylori*-induced, 71*t*–72*t*
 peptic, 71–72, 223*t*, 224*t*
 pressure, 181*t*, 184–187
 skin, 180–189, 181*t*
 stress, 72–73
 venous, 181*t*, 187–189
Ultracal, 116*t*
Ultracet. *See also* Tramadol with APAP
 for pain, 147*t*
Ultralente (insulin), 63*t*
Ultram. *See also* Tramadol
 for pain, 147*t*
 for painful neuropathy, 136
Ultravate (halobetasol propionate), 58*t*
Unasyn (ampicillin-sulbactam), 99*t*
Uniphyl. *See also* Theophylline-SR
 for asthma and COPD, 173*t*
Uniretic (moexipril with HCTZ), 37*t*
Univasc. *See also* Moexipril
 for HTN, 36*t*
Unna's boot, 188
Unoprostone (*Rescula*), 196*t*
Uracel (sodium salicylate), 124*t*
Urate crystal disease, 126
Urea, fractional excretion of (FEun), 107

Urecholine. See also Bethanechol
    for GERD, 71t
Urge incontinence. See also Urinary
    incontinence
    antihypertensive therapy and, 37t
    classification, 85
    and depression, 50
    drugs to treat, 87t
Urinary incontinence (UI), 85–88
    classification, 85
    drugs to treat, 87t–88t
    estrogen for, 87
    mixed, 85, 87t
    resources, 227
    stress, 85, 86, 88t
    urge, 37t, 50, 85, 87t
Urinary tract infection, 93–94
    recurrent, 179
Urine osmolality, 110
Urine sodium, 109
Urodynamic testing, 86
Urosepsis, 94
UroXatral (alfuzosin ER), 163
Urticaria, 55t
UV light, 54t
Uvulopalatopharyngoplasty, 192

V
Vaccines, 95
Vacuum tumescence devices (Catalyst
    Vacuum Device, Osbon-Erec Aid,
    Pos-T-Vac, Rejoyn), 178t
Vagifem (estradiol vaginal tablets), 179t
Vaginal bleeding, 140t
Vaginal candidiasis, 105t
Vaginal prolapse, 201
Vaginismus, 179
Valacyclovir (Valtrex), 95t
Valdecoxib (Bextra), 126t
Valerian, 13t
Valisone (betamethasone valerate), 57t
Valium. See also Diazepam
    recommended max dose, 221t
Valproic acid (Depacon, Depakene,
    Depakote)
    for bipolar disorders, 52t
    drug and metabolic interactions,
        11t–12t

    for epilepsy, 135t
Valsartan (Diovan)
    with HCTZ (Diovan-HCT), 37t
    for HTN, 36t
    target dose in HF, 29t
Valtrex (valacyclovir), 95t
Valvular heart disease
    anticoagulation for, 18t
    aortic stenosis, 39
Vancenase. See also Beclomethasone
    for allergic rhinitis or conjunctivitis,
        168t
Vanceril. See also Beclomethasone
    for asthma and COPD, 173t
Vancocin. See also Vancomycin
    for infectious diseases, 104t
Vancomycin (Vancocin)
    for antibiotic-associated diarrhea, 77
    for endocarditis prophylaxis, 161t
    for hospital-acquired pneumonia, 93
    for infectious diseases, 104t
    for nursing-home–acquired
        pneumonia, 93
    for UTI or urosepsis, 94
Vancomycin-resistant E faecium, 104t
Vantin. See also Cefpodoxime
    for infectious diseases, 101t
Vardenafil (LEVITRA)
    for BPH, 163
    for male sexual dysfunction, 178t
Vascular dementia, 45
Vaseline, 55t
Vaseretic (enalapril maleate with HCTZ),
    37t
Vasodilators
    for aortic stenosis, 39
    fall risks, 69t
    for HTN, 35t
Vasotec. See also Enalapril
    for HTN, 35t
Vasovagal syncope
    classification of, 40t
    evaluation of, 40
    management of, 40
Venlafaxine (Effexor, Effexor XR)
    for anxiety disorders, 22
    for depression, 49, 51t
    drug and metabolic interactions, 12t

## INDEX (CONT.)

Venlafaxine (*continued*)
  for hot flushes, 201
Venous filling time, 182
Venous leak syndrome, 177
Venous ulcers, 187–189
  wound characteristics, 181*t*
Ventilation, mechanical, 92
Ventilation, positive pressure, 170*t*
Ventilation-perfusion lung scans, 176*f*
*Ventolin* (albuterol), 172*t*
*Ventolin Rotacaps* (albuterol), 172*t*
Ventricular fibrillation (VF), 41
Ventricular tachycardia (VT), 41
Verapamil
  for AF, 38
  digoxin interactions, 11
  drug and metabolic interactions, 12*t*
  enteral nutrition interactions, 117
Verapamil hydrochloride with trandolapril
  *(Tarka)*, 37*t*
Verapamil SR *(Calan SR, Covera-HS,
  Isoptin SR, Verelan)*, 35*t*
*Verelan* (verapamil), 35*t*
Vertebral artery, postural impingement of,
  130*t*
Vertebral compression fractures, 120
Vertebroplasty, 139
Vertigo, 130*t*
*Vesprin* (trifluopromazine), 220*t*
Vestibular neuronitis, 130*t*
VF (ventricular fibrillation), 41
*VFEND* (voriconazole), 106*t*
*Viagra. See also* Sildenafil
  for BPH, 163
  for male sexual dysfunction, 178*t*
  for SSRI-induced sexual dysfunction,
    179
*Vibramycin. See also* Doxycycline
  for infectious diseases, 103*t*
*Vicodin. See also* Hydrocodone with
  APAP
  for pain, 146*t*
*Vicoprofen* (hydrocodone ibuprofen), 146*t*
*Vigilon* (hydrogel), 186*t*
VIN (vulvar intraepithelial neoplasia), 200
Viral conjunctivitis, 198

*Visken* (pindolol), 34*t*
Visual impairment, 194–198
  and falls, 68
  resources, 227
  screening, 159*t*
Visual testing, 194
Vitamin B$_{12}$
  for anemia associated with deficiency,
    84*f*
  deficiency, anemia of, 81, 84*f*
  deficiency, differential diagnosis, 165
  and hypoproliferative anemia, 82*f*
Vitamin C, 195
Vitamin D
  for chronic kidney failure, 108
  insufficiency, 108
  for osteoporosis, 138
  for prevention of falls, 67
Vitamin D$_2$ (ergocalciferol), 108
Vitamin E
  for ARMD, 195
  for cognitive dysfunction in AD, 47
  warfarin interactions, 18
Vitamin K
  drug interactions, 10
  warfarin interactions, 18
  for warfarin overdose, 19*t*
Vitamin supplements, 180
*Vivactil* (protriptyline)
  antidepressants to avoid, 51
  recommended max dose, 219*t*
  for sleep apnea, 192
*Vivelle* (transdermal estrogen), 203*t*
Voiding record, 86
*Voltaren* (diclofenac), 124*t*
*Voltaren-XR* (diclofenac), 124*t*
Volume depletion, 109
Volume overload, 108
Vomiting, 74–75
  antiemetics, 75*t*
  at end of life, 155
  and hyponatremia, 111
Voriconazole *(VFEND)*, 106*t*
VT (ventricular tachycardia), 41
Vulvar diseases, 200

*Vytorin* (ezetimibe/simvastatin combination), 31*t*

W
Walking
for claudication, 39
for dementia, 46
for PAD, 39
prescription, 162
Warfarin *(Coumadin, Carfin, Sofarin)*, 18–19. *See also* Anticoagulation
for acute MI, 26
for AF, 38
cessation before surgery, 19
COX-2 inhibitor interactions, 126*t*
drug and metabolic interactions, 12*t*
drug interactions, 11, 18
food interactions, 10
overdose, 19*t*
for PE, 176
for stroke prevention, 131
toremifene interactions, 199*t*
Warfarin-R, 11*t*
Water loss, pure, 110
Weakness
at end of life, 153
facial, 135*t*
and falls, 68
Weight conversions, 1*t*
Weight loss. *See also* Malnutrition
for GERD, 70
for HTN, 32
for osteoarthritis, 122
post MI, 27
for sleep apnea, 192
Weight training, 162
*WelChol* (colesevelam), 31*t*
*Wellbutrin. See also* Bupropion
for depression, 50*t*
*Wellbutrin SR. See also* Bupropion
for SSRI-induced sexual dysfunction, 179
for tobacco abuse, 17*t*
Wernicke's aphasia, 135*t*
*Vestcort* (hydrocortisone valerate), 57*t*
Westergren sedimentation rate, 1
"White coat" HTN, 32

Withholding or withdrawing therapy, 152–153
Women's health, 199–203
breast cancer, 140*t*, 199, 199*t*–200*t*
breast examination, 159*t*, 199
dyspareunia, 178–179
early menopause, 138
estrogen therapy, 201–202
mammography, 159*t*, 199
menopause, 178–179
osteoporosis, 36*t*, 138–140, 140*t*, 227
resources, 227
Wound assessment and treatment, 180
arterial ulcers, 182
diabetic foot ulcers, 182–184
pressure ulcers, 184–187
venous ulcers, 187–189
wound and pressure ulcer products, 184*t*
*Wytensin* (guanabenz), 34*t*

X
*Xalatan* (latanoprost), 196*t*
*Xanax. See also* Alprazolam
recommended max dose (anxiolytic), 221*t*
recommended max dose (hypnotic), 221*t*
Xerosis, 55*t*
Xerostomia, 10
*Xopenex* (levalbuterol), 172*t*

Y
Yoga, 162
Yohimbine, 179

Z
Z scores, 138
*Zaditor* (ketotifen), 169*t*
Zafirlukast *(Accolate)*, 174*t*
*Zagam* (sparfloxacin), 103*t*
Zaleplon *(Sonata)*, 191*t*
Zanamivir *(Relenza)*, 96*t*
*Zantac* (ranitidine), 71*t*
*Zaroxolyn. See also* Metolazone
for HTN, 33*t*
*Zebeta. See also* Bisoprolol
for HF, 28

**INDEX** (CONT.)

Zebeta (*continued*)
  for HTN, 34*t*
*Zefazone* (cefmetazole), 100*t*
*Zestoretic* (lisinopril with HCTZ), 37*t*
*Zestril. See also* Lisinopril
  for HTN, 36*t*
*Zetia* (ezetimibe), 31*t*
*Ziac* (bisoprolol fumarate with HCTZ), 37*t*
Zileuton (*Zyflo*), 174*t*
Zinc
  drug interactions, 10
  insulin (*Lente*), 63*t*
  for visual impairment, 195
Ziprasidone (*Geodon*)
  for delirium, 43
  drug and metabolic interactions, 12*t*
  for psychosis, 166*t*
*Zithromax. See also* Azithromycin
  for infectious diseases, 102*t*
*Zocor. See also* Simvastatin
  for dyslipidemia, 30*t*
*Zofran* (ondansetron), 155
*Zoladex* (goserelin acetate implant), 164*t*
Zoledronic acid
  for metastatic bone disease in breast
    cancer, 199
  for metastatic bone disease in
    prostate cancer, 164
*Zoloft. See also* Sertraline
  for depression, 50*t*
Zolpidem (*Ambien*)
  drug and metabolic interactions, 12*t*

  for sleep disorders, 191*t*
*Zonalon. See also* Doxepin
  for hives, 55*t*
*Zonegran* (zonisamide), 135*t*
Zonisamide (*Zonegran*), 135*t*
*ZORprin* (ASA), 124*t*
Zoster (shingles), 94–95
  antiviral treatments, 95*t*
  post-herpetic neuralgia, 95
*Zostrix. See also* Capsaicin
  for pain, 149*t*
  for painful neuropathy, 136
*Zosyn* (piperacillin-tazobactam), 100*t*
*Zovirax* (acyclovir), 95*t*
*Zyban. See also* Bupropion
  for depression, 50*t*
  for SSRI-induced sexual dysfunction,
    179
  for tobacco abuse, 17*t*
*Zydis. See also* Olanzapine
  for agitation, 47*t*
*Zyflo* (zileuton), 174*t*
*Zyloprim. See also* Allopurinol
  for chronic gout, 127*t*
*Zyprexa. See also* Olanzapine
  for agitation, 47*t*, 48*t*
  for delirium, 43
  for psychosis, 165*t*
  recommended max dose, 220*t*
*Zyrtec* (cetirizine), 167*t*
*Zyvox* (linezolid), 104*t*